Professional Examinations

D1810438

PART 3

Paper 3.7

Strategic Financial Management

EXAM KIT

ACCA
Approved Publisher

KAPLAN

PUBLISHING
FOULKS LYNCH

British Library Cataloguing-in-Publication Data

A catalogue record for this book is available from the British Library.

Published by:
Kaplan Publishing Foulks Lynch
Unit 2 The Business Centre
Molly Millars Lane
Wokingham
RG41 2QZ

ISBN 978 1 84390 904 0

© FTC Kaplan Ltd, December 2006

Printed and bound in Great Britain by William Clowes Ltd, Beccles, Suffolk

Acknowledgements

The past ACCA examination questions are the copyright of the Association of Chartered Certified Accountants. The original answers to the questions from June 1994 onwards were produced by the examiners themselves and have been adapted by Kaplan Publishing Foulks Lynch.

We are grateful to the Chartered Institute of Management Accountants and the Institute of Chartered Accountants in England and Wales for permission to reproduce past exam questions. The answers have been prepared by Kaplan Publishing Foulks Lynch.

KAPLAN PUBLISHING

CONTENTS

Section

INDEX TO QUESTIONS AND ANSWERS

Interest rate risk

The global economic environment and global financial management

SYLLABUS AND EXAM FORMAT

Format of the exam

		Number of marks
Section A:	2 compulsory questions	70
Section B:	Choice of 2 from 4 questions (15 marks each)	30
		100

Total time allowed: 3 hours

Aim

To ensure that candidates can exercise judgement and technique to make commercial value added decisions in strategic financial management and are able to adapt to factors affecting those decisions.

Objectives

On completion of this paper candidates should be able to:

- prepare reports for management explaining and evaluating the financial consequences of strategic decisions
- identify and evaluate appropriate sources of finance, their risks and costs
- assess potential investment decisions and strategies
- understand the impact of the global business environment on national and multinational organisations
- explain, demonstrate and recommend suitable risk management techniques
- understand the significance of cash management and the treasury function in the commercial environment
- select the techniques most appropriate to optimise the employment of financial resources and critically evaluate such techniques
- analyse and evaluate financial information relating to past and future business performance
- demonstrate the skills expected in Part 3.

Position of the paper in the overall syllabus

Candidates will require a thorough understanding of the financial management section of Paper 2.4 Financial Management and Control. Candidates will also be required to apply quantitative techniques covered in earlier papers.

Paper 3.7 develops the financial management elements of Paper 2.4 by:

- providing a more critical analysis of corporate governance

- examining the strategic implications of short-term and long-term financial planning

- in-depth analysis of risk management in both domestic and international contexts

- more rigorous analysis of investment decisions and the cost of capital, including CAPM and other models

- analysis of corporate growth and restructuring through mergers, acquisitions and other means

- introducing international dimensions of the treasury function

- considering the global economic environment and other influences on financial management decisions

- analysis of global financial management decisions

- introducing ethical considerations.

Paper 3.7 will draw upon strategic management and business planning issues covered in Paper 3.5 Strategic Business Planning and Development in the context of financial planning.

Paper 3.7 covers mergers, acquisitions and corporate restructuring from a financial perspective, areas covered from an accounting perspective in Paper 3.6 Advanced Corporate Reporting.

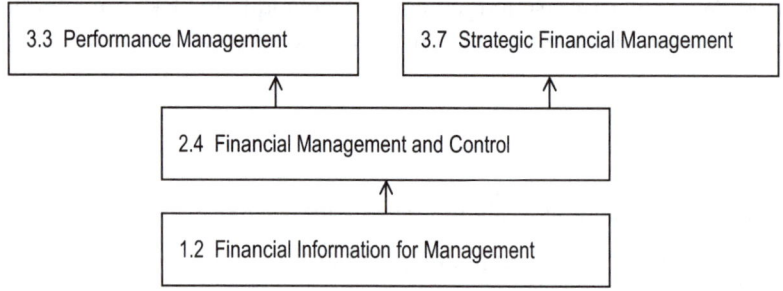

Syllabus content

1 Objectives and corporate governance

(a) The aims and objectives of an organisation and their impact on business planning

(b) Key stakeholders of an organisation: shareholders, lenders, directors, employees, customers, suppliers and the government

(c) Environmental issues and their impact on corporate objectives and governance

(d) The concept of goal congruence and how it might be achieved

(e) Key aspects of governance in the UK and internationally

(f) The implications of corporate governance for organisations

2 Strategy formulation

(a) The strategic planning process and its link with investment decisions

(i) the development and analysis of financial plans to meet agreed objectives

(ii) seeking, clarifying and confirming information (e.g. on the current or past business position through ratios or other forms of analysis) relevant to the achievement of business objectives

(iii) advising clients on the strategies that a company might use to expand or maintain its current market position, and on exit strategies

(iv) long-term financial planning including measures of value, profit, optimisation and utility

(v) the use of free cash flow in financial planning

(vi) techniques for valuing individual shares and other securities and for valuing a business, including EVA and SVA

(b) Strategic planning for multinationals

(i) entry and exit barriers

(ii) competitive advantage

3 Risk analysis

(a) Cost of capital

(i) the cost of equity (CAPM and dividend growth model)

(ii) the cost of debt

(iii) the weighted average cost of capital (WACC)

(iv) the impact of varying capital structures on the cost of capital

(b) Interest rate and foreign exchange risk

(i) the identification of interest rate and foreign exchange exposure

(ii) yield curves and their significance to financial managers

(iii) hedging risk using forwards, futures, options, swaps, FRAs and other products

(iv) the scope and benefit of financial engineering

4 Investment decisions

(a) Decision-making techniques

(i) detailed knowledge of discounted cash flow (NPV)

(ii) adjusted NPV (APV)

(iii) portfolio theory and CAPM and their value to managers

(iv) options embedded in investments (basic knowledge only)

(b) Expansion strategies

(i) organic growth, mergers and acquisitions

(ii) valuations for mergers and acquisitions

(iii) takeover and defence strategies

(iv) planning for post-merger success and audit

(c) Corporate reorganisation

(i) divestments

(ii) buy-outs and buy-ins

(iii) corporate restructuring

(iv) going private

(v) share repurchases

5 Treasury management and financial forecasting

(a) Methods of financing short- and long-term investment, including mergers and acquisitions

(b) The role of cash flow forecasting in business planning

(i) development and analysis of short-term financial plans

(c) Role of treasury function

(i) activities of treasury managers

(ii) centralised versus decentralised treasury functions

(d) Dividend policy

(i) influences on dividend policy

(ii) the effect of dividends upon company value

6 The global economic environment

(a) International factors affecting business developments

(i) trends in global competition

(ii) the role of multinational companies in the world economy

(iii) free trade, protectionism, trade agreements, common markets

(iv) role of World Bank and International Monetary Fund (IMF) and other international organisations

(v) economic relations between developed and developing countries including problems of debt and development

(vi) introduction of a single currency

(b) Exchange rate determination

(i) influences on exchange rates

(ii) models of exchange rate determination

(iii)   different forms of exchange rate system

7   Global financial management

(a)   Appraisal of overseas investment decisions

    (i)   alternative forms of foreign investment

    (ii)   the impact of overseas taxation (basic principles only)

    (iii)   overseas cost of capital and capital structure

    (iv)   forecasting future exchange rates

    (v)   political risk

(b)   Raising capital overseas

    (i)   international capital markets including the Euromarkets

    (ii)   overseas domestic capital markets

(iii)   international banking

(c)   Managing financial resources within a multinational group

    (i)   financial control within a group of companies

    (ii)   international cash management

    (iii)   international transfer pricing

    (iv)   performance measurement and evaluation

(d)   Management of international trade

    (i)   the management of the risks of international trade

    (ii)   the finance of international trade

8   Ethical consideration

(a)   Ethics and business conduct, including international ethical considerations

Excluded topics

The syllabus content outlines the areas for assessment. No areas of knowledge are specifically excluded from the syllabus.

Key areas of the syllabus

The key topic areas are as follows:

- investment decisions

- risk analysis

- global financial management

- treasury management

- financial forecasting

Wider reading is also desirable, especially regular study of relevant articles in the *Student Accountant*.

Additional information

Candidates need to be aware that questions involving knowledge of new examinable regulations will not be set until at least six months after the last day of the month in which the regulation was issued.

Examinable documents are listed in the 'Exam Notes' section of *Student Accountant*, usually appearing in the March and September issues three months before each exam.

ANALYSIS OF PAST PAPERS

June 2003

Section A

1 Decision about company closure, reconstruction or company sale.
2 Portfolio theory.

Section B

3 Interest rate caps and collars. Constructing a collar.
4 Short-term export finance: credit insurance, export factor, letter of credit.
5 Yield curve. Bond pricing.
6 Conflicts of interest between shareholders and bondholders. Bond covenants.

December 2003

Section A

1 DCF appraisal, overseas investment (with inflation and taxation). Issues of political risk and impact of blocked remittances.
2 Analysis of techniques that might be used to forecast corporate failure and consequent organisational implications. Estimates of free cash flow.

Section B

3 Examination of the validity of a financial forecast in the context of a growth via acquisition situation.
4 Hedging for a share portfolio. Stock index fixtures.
5 Black-Scholes model (option to develop and market a drug).
6 Influence on objectives of non-financial, ethical and environmental issues.

June 2004

Section A

1 Production of forecast pro-forma accounts for a four year period. Use of free cash flow and ratio analysis.
2 Alternative forms of foreign currency hedging. Issues relating to countertrade and the raising of international finance.

Section B

3 Estimating the cost of capital using internal and external sources of finance.
4 Analysis of risk and return in the context of division investment strategies.
5 Use of options to hedge an investment portfolio.
6 Analysis of the global debt problem and attempts to resolve it.

December 2004

Section A

1   Discussion of the weighted average cost of capital and adjusted present value. Report and calculations involving adjusted present value.
2   Analysis of a currency swap and comparison with swaption and currency option.

Section B

3   Comparison of the performance of two organisations over time using a variety of measure.
4   Comparison of remuneration packages for a managing director based upon alternative ways of assessing company performance, including use of share options and EVA.
5   Use of tax havens, and the impact of changing tax rules.
6   Preparation of a briefing document for a Board of Directors discussing issues that might influence a company's capital structure.

June 2005

Section A

1   Takeover bid involving evaluation of synergy using discounted cash flows, limitations of estimates used, factors influencing whether the bid will be accepted, an estimate of maximum bid and likely response and possible defences.
2   Evaluation of financing options.

Section B

3   Hedging interest rate risk using futures and FRAs.
4   Pension fund investment decisions.
5   Assessing political risk.
6   Exchange rate regimes and their implications for a multinational firm.

December 2005

Section A

1   Investment appraisal with calculations (NPV) and discussion (assumptions, other information required and non-financial factors).
2   Financial gearing with correction of given WACC calculations, revised calculations and discussion of plan to increase gearing.

Section B

3   Option valuation with discussion of decision to buy the option.
4   MBOs, including discussion of benefits, calculation of equity growth and evaluation of warrants proposals.
5   Hedging strategy for a multinational group, including netting off, forward contracts and options.
6   Discussion question on protectionism and the role of the WTO.

June 2006

Section A

1   Performance appraisal,
2   Forex risk hedging

Section B

3   Calculation of yield and price for zero coupon debentures. Using delta and theta.
4   Interest rate swaps.
5   Overseas investment appraisal and capital structure.
6   Discussion question covering dividend policy, overseas manufacturing and tax minimisation.

REVISION GUIDANCE

Planning your revision

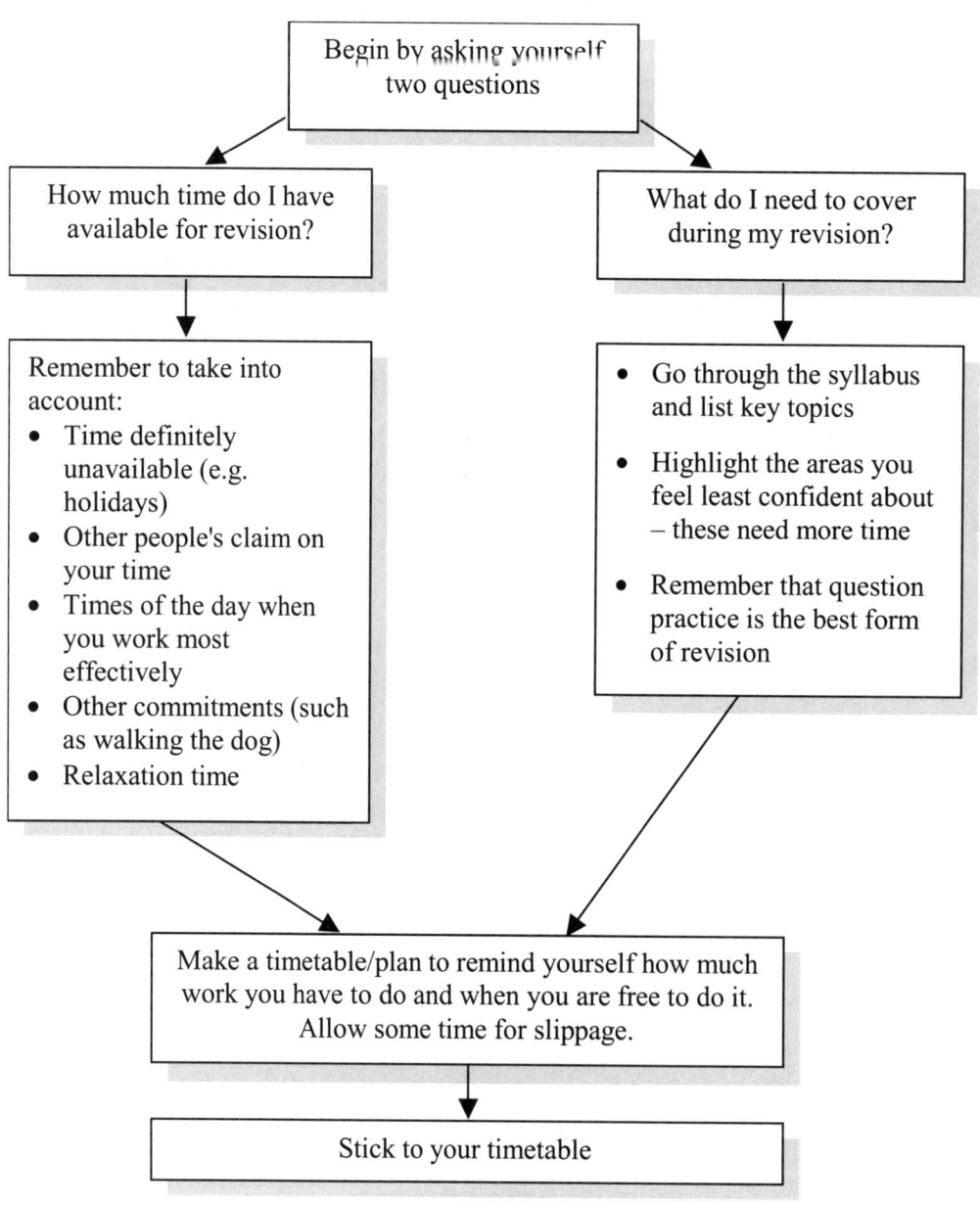

Begin by asking yourself two questions

How much time do I have available for revision?

What do I need to cover during my revision?

Remember to take into account:
- Time definitely unavailable (e.g. holidays)
- Other people's claim on your time
- Times of the day when you work most effectively
- Other commitments (such as walking the dog)
- Relaxation time

- Go through the syllabus and list key topics
- Highlight the areas you feel least confident about – these need more time
- Remember that question practice is the best form of revision

Make a timetable/plan to remind yourself how much work you have to do and when you are free to do it. Allow some time for slippage.

Stick to your timetable

Revision techniques

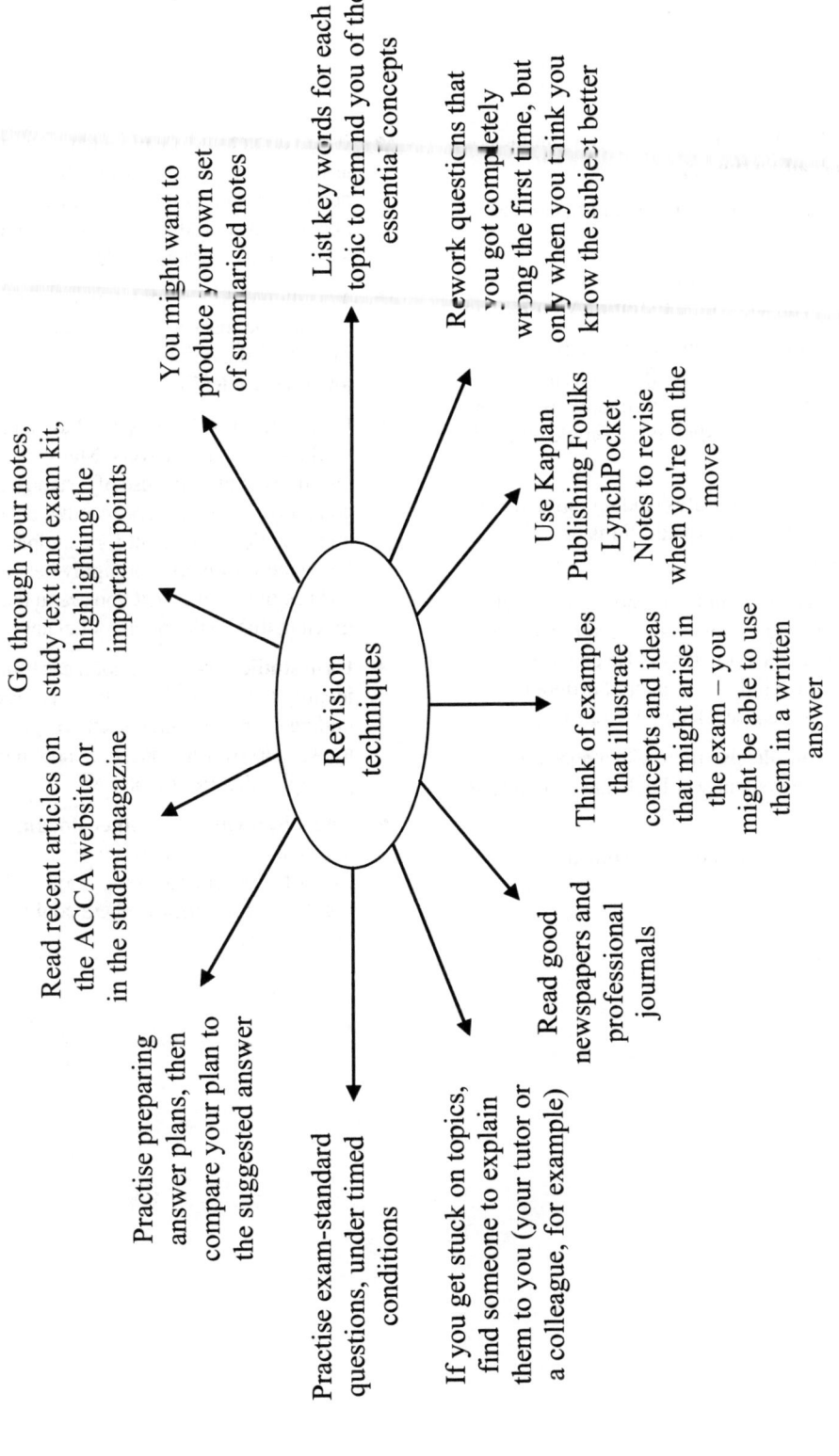

Revision techniques

List key words for each topic to remind you of the essential concepts

Rework questions that you got completely wrong the first time, but only when you think you know the subject better

You might want to produce your own set of summarised notes

Use Kaplan Publishing Foulks LynchPocket Notes to revise when you're on the move

Go through your notes, study text and exam kit, highlighting the important points

Think of examples that illustrate concepts and ideas that might arise in the exam – you might be able to use them in a written answer

Read recent articles on the ACCA website or in the student magazine

Read good newspapers and professional journals

Practise preparing answer plans, then compare your plan to the suggested answer

Practise exam-standard questions, under timed conditions

If you get stuck on topics, find someone to explain them to you (your tutor or a colleague, for example)

EXAM TECHNIQUES

- You might want to spend the first few minutes of the exam **reading the paper**.

- Where you have a **choice of question**, decide which questions you will do.

- Unless you know exactly how to answer the question, spend some time **planning** your answer.

- **Divide the time** you spend on questions in proportion to the marks on offer. One suggestion is to allocate 1½ minutes to each mark available, so a 10 mark question should be completed in 15 minutes.

- Spend the last **five minutes** reading through your answers and **making any additions or corrections**.

- **Essay questions**: Your essay should have a clear structure. It should contain a brief introduction, a main section and a conclusion. Be concise. It is better to write a little about a lot of different points than a great deal about one or two points.

- If you **get completely stuck** with a question, leave space in your answer book and **return to it later.**

- Stick to the question and **tailor your answer** to what you are asked. Pay particular attention to the verbs in the question.

- If you do not understand what a question is asking, **state your assumptions**. Even if you do not answer in precisely the way the examiner hoped, you should be given some credit, if your assumptions are reasonable.

- You should do everything you can to make things easy for the marker. The marker will find it easier to identify the points you have made if your **answers are legible**.

- **Computations**: It is essential to include all your workings in your answers. Many computational questions require the use of a standard format: company profit and loss account, balance sheet and cash flow statement for example. Be sure you know these formats thoroughly before the exam and use the layouts that you see in the answers given in this book and in model answers.

- **Case studies**: to write a good case study, first identify the area in which there is a problem, outline the main principles/theories you are going to use to answer the question, and then apply the principles/theories to the case.

- **Reports, memos and other documents**: some questions ask you to present your answer in the form of a report or a memo or other document. So use the correct format – there could be easy marks to gain here.

KAPLAN PUBLISHING

MATHEMATICAL TABLES

Formulae

Ke   (i) $E(r_j) = r_f + [E(r_m) - r_f]\beta_j$

     (ii) $\dfrac{D_1}{P_0} + g$

WACC $Ke_g \dfrac{E}{E+D} + Kd(1-t)\dfrac{D}{E+D}$

or $Ke_u \left(1 - \dfrac{Dt}{E+D}\right)$

2 asset portfolio

$$\sigma_p = \sqrt{\sigma_a^2 x^2 + \sigma_b^2 (1-x)^2 + 2x(1-x)p_{ab}\sigma_a\sigma_b}$$

Purchasing power parity $\dfrac{i_f - i_{uk}}{1 + i_{uk}}$

$$\beta_a = \beta_e \dfrac{E}{E+D(1-t)} + \beta_d \dfrac{D(1-t)}{E+D(1-t)}$$

Call price for a European option = $P_s\,N(d_1) - Xe^{-rT}\,N(d_2)$

$$d_1 = \frac{ln(Ps/X) + rT}{\sigma\sqrt{T}} + 0.5\,\sigma\sqrt{T}$$

$$d_2 = d_1 - \sigma\sqrt{T}$$

Put call parity $P^P = P^C - P^S + Xe^{-rT}$

(handwritten annotations)

Ps – share price
X – xercase price
r – ~~Ask free rate~~ rate
t – time
σ = risk

Present value table

Present value of 1 i.e. $(1+r)^{-n}$ where r = discount rate, n = number of periods until payment

Discount rate (r)

Periods

(n)	1%	2%	3%	4%	5%	6%	7%	8%	9%	10%	
1	0.990	0.980	0.971	0.962	0.952	0.943	0.935	0.926	0.917	0.909	1
2	0.980	0.961	0.943	0.925	0.907	0.890	0.873	0.857	0.842	0.826	2
3	0.971	0.942	0.915	0.889	0.864	0.840	0.816	0.794	0.772	0.751	3
4	0.961	0.924	0.888	0.855	0.823	0.792	0.763	0.735	0.708	0.683	4
5	0.951	0.906	0.863	0.822	0.784	0.747	0.713	0.681	0.650	0.621	5
6	0.942	0.888	0.837	0.790	0.746	0.705	0.666	0.630	0.596	0.564	6
7	0.933	0.871	0.813	0.760	0.711	0.665	0.623	0.583	0.547	0.513	7
8	0.923	0.853	0.789	0.731	0.677	0.627	0.582	0.540	0.502	0.467	8
9	0.914	0.837	0.766	0.703	0.645	0.592	0.544	0.500	0.460	0.424	9
10	0.905	0.820	0.744	0.676	0.614	0.558	0.508	0.463	0.422	0.386	10
11	0.896	0.804	0.722	0.650	0.585	0.527	0.475	0.429	0.388	0.350	11
12	0.887	0.788	0.701	0.625	0.557	0.497	0.444	0.397	0.356	0.319	12
13	0.879	0.773	0.681	0.601	0.530	0.469	0.415	0.368	0.326	0.290	13
14	0.870	0.758	0.661	0.577	0.505	0.442	0.388	0.340	0.299	0.263	14
15	0.861	0.743	0.642	0.555	0.481	0.417	0.362	0.315	0.275	0.239	15

(n)	11%	12%	13%	14%	15%	16%	17%	18%	19%	20%	
1	0.901	0.893	0.885	0.877	0.870	0.862	0.855	0.847	0.840	0.833	1
2	0.812	0.797	0.783	0.769	0.756	0.743	0.731	0.718	0.706	0.694	2
3	0.731	0.712	0.693	0.675	0.658	0.641	0.624	0.609	0.593	0.579	3
4	0.659	0.636	0.613	0.592	0.572	0.552	0.534	0.516	0.499	0.482	4
5	0.593	0.567	0.543	0.519	0.497	0.476	0.456	0.437	0.419	0.402	5
6	0.535	0.507	0.480	0.456	0.432	0.410	0.390	0.370	0.352	0.335	6
7	0.482	0.452	0.425	0.400	0.376	0.354	0.333	0.314	0.296	0.279	7
8	0.434	0.404	0.376	0.351	0.327	0.305	0.285	0.266	0.249	0.233	8
9	0.391	0.361	0.333	0.308	0.284	0.263	0.243	0.225	0.209	0.194	9
10	0.352	0.322	0.295	0.270	0.247	0.227	0.208	0.191	0.176	0.162	10
11	0.317	0.287	0.261	0.237	0.215	0.195	0.178	0.162	0.148	0.135	11
12	0.286	0.257	0.231	0.208	0.187	0.168	0.152	0.137	0.124	0.112	12
13	0.258	0.229	0.204	0.182	0.163	0.145	0.130	0.116	0.104	0.093	13
14	0.232	0.205	0.181	0.160	0.141	0.125	0.111	0.099	0.088	0.078	14
15	0.209	0.183	0.160	0.140	0.123	0.108	0.095	0.084	0.074	0.065	15

Annuity table

Present value of an annuity of 1 i.e. $\dfrac{1-(1+r)^{-n}}{r}$ where r = discount rate, N = number of periods

Discount rate (r)

Periods

(n)	1%	2%	3%	4%	5%	6%	7%	8%	9%	10%	
1	0.990	0.980	0.971	0.962	0.952	0.943	0.935	0.926	0.917	0.909	1
2	1.970	1.942	1.913	1.886	1.859	1.833	1.808	1.783	1.759	1.736	2
3	2.941	2.884	20829	2.775	2.723	2.673	2.624	2.577	2.531	2.487	3
4	3.902	3.808	3.717	3.630	3.546	3.465	3.387	3.312	3.240	3.170	4
5	4.853	4.713	4.580	4.452	4.329	4.212	4.100	3.993	3.890	3.791	5
6	5.795	5.601	5.417	5.242	5.076	4.917	4.767	4.623	4.486	4.355	6
7	6.728	6.472	6.230	6.002	5.786	5.582	5.389	5.206	5.033	4.868	7
8	7.652	7.325	7.020	6.733	6.463	6.210	5.971	5.747	5.535	5.335	8
9	8.566	8.162	7.786	7.435	7.108	6.802	6.515	6.247	5.995	5.759	9
10	9.471	8.983	8.530	8.111	7.722	7.360	7.024	6.710	6.418	6.145	10
11	10.37	9.787	9.253	8.760	8.306	7.887	7.499	7.139	6.805	6.495	11
12	11.26	10.58	9.954	9.385	8.863	8.384	7.943	7.536	7.161	6.814	12
13	12.13	11.35	10.63	9.986	9.394	8.853	8.358	7.904	7.487	7.103	13
14	13.00	12.11	11.30	10.56	9.899	9.295	8.745	8.244	7.786	7.367	14
15	13.87	12.85	11.94	11.12	10.38	9.712	9.108	8.559	8.061	7.606	15

(n)	11%	12%	13%	14%	15%	16%	17%	18%	19%	20%	
1	0.901	0.893	0.885	0.877	0.870	0.862	0.855	0.847	0.840	0.833	1
2	1.713	1.690	1.668	1.647	1.626	1.605	1.585	1.566	1.547	1.528	2
3	2.444	2.402	2.361	2.322	2.283	2.246	2.210	2.174	2.140	2.106	3
4	3.102	3.037	2.974	2.914	2.855	2.798	2.743	2.690	2.639	2.589	4
5	3.696	3.605	3.517	3.433	3.352	3.274	3.199	3.127	3.058	2.991	5
6	4.231	4.111	3.998	3.889	3.784	3.685	3.589	3.498	3.410	3.326	6
7	4.712	4.564	4.423	4.288	4.160	4.039	3.922	3.812	3.706	3.605	7
8	5.146	4.968	4.799	4.639	4.487	4.344	4.207	4.078	3.954	3.837	8
9	5.537	5.328	5.132	4.946	4.772	4.607	4.451	4.303	4.163	4.031	9
10	5.889	5.650	5.426	5.216	5.019	4.833	4.659	4.494	4.339	4.192	10
11	6.207	5.938	5.687	5.453	5.234	5.029	4.836	4.656	4.486	4.327	11
12	6.492	6.194	5.918	5.660	5.421	5.197	4.988	4.793	4.611	4.439	12
13	6.750	6.424	6.122	5.842	5.583	5.342	5.118	4.910	4.715	4.533	13
14	6.982	6.628	6.302	6.002	5.724	5.468	5.229	5.008	4.802	4.611	14
15	7.191	6.811	6.462	6.142	5.847	5.575	5.324	5.092	4.876	4.675	15

Standard normal distribution table

	0.00	0.01	0.02	0.03	0.04	0.05	0.06	0.07	0.08	0.09
0.0	0.0000	0.0040	0.0080	0.0120	0.0160	0.0199	0.0239	0.0279	0.0319	0.0359
0.1	0.0398	0.0438	0.0478	0.0517	0.0557	0.0596	0.0636	0.0675	0.0714	0.0753
0.2	0.0793	0.0832	0.0871	0.0910	0.0948	0.0987	0.1026	0.1064	0.1103	0.1141
0.3	0.1179	0.1217	0.1255	0.1293	0.1331	0.1368	0.1406	0.1443	0.1480	0.1517
0.4	0.1554	0.1591	0.1628	0.1664	0.1700	0.1736	0.1772	0.1808	0.1844	0.1879
0.5	0.1915	0.1950	0.1985	0.2019	0.2054	0.2088	0.2123	0.2157	0.2190	0.2224
0.6	0.2257	0.2291	0.2324	0.2357	0.2389	0.2422	0.2454	0.2486	0.2517	0.2549
0.7	0.2580	0.2611	0.2642	0.2673	0.2703	0.2734	0.2764	0.2794	0.2823	0.2852
0.8	0.2881	0.2910	0.2939	0.2967	0.2995	0.3023	0.3051	0.3078	0.3106	0.3133
0.9	0.3159	0.3186	0.3212	0.3238	0.3264	0.3289	0.3315	0.3340	0.3365	0.3389
1.0	0.3413	0.3438	0.3461	0.3485	0.3508	0.3531	0.3554	0.3577	0.3599	0.3621
1.1	0.3643	0.3665	0.3686	0.3708	0.3729	0.3749	0.3770	0.3790	0.3810	0.3830
1.2	0.3849	0.3869	0.3888	0.3907	0.3925	0.3944	0.3962	0.3980	0.3997	0.4015
1.3	0.4032	0.4049	0.4066	0.4082	0.4099	0.4115	0.4131	0.4147	0.4162	0.4177
1.4	0.4192	0.4207	0.4222	0.4236	0.4251	0.4265	0.4279	0.4292	0.4306	0.4319
1.5	0.4332	0.4345	0.4375	0.4370	0.4382	0.4394	0.4406	0.4418	0.4429	0.4441
1.6	0.4452	0.4463	0.4474	0.4484	0.4495	0.4505	0.4515	0.4525	0.4535	0.4545
1.7	0.4554	0.4564	0.4573	0.4582	0.4591	0.4599	0.4608	0.4616	0.4625	0.4633
1.8	0.4641	0.4649	0.4656	0.4664	0.4671	0.4678	0.4686	0.4693	0.4699	0.4706
1.9	0.4713	0.4719	0.4726	0.4732	0.4738	0.4744	0.4750	0.4756	0.4761	0.4767
2.0	0.4772	0.4778	0.4783	0.4788	0.4793	0.4798	0.4803	0.4808	0.4812	0.4817
2.1	0.4821	0.4826	0.4830	0.4834	0.4838	0.4842	0.4846	0.4850	0.4854	0.4857
2.2	0.4861	0.4864	0.4868	0.4871	0.4875	0.4878	0.4881	0.4884	0.4887	0.4890
2.3	0.4893	0.4896	0.4898	0.4901	0.4904	0.4906	0.4909	0.4911	0.4913	0.4916
2.4	0.4918	0.4920	0.4922	0.4925	0.4927	0.4929	0.4931	0.4932	0.4934	0.4936
2.5	0.4938	0.4940	0.4941	0.4943	0.4945	0.4946	0.4948	0.4949	0.4951	0.4952
2.6	0.4953	0.4955	0.4956	0.4957	0.4959	0.4960	0.4961	0.4962	0.4963	0.4964
2.7	0.4965	0.4966	0.4967	0.4968	0.4969	0.4970	0.4971	0.4972	0.4973	0.4974
2.8	0.4974	0.4975	0.4976	0.4977	0.4977	0.4978	0.4979	0.4979	0.4980	0.4981
2.9	0.4981	0.4982	0.4982	0.4983	0.4984	0.4984	0.4985	0.4985	0.4986	0.4986
3.0	0.4987	0.4987	0.4987	0.4988	0.4988	0.4989	0.4989	0.4989	0.4990	0.4990

This table can be used to calculate $N(d_i)$, the cumulative normal distribution functions needed for the Black-Scholes model of option pricing. If $d_i > 0$, add 0.5 to the relevant number above. If $d_i < 0$, subtract the relevant number above from 0.5.

Section 1

PRACTICE QUESTIONS

OBJECTIVES AND CORPORATE GOVERNANCE

1   INFLUENCE ON OBJECTIVES

Discuss, and provide examples of, the types of non-financial, ethical and environmental issues that might influence the objectives of companies. Consider the impact of these non-financial, ethical and environmental issues on the achievement of primary financial objectives such as the maximisation of shareholder wealth.   **(15 marks)**

2   BONDS AND COVENANTS

(a)   Discuss why conflicts of interest might exist between shareholders and bondholders.
(8 marks)

(b)   Provide examples of covenants that might be attached to bonds, and briefly discuss the advantages and disadvantages to companies of covenants.   **(7 marks)**

(Total: 15 marks)

3   CORPORATE GOVERNANCE

The following are extracts from the corporate governance guidelines issued by a UK plc:

(i)   All auditors' fees, including fees for services other than audit, should be fully disclosed in the annual report. In order to ensure continuity of standards the same audit partner, wherever possible, should be responsible for a period of at least three years.

(ii)   The board shall establish a remuneration committee comprising 50% executive directors, and 50% non-executive directors. A non-executive director shall chair the committee.

(iii)   The Chairman of the company may also hold the position of Chief Executive, although this shall not normally be for a period of more than three years.

(iv)   The annual report shall fully disclose whether principles of good corporate governance have been applied.

(v)   No director shall hold directorships in more than twenty companies.

(vi)   Directors should regularly report on the effectiveness of the company's system of internal control.

Required:

(a)   Discuss the extent to which each of points (i) – (vi) is likely to comply with corporate governance systems such as the UK Combined Code.   **(9 marks)**

(b) Prepare a brief report advising senior managers of your company who are going to work in subsidiaries in Germany, Japan and the USA of the main differences in corporate governance between the UK and any TWO of the above countries, and possible implications of the differences for the managers. **(6 marks)**

(Total: 15 marks)

STRATEGY FORMULATION INCLUDING VALUATION OF SECURITIES

4 FINANCING MIX

(a) Discuss the main factors that should be taken into account when developing a short-term financial plan. **(5 marks)**

(b) Beppan plc's current assets are 65% of its total assets. The company is considering what mix of short-term and long-term financing to use. The UK yield curve is currently downward sloping, largely because of expectations that the UK will join the single currency eurozone in a few years' time. The company's managing director has suggested that, given the shape of the yield curve, at least 90% of financing needs should be from medium to long-term sources.

Required:

Discuss the advantages and disadvantages of the managing director's suggestion regarding the financing mix that the company should use. **(5 marks)**

(Total: 10 marks)

5 CORPORATE FAILURE

Assume that 'now' is December 20X3.

The managing director of Snowwell plc has received an unsolicited letter from a reputable organisation specialising in the prediction of corporate failure, which suggests that Snowwell has been identified as a probable failing company. The organisation has offered to supply details of the full report on Snowwell for £100,000.

Given the collapse of many companies' share prices during the last few years, the managing director of Snowwell is concerned that if the contents of the report become public knowledge, Snowwell's share price could also fall.

He has also read about various models which use combinations of financial ratios to attempt to predict corporate failure, including a leading business school's S_0 model (developed in 20X1) which produces a score based upon the following equation:

$$S_0 = 3.5S_1 + 1.8S_2 + 0.25S_3 + 0.69S_4$$

where:

S_1 = Earnings before interest and tax/market value of equity

S_2 = Working capital/medium and long term capital employed

S_3 = Market value of equity/market value of debt

S_4 = The present value to infinity of current operating free cash flow/turnover

According to the S_0 system, a company scoring less than 1 has a high probability of failure; a score of 1 – 2 suggests remedial action is necessary to improve corporate financial performance; and a score of over 2 means that a company has a high probability of survival for at least three years, which is the maximum claimed prediction period for the model.

The latest summarised accounts of Snowwell plc are shown below:

BALANCE SHEETS AS AT

	31 March 20X3		31 March 20X2	
Fixed assets	£ million	£ million	£ million	£ million
Land and buildings (net)		211		196
Other fixed assets (net)		247		235
		458		431
Current assets				
Stock	156		127	
Debtors	32		34	
Cash	5		3	
		193		164
Creditors: amounts falling due within 1 year				
Creditors	196		166	
Dividend	12		12	
Taxation	7		10	
		(215)		(188)
Creditors: amounts falling due after more than 1 year				
14% loan stock redeemable December 20X6 (£100 par)		(150)		(150)
Floating rate bank term loans		(94)		(64)
		192		193
Shareholders funds				
Ordinary shares (50 pence par)		75		75
Reserves		117		118
		192		193

PROFIT AND LOSS ACCOUNTS FOR THE YEARS ENDING

	31 March 20X3	31 March 20X2
	£ million	£ million
Turnover	620	580
Earnings before interest and tax	43	52
Interest	20	18
Profit before tax	23	34
Taxation	7	10
Available to shareholders	16	24
Dividend	17	17
Retained earnings	(1)	7

Additional information:

(i)   The share price of Snowwell plc is currently 232 pence.

(ii)   The current redemption yield on loan stock of similar risk to that of Snowwell is 8%, which is also the current interest rate of the floating rate term loan.

(iii)   Snowwell needs to invest approximately £35 million per year to maintain operations at current levels.

(iv)   Tax allowable depreciation in 20X3 was £38 million.

(v)   Snowwell's cost of equity is estimated to be 12%.

(vi)   Corporate tax is at the rate of 30% per year.

(vii)   The average gearing of Snowwell's industry is 50% (measured by the market value of medium and long-term debt related to the market value of equity).

(viii) Snowwell's turnover is mostly retail sales of high quality jewellery and watches.

Required:

You have been requested by the managing director of Snowwell plc to prepare a briefing document that includes:

(a)   An estimate of the S_0 score for Snowwell plc.   **(11 marks)**

(b)   A discussion of the significance of this score for Snowwell plc.   **(4 marks)**

(c)   A brief discussion of alternative ways of assessing whether or not Snowwell plc is likely to experience financial distress and/or corporate failure.   **(4 marks)**

(d)   Recommendations as to whether or not Snowwell should take any action based upon your findings in (a) – (c) above and any other relevant information or analysis

                                                                                      (7 marks)

(e)   A discussion as to whether or not Snowwell should purchase the full report for £100,000.   **(4 marks)**

                                                                            (Total: 30 marks)

6   NOIFA LEISURE PLC

Extracts from the annual report of Noifa Leisure plc are shown below:

Chairman's report

'The group's financial position has never been stronger. Turnover has risen 209% and the share price has almost doubled during the last four years, between 20X6 and 20X9. Since the end of the financial year the company has acquired Beddall Hotels for £100 million, financed at only 9% per year by a Euro floating rate loan which has little risk. Our objective is to become the largest hotel group in the United Kingdom within five years.'

Profit and loss account summaries for the years ending 31 December

	20X6 £m	20X7 £m	20X8 £m	20X9 £m
Turnover	325	370	490	680
Operating profit	49	60	75	92
Investment income	18	10	3	1
	67	70	78	93
Interest payable	14	16	24	36
Profit before tax	53	54	54	57

	20X6 £m	20X7 £m	20X8 £m	20X9 £m
Taxation	20	19	19	20
Profit after taxation	33	35	35	37
Extraordinary items[1]	(3)	–	–	4
Profit attributable to shareholders	30	35	35	41
Dividends	12	12	12	12
Retained earnings	18	23	23	29

[1] Loss/gain on disposal of fixed assets

Balance sheet summaries as at 31 December

	20X6 £m	20X7 £m	20X8 £m	20X9 £m
Fixed assets				
Tangible assets	165	260	424	696
Investments	120	68	20	4
	285	328	444	700
Current assets				
Stock	40	45	70	110
Debtors	56	52	75	94
Cash	2	3	4	5
	98	100	149	209
Less: Current liabilities				
Trade creditors	82	94	130	176
Taxation	18	19	19	20
Overdraft	-	-	42	68
Other	15	24	28	42
	115	137	219	306
Total assets less current liabilities	268	291	374	603
Financed by:				
Ordinary shares (10 pence nominal value)	50	50	50	50
Share premium	22	22	22	22
Revaluation reserve	-	-	-	100
Revenue reserves	74	97	120	149
Shareholders' funds	146	169	192	321
Bank loans	42	42	102	102
13% debenture (9 years to redemption)	80	80	80	180
	268	291	374	603

Analysis by type of activity

	20X6		20X7		20X8		20X9	
	Turnover	*Profit[1]*	*Turnover*	*Profit*	*Turnover*	*Profit*	*Turnover*	*Profit*
	£m	£m	£m	£m	£m	£m	£m	£m
Hotels	196	36	227	41	314	37	471	45
Theme park	15	(3)	18	(2)	24	3	34	5
Bus company	24	6	28	8	38	14	46	18
Car hire	43	7	45	8	52	12	62	15
Zoo[2]	5	(1)	6	(1)	9	0	10	(1)
Waxworks	10	1	11	3	13	4	14	5
Publications	32	3	35	3	40	5	43	5
	325	49	370	60	490	75	680	92

[1]Operating profit before taxation.

[2]The zoo was sold during 20X9.

	20X6	20X7	20X8	20X9
Noifa plc average share price (pence)	82	104	120	159
FT 100 Share Index	1,500	1,750	1,800	2,300
Leisure industry share index	178	246	344	394
Leisure industry PE ratio	10:1	12:1	19:1	25:1

Required:

In his report the chairman stated that 'the group's financial position has never been stronger.' From the viewpoint of an external consultant appraise whether you agree with the chairman. Discussion of the group's financing policies and strategic objective, with suggestions as to how these might be altered, should form part of your appraisal. Relevant calculations must be shown.

(30 marks)

7 COMPANY'S SHARES

Your managing director has just attended a meeting with an investment analyst who has suggested that your company's shares are overvalued by 10%. The data used by the investment analyst in her calculations is shown below. ('Now' is June 20X4).

Year	Total dividends £000	Number of shares	Total earnings £000
20X0	5,680	28,600,000	18,260
20X1	6,134	28,600,000	21,320
20X2	8,108	35,000,000	26,710
20X3	10,007	40,000,000	28,620

Your company's current share price is 645 pence and the cost of equity is estimated to be 12.5%.

Required:

Prepare a brief report for the managing director discussing whether or not your company's shares are likely to be overvalued. Relevant calculations should form part of your report.

(10 marks)

8 BNG PLC

Investor of bonds

'Now' is the end of December 2003.

BNG plc has a number of long-term fixed interest financial investments. The company's treasury team has received data on two other bonds and is considering whether or not to replace an investment in the bonds of Magnacorp with either bonds of Suprafirm or Grandit. *— assumes market is efficient*

Details of the bonds are presented below:

	Magnacorp	Suprafirm	Grandit
Annual coupon *Interest only!!*	8.125%	6.5%	7.8%
Maturity date	*10yrs* 31/12/2013	*10yrs* 31/12/2013	*4yrs* 31/12/2007
Credit rating (Standard & Poor's)	A–	BBB+	A–
Market price £	107.8	93.1	105.83
Yield to redemption K_D *Total return*	7.0%	7.5%	6.0%
Redemption price £	100	100	100

Capital Loss

Required:

(a) Prepare reasoned advice to BNG plc as to whether or not the bonds of Magnacorp should be replaced. **(3 marks)**

(b) Evaluate whether or not the market price of Grandit's bonds in the above table is what would be expected from the company's other data. **(3 marks)**

(c) Discuss whether or not your advice in (a) above would change if the yield curve is upward sloping but BNG plc's treasury team expect interest rates to fall, with medium-term interest rates expected to fall by more than long-term interest rates. **(4 marks)**

(Total: 10 marks)

9 TOUTPLUT INC

— EVA for 2 years

Assume that 'now' is June 20X4.

The managers of Toutplut Inc were surprised at a recent newspaper article which suggested that the company's performance in the last two years had been poor. The CEO commented that turnover had increased by nearly 17% and pre-tax profit by 25% between the last two financial years, and that the company compared well with others in the same industry.

Profit and loss account extracts for the year

	20X2	20X3
	$ million	$ million
Turnover	326	380
Pre-tax accounting profit *(Note)*	67	84
Taxation	23	29
Profit after tax	44	55
Dividends	15	18
Retained earnings	29	37

Balance sheet extracts for the year ending

	20X2	20X3
	$ million	$ million
Fixed assets	120	156
Net current assets	130	160
	250	316
Financed by:		
Shareholders' funds	195	236
Medium and long-term bank loans	55	80
	250	316

Economic dep = accounting dep added back ✓

Note: After deduction of the economic depreciation of the company's fixed assets. This is also the depreciation used for tax purposes. *Do not add back or subtract depre*

Other information:

Opening capital employed

Total value + Addback 10 each year

(i) Toutplut had non-capitalised leases valued at $10 million in each year 20X1 – 20X3.

(ii) Balance sheet capital employed at the end of 20X1 was $223 million.

(iii) The company's pre-tax cost of debt was estimated to be 9% in 20X2, and 10% in 20X3. *Kd*

(iv) The company's cost of equity was estimated to be 15% in 20X2 and 17% in 20X3. *Ke*

(v) The target capital structure is 60% equity, 40% debt. *Gearing*

(vi) The effective tax rate was 35% in both 20X2 and 20X3. *Tax*

Ignore — (vii) Economic depreciation was $30 million in 20X2 and $35 million in 20X3.

Add back gross — (viii) Other non-cash expenses were $10 million per year in both 20X2 and 20X3.

Add back Net — (ix) Interest expense was $4 million in 20X2 and $6 million in 20X3.

Required:

(a) Estimate the Economic Value Added (EVA) for Toutplut Inc for both 20X2 and 20X3. State clearly any assumptions that you make. Comment upon the performance of the company. **(7 marks)**

(b) Explain the relationship between economic value added and net present value. *PV of EVA = NPV in theory* **(2 marks)**

(c) Briefly discuss the advantages and disadvantages of EVA. **(6 marks)**

Pg 100 **(Total: 15 marks)**

10 WURRALL PLC

The board of directors of Wurrall plc has requested the production of a four-year financial plan. The key assumptions behind the plan are:

(i) Historically, sales growth has been 9% per year. Uncertainty about future economic prospects over the next four years from 2005–2008 however implies that this growth rate will reduce by 1% per year after the financial year 2005 (e.g. to 8% in 2006). After four years, growth is expected to remain constant at the 2008 rate.

(ii) Cash operating costs are estimated to be approximately 68% of sales.

(iii) Tax allowable depreciation for the past few years has been approximately 15% of the net book value of plant and machinery at year end. This is expected to continue for the next few years.

(iv) Stocks, debtors, cash in hand and 'other creditors' are assumed to increase in proportion to the increase in sales.

(v) Investment in, and net book value of, plant and machinery is expected to increase in line with sales. No investment is planned in other fixed assets other than a refurbishment of buildings at an estimated cost of £40 million in late 2007.

(vi) Any change in interest paid as a result of changes in borrowing may be assumed to be effective in the next year. Wurrall plans to meet any changes in financing needs, with the exception of the repayment of the fixed rate loan, by adjusting its overdraft.

(vii) Wurrall currently pays 7% per annum interest on its short-term borrowing.

(viii) Corporation tax is expected to continue at its present rate over the next four years.

(ix)   For the last few years the company's dividend policy has been to pay a constant percentage of earnings after tax. No changes in this policy are planned.

(x)   Wurrall has borrowed extensively from the banking system, and covenants exist that prevent the company's gearing (book value of total loans to book value of total loans plus equity) exceeding 40% for a period of more than one year.

(xi)   The company's managing director has publicly stated that both profits before tax and Wurrall's share price should increase by at least 100% during the next four years.

Summarised financial accounts of Wurrall plc:
Profit and loss account for the year ended March 2004

	£ million
Turnover	1,639
Operating costs before depreciation	(1,225)
EBITDA	414
Tax allowable depreciation	(152)
EBIT	262
Net interest payable	(57)
Profit on ordinary activities before tax	205
Tax on ordinary activities (30%)	(62)
Dividends	(80)
Amount transferred to reserves	63

Balance sheet as at 31 March 2004

	£ million
Fixed assets	
Land and buildings	310
Plant and machinery (net)	1,012
Investments (i)	32
	1,354
Current assets	
Stocks	448
Debtors	564
Cash in hand and short-term deposits	20
	1,032
Creditors: amounts falling due within one year	
Short term loans and overdrafts	230
Other creditors	472
	(702)
Creditors: amounts falling due after one year:	
Borrowings (8% fixed rate) (ii)	(580)
	1,104
Capital and reserves	
Called up share capital (10 pence par)	240
Reserves	864
	1,104

(i)   The investments yield negligible interest

(ii)   Borrowings are scheduled to be repaid at the end of 2006 and will be refinanced with a similar type of loan in 2006.

The company's current share price is 210 pence, and its weighted average cost of capital is 11%.

Required:

(a)   Produce pro forma balance sheets and profit and loss accounts for each of the next four years. Clearly state any assumptions that you make.   **(12 marks)**

(b)   Critically discuss any problems or implications of the assumptions that are made in each of points (i) to (iv) and point (ix) in the question.   **(8 marks)**

(c)   Using free cash flow analysis, evaluate and discuss whether or not the managing director's claims for the future share price are likely to be achievable. (The operating cash flow element of free cash flow may be estimated by: EBIT(1-t) plus depreciation.)   **(10 marks)**

(d)   Using financial ratios or other forms of analysis, highlight any potential financial problems for the company during this period. Discuss what actions might be taken with respect to these problems.   **(10 marks)**

(Total: 40 marks)

11   REMUNERATION

The remuneration committee of a plc is discussing the remuneration package that might to be offered to the company's new managing director. Members of the committee have expressed different opinions. These include:

(i)   The managing director must be offered a salary at least 20% more than the average of similar sized companies in order to attract the best candidates.

(ii)   It is essential to offer a salary linked to turnover.

(iii)   The managing director should be offered share options, exercisable in one year's time, on at least 3,000,000 shares, at an exercise price of 25% below the current market price of 120 pence.

(iv)   Remuneration should be a basic salary plus a proportion of the economic value added (EVA®) of the company. 1.5% per year was the suggested proportion.

In the ensuing debate one committee member stated that a friend had recently bought one year European style put options on the company's shares at a price of 35 pence. The options to be granted to the new managing director would therefore be worth several million pounds. Such generosity would not be well received given recent newspaper commentary about the excessive remuneration of senior managers in some companies.

Relevant company and market data is shown below:

Year ended 31 March 2004

	£ million
Turnover	546
Cost of sales	(369)
Depreciation	(52)
Advertising	(10)
Net interest	(26)
Profit before tax	89

Taxation	(27)	
Available to shareholders *PAT*	62	

	Opening £ million	Closing
	31 March 2003	31 March 2004
Capital employed	420	458

Notes:

(i)   Accounting depreciation is approximately equal to economic deprecation. *Cashflow*

(ii)   Advertising has been £10 million per year for the last four years. *x 4 yrs = 40*

(iii)   The company's cost of equity is 12%

(iv)   The company's weighted average cost of capital is 9.5% — *WACC*

(v)   The risk free rate is 4%

(vi)   The corporate tax rate is 30%

Required:

(a)   Discuss the relative merits of each of the four suggestions.   **(6 marks)**

(b)   Some committee members have expressed concern about how much some of the suggestions might cost the company.

   For both the share option and EVA® suggestions, estimate the potential cost to the company, and comment on your findings. For EVA® the estimate should be based upon the most recent relevant published data.   **(9 marks)**

   (Total: 15 marks)

PORTFOLIO THEORY AND CAPM

12   PORTFOLIO RISK AND RETURN (MALTEC)

Maltec plc is a company that has diversified into five different industries in five different countries. The investments are each approximately equal in value. The company's objective is to reduce risk through diversification, and it believes that the return on any investment is not correlated with the return on any other investment. The estimated risk and return (in present value terms) of the five investments are shown below:

Investments	Total Risk (% standard deviation)	Return (%)
1	8	14
2	10	16
3	7	12
4	4	9
5	16	22

Required:

(a)   Estimate the risk and return of the portfolio of five investments, and briefly explain the significance of your results.   **(5 marks)**

(b)   Discuss the validity to investors of Maltec's objective for risk reduction through international diversification.   **(5 marks)**

   (Total: 10 marks)

13 ALPHA VALUES

You have purchased the following data from an investment bank.

Company	Forecast total equity return	Standard deviation of total equity return	Covariance with market return
Dedton	16%	6.3%	32%
Paralot	12%	4.8%	19%
Sunout	14%	4.7%	24%
Rangon	19%	6.9%	43%

The market return and market standard deviation are 14.5% and 5% respectively, and the risk free rate is 6%. Returns and all other data relate to a one year period.

Required:

(a) Estimate the 'alpha' values for each of these companies' shares and explain what use alpha values might be to financial managers. **(6 marks)**

(b) Briefly discuss reasons for the existence of alpha values, and whether or not the same alpha values would be expected to exist in one years time. **(4 marks)**

(Total: 10 marks)

14 PHANTOM PLC

Phantom plc wishes to buy £1 million of shares in each of two companies from a choice of three companies that it might wish to acquire at some future date. The companies are in different industries. Historic five year data on the risk and returns of the three companies are shown below.

	Average annual returns	Standard deviation of returns
Mangeit Foods	11%	17%
Altalk Communications	20%	29%
Legi Printers	14%	21%

Correlation coefficients between returns

Mangeit and Altalk	0.00
Altalk and Legi	0.40
Mangeit and Legi	0.62

An adviser to Phantom plc has suggested that the decision about which shares to buy should be based upon selecting the most efficient portfolio of two shares.

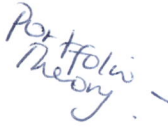

Required:

(a) Estimate which of the possible portfolios is the most efficient. **(5 marks)**

(b) Discuss whether or not Phantom plc's strategy should be to purchase the most efficient portfolio of two shares. **(5 marks)**

(Total: 10 marks)

15 MUNXAY PLC

Munxay plc is comprised of only four major investment projects, details of which are as follows:

Project	% of company market value	Annual % return during the last five years	Risk % standard deviation	Correlation with the market
1	28	10	15	0.55
2	17	18	20	0.75
3	31	15	14	0.84
4	24	13	18	0.62

The risk free rate is expected to be 5% per year, the market return 14% per year, and the standard deviation of market returns 13%.

Required:

(a) Assume that Munxay plc's shares are currently priced based upon the assumption that the last five years' experience of returns will continue for the foreseeable future. Evaluate whether or not the share price of Munxay plc is undervalued or overvalued.

(5 marks)

(b) Discuss why your results in (a) above might not correctly identify whether or not the share price of Munxay plc is undervalued or overvalued. **(5 marks)**

(Total: 10 marks)

16 HASDER PLC

Hasder plc currently operates only in the UK, but is considering diversifying its activities internationally into either Europe or East Asia, the latter including several developing economies. Estimates have been obtained of the likely risk and return of investments in these parts of the world, which are expected to vary during different economic states of the UK. After either diversification approximately 30% of the market value of the company would be represented by overseas investments.

UK economic state	Probability	Expected % IRR return		
		Invest in Europe	Invest in East Asia	Invest in UK
Low growth	0.3	7	2	6
Average growth	0.5	12	30	13
Rapid growth	0.2	21	15	17

Standard deviation of expected returns:

Europe	4.86
East Asia	12.26
UK	4.03

Covariances of expected returns:

UK/Europe	17.89
UK/East Asia	31.98

Members of Hasder's board of directors have different views about such diversification.

Director A believes that the company should focus exclusively upon the UK market as it always has, because 'overseas investments are too risky'.

Director B believes that overseas diversification will offer the company the opportunity to achieve a much better combination of risk and return than purely domestic investments, and 'will open up new opportunities'.

Director C considers that overseas investments are expensive, and overseas diversification will not be valued by shareholders who could easily achieve such diversification themselves.

Director D is in favour of the diversification, but considers East Asia to be a much better alternative than Europe.

Director E is also in favour of East Asia, but suggests that a much higher proportion of the company's activities should be located there, possibly between 50% and 70%.

Required:

(a)   Discuss the views of each of the five directors. Include in your discussion relevant calculations regarding portfolio risks and returns. What other factors might influence the investment decision?

State clearly any assumptions that you make.   **(25 marks)**

(b)   Estimate and explain the implications of the correlation coefficients between:

(i)   UK/Europe; and

(ii)   UK/East Asia.   **(6 marks)**

(c)   Hasder plc has also purchased CAPM-based risk and return estimates from an investment bank.

	Relevant market return	*Relevant risk free rate*	*Relevant investment beta*
Europe	13%	5%	0.85
East Asia	18%	8%	1.32

Assuming this information is accurate, show how it might be used to assist the diversification decision.   **(4 marks)**

(Total: 35 marks)

17   WONPAR PLC

Wonpar plc wishes to invest £5 million in ordinary shares for a period of up to five years. The company's directors are debating about in which country(ies) to invest.

Director 1 suggests investing in France because it has a relatively high expected return and a low standard deviation of returns.

Director 2 suggests Singapore, as it has the lowest correlation coefficient with the UK stock market.

Correlation coefficients between stock market returns

	UK	USA	France	Japan	Singapore	Hong Kong
UK	–					
USA		0.62	–			
France	0.74	0.49	–			
Japan	0.36	0.43	0.37	–		
Singapore	0.25	0.32	0.41	0.56	–	
Hong Kong	0.44	0.52	0.49	0.67	0.71	–

	Average return (%)	Standard deviation (%)	Beta
UK	12.8	6.3	0.94
USA	11.9	7.2	0.98
France	13.0	4.6	1.06
Singapore	12.9	10.3	1.17
Hong Kong	15.3	14.2	1.32

Notes:

(1)   The world beta is 1

(2)   Average returns have been adjusted for currency changes relative to the pound

Required:

Prepare a brief report that:

(a)   discusses the possible benefits of international portfolio investment, and

(b)   comments upon the validity of each of the two directors' suggestions.

Additional calculations are NOT required as part of the report.   **(10 marks)**

18   DELTA HEDGE (UNIGLOW)

(a)   Briefly discuss the meaning and importance of the terms 'delta', 'theta', and 'vega' (also known as kappa or lambda) in option pricing.   **(5 marks)**

(b)   Assume that your company has invested in 100,000 shares of Uniglow plc, a manufacturer of light bulbs. You are concerned about the recent volatility in Uniglow's share price due to the unpredictable weather in the United Kingdom. You wish to protect your company's investment from a possible fall in Uniglow's share price until winter in three months' time, but do not wish to sell the shares at present. No dividends are due to be paid by Uniglow during the next three months.

Market data:

Uniglow's current share price: 200 pence

Call option exercise price: 220 pence

Time to expiry: 3 months

Interest rate (annual): 6%

Volatility of Uniglow's shares 50% (standard deviation per year)

Assume that option contracts are for the purchase or sale of units of 1,000 shares.

Required:

(i)   Devise a delta hedge that is expected to protect the investment against changes in the share price until winter. Delta may be estimated using N(d1).   **(8 marks)**

(ii)   Comment upon whether or not such a hedge is likely to be totally successful.   **(2 marks)**

(Total: 15 marks)

19 BLACK-SCHOLES (AVT)

(a) Discuss how a decrease in the value of each of the determinants of the option price in the Black-Scholes option-pricing model for European options likely to change the price of a call option.   **(6 marks)**

(b) AVT plc is considering the introduction of an executive share option scheme.

The scheme would be offered to all middle managers of the company. It would replace the existing scheme of performance bonuses linked to the post-tax earnings per share of the company. Such bonuses in the last year ranged between £5,000 and £7,000. If the option scheme is introduced new options are expected to be offered to the managers each year.

It is proposed for the first year that all middle managers are offered options to purchase 5,000 shares at a price of 500 pence per share, after the options have been held for one year. Assume that the tax authorities allow the exercise of such options after they have been held for one year. If the options are not exercised at that time they will lapse.

The company's shares have just come ex-div and have a current market price of 610 pence. The dividend paid was 25 pence share, a level that has remained constant for the last three years. Assume that dividends are only paid annually.

The company's share price has experienced a standard deviation of 38% during the last year.

The short-term risk-free interest rate is 6% annum.

Required:

(i) Discuss the relative merits for the company of the existing bonus scheme and the proposed share option scheme.   **(6 marks)**

(ii) Evaluate whether or not the proposed share option scheme is likely to be attractive to middle managers of AVT plc.   **(11 marks)**

(iii) When told of the scheme one manager stated that he would rather receive put options than call options, as they would be more valuable to him.

(1) Discuss whether or not AVT should agree to offer him put options.

(3 marks)

(2) Calculate whether or not he is correct in his statement that put options would be more valuable to him.   **(4 marks)**

(Total: 30 marks)

20 CHANCIT PLC

The board of directors of Chancit plc is concerned that two of its divisions appear to be significantly less successful in their capital investments than the company's other divisions. Investment ideas are normally generated by senior divisional managers, and then approved or rejected by the main board. An external consultant has suggested that the divisions' performance might be related to the attitude to risk of senior divisional managers. The consultant has tested such attitude and produced tables of equal satisfaction under different risk/return conditions, for both of the divisions' managers.

Division 1

Expected NPV	Risk (σ)
£1,000,000 with certainty	0
80% chance of £1.3m, 20% chance of £700,000	0.24
60% chance of £1.8m, 40% chance of £300,000	0.74
40% chance of £2.5m, 60% chance of £100,000	1.08
20% chance of £3.0m, 80% chance of (£100,000)	1.24
10% chance of £4.0m, 90% chance of (£200,000)	1.26

Division 2

Expected NPV	Risk (σ)
£1,000,000 with certainty	0
85% chance of £1.3m, 15% chance of £700,000	0.21
75% chance of £1.8m, 25% chance of £300,000	0.65
50% chance of £2.5m, 50% chance of £100,000	1.20
35% chance of £3.0m, 65% chance of (£100,000)	Not yet estimated
20% chance of £4.0m, 80% chance of (£200,000)	Not yet estimated

Required:

(a) Analyse the data in the tables and discuss the possible implications of the data for the success of these two divisions' investments. **(8 marks)**

(b) Discuss what actions the board of directors of Chancit might take in response to your findings in (a). **(3 marks)**

(c) Discuss any possible problems with the method of analysis used in (a). **(4 marks)**

(Total: 15 marks)

21 PENSION FUND

The managers of a pension fund follow an active portfolio management strategy. They try to purchase shares and bonds that show a positive abnormal return (positive alpha factor in the case of shares). The pension fund is required by law to hold at least 40% of its investments in bonds. £100 million is currently available for investment.

Three shares and three bonds are being considered for purchase.

The required return on bonds may be measured using a model similar to the capital asset pricing model, where beta is replaced by the relative duration of the individual bond (Di) and the bond market portfolio (Dm). This is shown as Di/Dm

Shares:	Expected return (%)	Standard deviation of returns	Correlation coefficient of returns with the market
Equity market	10.5	15	1
Flitter plc	11.0	25	0.76
Polgin plc	9.5	18	0.54
Scruntor plc	13.5	35	0.63

Bonds:	Duration (years)	Coupon (%)	Redemption yield (%)
Bond market	7.5	-	5.8
UK Government	1.5	8	4.5
Supragow plc	8.6	6	5.3
Teffon plc	14.2	9	7.2

Note: the risk-free rate is 4%

Required:

(a) Evaluate whether or not any of the shares or bonds are expected to offer a positive abnormal return. **(7 marks)**

(b) The pension fund currently has the maximum permitted investment in shares and wishes to continue this strategy. It has a market value of £1,000 million and a beta of 0.62.

Calculate the required return from the pension fund if any shares and bonds with positive abnormal returns are purchased.

State clearly any assumptions that you make. **(3 marks)**

(c) Discuss possible problems with the pension fund's investment strategy. **(5 marks)**

(Total: 15 marks)

22   DAYLON PLC

The managers of Daylon plc are reviewing the company's investment portfolio. About 15% of the portfolio is represented by a holding of 5,550,000 ordinary shares of Mondglobe plc. The managers are concerned about the effect on portfolio value if the price of Mondglobe's shares should fall, and are considering selling the shares. Daylon's investment bank has suggested that the risk of Mondglobe's shares falling by more than 5% from their current value could be protected against by buying an over the counter option. The investment bank is prepared to sell an appropriate six month option to Daylon for £250,000.

Other information:

(i) The current market price of Mondglobe's ordinary shares is 360 pence.

(ii) The annual volatility (variance) of Mondglobe's shares for the last year was 169%.

(iii) The risk free rate is 4% per year.

(iv) No dividend is expected to be paid by Mondglobe during the next six months.

Required:

(a) Evaluate whether or not the price at which the investment bank is willing to sell the option is a fair price. **(10 marks)**

(b) Discuss what factors Daylon should consider before deciding whether or not to purchase the option. **(5 marks)**

(Total: 15 marks)

COST OF CAPITAL AND RISK ANALYSIS

23   BENTRAS

The finance director of Bentras plc wishes to find the company's optimal capital structure.

The cost of debt varies according to the company's credit rating, which itself depends, amongst other factors, upon the level of gearing of the company.

% debt (debt/(debt + equity))	Likely credit rating	Pre tax cost of debt
10	AAA	6.5%
20	AA	7.1%
30	A	7.8%
40	BBB	8.5%
50	BB	10%
60	B	12%
70	C	15%

The company's ungeared equity beta (asset beta) is 0.85.

The risk free rate is 6% per annum, and the market return 14% per annum.

Corporate taxation is at the rate of 30% per year.

Required:

↗Lowest WACC.

(a)   Estimate the company's optimal weighted average cost of capital. State clearly any assumptions that you make.   **(8 marks)**

(b)   Recommend whether or not the company should adopt the optimal capital structure identified in (a) above. Discuss what factors might influence the capital structure decision.   **(7 marks)**

(Total: 15 marks)

24   NETRA PLC

The finance director of Netra plc, a company listed on the AIM (Alternative Investment Market), wishes to estimate what impact the introduction of debt finance is likely to have on the company's overall cost of capital. The company is currently financed only by equity. — Ungeared

Netra plc summarised capital structure

	£000
Ordinary shares (25 pence par value)	500 ✻ 25p = 2000
Reserves	1,100
	1,600

The company's current share price is 420 pence, and up to £4 million of fixed rate five year debt could be raised at an interest rate of 10% per annum. The corporate tax rate is 33%. →

Netra's current earnings before interest and tax are £2.5 million. These earnings are not expected to change significantly for the foreseeable future.

The company is considering raising either: →Debt

(i)   £2 million in debt finance

(ii)   £4 million in debt finance

In either case the debt finance will be used to repurchase ordinary shares. (Share buy back)

Required:

(a)   Using Miller and Modigliani's model in a world with corporate tax, estimate the impact on Netra's cost of capital of raising:

Fill in
formulae

(i)   £2 million and   ⎤ Debt

(ii)   £4 million in debt finance.   ⎦

State clearly any assumptions that you make.   **(6 marks)**

(b)   Briefly discuss whether or not the estimates produced in part (a) are likely to be accurate.   **(4 marks)**

(Total: 10 marks)

25   CONVERTIBLE DEBENTURE

Your company is considering the possible effect on its cost of capital if conversion of a convertible debenture occurs. Stock market prices have recently been very volatile, and could easily rise or fall by 10% or more during the next two months. The convertible is a £20 million 8% debenture with four years to maturity, which was originally issued at its par value (face value) of £100. The debenture may be converted into 20 ordinary shares during the next two months only. The debenture's current market price is £110. Redemption in four years' time would be at the par value of £100. The company has other debt with a market value of £23 million.

Your company could currently issue straight debt at par of £100 with a redemption yield of 9%.

The company's current share price is 520 pence, the market value of ordinary shares is £180 million, and financial gearing 80% equity to 20% debt (by market values).

The systematic risk of the company's equity is similar to that of the market, and is thought to be unlikely to change in the near future.

The market return is 15%.

The corporate tax rate is 30%.

Required:

Assuming that no major changes in interest rates occur during the next two months, estimate the impact on the company's cost of capital if:

(a) the company's share price in two months' time is 470 pence, and no conversion takes place

(b) the company's share price in two months' time is 570 pence, and conversion takes place.

State clearly any other assumptions that you make.

Comment on your findings.   **(10 marks)**

26 KULPAR

The finance director of Kulpar plc is concerned about the impact of capital structure on the company's value, and wishes to investigate the effect of different capital structures.

He is aware that as gearing increases the required return on equity will also increase, and the company's interest cover is likely to decrease. A decrease in interest cover could lead to a change in the company's credit rating by the leading rating agencies. He has been informed that the following changes are likely:

Interest cover	Credit rating	Cost of long term debt
More than 6.5	AA	8.0%
4.0 – 6.5	A	9.0%
1.5 – 4.0	BB	11.0%

(handwritten annotations: – pre tax. – free debt. Traditional gearing)

The company is currently rated A.

Summarised financial data:

	£ million
Net operating income	110
Depreciation	20
Earnings before interest and tax	90
Interest	22
Taxable income	68
Tax (30%)	20.4
Net income	47.6
Capital spending	20

Market value of equity is £458 million, and of debt £305 million.

Kulpar's equity beta is 1.4. The beta of debt may be assumed to be zero.

The risk free rate is 5.5% and the market return 14%.

The company's growth rate of cash flow may be assumed to be constant and to be unaffected by any change in capital structure.

Required:

(a)   Determine the likely effect on the company's cost of capital and corporate value if the company's capital structure was:

(i)   80% equity, 20% debt by market values

(ii)   40% equity, 60% debt by market values.

Recommend which capital structure should be selected.

Any change in capital structure would be achieved by borrowing to repurchase existing equity, or by issuing additional equity to redeem existing debt as appropriate.

The current total firm value (market value of equity plus market value of debt) is consistent with the growth model (CF1/(k – g)) applied on a corporate basis. CF1 is next year's free cash flow, k is the weighted average cost of capital (WACC), and g the expected growth rate.

Company free cash flow may be estimated using EBIT(1 – t) + depreciation – capital spending.

State clearly any other assumptions that you make.   **(20 marks)**

(b)   Discuss possible reasons for errors in the estimates of corporate value in part (a) above.   **(10 marks)**

                                                                                        (Total: 30 marks)

27   BOND PRICES

(a)   Briefly discuss possible reasons for an upward sloping yield curve.   **(4 marks)**

(b)   Assume that 'now' is June 2004.

The financial manager of Gaddes plc's pension fund is reviewing strategy regarding the fund. Over 60% of the fund is invested in fixed rate long-term bonds. Interest rates are expected to be quite volatile for the next few years.

Among the pension fund's current investments are two AAA rated bonds:

(i)   Zero coupon June 2019

(ii)   12% Gilt June 2019 (interest is payable semi-annually)

The current annual redemption yield (yield to maturity) on both bonds is 6%. The semi-annual yield may be assumed to be 3%. Both bonds have a par value and redemption value of £100.

Required:

(i)   Estimate the market price of each of the bonds if interest rates (yields):

(a)   increase by 1%

(b)   decrease by 1%.

The changes in interest rates may be assumed to be parallel shifts in the yield curve (yield changes by an equal amount at all points of the yield curve).

                                                                                        (6 marks)

(ii) Comment upon and briefly explain the size of the expected price movements from the current prices, and how such changes in interest rates might affect the strategy of the financial manager with respect to investing in the two bonds.

(3 marks)

(iii) How might the bond investment strategy of the financial manager be affected if the yield curve was expected to steepen (the gap between short- and long-term interest rates to widen), and interest rates are expected to rise? **(2 marks)**

(Total: 15 marks)

28   CAPITAL STRUCTURE STRATEGY

Prepare a briefing document for a board of directors discussing issues that might influence a company's capital structure strategy. **(15 marks)**

29   MCTEE PLC

McTee plc is a Scottish manufacturer of golf clubs. The company has decided to purchase an existing golf club manufacturer in the State of Florida, USA. The purchase will cost an agreed $72 million for fixed assets and equipment, and in addition $8 million of working capital will be needed. No additional external funding for the proposed US subsidiary is expected to be needed for at least five years, and sales from the subsidiary would be exclusively to the US market. McTee has no other foreign subsidiaries, and the company's managers are considering how to finance the US investment. McTee's bank has advised that, taking into account McTee's credit rating, the following alternatives might be possible, with finance available up to the amount shown:

(i) A one for four rights issue, at a price of 280 pence per share. Underwriting and other costs are expected to be 5% of the gross amount raised.

(ii) Five year Sterling 7% fixed rate secured bank term loan of up to £50 million, initial arrangement fee 1%.

(iii) $15 million one year commercial paper, issued at $US LIBOR plus 1.5%. This could be renewed on an annual basis. An additional 0.5% per year would be payable to a US bank for a back-up line of credit.

(iv) 80 million Swiss Franc five year fixed rate secured bank loan at 2.5%. This may be swapped into fixed rate $ at an additional annual interest rate of 2.3%. An upfront fee of 3.0% is also payable.

(v) £42 million 10-year Sterling Eurobond issue at 6.85%. This may be swapped into $ at an annual interest rate of 4.95%. Eurobond issue costs of 2%, and upfront swap costs of 1.7% would also be payable.

(vi) $40 million floating rate six year secured term loan from a US bank, at $US LIBOR plus 3%.

No currency swaps are available other than those shown. Currency swaps would involve swapping the principal at the current spot exchange rate, with the reversal of the swap at the same rate at the swap maturity date.

$US LIBOR is currently 3%.

Exchange rates:

	Spot	One year forward
$/£	1.7985 – 1.8008	1.7726 – 1.7746
SF/£	2.256 – 2.298	2.189 – 2.205

McTee's current balance sheet is summarised below.

	£m
Fixed assets	117.8
Investments	8.1
Current assets	98.1
Creditors: amounts falling due within one year	
Loan and other borrowings	(38.0)
Other creditors	(48.6)
	137.4
Creditors: amounts falling due after more than one year	
Medium and long-term bank loans	30.0
8% Bond 20X9 (par value £100)	18.0
	48.0
Capital and reserves	
Ordinary shares (25 pence par value)	20.0
Reserves	69.4
	137.4

A covenant exists that prevents the book value of McTee's debt finance from exceeding 50% of total assets. McTee's current dividend per share is 22.2 pence and dividend growth is approximately 4% per year. The company's current share price is 302 pence.

Interest payments on debt financing may be assumed to be made annually at the end of the year. Corporate tax in the UK, USA and Switzerland is at a rate of 30%. Issue costs and fees such as swap fees are not tax allowable.

Required:

(a) Discuss the factors that McTee should consider before deciding how to finance the proposed US subsidiary. **(10 marks)**

(b) Prepare a report discussing and evaluating each of the six possible sources of finance, and provide a reasoned recommendation of which source, or combination of sources, McTee should use. Supporting calculations, including costs, should be provided wherever relevant. **(20 marks)**

(Total: 30 marks)

30 SEMER PLC

A proposal has been put to the board of directors of Semer plc that the company should increase its capital gearing to at least 50%, in order to reduce the company's cost of capital and increase its market value.

The managing director of Semer is not convinced by the logic of the proposal, or the accuracy of the calculations, but is unable to explain the reasons for his reservations.

A summary of the proposal and its implications is shown overleaf.

Proposal to increase the capital gearing of Semer plc

The company's current weighted average cost of capital is estimated to be 10.6%. If the proportion of debt is increased to 50% of total capital, by the repurchase of ordinary shares at their current market value, the cost of capital may be reduced to 9.9%. A reduced cost of capital means that the value of the company will increase which will be welcomed by our shareholders. Calculations supporting the above proposal are shown below:

Existing cost of capital

Cost of equity using the capital asset pricing model:

$4\% + (10.5\% - 4\%)\,1.2 = 11.8\%$

Cost of debt: 8%

Weighted average cost of capital:

$$11.8\% \times \frac{£350m}{£519m} + 8\% \times \frac{£169m}{£519m} = 10.56\%$$

Estimated new cost of capital:

$$11.8\% \times \frac{£259.5m}{£519m} + 8\% \times \frac{£259.5m}{£519m} = 9.90\%$$

Impact on the value of the company:

Current value $\dfrac{£60m}{0.1056} = £568$ million

Expected new value $\dfrac{£60m}{0.099} = £606$ million

Other information:

(i)   Most recent summarised balance sheet

Semer plc	£ million
Fixed assets (net)	442
Current assets	345
Less current liabilities	(268)
	519
Issued ordinary shares (50 pence par)	80
Reserves	270
Liabilities falling due after one year:	
Bank loans	119
8% debenture 2010 (£100 par value)	50
	519

(ii)   The current price of Semer's ordinary shares is 410 pence.

(iii)   The market price of one 8% debenture 2010 is £112.

(iv)   The market return is 10.5% and the risk free rate 4.0%.

(v)   Semer's equity beta is 1.2.

(vi)   Semer currently pays £15 million in dividends.

(vii)   The corporate tax rate is 30%.

(viii) The company currently generates a free cash flow of £60 million per year, which is expected to increase by approximately 3% per year.

Required:

(a)   What, if any, are the mistakes in the proposal? Correcting for any mistakes produce revised estimates of the company's *current* cost of capital and *current* value. Brief explanation of the reasons for any revisions should be included.   **(15 marks)**

(b)   Assuming that the cost of equity and cost of debt do not alter, estimate the effect of the share repurchase on the company's cost of capital and value.   **(5 marks)**

(c)   Acting as an external consultant to Semer, discuss the validity of the proposed strategy to increase gearing, and explain whether or not the estimates produced in (b) above are likely to be accurate.   **(10 marks)**

(Total: 30 marks)

INVESTMENT DECISIONS: DECISION-MAKING TECHNIQUES

31   DARON

Assume that 'now' is December 2003.

The senior managers of Daron, a company located in a European country, are reviewing the company's medium term prospects. The company is in a declining industry, and is heavily dependent on a single product. Sales volume is likely to fall for the next few years. A general election will take place in the near future and the managers believe that the future level of inflation will depend upon the result of the election. Inflation is expected to remain at approximately 5% per year if political party A wins the election, or will quickly move to approximately 10% per year if party B wins the election. Opinion polls suggest that there is a 40% chance of party B winning. An increase in the level of inflation is likely to reduce the volume of sales of Daron.

Projected financial data for the next five years, including expected inflation where relevant, are shown opposite.

Political party A wins, inflation 5% per year

	$ million				
	2004	*2005*	*2006*	*2007*	*2008*
Operating cash flows:					
Sales	28	29	26	22	19
Variable costs	17	18	16	14	12
Fixed costs	3	3	3	3	3
Other financial data:					
Incremental working capital*	-	(1)	(2)	(3)	(3)
Tax allowable depreciation	4	3	3	2	1

Political party B wins, inflation 10% per year

	$ million				
	2004	*2005*	*2006*	*2007*	*2008*
Operating cash flows:					
Sales	30	26	24	20	16
Variable costs	18	16	15	12	11
Fixed costs	3	3	4	4	4
Other financial data:					
Incremental working capital*	1	(2)	(2)	(3)	(3)
Tax allowable depreciation	4	3	3	2	1

*A bracket signifies a decrease in working capital.

Tax allowable depreciation will be negligible after 2008 in both cases.

Cash flows after year 2008, excluding tax savings from tax allowable depreciation, are expected to be similar to year 2008 cash flows for a period of five years, after which substantial new fixed investment would be necessary in order to continue operations.

Working capital will remain approximately constant after the year 2008.

Corporate taxation is at a rate of 30% per year, and is expected to continue at this rate. Tax may be assumed to be payable in the year that the income arises.

Daron's current ordinary share price is 92 centos (100 centos = $1).

Summarised balance sheet of Daron plc as at 31 March 2003

	$ million
Tangible fixed assets	24
Net current assets	12
Total assets less current liabilities	36
Loans and other borrowings falling due after one year	14
Capital and reserves:	
Called up share capital (25 centos par value)	5
Reserves	17
	36

The company can currently borrow long term from its bank at an interest rate of 10% per year. This is likely to quickly rise to 15.5% per year if the political party B wins the election.

The real risk free rate (i.e. excluding inflation) is 4% and the real market return is 10%.

Daron's equity beta is estimated to be 1.25. This is not expected to significantly change if inflation increases.

Three alternatives are available to the managers of Daron:

(i) Recommend the sale of the company now. An informal, unpublicised, offer of $20 million for the company's shares has been received from a competitor.

(ii) Continue existing operations, with negligible capital investment for the foreseeable future.

(iii) If the political party A wins the election, diversify operations by buying a going concern in the hotel industry at a cost of $9 million. The purchase would be financed by the issue of 10% convertible debentures. Issue costs are 2% of the gross sum raised. Daron has no previous experience of the hotel industry.

Financial projections of the hotel purchase

$ million

	2004	2005	2006	2007	2008
Turnover	9	10	11	12	13
Variable costs	6	6	7	7	8
Fixed costs	2	2	2	2	2
Other financial data:					
Incremental working capital	1	-	-	1	-

Tax allowable depreciation is negligible for the hotel purchase. The after tax realisable value of the hotel at the end of year 2008 is expected to be $10 million, including working capital. The systematic risk of operating the hotels is believed to be similar to that of the company's existing operations.

Required:

(a) Using the above data, prepare a report advising the managers of Daron which, if any, of the three alternatives to adopt. Include in your report comment on any weaknesses/limitations of your data analysis. Relevant calculations, including:

(i) estimates of the present values of future cash flows from existing operations, and

(ii) the estimated adjusted present value of diversifying into the hotel industry should form appendices to your report.

The book value and market value of debt may be assumed to be the same. State clearly any other assumptions that you make. **(32 marks)**

Approximately 20 marks are available for calculations and 12 for discussion.

(b) Details of the possible convertible debenture issue for the purchase of the hotel are shown below:

10% $100 convertible debentures 2017, issued and redeemable at par. The debentures are convertible into 60 ordinary shares at any date between 1 January 2009 and 31 December 2011. The debentures are callable for conversion by the company subject to the company's ordinary share price exceeding 200 centos between 1 January 2009 and 31 December 2011, and puttable for redemption by the debenture holders if the share price falls below 100 centos between the same dates.

Discuss the implications for Daron if the diversification is financed with convertible debentures with these terms. **(8 marks)**

(Total: 40 marks)

32 TOVELL PLC

The selection of appropriate discount rates for capital investments has frequently been a problem for the finance director of Tovell plc. The company has adopted a strategy of diversification into many different industries, in order to reduce risk for the company's shareholders. This has resulted in frequent changes in the company's gearing level and widely fluctuating risks of individual investments.

The current project under appraisal, an investment in the fast food industry where Tovell has no other investments, is expected to generate pre-tax operating cash flows of £420,000 in the first year, rising by 5% per year for the five year expected life of the project. After five years the land and buildings are expected to have a realisable value of £1,250,000 (after any tax effects), the same as their original cost, but in order to continue operations major new investment in equipment would be required at that time. Other fixed assets would have negligible value after five years. The total initial outlay of the project (net of issue costs) is £2.3 million, and all but the land and buildings attracts a 25% per year capital allowance on a reducing balance basis.

The project would be financed by a £800,000 fixed rate loan from a regional development agency at a subsidised interest rate of 6% per year, 3% less than Tovell could borrow at in the capital market. The remainder of the finance would be provided by an underwritten rights issue at a 10% discount on current market price, with total underwriting and issue costs of 5% of gross proceeds. The investment is believed to add £1 million to the company's debt capacity.

Current financial data for Tovell and the fast food industry includes:

	Tovell plc	Fast food industry (average)
P/E ratio	12	20
Dividend yield	5%	3%
Equity beta	1.1	1.4
Debt beta	0.2	0.25
Gearing (debt/equity):		
Book values	1.1 to 1	1.6 to 1
Market values	0.4 to 1	1 to 1
Share price	470 pence	n/a
Number of ordinary shares	3.5 million	n/a

The corporate tax rate is currently 30% per year, and tax is payable one year in arrears.

Treasury bills are currently yielding 5% per year after tax, and the return required by well diversified investors is 12.5% per year.

Required:

(a) Provide a reasoned explanation as to whether you would support the company's strategy of diversifying into many different industries. **(8 marks)**

(b) Prepare a report for the finance director of Tovell plc advising on the financial viability of the proposed fast food investment. Include in the report an assessment of the limitations of the method of appraisal that you have used. Supporting calculations should form an appendix to your report. **(22 marks)**

(Total: 30 marks)

33 WICKERN PLC

Assume that 'now' is the end of 2003.

Four years ago Wickern plc, a UK quoted company, invested in an ice-skating rink in the European country of Movania. The capital cost was 60 million Movanian francs (MF), or £8 million at the exchange rate at the time. The rink is used most of the time for public skating sessions, but is also used by an ice hockey team and for concerts.

When the investment occurred the rink had an expected working life of eight years, after which significant new investment would be needed. If no new investment were to take place the building and the site at the end of 2007 would have an estimated value of 12 million euros (the Movanian franc equivalent of this euro realisable value has not changed since the original cash flow projections). Any new capital investment in 2007 would cost an estimated 50 million euros and could lead to annual incremental after tax cash flows of between €7.5 million and €10 million for the next ten years.

The value of the land and building if sold now is €15 million.

The corporate tax rate between 2000 and 2003 was 30% in the UK, and 35% in Movania. It was announced in December 2003 that the Movania tax rate would be reduced to 28.5% in 2004 in a move to promote greater tax harmonisation in Europe. The UK tax rate is expected to remain at 30% for the foreseeable future. A bilateral tax treaty exists between the UK and Movania, where any tax suffered in Movania will be fully available for credit in the UK.

Wickern plc has had other profitable capital investments in Movania since before 2000, and pays the full rate of taxation in Movania.

Original forecast operating cash flows

Movanian francs (million)

	2000	2001	2002	2003	2004	2005	2006	2007
Inflows from:								
Public ice-skating	13.5	14.2	15.0	15.7	16.5	17.2	18.0	18.7
Ice hockey matches	18.0	18.5	19.0	19.5	20.0	20.5	21.0	21.5
Concerts	7.5	11.0	11.0	11.0	13.5	13.5	13.5	13.5
	39.0	43.7	45.0	46.2	50.0	51.2	52.5	53.7
Outflows from:								
Public ice-skating	7.5	7.5	7.5	7.5	7.5	7.5	7.5	7.5
Ice hockey matches	3.0	3.0	3.0	3.0	3.0	3.0	3.0	3.0
Concerts	1.5	1.5	1.5	1.5	1.5	1.5	1.5	1.5
General overheads	11.2	11.2	13.5	13.5	13.5	15.7	15.7	15.7
Tax allowance depreciation	7.5	7.5	7.5	7.5	7.5	7.5	7.5	7.5
	30.7	30.7	33.0	33.0	33.0	35.2	35.2	35.2
Taxable net cash flows	8.3	13.0	12.0	13.2	17.0	16.0	17.3	18.5
Taxation (35%)	(2.9)	(4.6)	(4.2)	(4.6)	(6.0)	(5.6)	(6.1)	(6.5)
Remittable to the UK	12.9	15.9	15.3	16.1	18.5	17.9	18.7	19.5

£ (million)

	2000	2001	2002	2003	2004	2005	2006	2007
Remittable to the UK	1.72	2.12	2.04	2.15	2.47	2.39	2.49	2.60

The original cash flow forecasts subsequently proved to be inaccurate, and at the end of 2003 the actual cash flows for the first four years were produced for analysis, together with new cash flow forecasts for the next four years.

Actual (2000-2003) and revised projected future operating cash flows (post 2003)

Moldavian francs (million)

	2000	2001	2002	2003
Inflows from:				
Public ice-skating	11.2	12.0	12.0	12.0
Ice hockey matches	11.2	11.2	12.0	13.5
Concerts	6.0	7.5	6.0	11.2
	28.4	30.7	30.0	36.7
Outflows from:				
Public ice-skating	7.5	7.5	7.5	7.5
Ice hockey matches	3.0	3.0	3.0	3.0
Concerts	3.0	3.0	3.0	3.0
General overheads	13.5	13.5	14.2	14.2
Tax allowance depreciation	7.5	7.5	7.5	7.5
	34.5	34.5	35.2	36.7

Taxable net cash flows	(6.1)	(3.8)	(5.2)	0
Taxation (35%)	2.1	1.3	1.8	0
	(4.0)	(2.5)	(3.4)	0
Add back depreciation	7.5	7.5	7.5	7.5
Remittable to the UK	3.5	5.0	4.1	7.5

[handwritten: Francs — next to Add back depreciation row]

Cash flows in sterling   £ (million)

[handwritten: X Rates 7.95 ... 11.03]

	2000	2001	2002	2003
Remittable to the UK	0.44	0.56	0.41	0.68

[handwritten left margin: Franc depreciated ∴ less in £ / Ignores economic risk]

€ (million)

	2004	2005	2006	2007
Inflows from:				
Public ice-skating	2.1	2.1	2.1	2.1
Ice hockey matches	2.3	2.3	2.3	2.3
Concerts	2.0	2.0	2.0	2.0
	6.4	6.4	6.4	6.4
Outflows from:				
Public ice-skating	1.1	1.1	1.1	1.1
Ice hockey matches	0.5	0.5	0.5	0.5
Concerts	0.7	0.7	0.7	0.7
General	2.3	2.3	2.3	2.3
Tax allowance depreciation	1.1	1.1	1.1	1.1
	5.7	5.7	5.7	5.7
Taxable net cash flows	0.7	0.7	0.7	0.7
Taxation (28.5%)	(0.2)	(0.2)	(0.2)	(0.2)

[handwritten above "Taxable net cash flows": profits]

[handwritten left margin: PPPT / Estimate future spot rates]

Inflation in the eurozone (of which Movania has just become a member) is at the rate of 5% per year and in the UK 2% per year. These rates are expected to continue unless the UK joints the eurozone bloc and the euro replaces the pound sterling. The UK is not expected to join the eurozone until at least 2007.

Since the end of the 2001 the Movanian franc has had an irrevocable conversion rate with the euro of MF6.55957/€1. The spot rate at the end of 2003 is €1.69/£1. *[handwritten: Now]*

[handwritten left margin: WACC]

The beta of the investment in 2000 was estimated to be 1.125. The risk free rate was 7% and the market return 15%. At the end of 2003 the beta of the investment has been re-evaluated at 0.95, the risk free rate is 6% and the market return is 13.5%.

Required:

[handwritten: risk has changed / investment decision / variance on PV]

(a) Analyse the financial performance of the ice-skating rink between 2000 and 2003 inclusive. Included in your analysis discussion of reasons why the actual cash flows differed from those forecast. Recommend what corrective action might be taken.

(15 marks)

[handwritten left margin: 3 decisions]

(b) Prepare a report for the board of Wickern plc discussing whether or not the ice-skating rink should be sold now, retained for another four years or retained indefinitely. All relevant assumptions and calculations should be included in the report (or as an appendix to it).

(15 marks)

(c) Discuss what other factors should be considered in order to assist the decision process.

[handwritten: ART IS Real Risk]

(10 marks)

(Total: 40 marks)

34 JETTER PLC *Exam Date June 2002*

Summarised financial details of Jetter plc are shown below:

Extract from the profit and loss account

	£ million
Turnover	582
Profit before tax	93
Taxation (30%)	(28)
Profit after tax	65
Dividends	(26)
Retained earnings	39

Extract from the balance sheet

	£ million
Fixed assets (net)	210
Current assets	186
Current liabilities	(153)
	243
Financed by:	
Ordinary shares (25 pence par)	50 *200m shares*
Reserves	122 *Book value ∴ Ignore*
12% debentures June 2006	71 *- reedemable → IRR*
	243

The company's ordinary shares are currently trading at £2.20, and the debentures at £105.50. The debenture is redeemable at its par value of £100 in four years time   *100*

The company's equity beta is 1.25.

Shareholder get dividend, Capital gain + Loss.

Jetter plc is considering investing in one of three projects. The company has £50 million that is currently earning 5.8% in short-term money market deposits. Any surplus funds after the investment in one of the projects will continue to be invested in the money market.

The company has employed an external consultant to estimate risk/return data relevant to the three projects.

	Project 1	Project 2	Project 3
Investment cost (£ million)	35	40	28
Estimated correlation of returns with the market	0.76	0.63	0.58 *→β*
Standard deviation of returns	8.4%	4.6%	14.3%
Expected return (IRR)	15%	11%	17%

Market return 15% per annum

Market standard deviation of returns 6.9%

Risk free rate 6% per annum

Required:

(a)   Evaluate which project should be selected. Do not use information provided later in the question requirements in your evaluation.

State clearly any assumptions that you make in all parts of this question.   **(8 marks)**

(b)   If it was later calculated that the profitability index for project 2 was 1.3, based upon equal cash inflows of £16 million per year from the project for four years, what does this imply about the accuracy of the beta estimated for the project?   **(5 marks)**

(c)   Estimate Jetter's cost of capital prior to undertaking the investment. Briefly discuss (do not calculate) what effect the project selected in (a) is likely to have on Jetter's cost of capital. The profitability index of 1.3 also relates to this part of the question.

(8 marks)

(d)   The consultant has suggested that beta estimates should be adjusted by using the formula: $(0.67 \times \text{unadjusted beta}) + 0.33)$ in any estimate of required returns.

   (i)   Briefly discuss the reason for using an adjusted beta such as this.   **(3 marks)**

   (ii)   Calculate whether or not your choice of project in (a) above would have altered using adjusted betas.   **(3 marks)**

(e)   Discuss the advantages and disadvantages of using the Capital Asset Pricing Model and the Arbitrage Pricing Theory in investment appraisal.   **(8 marks)**

(Total: 35 marks)

35   STRAYER PLC

The managers of Strayer plc are investigating a potential £25 million investment. The investment would be a diversification away from existing mainstream activities and into the printing industry. £6 million of the investment would be financed by internal funds, £10 million by a rights issue and £9 million by long term loans. The investment is expected to generate pre-tax net cash flows of approximately £5 million per year, for a period of ten years. The residual value at the end of year ten is forecast to be £5 million after tax. As the investment is in an area that the government wishes to develop, a subsidised loan of £4 million out of the total £9 million is available. This will cost 2% below the company's normal cost of long-term debt finance, which is 8%. (6%)

Strayer's equity beta is 0.85, and its financial gearing is 60% equity, 40% debt by market value. The average equity beta in the printing industry is 1.2, and average gearing 50% equity, 50% debt by market value. The risk free rate is 5.5% per annum and the market return 12% per annum. Issue costs are estimated to be 1% for debt financing (excluding the subsidised loan), and 4% for equity financing. These costs are not tax allowable.

The corporate tax rate is 30%.

Required:

(a)   Estimate the Adjusted Present Value (APV) of the proposed investment.   **(12 marks)**

(b)   Comment upon the circumstances under which APV might be a better method of evaluating a capital investment than Net Present Value (NPV).   **(3 marks)**

(Total: 15 marks)

36   AVTO

Avto plc is considering an investment in Terrania, a country with a population of 60 million that has experienced twelve changes of government in the last ten years. The investment would cost 580 million Terranian francs for machinery and other equipment, and an additional 170 million francs would be necessary for working capital.

Terrania has a well-trained, skilled labour force and good communications infrastructure, but has suffered from a major disease in its main crop, the banana, and the effect of cheaper labour in neighbouring countries.

Terrania is heavily indebted to the IMF and the international banking system, and it is rumoured that the IMF is unwilling to offer further assistance to the Terranian government.

The Terranian government has imposed temporary restrictions on the remittance of funds from Terrania on three occasions during the last ten years.

The proposed investment would be in the production of recordable DVD players, which are currently manufactured in the UK, mainly for the European Union market. If the Terranian investment project was undertaken the existing UK factory would either be closed down or downsized. Avto plc hopes to become more competitive by shifting production from the UK.

Additional information:

(i) UK corporate tax is at the rate of 30% per year, and Terranian corporate tax at the rate of 20% per year, both payable in the year that the tax charge arises. Tax allowable depreciation in Terrania is 25% per year on a reducing balance basis. A bilateral tax treaty exists between Terrania and the UK.

(ii) The after-tax realisable value of the machinery and other equipment after four years is estimated to be 150 million Terranian francs.

(iii) £140,000 has recently been spent on a feasibility study into the logistics of the proposed Terranian investment. The study reported favourably on this issue.

(iv) The Terranian government has offered to allow Avto plc to use an existing factory rent free for a period of four years on condition that Avto employs at least 300 local workers. Avto has estimated that the investment would need 250 local workers. Rental of the factory would normally cost 75 million Terranian francs per year before tax.

(v) Almost all sales from Terranian production will be to the European Union priced in euros.

(vi) Production and sales are expected to be 50,000 units per year. The expected year 1 selling price is 480 euros per unit.

(vii) Unit costs throughout year 1 are expected to be:

Labour: 3,800 Terranian (T) francs based upon using 250 workers
Local components: 1,800 T francs
Component from Germany: 30 euros
Sales and distribution: 400 T francs

(viii) Fixed costs in year 1 are 50 million T francs.

(ix) Local costs and the cost of the German component are expected to increase each year in line with Terranian and EU inflation respectively. Due to competition, the selling price (in euros) is expected to remain constant for at least four years.

(x) All net cash flows arising from the proposed investment in Terrania would be remitted at the end of each year back to the UK.

(xi) If the UK factory is closed Avto will face tax-allowable redundancy and other closure costs of £35 million. Approximately £20 million after tax is expected to be raised from the disposal of land and buildings.

(xii) If Avto decides to downsize rather than close its UK operations then tax-allowable closure costs will amount to £20 million, and after-tax asset sales to £10 million. Pre-tax net cash flows from the downsized operation are expected to be £4 million per year, at current values. Manufacturing capacity in Terrania would not be large enough to supply the market previously supplied from the UK if downsizing does not occur.

(xiii) The estimated beta of the Terranian investment is 1.5 and of the existing UK investment is 1.1.

(xiv) The relevant risk-free rate is 4.5% and market return 11.5%.

(xv) Money market investment in Terrania is available to Avto paying a rate of interest equivalent to the Terranian inflation rate.

(xvi) Forecast % inflation levels:

Purchasing Price Parity

$PPP = \dfrac{1 + i^{sc}}{1 + i^{nd}}$

	UK and the EU	Terrania
Year 1	2%	20%
Year 2	3%	15%
Year 3	3%	10%
Year 4	3%	10%
Year 5	3%	10%

franc depreciate

high inflation

think - 4 year project

(xvii) Spot exchange rates:

Terranian francs/£1	36.85
Terranian francs/euros	23.32

Overseas NPV

ART is REAL RISK

– Transfer – mgt fee – pricing

Required:

PV

(a) Prepare a financial appraisal of whether or not Avto plc should invest in Terrania and close or downsize its UK factory. State clearly all assumptions that you make.

(b) Discuss the wider commercial issues that the company should consider, in addition to the financial appraisal, before making its decision on whether to invest. *political risk*

(c) Estimate the possible impact of blocked remittances in Terrania for the planning horizon of four years, and discuss how Avto might react to blocked remittances.

(**28 marks** in total are available for calculations, and **12 marks** for discussion)

(**40 marks**)

37   FUELIT PLC

Fuelit plc is an electricity supplier in the UK. The company has historically generated the majority of its electricity using a coal fuelled power station, but as a result of the closure of many coal mines and depleted coal resources, is now considering what type of new power station to invest in. The alternatives are a gas fuelled power station, or a new type of efficient nuclear power station.

Both types of power station are expected to generate annual revenues at current prices of £800 million. The expected operating life of both types of power station is 25 years.

Financial estimates:

	£ million	
	Gas	Nuclear
Building costs	600	3,300
Annual running costs (at current prices):		
Labour costs	75	20
Gas purchases	500	-
Nuclear fuel purchases	-	10
Sales and marketing expenses	40	40
Customer relations	5	20
Interest expense	51	330
Other cash outlays	5	25
Accounting depreciation	24	132

Other information:

(i) Whichever power station is selected, electricity generation is scheduled to commence in three years time.

(ii) If gas is used most of the workers at the existing coal fired station can be transferred to the new power station. After tax redundancy costs are expected to total £4 million in year four. If nuclear power is selected fewer workers will be required and after tax redundancy costs will total £36 million, also in year four.

(iii) Both projects would be financed by Eurobond issues denominated in Euros. The gas powered station would require a bond issue at 8.5% per year, the bond for the nuclear project would be at 10% reflecting the impact on financial gearing of a larger bond issue.

(iv) Costs of building the new power stations would be payable in two equal instalments in one and two years time.

(v) The existing coal fired power station would need to be demolished at a cost of £10 million in three years time.

(vi) The company's equity beta is expected to be 0.7 if the gas station is chosen and 1.4 if the nuclear station is chosen. Gearing (debt to equity plus debt) is expected to be 35% with gas and 60% with nuclear fuel.

(vii) The risk free rate is 4.5% per year and the market return is 14% per year. Inflation is currently 3% per year in the UK and an average of 5% per year in the member countries of the eurozone in the European Union.

(viii) Corporate tax is at the rate of 30%, payable in the same year that the liability arises.

(ix) Tax allowable depreciation is at the rate of 10% per year on a straight line basis.

(x) At the end of twenty-five years of operations the gas plant is expected to cost £25 million (after tax) to demolish and clean up the site. Costs of decommissioning the nuclear plant are much less certain, and could be anything between £500 million and £1,000 million (after tax) depending upon what form of disposal is available for nuclear waste.

Required:

(a) Estimate the expected NPV for **each of** the investment in a gas fuelled power station and the investment in a nuclear fuelled power station.

State clearly any assumptions that you make.

Note: It is recommended that annuity tables are used wherever possible **(20 marks)**

(b) Discuss other information that might assist the decision process. **(8 marks)**

(c) An external advisor has suggested that the discount rate for the costs of decommissioning the nuclear power station should be adjusted because of their risk. Discuss whether or not this discount rate should be increased or decreased. **(4 marks)**

(d) Explain the significance of the existence of real options to the capital investment decision, and briefly discuss examples of real options that might be significant in the power station decision process. **(8 marks)**

(Total: 40 marks)

38 UTOPIA HOTEL GROUP

The Utopia hotel group is considering building a new luxury hotel in the English resort of Torquay. The hotel would have a cost of £50 million, ten percent of which is payable immediately, 50% payable in one years time and the balance on completion in approximately two years time. This expenditure is eligible for tax allowable depreciation on a straight line basis at the rate of 2.5% per year. Corporate taxes are levied at the rate of 33% per year, payable in the year that income arises. Working capital of £1.5 million will be required from the start of year three.

The hotel is planned with 300 bedrooms. On average, when a bedroom is occupied, 1.4 people per night are expected to occupy a room. The average room charge per night is expected to be £100, which is valid whether one or more persons use the room. In addition on average £40 per person per day is expected to be spent on food and drink, and £15 per person per day on other hotel facilities. Based upon previous experience the profit margin on food and drink is expected to be 40%, and on other facilities, 30%.

Non-resident guests are expected to provide an annual contribution to cash flow of £1 million per year.

Annual outlays are expected to be:	£000
Staff	4,000
Services (gas, electricity, water, local building taxes etc.)	1,800
Maintenance and other costs	400

Every five years the hotel would require major redecoration and refurbishment, at a cost of approximately £10 million. These costs are tax allowable in the year incurred.

The group evaluates its hotels over a fifteen operating years time horizon. At the end of fifteen years of operation the hotel is expected to have an after tax value of £60 million, before any end of period refurbishment, and excluding working capital.

All revenues, costs and values are estimated at current prices, and take no account of inflation.

The group is not sure what occupancy rate (the percentage of rooms occupied per night) the hotel would have.

Utopia Hotels – summarised capital structure (current)

	£ million
Net assets	740
Financed by:	
Issued ordinary shares (25 pence par)	120
Reserves	270
12% debentures	200
Bank floating rate term loans	150
	740

The 12% debentures are redeemable at par in thirteen years' time.

The ordinary shares are currently trading at 345 pence per share, and the debentures at £114.

The group believes that it can issue new long dated debentures at a gross yield of 3% above the risk free rate. The systematic risk of the group's shares is 80% of that of the market, and the market return is estimated to be 15%. The new hotel is not expected to significantly affect the group's business risk or financial risk.

The current level of inflation is 3.8% per year and this is expected to continue for the foreseeable future.

Required:

(a) Evaluate what occupancy rate the hotel would need to achieve in order to be financially viable, and comment upon your findings.

State clearly any assumptions that you make. **(25 marks)**

(b) Discuss how accurate your evaluation is likely to be and explain which parts of your evaluation could be subject to significant error. **(7 marks)**

(c)   One of the directors of Utopia is concerned about the use of the capital asset pricing model (CAPM) in the evaluation of the proposed hotel, as she has heard that many of the model's assumptions are unrealistic. She suggests the use of the arbitrage pricing theory as an alternative to CAPM.

Prepare a brief report for the Board of Directors of Utopia which discusses this suggestion, and advise whether or not it should be agreed.   **(8 marks)**

(Total: 40 marks)

39   MOVER PLC

'Now' is June 2004.

You have been asked to provide preliminary advice on whether or not your company's pension fund should make an investment in the shares of Mover plc, a large construction company which is leading a consortium that is proposing to build a rail tunnel between Gibraltar and Morocco. The tunnel is scheduled to open in 2009. The only information available to you at this time is the cash flow projections published by the tunnel consortium.

Projected net cash flows of the tunnel project:

	£ million
2005	(450)
2006	(500)
2007	(550)
2008	(650)
2009	(200)
2010	200
2011	300
2012	320
2013	340
2014	360
2015	400
Each year after 2015	400

All projections exclude inflation, which is expected to remain at approximately 4% per year.

Required:

Undertake an analysis of the proposed tunnel project and advise on whether or not the pension fund should invest in shares of Mover plc. Relevant calculations must be shown.

State clearly *all* assumptions that you make. In this question ONLY reasoned assumptions regarding a discount rate are encouraged.   **(10 marks)**

40   WACC

(a)   Discuss the merits and potential problems of using each of the weighted average cost of capital and adjusted present value to aid the evaluation of proposed capital investments.   **(8 marks)**

(b)   Trosoft pte ltd is a Singapore based company specialising in the development of business software. The company's managers believe that its future growth potential in the software sector is limited, and are considering diversifying into other activities. One suggestion is Internet auctions, and a member of the management team has produced the following draft financial proposal.

Internet auctions project

| | | | S$000 | | |
Year	0	1	2	3	4
Auction fees	–	4,300	6,620	8,100	8,200
Outflows:					
IT maintenance costs	–	1,210	1,850	1,920	2,125
Telephone	–	1,215	1,910	2,230	2,420
Wages	–	1,460	1,520	1,680	1,730
Salaries	–	400	550	600	650
Allocated head office overhead	–	85	90	95	100
Marketing	500	420	200	200	–
Royalty payments for use of technology	680	500	300	200	200
Market Research	110				
Rental of premises		280	290	300	310
Total outflows	1,290	5,570	6,710	7,225	7,535
Profit before tax	(1,290)	(1,270)	(90)	875	665
Tax	316	311	22	(214)	(163)
Other outflows:					
IT infrastructure	2,700				
Working capital	400	24	24	25	26
Net flows	(4,074)	(983)	(92)	636	476

Additional information:

(i) All data include the estimated effects of inflation on costs and prices wherever relevant. Inflation in Singapore is forecast to be 2% per year for the foreseeable future.

(ii) The investment in IT infrastructure and the initial working capital will be financed by a 6 year 5.5% fixed rate term loan. Other year 0 outlays will be financed from existing cash flows.

(iii) The Singapore government is expected to give a 1% per year subsidy to the cost of the loan to support the creation of jobs associated with this project.

(iv) Highly skilled IT staff would need to be taken from other activities resulting in a loss of S$80,000 per year pre-tax contribution for three years.

(v) Head office cash flows for overheads will increase by S$50,000 as a result of the project in year one, rising by S$5,000 per year after year one.

(vi) Corporate tax is at a rate of 24.5% per year, payable in the year that the tax liability arises. The company has other profitable projects.

(vii) Tax allowable depreciation on IT infrastructure is 20% for the first year, and straight line thereafter. The IT infrastructure has an expected working life of six years after which major new investment would be required.

(viii) The company's current weighted average cost of capital is 7.8%.

(ix) The company's equity beta is 1.05.

(x) The average equity beta of companies in the Internet auctions sector is 1.42.

(xi) The market return is 9.5% per year and the risk free rate 4% per year.

(xii) Trosoft's capital gearing is:

Book value 55% equity, 45% debt

Market value 70% equity, 30% debt

(xiii) The average gearing of companies in the Internet auction sector is 67% equity, 33% debt by market values.

(xiv) The market research survey was undertaken three weeks ago.

(xv) After tax operating net cash flows after year 4 are expected to stay approximately constant in real terms. The royalty payment will remain at S$200,000 in money terms.

(xvi) Issue costs on debt are 1.5%. These costs are not tax allowable.

Required:

Acting as an external consultant you have been asked to prepare a report on the proposed diversification of the company into Internet auctions. The report must include a revised financial analysis. You should use the adjusted present value method for this purpose. Include in your report discussion of other financial and nonfinancial factors, including real options, that Trosoft might consider prior to making the investment decision.   **(32 marks)**

(23 marks are available for calculations of the APV and 9 marks for discussion)

(Total: 40 marks)

41   TAX RULES

(a)   Briefly discuss possible advantages to a multinational company from using a holding company based in a tax haven.   **(4 marks)**

(b)   Boxless plc has subsidiaries in three overseas countries, Annovia, Cardenda and Sporoon. Corporate taxes for the three countries are shown below:

	Corporate income tax rate	*Withholding tax on dividends*	*% of after tax income remitted to the UK*
Annovia	40%	10%	70
Cardenda	25%	–	40
Sporoon	20%	5%	80

The UK corporate tax rate is 30%, and bilateral tax treaties exist between the UK and each of the three countries. Under the treaties, any corporate tax paid overseas on income remitted to the UK may be credited against UK tax liability. Boxless currently remits income from its overseas subsidiaries direct to the UK parent company.

The UK government currently only taxes income from multinational companies' overseas subsidiaries when such income is remitted to the UK. UK tax liability is based upon the grossed up dividend distributions to the UK (grossed up at the local tax rate and before deduction of any withholding tax).

The UK government is now considering taxing the gross income earned by overseas subsidiaries. If such gross income were to be taxed, credit against UK tax liability would be available for all corporate tax paid overseas.

Required:

(i)   Estimate the impact on the cash flows of Boxless if the UK government alters the tax rules as detailed above.

Assume that the taxable income in each of the subsidiaries is the equivalent of £100,000.   **(7 marks)**

(ii)   For each of the current and possible new tax rules, evaluate what benefit, if any, Boxless would experience if it were to transfer income from its overseas subsidiaries to the parent company via a tax haven holding company. Assume that the UK tax authorities would then treat all income from overseas subsidiaries as coming from a single source, the tax haven holding company. Comment upon your results. **(4 marks)**

(Total: 15 marks)

42   NOVOROAST PLC

Novoroast plc manufactures microwave ovens which it exports to several countries, as well as supplying the home market. One of Novoroast's export markets is a South American country, which has recently imposed a 40% tariff on imports of microwaves in order to protect its local 'infant' microwave industry. The imposition of this tariff means that Novoroast's products are no longer competitive in the South American country's market, but the government there is willing to assist companies wishing to undertake direct investment locally. The government offers a 10% grant towards the purchase of plant and equipment, and a three-year tax holiday on earnings. Corporate tax after the three-year period would be paid at the rate of 25% in the year that the taxable cash flow arises.

Novoroast wishes to evaluate whether to invest in a manufacturing subsidiary in South America, or to pull out of the market altogether.

The total cost of an investment in South America is 155 million pesos (at current exchange rates), comprising:

- 50 million pesos for land and buildings

- 60 million pesos for plant and machinery (all of which would be required almost immediately)

- 45 million pesos for working capital

20 million pesos of the working capital will be required immediately and 25 million pesos at the end of the first year of operation. Working capital needs are expected to increase in line with local inflation.

The company's planning horizon is five years.

Plant and machinery is expected to be depreciated (tax allowable) on a straight-line basis over five years, and is expected to have negligible realisable value at the end of five years. Land and buildings are expected to appreciate in value in line with the level of inflation in the South American country.

Production and sales of microwaves are expected to be 8,000 units in the first year at an initial price of 1,450 pesos per unit, 60,000 units in the second year, and 120,000 units per year for the remainder of the planning horizon.

In order to control the level of inflation, legislation exists in the South American country to restrict retail price rises of manufactured goods to 10% per year.

Fixed costs and local variable costs, which for the first year of operation are 12 million pesos and 600 pesos per unit respectively, are expected to increase by the previous year's rate of inflation.

All components will be produced or purchased locally except for essential microchips which will be imported from the UK at a cost of £8 per unit, yielding a contribution to the profit of the parent company of £3 per unit. It is hoped to keep this sterling cost constant over the planning horizon.

Corporate tax in the UK is at the rate of 30% per year, payable in the year the liability arises. A bi-lateral tax treaty exists between the UK and the South American country, which permits the offset of overseas tax against any UK tax liability on overseas earnings. In periods of tax holiday assume that no UK tax would be payable on South American cash flows.

Summarised group data:

Novoroast plc, summarised balance sheet	£ million
Fixed assets (net)	440
Current assets	370
Less current liabilities	(200)
	610
Financed by:	
£1 ordinary shares	200
Reserves	230
	430
6% Eurodollar bonds, eight years until maturity	180
	610

Novoroast's current share price is 410 pence per share, and current bond price is $800 per bond ($1,000 par and redemption value).

Forecast inflation rates

	UK	South American country
Present	4%	20%
Year 1	3%	20%
Year 2	4%	15%
Year 3	4%	15%
Year 4	4%	15%
Year 5	4%	15%

Foreign exchange rates

	Peso/£
Spot	13.421
1 year forward	15.636

Novoroast plc believes that if the investment is undertaken the overall risk to investors in the company will remain unchanged.

The company's beta coefficients have been estimated as equity 1.25, debt 0.225.

The market return is 14% per annum and the risk free rate is 6% per annum.

Existing UK microwave production, currently produces an after tax net cash flow of £30 million pounds per annum. This is expected to be reduced by 10% if the South American investment goes ahead (after allowing for the diversion of some production to other EU countries). Production is currently at full capacity in the UK.

Required:

(a) Prepare a report advising whether or not Novoroast plc should invest in the South American country.

- Include in your report a discussion of the limitations of your analysis.

- What other information would be useful to assist the decision process?

- All relevant calculations must be shown in your report or as an appendix to it.

- State clearly any assumptions that you make.

Approximately 20 marks are available for calculations and 10 for discussion.

(30 marks)

(b) If, once the investment had taken place, the government of the South American country imposed a block on the remittance of dividends to the UK, discuss how Novoroast might try to avoid such a block on remittances. **(5 marks)**

(c) Briefly discuss ethical issues that might need to be considered as part of a multinational company's investment decision process. **(5 marks)**

(Total: 40 marks)

43 SLEEPON HOTELS PLC

Sleepon Hotels plc owns a successful chain of hotels. The company is considering diversifying its activities through the construction of a theme park near London. The theme park would have a mixture of family activities and adventure rides. Sleepon has just spent £230,000 on market research into the theme park, and is encouraged by the findings.

The theme park is expected to attract an average of 15,000 visitors per day for at least four years, after which major new investment would be required in order to maintain demand. The price of admission to the theme park is expected to be £18 per adult and £10 per child. 60% of visitors are forecast to be children. In addition to admission revenues, it is expected that the average visitor will spend £8 on food and drinks, (of which 30% is profit), and £5 on gifts and souvenirs, (of which 40% is profit). The park would open for 360 days per year.

All costs and receipts (excluding maintenance and construction costs and the realisable value) are shown at current prices; the company expects all costs and receipts to rise by 3% per year from current values.

The theme park would cost a total of £400 million and could be constructed and working in one year's time. Half of the £400 million would be payable immediately, and half in one year's time. In addition working capital of £50 million will be required from the end of year one. The after tax realisable value of fixed assets is expected to be between £250 million and £300 million after four years of operation.

Maintenance costs (excluding labour) are expected to be £15 million in the first year of operation, increasing by £4 million per year thereafter. Annual insurance costs are £2 million, and the company would apportion £2.5 million per year to the theme park from existing overheads. The theme park would require 1,500 staff costing a total of £40 million per annum (at current prices). Sleepon will use the existing advertising campaigns for its hotels to also advertise the theme park. This will save approximately £2 million per year in advertising expenses.

As Sleepon has no previous experience of theme park management, it has investigated the current risk and financial structure of the closest UK theme park competitor, Thrillall plc. Details are summarised below.

Thrillall plc, summarised balance sheet

	£ million
Fixed assets (net)	1,440
Current assets	570
Less current liabilities	(620)
	1,390
Financed by:	
£1 ordinary shares	400
Reserves	530
	930
Medium and long term debt	460
	1,390

Other information:

(i)   Sleepon has access to a £450 million Eurosterling loan at 7.5% fixed rate to provide the necessary finance for the theme park.

(ii)   £250 million of the investment will attract 25% per year capital allowances on a reducing balance basis.

(iii)   Corporate tax is at a rate of 30%.

(iv)   The average stock market return is 10% and the risk free rate 3.5%.

(v)   Sleepon's current weighted average cost of capital is 9%.

(vi)   Sleepon's market weighted gearing if the theme park project is undertaken is estimated to be 61.4% equity, 38.6% debt.

(vii)   Sleepon's equity beta is 0.70.

(viii) The current share price of Sleepon is 148 pence, and of Thrillall 386 pence.

(ix)   Thrillall's medium and long term debt comprises long term bonds with a par value of £100 and current market price of £93.

(x)   Thrillall's equity beta is 1.45.

Required:

Prepare a report analysing whether or not Sleepon should undertake the investment in the theme park. Your report should include a discussion of what other information would be useful to Sleepon in making the investment decision. All relevant calculations must be included in the report or as an appendix to it. State clearly any assumptions that you make.

(Approximately 28 marks are available for calculations and 12 for discussion)

(40 marks)

EXPANSION STRATEGIES AND CORPORATE REORGANISATION

44   SYNERGIES

You have been asked to produce a briefing memo for senior management at your company on the subject of mergers and acquisitions. Your memo should identify and discuss:

(a)   Possible synergies that might occur in mergers and acquisitions.   **(7 marks)**

(b)   Potential problems in the achievement of synergies.   **(4 marks)**

(c)   Whether or not mergers and acquisitions should be undertaken to achieve corporate diversification only.   **(4 marks)**

(Total: 15 marks)

45 LACETO PLC

(a) Laceto plc, a large UK based retail group specialising in the sale of clothing and electrical goods is currently considering a takeover bid for a competitor in the electrical goods sector, Omnigen plc, whose share price has fallen by 205 pence during the last three months.

Summarised data for the financial year to 31 March 20X1:

	£ million	
	Laceto	*Omnigen*
Turnover	420	180
Profit before tax (after interest payments)	41	20
Taxation	12	6
Fixed assets (net)	110	63
Current assets	122	94
Current liabilities	86	71
Medium and long-term liabilities	40	12
Shareholders' funds	106	74

The share price of Laceto is currently 380 pence, and of Omnigen 410 pence. Laceto has 80 million issued ordinary shares and Omnigen 30 million. Typical of Laceto's medium and long-term liabilities is a 12% debenture with three years to maturity, a par value £100, and a current market price of £108.80.

The finance team of Laceto has produced the following forecasts of financial data for the activities of Omnigen if it is taken over.

Financial year	20X2	20X3	20X4	20X5
	£ million			
Net sales	230	261	281	298
Cost of goods sold (50%)	115	131	141	149
Selling and administrative expenses	32	34	36	38
Capital allowances (total)	40	42	42	42
Interest	18	16	14	12
Cash flow needed for asset replacement and forecast growth	50	52	55	58

Corporate taxation is at the rate of 30% per year, payable in the year that the taxable cash flow occurs. The risk-free rate is 6% per year and market return 14% per year. Omnigen's current equity beta is 1.2. This is expected to increase by 0.1 if the company is taken over as Laceto would increase the current level of capital gearing associated with the activities of Omnigen. Laceto's gearing post acquisition is expected to be between 18% and 23% (debt to debt plus equity by market values), depending upon the final price paid for Omnigen.

Post-takeover cash flows of Omnigen (after replacement and growth expenditure) are expected to grow at between 3% and 5% per year after 20X5.

Additional notes:

(i) The realisable value of Omnigen's assets, net of all debt repayments, is estimated to be £82 million.

(ii) The P/E ratios of two of Omnigen's quoted competitors in the electrical industry are 13:1 and 15:1 respectively.

Required:

Discuss and evaluate what price, or range of prices, Laceto should offer to purchase the shares of Omnigen. State clearly any assumptions that you make. **(25 marks)**

Approximately 17 marks are for calculations and 8 for discussion.

Before making a bid for Omnigen the managing director of Laceto hears a rumour that a bid for Laceto might be made by Agressa.com plc, an internet retailer specialising in the sale of vehicles and electrical goods. Summarised financial data for Agressa.com are shown below.

Agressa.com	£ million
Turnover	190
Operating profit	12
Interest	4
Taxation	2
Fixed assets (net)	30
Current assets	80
Current liabilities	30
Medium and long-term liabilities	40
Shareholders' funds	40

Agressa's current share price is £26.50, and the company has 15 million issued ordinary shares.

Required:

(b)   Prepare a brief report for the managing director of Laceto which analyses how Laceto might defend itself from a takeover bid from Agressa.com.   **(8 marks)**

(c)   Discuss how the method of payment of the potential takeovers in (a) and (b) above might effect the success or failure of the bids.   **(7 marks)**

(Total: 40 marks)

46   OBERBERG AG

(a)   Discuss the advantages to a company of establishing an overseas operating subsidiary by either

(i)   organic growth, or

(ii)   acquisition.   **(8 marks)**

(b)   'Now' is December 20X2.

The Board of Directors of Intergrand plc wishes to establish an operating subsidiary in Germany through the acquisition of an existing German company. Intergrand has undertaken research into a number of German quoted companies, and has decided to attempt to purchase Oberberg AG. Initial discussions suggest that the directors of Oberberg AG may be willing to recommend the sale of 100% of the company's equity to Intergrand for a total cash price of €115 million, payable in full on acquisition.

Oberberg has provided the managers of Intergrand with internal management information regarding accounting/cash flow projections for the next four years.

The projections are in money/nominal terms.

	Oberberg AG, financial projections			
	€ (million)			
Year	*20X3*	*20X4*	*20X5*	*20X6*
Sales	38.2	41.2	44.0	49.0
Labour	11.0	12.1	13.0	14.1
Materials	8.3	8.7	9.0	9.4
Overheads	3.2	3.2	3.3	3.4
Interest	2.5	3.0	3.5	3.8
Tax-allowable depreciation	6.3	5.8	5.6	5.2
	31.3	32.8	34.4	35.9

Taxable profit	6.9	8.4	9.6	13.1
Taxation (25%)	1.7	2.1	2.4	3.3
Incremental operating working capital	0.7	0.9	1.0	2.0
Replacement investment	4.2	4.2	4.2	4.2
Investment for expansion	-	-	9.0	-

**Oberberg AG, pro forma summarized P & L account
for the year ending 31 December 20X2**

	€ (million)
Sales	35.8
Operating expenses	21.1
Interest expense	3.4
Depreciation	6.2
	30.7
Taxable profit	5.1
Taxation (25%)	1.3
Profit after tax	3.8

Oberberg AG pro forma summarised balance sheet as at 31 December 20X2

	€ (million)
Fixed assets	73.2
Current assets	58.1
Current liabilities	(40.3)
	91.0
Financed by:	
Ordinary shares (€100 par value)	15.0
Reserves	28.0
Medium and long term bank loans	30.0
8% Bond 20X9 (par value €1,000)	18.0
	91.0

Notes:

(i) The spot exchange rate between the Euro and pound is €1.625/£1.

(ii) Inflation is at 4% per year in the UK, and 2% per year in the Eurozone. This differential is expected to continue unless the UK joins the Eurozone.

(iii) The market return is 11% and the risk-free rate is 4%.

(iv) Oberberg's equity beta is estimated to be 1.4.

(v) Oberberg's 8% bond is currently priced at €1,230, and its ordinary share price is €300.

(vi) Post-merger rationalisation will involve the sale of some fixed assets (non-current assets) of Oberberg in 20X3 with an expected after tax market value of €8 million.

(vii) Synergies in production and distribution are expected to yield €2 million per annum before tax from 20X4 onwards.

(viii) £175,000 has already been spent researching into possible acquisition targets.

(ix) The purchase of Oberberg will provide publicity and exposure in Germany for the Intergrand name and brand. This extra publicity is believed to be the equivalent of Intergrand spending €1 million per year on advertising in Germany.

(x) The weighted average cost of capital of Intergrand is 10%.

(xi) After-tax cash flows of Oberberg after 20X6 are expected to grow at approximately 2% per year.

(xii) Oberberg does not plan to issue or redeem any equity or medium- and long-term debt prior to 20X6.

(xiii) After-tax redundancy costs as a result of the acquisition are expected to be €5 million, payable almost immediately.

(xiv) Operating working capital comprises debtors and stock less creditors (receivables plus inventory less payables). It excludes short-term loans.

(xv) Current liabilities include negligible amounts of short-term loans.

(xvi) The corporate tax rate in Germany is 25%, and in the UK 30%. A bilateral tax treaty exists between the two countries whereby tax paid in one country may be credited against any tax liability in the other country.

(xvii) If Intergrand acquires Oberberg, existing exports to Germany yielding a pre-tax cash flow of £800,000 per annum will be lost. It is hoped that about half of these exports can be diverted to the French market.

Required:

Intergrand has suggested that Oberberg should be valued based upon the expected present value (to infinity) of the operating free cash flows of Oberberg. These would be discounted at an all-equity rate, and adjusted by the present value of all other relevant cash flows, discounted at an appropriate rate(s).

Acting as a consultant to Intergrand plc, prepare a report evaluating whether or not Intergrand should offer the €115 million required to acquire Oberberg AG. Include in your report discussion of other commercial and business factors that Intergrand should consider prior to making a final decision.

State clearly any other assumptions that you make. **(32 marks)**

Approximately 22 marks are available for calculations and 10 for discussion.

(Total: 40 marks)

47 ROMAGE PLC

Romage plc has two major operating divisions, manufacturing and property sales with turnovers of £260 million and £620 million respectively.

Balance sheet for Romage plc

	£ million
Land and buildings	80
Plant and machinery	140
Current assets	250
Current liabilities	180
	290
Financed by:	
Ordinary shares (25 pence par)	50 ÷ 25 = 200m shares
~~Reserves~~	130 Book value
Secured term loan MV of Debt	60
13% debentures redeemable at par in 15 years' time	50 ∴ IRR
	290

Summarised cash flow data for Romage plc

	£ million
Cash turnover	880
Divisional operating expenses	803
Central costs	8
Interest	11
Taxation	14
Dividends	15

The company's current share price is 296 pence, and the market value of a debenture is £131.

Projected real (i.e. excluding inflation) pre tax financial data (£million) of the two divisions are:

Year	1	2	3	4	5	6 onwards
Manufacturing						
Operating net cash flows	45	48	50	52	57	60
Allocated central costs	4	4	4	4	4	4
Tax allowable depreciation	10	8	7	8	8	8
Property sales						
Operating net cash flows	32	40	42	44	46	50
Allocated central costs	4	3	3	3	3	3
Tax allowable depreciation	5	5	5	5	5	5

[handwritten annotation: Capital allowance]

Corporate taxation is at the rate of 31% per year, payable in the year that the relevant cash flow arises.

Inflation is expected to remain at approximately 3% per year.

[handwritten annotation: includes inflation]

The risk free rate is 5.5% and the market return 14%.

Romage's equity beta is 1.15.

The company is considering a demerger whereby the two divisions are floated separately on the stock market. The debenture would be serviced by the property division and the term loan by the manufacturing division. The existing equity would be split evenly between the divisions, although new ordinary shares would be issued to replace existing shares.

The average equity betas in the manufacturing and property sectors are 1.3 and 0.9 respectively, and the gearing levels in manufacturing and property sales by market values are 70% equity, 30% debt and 80% equity, 20% debt respectively.

Notes

(1) Allocated central costs reflect actual cash flows. If a demerger occurs these costs would rise to £6 million per year for each company.

(2) A demerger would involve a one-off after tax cost of £16 million in year one which would be split evenly between the two companies. There would be no other significant impact on expected cash flows.

(3) The current cost of the debenture and term loan are almost identical.

(4) The debenture is redeemable at par.

Required:

(a) Discuss the potential advantages for Romage plc of undertaking the divestment of one of its divisions by means of

   (1) a sell-off and

   (2) a demerger *exc inflation* **(8 marks)**

(b) Using real cash flows, evaluate whether or not it is expected to be financially advantageous to the original shareholders of Romage plc for the company to separately float the two divisions on the stock market. Your evaluation should use both a 15 year time horizon and an infinite time horizon.

annuity   *perpetuity*

In any gearing estimates the manufacturing division may be assumed to comprise 55% of the market value of equity of Romage plc, and the property sales division 45%.

State clearly any additional assumptions that you make. **(24 marks)**

(c) Discuss what additional information and analysis would assist the decision process.

Goodard Gift **(8 marks)**

(Total: 40 marks)

48 PEDER AND TULEN

The total values (equity plus debt) of two companies, Peden and Tulen are expected to fluctuate according to the state of the economy.

	Economic state		
	Recession	*Slow growth*	*Rapid growth*
Probability	0.15	0.65	0.20
Total values			
Peden (£m)	42	55	75
Tulen (£m)	63	80	120

Peden currently has £45 million of debt, and Tulen £10 million of debt.

Required:

If the two companies were to merge, and assuming that no operational synergy occurs as a result of the merger, calculate the expected value of debt and equity of the merged company. Explain the reason for any difference that exists from the expected values of debt and equity if they do not merge. **(10 marks)**

49 OAKTON PLC

(a) Explain why synergy might exist when one company merges with or takes over another company. **(6 marks)**

(b) Oakton plc, a company quoted on the London Stock Exchange, has cash balances of £23 million which are currently invested in short-term money market deposits. The cash is intended to be used primarily for strategic acquisitions, and the company has formed an acquisition committee with a remit to identify possible acquisition targets. The committee has suggested the purchase of Mallard plc, a company in a different industry, that is quoted on the AIM (Alternative Investment Market). Although Mallard is quoted, approximately 50% of its shares are still owned by three directors. These directors have stated that they might be prepared to recommend the sale of Mallard, but they consider that its shares are worth £22 million in total.

Summarised financial data

	Oakton plc £000		Mallard plc £000
Turnover	480,000		38,000
Pre tax operating cash flow	51,000		5,300
Taxation (33%)	16,830		1,749
Post tax operating cash flow	34,170		3,551
Dividend	11,000		842
Fixed assets (net)	168,000		8,400
Current assets	135,000		4,700
Current liabilities	99,680		3,900
	203,320		9,200
Financed by			
Ordinary shares (25 pence par)	10,000	(Mallard 10 pence par)	500
Reserves	158,320		5,200
12% Debentures 2006	20,000		–
10% Bank term loan	15,000		
		Recent 11% bank loan	3,500
	203,320		9,200
Current share price	785 pence		370 pence
Earnings yield	10.9%		19.2%
Average dividend growth during the last five years	7% p.a.		8% p.a.
Equity beta	0.95		0.8
Industry data:			
Average P/E ratio	10:1		6:1
Average P/E of companies recently taken over, based upon the offer price	12:1		7:1

The risk free rate of return is 6% per annum and the market return 14% per annum.

The rate of inflation is 2.4% per annum and is expected to remain at approximately this level.

Expected effects of the acquisition would be:

(i) 50 employees of Mallard would immediately be made redundant at an after tax cost of £1.2 million. Pre-tax annual wage savings are expected to be £750,000 (at current prices) for the foreseeable future.

(ii) Some land and buildings of Mallard would be sold for £800,000 (after tax).

(iii) Pre-tax advertising and distribution savings of £150,000 per year (at current prices) would be possible.

(iv) The three existing directors of Mallard would each be paid £100,000 per year for three years for consultancy services. This amount would not increase with inflation.

Required:

Estimate the value of Mallard based upon:

(i) The use of comparative P/E ratios

(ii) The dividend valuation model

(iii) The present value of relevant operating cash flows over a 10 year period and critically discuss the advantages and disadvantages of *each* of the three valuation methods.

Recommend whether or not Oakton should offer £22 million for Mallard's shares.

Approximately 8 marks are available for discussion. **(20 marks)**

(c) Briefly discuss the factors that might influence whether or not Oakton plc uses its *cash balances*, rather than shares or bonds to make payment for Mallard. **(4 marks)**

(Total: 30 marks)

50   DRICOM PLC

Assume that 'now' is December 2003.

Dricom plc is a manufacturer of mobile phones. The company was successful in the mid 1990s, and established a small chain of retail shops in major UK cities. In 2001–02 the company's new products experienced reliability problems and competition from technologically superior products, causing sales to fall by forty percent from 2000–01 levels. This lead to substantial losses being made in both 2001–02 and 2002–03.

The company's managers are confident that the technical problems can be overcome, but this will require an investment of £2.25 million for new automated equipment and quality monitoring machinery. Dricom's bank, BXT Bank, is concerned about the company's recent performance, and a new debt or equity issue on the stock market is not possible. Without the new investment Dricom is unlikely to be competitive, and might not survive the next financial year. With the new investment profits before interest and tax are forecast to be at least £750,000 per year from 2004–05 for at least five years.

Dricom plc

Summarised balance sheet as at 30 September 2003

	£000
Land and buildings	1,500
Plant and machinery (net)	2,100
	3,600
Current assets	
Stocks	1,340
Debtors	1,090
Cash at bank and in hand	35
Total current assets	2,465
Creditors: amounts falling due within one year	
Overdraft	620
Other creditors	940
	1,560
Total assets less current liabilities	4,505

Creditors: amounts falling due after more than one year

Term loan (from BXT Bank)	800
9% debenture 2016	500
8% convertible debenture 2005	1,000
10% loan stock 2011	500
	2,800

Capital and reserves

Called up share capital (£1 par value)	1,000
Share premium account	945
Revenue reserves	(240)
Total shareholders' funds	1,705
Total capital employed	4,505

Notes

(1) The 9% straight debenture is secured by a fixed charge on the company's main factory building, the convertible debenture and term loan by a floating charge on fixed assets. The loan stock and overdraft are unsecured.

(2) The land and buildings are believed to have a realisable value 20% less than their net book value.

(3) If the company ceased trading stocks would be sold at 50% of their book value.

(4) The new equipment would result in fifty staff being made redundant, with an immediate after tax cost of £500,000. If the company were to be liquidated after tax redundancy payments would total £1 million. Redundancy payments may be assumed to rank before unsecured creditors.

(5) Obsolete machinery with a net book value of £800,000 will be sold for £300,000 irrespective of whether or not the new investment takes place. The remainder of the plant and machinery could be disposed of at net book value. All disposal values are after tax.

(6) The overdraft currently costs 10% per year and the bank term loan 12% per year.

(7) The company's current share price is 23 pence, loan stock price £78, straight debenture price £90 and convertible debenture price £94. All marketable debt has a par and redemption value of £100.

Dricom's finance director believes that a corporate restructuring could solve the company's problems, and has made the following proposals:

(i) Existing shareholders are to be offered 28 pence per share to redeem their shares, which would then be cancelled.

(ii) £1 million would be provided by a venture capital organisation in return for 700,000 new 25 pence par value ordinary shares.

(iii) The company's directors and employees would subscribe to 500,000 new 25 pence ordinary shares at a price of 150 pence per share.

(iv) The convertible debenture is to be replaced by new ordinary shares (par value 25 pence), with 60 ordinary shares for every £100 nominal value loan stock.

(v) The term loan is to be renegotiated with the bank and the total amount of the loan increased to £2 million. This would have an expected interest charge of 13% per annum. A floating charge on fixed assets would be offered on the overdraft.

(vi) All other long-term loans would remain unchanged.

Apart from the directors, none of the above parties have yet been consulted regarding the proposed reconstruction.

Following a reconstruction no corporate tax is expected to be paid for at least two years. The corporate tax rate is 33%.

The average price/earnings ratio in Dricom's industry is 12:1.

Required:

Acting as a consultant to Dricom plc prepare a report evaluating whether or not the suggested scheme of reconstruction is likely to succeed.

A full pro forma balance sheet is not required as part of your evaluation. State clearly any assumptions that you make. **(30 marks)**

51 RAYSWOOD PLC

In a recent meeting of the board of directors of Rayswood plc the chairman proposed the acquisition of Pondhill plc. During his presentation the chairman stated that. '*As a result of this takeover we will diversify our operations and our earnings per share will rise by 13%, bringing great benefits to our shareholders.*'

No bid has yet been made, and Rayswood currently owns only 2% of Pondhill.

A bid would be based on a share for share exchange, which would be one Rayswood share for every six Pondhill shares.

Financial data for the two companies include:

	Rayswood	Pondhill
	£m	£m
Turnover	56.0	42.0
Profit before tax	12.0	10.0
Profit available to		
ordinary shareholders	7.8	6.5
Dividends	3.2	3.4
Retained earnings	4.6	3.1
Issued ordinary shares	20m	15m
Market price per share	320 pence	45 pence

Rayswood 50 pence par value, Pondhill 10 pence par value.

A non-executive director has recently stated that he believes 'the share price of Rayswood will rapidly increase to £3.61 following the announcement of the bid.'

Required:

Explain whether you agree with the chairman's and the non-executive director's assessment of the benefits of the proposed takeover.

Support your explanation with relevant calculations, including your assessment of the likely post acquisition share price of Rayswood if the bid is successful.

State clearly any assumptions that you make. **(15 marks)**

52   PRICUT PLC

The directors of Pricut plc, a food retailer with 20 superstores, are proposing to make a takeover bid for Verlot plc, a company with six superstores in the north of England. Pricut will offer four of its ordinary shares for every three ordinary shares of Verlot. The bid has not yet been made public.

Handwritten annotations: P 4   V 3 ; P+V = E Total value ; Calculate theoretical price ∴ post merger share price ; Gearing → financial risk ; Gearing 3/4 ; 75 ÷ 0.25 = 300m shares ; 20 ÷ 0.5 = 40m shares

Summarised accounts
Balance sheets as at 31 March 20X3

	Pricut plc £ million	Verlot plc £ million
Land and buildings (net)	483	42.3
Fixed assets (net)	150	17.0
	633	59.3
Current assets		
Stock	328	51.4
Debtors	12	6.3
Cash	44	5.3
	384	63.0
Creditors: amounts falling due in less than one year		
Creditors	447	46.1
Dividend	12	2.0
Taxation	22	2.0
	(481)	(50.1)
Creditors: amounts falling due after more than one year		
14% loan stock	(200)	–
Floating rate bank term loans	(114)	(17.5)
	222	54.7
Shareholders funds		
Ordinary shares (25 pence par)	75	
Ordinary shares (50 pence par)		20.0
Reserves	147	34.7
	222	54.7

Profit and loss accounts
for the year ending 31 March 20X3

Company's ability to pay interest (handwritten)

Interest cover less than 3 times (handwritten)

Average interest cover 3:1 (handwritten)

	Pricut plc £ million	Verlot plc £ million
Turnover	1,130	181
Earnings before interest and tax	115	14
Net interest	40	2
Profit before tax	75	12
Taxation	25	4
Available to shareholders	50	8
Dividend	24	5
Retained earnings	26	3

2.9:1 (handwritten)

Interest cover $\frac{14}{2} = 7$ *times* (handwritten)

The share price of Pricut plc is currently 232 pence, and of Verlot plc 295 pence. The loan stock price of Pricut plc is £125.

Recent annual growth trends:	Pricut plc	Verlot plc
Dividends *per share see Q7.*	7%	8%
EPS	7%	10%

Rationalisation following the acquisition will involve the following transactions (all net of tax effects): *Synergy after tax* (handwritten)

(i)   Sale of surplus warehouse facilities £6.8 million.

(ii)   Redundancy payments £9.0 million. *cost* (handwritten)

(iii)   Wage savings of £2.7 million per year for at least five years. *Annuity ∴ Need disc rate* (handwritten) *PV of synergy* (handwritten)

Pricut's cost of equity is estimated to be 14.5%, and weighted average cost of capital 12%. Verlot's cost of equity is estimated to be 13%. *of acquirer* (handwritten)

Required:

How the shareholder's wealth might be affected. (handwritten)

(a)   Discuss and evaluate whether or not the bid is likely to be viewed favourably by the shareholders of both Pricut plc and Verlot plc. Include discussion of the factors that are likely to influence the views of the shareholders.

All relevant calculations must be shown.   **(14 marks)**

(b)   Discuss the possible effects on the likely success of the bid if the offer terms were to be amended to a choice of one new Pricut plc ten year zero coupon debenture redeemable at £100 for every ten Verlot plc shares, or 325 pence per share cash. Pricut plc could currently issue new ten year loan stock at an interest rate of 10%.

All relevant calculations must be shown.   **(8 marks)**

(c)   The directors of Verlot plc have decided to fight the bid and have proposed the following measures:

(i)   announce that their company's profits are likely to be doubled next year

(ii)   alter the articles of association to require that at least 75% of shareholders need to approve an acquisition

(iii) persuade, for a fee, a third party investor to buy large quantities of the company's shares

    (iv)   introduce an advertising campaign criticising the performance and management ability of Pricut plc

    (v)   revalue fixed assets to current values so that shareholders are aware of the company's true market values.

Required:

Acting as a consultant to the company give reasoned advice on whether or not the company should adopt each of these measures. **(8 marks)**

(Total: 30 marks)

53   PERFORMANCE ASSESSMENT

Assume that an important UK based client has asked you to review the performance of two overseas companies in which he is thinking of investing. Both companies are claiming to have been successful during the last four years. One company is located in the country of Asertia, the other in Knowland.

Company 1 in Asertia — Lire (million)

	2000	2001	2002	2003
Turnover	432	567	693	810
Profit after tax	55	76	102	126
Share price (lire)	1,058	1,330	1,620	2,001
Equity beta				1.55

Company 2 in Knowland — Francs (000)

	2000	2001	2002	2003
Turnover	12,000	12,430	13,100	14,569
Profit after tax	1,840	2,004	2,320	2,540
Share price (francs)	236	192	204	229
Equity beta				0.98

Data for the two countries:

Asertia

	2000	2001	2002	2003
Retail price (inflation) index	450.3	610.2	773.1	924.2
Stock market index	5,005	6,002	7,450	9,470
Risk free rate				19%

Knowland

	2000	2001	2002	2003
Retail price (inflation) index	100	104.3	107.1	110.8
Stock market index	10,200	8,896	9,320	9,457
Risk free rate				4%

The equity betas and the risk free rate were estimated over the period 2000–2003.

Required:

    (a)   Prepare a report for the client discussing the performance of the two companies. Relevant calculations should be included in the report. **(10 marks)**

    (b)   Discuss what other information would be useful to assess the performance of the two companies. **(5 marks)**

(Total: 15 marks)

54   PAXIS

Paxis plc will soon announce a takeover bid for Wragger plc, a company in the same industry. The initial bid will be an all share bid of four Paxis shares for every five Wragger shares.

The most recent annual data relating to the two companies are shown below:

	£000	
	Paxis	*Wragger*
Sales revenue	13,333	9,400
Operating costs	(8,683)	(5,450)
Tax allowable depreciation	(1,450)	(1,100)
Earnings before interest and tax	3,200	2,850
Net interest	(715)	(1,660)
Taxable income	2,485	1,190
Taxation (30%)	(746)	(357)
After tax income	1,739	833
Dividend	(870)	(458)
Retained earnings	869	375

Other information:

	Paxis	*Wragger*
Annual replacement capital expenditure (£000)	1,600	1,240
Expected annual growth rate in sales, operating costs (including depreciation), replacement investment and dividends for the next four years	5%	6.5%
Expected annual growth rate in sales, operating costs (incuding depreciation), replacement investment and dividends after four years	4%	5%
Gearing (long term debt/long term debt plus equity by market value)	30%	55%
Market price per share (pence)	298	192
Number of issued shares (million)	7	8
Current market cost of fixed interest debt	6%	7.5%
Equity beta	1.18	1.38
Risk free rate	4%	
Market return	11%	

The takeover is expected to result in cost savings in advertising and distribution, reducing the operating costs (including depreciation) of Paxis from 76% of sales to 70% of sales. The growth rate of the combined company is expected to be 6% per year for four years, and 5% per year thereafter. Wragger's debt obligations will be taken over by Paxis. The corporate tax rate is expected to remain at 30%.

Sales and costs relevant to the decision may be assumed to be in cash terms.

Required:

(a) Using free cash flow analysis for each individual company and the potential combined company, estimate how much synergy is expected to be created from the takeover. State clearly any assumptions that you make.

Note: The weighted average cost of capital of the combined company may be assumed to be the market weighted average of the current costs of capital of the individual companies, weighted by the current market value of debt and equity of the combined company, with the equity of Wragger adjusted for the effect of the bid price.

(20 marks)

(b) Discuss the limitations of the above estimates.

(6 marks)

(c) Discuss the factors that might influence whether the initial bid is likely to be accepted by the shareholders of Wragger plc.

(4 marks)

(d) Estimate by how much the bid might be increased without the shareholders of Paxis suffering a fall in their expected wealth, and discuss whether or not the directors of Paxis should proceed with the bid.

(5 marks)

(e) Once the bid is announced, discuss what defences Wragger plc might use against the bid by Paxis plc.

(5 marks)

(Total: 40 marks)

55   REFLATOR PLC

A division of Reflator plc has recently experienced severe financial difficulties. The management of the division is keen to undertake a buy-out, but in order for the buyout to succeed it needs to attract substantial finance from a venture capital organisation. Reflator plc is willing to sell the division for £2.1 million, and the managers believe that an additional £1 million of capital would need to be invested in the division to create a viable going concern.

Possible financing sources:

Equity from management £500,000, in 50 pence ordinary shares.

Funds from the venture capital organisation:

Equity £300,000, in 50 pence ordinary shares

Debt: 8.5% fixed rate loan £2,000,000

9% subordinated loan with warrants attached £300,000.

The warrants are exercisable any time after four years from now at the rate of 100 ordinary shares at the price of 150 pence per share for every £100 of subordinated loan.

The principal on the 8.5% fixed rate loan is repayable as a bullet payment at the end of eight years. The subordinated loan is repayable by equal annual payments, comprising both interest and principal, over a period of six years.

The division's managers propose to keep dividends to no more than 15% of profits for the first four years.

Independently produced forecasts of earnings before tax and interest after the buy-out are shown below:

	£000			
Year	1	2	3	4
EBIT	320	410	500	540

Corporate tax is at the rate of 30% per year.

The managers involved in the buy-out have stated that the book value of equity is likely to increase by about 20% per year during the first four years, making the investment very attractive to the venture capital organisation. The venture capital organisation has stated that it is interested in investing, but has doubts about the forecast growth rate of equity value, and would require warrants for 150 shares per £100 of subordinated loan stock rather than 100 shares.

Required:

(a) Briefly discuss the potential advantages of management buy-outs. **(5 marks)**

(b) On the basis of the above data, estimate whether or not the book value of equity is likely to grow by 20% per year. **(7 marks)**

(c) Evaluate the possible implication of the managers agreeing to offer warrants for 150 ordinary shares per £100 of loan stock. **(3 marks)**

(Total: 15 marks)

TREASURY MANAGEMENT

56   TYR PLC

Summarised financial data for TYR plc is shown below:

TYR plc

Year	Post-tax earnings (£ million)	Dividends (£ million)	Issued shares (million)	Share price (pence)
20X1	86.2	34.5	180	360
20X2	92.4	36.2	180	410
20X3	99.3	37.6	180	345
20X4	134.1	51.6	240	459
20X5	148.6	53.3	240	448

Year	All-share index	Inflation rate
20X1	2895	6%
20X2	3300	5%
20X3	2845	4%
20X4	2610	3%
20X5	2305	3%

TYR's cost of equity is estimated to be 11%.

Required:

(a) Explain, with supporting numerical evidence, the current dividend policy of TYR plc, and briefly discuss whether or not this appears to be successful. **(6 marks)**

(b) Identify and consider additional information that might assist the managers of TYR in assessing whether the dividend policy has been successful. **(4 marks)**

(c) Evaluate whether or not the company's share price at the end of 20X5 was what might have been expected from the Dividend Growth Model. Briefly discuss the validity of your findings. **(5 marks)**

(Total: 15 marks)

57 DISCOS PLC

Discos plc is negotiating an export contract with a customer in a developing country, Xeridia. Discos has not exported to the country before, and is concerned both about the risk of late or non-payment for the exports, and about the foreign exchange risks associated with the Xeridian peso. The contract specifies that Discos should receive 55 million Xeridian pesos in three months' time. Discos will require short-term finance for the full value of the exports.

Exchange rates (peso/£)

Spot	32.34 – 32.89
3 months forward	33.82 – 34.55
6 months forward	35.17 – 35.90

Current short-term UK interest rates available to Discos plc:

Borrowing	6.5%
Investing	5.3%

Discos is considering three different ways of protecting against the foreign trade risk:

(i)   Insure the deal with Protect Trade plc and undertake a forward market hedge. An insurance policy is available at a cost of 1.25% of the spot sterling equivalent of the export value. The policy gives the following protection: 95% cover against non-payment as a result of political actions by a foreign government; 90% cover against other non-payment. Any payment by the insurer would be after six months.

(ii)   Use the services of a non-recourse export factor. The factor will guarantee that £1,590,000 is paid in three months' time if the customer pays on time, or £1,530,000 in six months' time if the customer makes a late payment or defaults. The factor is prepared to provide immediate trade finance of up to 80% of the value of the guaranteed sum, at an interest rate of 6.3%. The factor charges an administration fee of 2.5% of the sum guaranteed.

(iii) Use a confirmed, irrevocable, documentary letter of credit. The letter of credit would include a 90-day bank bill of exchange that may be immediately discounted in the Xeridian money market at an annual rate of 25%, which is the short term borrowing rate in Xeridia. The fees associated with the letter of credit are £30,000.

Discos has been advised that there is at least a 5% chance of late payment after six months or default by the client. The Xeridian government is not expected to take any action that is detrimental to foreign trade during the next six months.

Required:

Discuss the advantages and disadvantages of each alternative, and recommend which should be selected. Relevant calculations should support your discussion. State clearly any assumptions that you make.   **(15 marks)**

58 NTC PLC

(a)   Discuss the advantages and disadvantages of centralised treasury management for multinational companies.   **(8 marks)**

(b)   NTC plc is a UK multinational with subsidiaries in Spain, Hong Kong and the USA. Transactions between companies within the group have historically been in all of the currencies of the countries where the companies are located and have not been centrally co-ordinated, with the currency of the transaction varying in each deal.

Transactions due in approximately three months' time are shown below. All receipts and payments are in thousand units of the specified currencies. *Per £*

Assume that it is now mid-June.

Payments (read down)

Receipts (read across)	UK	Spain	Hong Kong	USA
UK	–	€210	HK$720	US$110
Spain	£100	–	€80	–
Hong Kong	HK$400	–	–	–
USA	US$430	€120	HK$300	–

Exchange rates:

	US$/£	Euro/£	HK$/£
Spot	1.4358–1.4366	1.6275–1.6292	11.1987–11.2050
3 months forward	1.4285–1.4300	1.6146–1.6166	11.1567–11.1602

Buy – sell *Buy – sell* *Buy – sell.*

— Forward Hedge.

Note:

The Hong Kong dollar is pegged against the US dollar. *fixed*

Interest rates available to NTC and its subsidiaries (annual %): — money market

	Borrowing	Investing
UK	6.9	6.0
Spain	5.3	4.5
Hong Kong	n.a.	6.1
USA	6.2	5.4

Currency options — Direct quote — Options

Philadelphia Stock exchange £/$ options, £31,250 contracts. Premium is in cents per £

$/£

	Calls			**Puts**		
Exercise price	July	August	September	July	August	September
1.42	1.42	2.12	2.67	0.68	1.42	2.15
1.43	0.88	1.60	1.79	1.14	1.92	3.12
1.44	0.51	1.19	1.42	1.77	2.51	4.35

In $ per £

If starts with 1 it's in $ per £

Option premiums are payable upfront. Contracts may be assumed to expire at the end of the relevant month.

Required: cc = £

Group context.

(i) The parent company is proposing that inter-company payments should be settled in sterling via multilateral netting. Demonstrate how this policy would reduce the number of transactions. (Foreign exchange spot mid-rates may be used for this purpose.) **(6 marks)**

Company context

(ii) If payments were to continue to be made in various currencies, illustrate three methods by which the UK parent company might hedge its transaction exposures for the next three months. Discuss, showing relevant calculations, which method should be selected. Include in your discussion an evaluation of the circumstances in which currency options would be the preferred choice. (*Note*: NTC plc wishes to minimise the transaction costs of hedging.)

(15 marks)

(c) NTC plc has been approached by a Russian company that wishes to purchase goods from NTC plc in exchange for wheat. The Russian currency is not freely convertible.

Discuss the potential advantages and disadvantages of such countertrade to NTC plc.

(6 marks)

(Total: 35 marks)

59   ELECTRONICS COMPANY

Assume that 'now' is June 2003.

The following data relates to a large company operating in the electronics industry.

	1998	1999	2000	2001	2002
After tax earnings (£ million)	130	195	255	295	472
Dividend per share (pence)	9.75	11.0	12.75	14.0	15.5
Number of ordinary shares (million)	508	600	650	695	930
Average share price (pence)	740	875	690	820	1,012
Net capital investment (£ million)	210	270	340	410	520
Annual increase in inflation (%)	4	4	3	3	3

A major institutional shareholder has criticised the level of dividend payment of the company suggesting that it should be substantially increased.

Required:

(a)   Briefly discuss the factors that are likely to influence the company's dividend policy.

(6 marks)

(b)   Discuss whether or not the institutional shareholder's criticism is likely to be valid.

(4 marks)

(Total: 10 marks)

60   TOUTEN PLC

Touten plc is a UK registered multinational company with subsidiaries in 14 countries in Europe, Asia and Africa. The subsidiaries have traditionally been allowed a large amount of autonomy, but Touten plc is now proposing to centralise most of group treasury management operations.

Required:

Acting as a consultant to Touten plc prepare a memo suitable for distribution from the group finance director to the senior management of each of the subsidiaries explaining:

- the potential benefits of treasury centralisation

- how the company proposes to minimise any potential problems for the subsidiaries that might arise as a result of treasury centralisation.   **(10 marks)**

61   SHARE BUY-BACKS AND STOCK SPLITS

Discuss the main feature of:

(i)   corporate share purchase repurchases (buy-backs) and

(ii)   share (stock) splits,

and why companies might use them. Include in your discussion comment on the possible effects on share price of share repurchases and share (stock) splits in comparison to the payment of dividends.   **(15 marks)**

FOREIGN EXCHANGE RISK

62   VERTID LTD

In an attempt to recover from the economic recession, Vertid Ltd, a company employing 30 workers in the UK Midlands, is starting to trade with two foreign countries, Werland and Thodia. Competitively priced components have been purchased from Werland, with payment of 3,000,000 Werland francs due in three months time. Goods have been sold to Thodia and receipts of 3,500,000 Thodian pesos are due to be received in six months time.

The managing director of Vertid is concerned that the company cannot afford to lose money on the two deals, as the company's poor cash flow situation has been the subject of recent discussions with the company's bank. Vertid's overdraft is currently approaching its agreed limit, and the bank has indicated that it is unlikely that the overdraft facility will be increased in the near future.

The managing director asked his sales manager for a brief report discussing the likely foreign exchange risk to be faced when trading with Werland and Thodia. The sales manager has stated that there is likely to be substantial foreign exchange risk in trading with Werland, but little risk in trading with Thodia, whose currency is directly linked to the US dollar.

The US dollar in recent months has been quite stable relative to sterling:

Exchange rates

Spot market

290 – 294 Werland francs/£1

1.4640 – 1.4690 US\$/£1

220 – 228 Thodian pesos/US\$1

Forward market US\$/£1

3 months forward 0.98 – 1.15 cents dis

6 months forward 1.70 – 1.86 cents dis

No forward market exists for the Werland franc or Thodian peso.

Current inflation rates

United Kingdom	3%
USA	6%
Werland	12%
Thodia	20%

Current annual interest rates that are available to Vertid

	Investing	*Borrowing*
£ sterling	4.5%	10%
US\$	6%	12%
Werland francs	12.5%	–
Thodian pesos	15%	–

OTC European currency call options are available for Werland francs at a premium of 25 francs/£1 with an exercise price of 300 francs/£1 and a three month maturity date.

The managing director of Vertid wishes to develop a strategy for:

(i)   protecting against *any form* of risk that these deals involve

(ii)   financing the overseas trade deals.

Required:

You have been asked as a consultant to:

(a) Explain whether or not the views of the sales manager regarding exchange risk are likely to be correct. **(9 marks)**

(b) Prepare a report discussing how the managers of Vertid might protect the company against *all* of the risks of each of the foreign deals. Relevant calculations should support your report. **(25 marks)**

(c) Outline what alternatives might be available to Vertid Ltd to finance the two trade deals. **(6 marks)**

(Total: 40 marks)

63 SOMAX PLC

Assume that 'now' is June 2003.

(a) Somax plc wishes to raise 260 million Swiss francs in floating rate finance for a period of five years. Discuss the advantages and disadvantages of raising such funds through:

    (i) Direct borrowing from a domestic banking system such as the Swiss domestic banking system. (Detailed knowledge of the Swiss banking system is not required.)

    (ii) The Euromarket **(10 marks)**

(b) The funds are to be used to establish a new production plant in Switzerland. Somax evaluates its investments using NPV, but is not sure what cost of capital to use in the discounting process.

The company is also proposing to increase its equity finance in the near future for UK expansion, resulting overall in little change in the company's market weighted capital gearing. The summarised financial data for the company before the expansion are shown below:

Profit and loss account for the year ending 31 March 2003

	£ million
Turnover	1,984
Gross profit	432
Profit after tax	81
Dividends	37
Retained earnings	44

Balance sheet as at 31 March 2003

	£ million
Fixed assets (net)	846
Working capital	350
	1,196
Medium and long-term loans[1]	(210)
	986
Shareholders' funds	
Issued ordinary shares (50 pence par)	225
Reserves	761
	986

[1] Including £75m 14% fixed rate bonds due to mature in five years time and redeemable at £100. The current market price of these bonds is £119.50. Other

medium and long-term loans are floating rate UK bank loans at bank base rate plus 1%.

Corporate tax may be assumed to be at the rate of 33% in both the UK and Switzerland.

The company's ordinary shares are currently trading at 376 pence.

Somax's equity beta is estimated to be 1.18. The systematic risk of debt may be assumed to be zero.

The risk free rate is 7.75% and market return 14.5%. Bank base rate is currently 8.25%.

The estimated equity beta of the main Swiss competitor in the same industry as the new proposed plant in Switzerland is 1.5, and the competitor's capital gearing is 35% equity, 65% debt by book values, and 60% equity, 40% debt by market values.

	Exchange rates
Spot	SFr2.3245-2.3300/£1
6 months forward	SFr2.2955-2.3009/£1

Somax can borrow in Swiss francs at a floating rate of between 5.75% and 6% depending upon which form of borrowing is selected (i.e. in the Euromarkets or the Swiss domestic market).

SFr LIBOR is currently 5%.

The interest rate parity theorem may be assumed to hold.

Required:

Estimate the STERLING cost of capital that Somax should use as the discount rate for its proposed investment in Switzerland.

State clearly any assumptions that you make. **(12 marks)**

(c)   Somax's bank has suggested a five year interest rate swap as an alternative to direct SFr borrowing. Somax would issue a five year sterling fixed rate bond, and make the following swap with a Swiss company that is also a client of the bank.

Somax would pay the Swiss company SFr LIBOR + 1% per year.

The Swiss company would pay Somax 9.5% per year.

A 0.2% per year fee would also be payable by each company to the bank. There will be an exchange of principal now, and in five years time, at todays middle spot foreign exchange rate. The Swiss company can borrow fixed rate sterling at 10.5% per annum, and floating rate SFr finance at SFr LIBOR + 1.5%.

Required:

(i)   Estimate the annual interest cost to Somax of issuing a five year sterling fixed rate bond, and calculate whether the suggested swap would be of benefit to both Somax plc and the Swiss company. **(10 marks)**

(ii)   Excluding cheaper finance, discuss the possible benefits, and the possible risks of such a swap for the two companies and the intermediary bank. **(8 marks)**

(Total: 40 marks)

64 ITALIAN GLASS

You have been asked to give advice to a medium sized glass manufacturer in Italy that is tendering for an order in Kuwait. The tender conditions state that payment will be made in Kuwait dinars in 18 months from now. The company is unsure as to what price to tender. The marginal cost of producing the glass at that time is estimated to be €350,000 and a 25% mark-up is normal for the company.

Exchange rates

Dinar/€1

Spot   3.2800 – 3.3000

No forward rate exists for 18 months time.

	Eurozone	Kuwait
Annual inflation rates	9%	3%
Annual interest rates available to the glass manufacturer:		
Borrowing	14%	9%
Lending	9%	3.5%

Required:

Discuss how the glass manufacturer might protect itself against foreign exchange rate changes, and recommend what tender price should be used.   **(10 marks)**

65 VTW PLC

The managers of VTW plc are discussing whether or not to set up a foreign subsidiary in a South American country. The government of the country has recently changed, and the country's new leaders have stated that they intend to introduce economic policies to improve the balance of payments. VTW is concerned that one of these measures could be to block the remittance of dividends from the South American country to the UK. VTW expects to remit about 180 million pesos per year to the UK if the government does not intervene. Blocked funds may be invested internally within the South American country, but the government is likely to control domestic interest rates.

The investment in the South American subsidiary has an expected NPV of £2 million. The peso is expected to devalue by approximately 10% per year relative to the pound. VTW used a discount rate of 20% per year in the appraisal of its South American capital investment. The current spot exchange rate is 20 pesos/£1.

Required:

(a)   Assuming that the government blocks the remittance of dividends for a period of three years, estimate the approximate interest rate that would have to exist in the South American country for the proposed investment to remain financially viable. Taxation may be ignored.   **(6 marks)**

(b)   Briefly discuss methods by which VTW might try to avoid the block on the remittance of dividends.   **(4 marks)**

(Total: 10 marks)

66   HERLER PLC

Assume that 'now' is December 2003.

Herler plc has agreed to undertake an eighteen-month construction project in the country of Surkaya. Payments to Herler will be made 25% as an immediate down payment, 25% in six months time, 15% in one year's time and the balance upon completion. The purchaser in Surkaya has no access to sterling or other leading currencies as the country is experiencing balance of payments problems, cannot readily borrow internationally, and has only small foreign currency reserves. Payment for the project is therefore to be made in the local currency, the Surkayan franc. The total price of the construction is 8 billion (8,000 million) Surkayan francs.

Inflation in Surkaya is currently at the rate of 250 percent per year, which is not expected to significantly change in the near future. Inflation in the UK is 5% per year.

The management of Herler plc when costing the construction project allowed for a 100% contribution to variable costs at each payment stage, at 1 December 2003 spot exchange rates. Almost all variable costs are incurred in sterling. Fixed costs are negligible. The company's discount rate for this construction project is 12%.

Spot rate December 1 2003

   2,400 Surkayan francs/£1

No forward market exists beyond three months, and Herler has no access to Surkayan money or capital markets.

Required:

(a)   Estimate the likely financial result for Herler plc of the construction project.

   State clearly any assumptions that you make.   **(6 marks)**

(b)   Suggest what actions Herler plc might have taken prior to agreeing the contract to reduce foreign exchange risk.   **(4 marks)**

   (Total: 10 marks)

67   KYT INC

Assume that it is now 30 June. KYT Inc is a company located in the USA that has a contract to purchase goods from Japan in two months time on 1 September. The payment is to be made in yen and will total 140 million yen.

The managing director of KYT Inc wishes to protect the contract against adverse movements in foreign exchange rates, and is considering the use of currency futures. The following data are available.

Spot foreign exchange rate:

   Yen/$ 128.15   — currency futures.

Yen currency futures contracts on SIMEX (Singapore Monetary Exchange).

   Contract size 12,500,000 yen. Contract prices are in US$ per yen.

   Contract prices:

   September 0.007985

   December 0.008250

Assume that futures contracts mature at the end of the month.

Required:

(a) Illustrate how KYT might hedge its foreign exchange risk using currency futures.

(3 marks)

(b) Show what basis risk is involved in the proposed hedge. **(2 marks)**

(c) Assuming the spot exchange rate is 120 yen/$1 on 1 September and that basis risk decreases steadily in a linear manner, calculate what the result of the hedge is expected to be. Briefly discuss why this result might not occur. Margin requirements and taxation may be ignored. **(5 marks)**

(Total: 10 marks)

68 PARTICIPATING CURRENCY OPTION

Your UK based company has won an export order worth $1.8 million from the USA. Payment is due to be made to you in dollars in six months time. It is now 15 November. You wish to protect the exchange rate risk with currency options, but do not wish to pay an option premium of more than £10,000.

Your bank has suggested using a participating currency option which has no premium. The option would allow a worst case exchange rate at which the option could be exercised of $1.65/£1. If the contract moved in your favour then the bank would share (participate in) the profits, and would take 50% of any gains relative to the current spot exchange rate.

You also have access to currency options on the Philadelphia Stock Exchange.

Current option prices are:

Sterling contacts, £31,250 contract size. Premium is in US cents per £1.

		Calls			Puts	
Exercise price	Dec	March	June	Dec	March	June
1.55	6.8	7.9	10.1	0.2	0.5	0.9
1.60	2.1	3.8	5.3	1.9	3.1	4.0
1.65	0.6	0.9	1.1	5.1	7.2	9.6
1.70	0.1	0.2	0.4	10.1	12.3	14.1

The current spot rate is $1.6055 – 1.6100/£1. Any option premium would be payable immediately.

Required:

Evaluate whether a participating option or traded option is likely to offer a better foreign exchange hedge. **(10 marks)**

69 POLYTOT PLC

Assume that it is now 1 July. Polytot plc has received an export order valued at 675 million pesos from a company in Grobbia, a country that has recently been accepted into the World Trade Organisation, but which does not yet have a freely convertible currency.

The Grobbian company only has access to sufficient $US to pay for 60% of the goods, at the official $US exchange rate. The balance would be payable in the local currency, the Grobbian peso, for which there is no official foreign exchange market. Polytot is due to receive payment in four months' time and has been informed that an unofficial market in Grobbian pesos exists in which the peso can be converted into pounds. The exchange rate in this market is 15% worse for Polytot than the 'official' rate of exchange between the peso and the pound.

Exchange rates:

Buy $ $/£ Sell $ *Buy £* *Sell £ Dec*

Spot	1.5475 – 1.5510
3 months forward	1.5362 – 1.5398
1 year forward	1.5140 – 1.5178
	Grobbian peso/£
Official spot rate	156.30
	Grobbian peso/$
Official spot rate	98.20

— forward market

Philadelphia SE £/$ options £31,250 (cents per pound) *— options*

	CALLS			PUTS		
	Sept	Dec	March	Sept	Dec	March
1.5250	2.95	3.35	3.65	2.00	3.25	4.35
1.5500	1.80	2.25	2.65	3.30	4.60	5.75
1.5750	0.90	1.40	1.80	4.90	6.25	7.35
1.6000	0.25	0.75	1.10	6.75	8.05	9.15

£/$ Currency futures (CME, £62,500) *— futures .*

September   1.5350

December   1.5275

Assume that options and futures contracts mature at the relevant month end.

Required:

(a) Discuss the alternative forms of currency hedge that are available to Polytot plc and calculate the expected revenues, in £ sterling, from the sale to the company in Grobbia as a result of each of these hedges. Provide a reasoned recommendation as to which hedge should be selected. **(17 marks)**

(b) The Grobbian company is willing to undertake a countertrade deal whereby 40% of the cost of the goods is paidfor by an exchange of three million kilos of Grobbian strawberries. A major UK supermarket chain has indicated that it would be willing to pay between 50 and 60 pence per kilo for the strawberries.

Discuss the issues that Polytot should consider before deciding whether or not to agree to the countertrade. **(6 marks)**

(c) The Grobbian company has asked for advice in using the Euromarkets to raise international finance.

Required:

Provide a briefing memo for the company discussing the advantages of the Euromarkets, and any potential problems for the Grobbian company in using them.

(7 marks)

(Total: 30 marks)

70   CURRENCY SWAPS

(a) From the perspective of a corporate financial manager, discuss the advantages and potential problems of using currency swaps. **(8 marks)**

(b) Galeplus plc has been invited to purchase and operate a new telecommunications centre in the republic of Perdia. The purchase price is 2,000 million rubbits. The Perdian government has built the centre in order to improve the country's infrastructure, but has currently not got enough funds to pay money owed to the local constructors. Galeplus would purchase the centre for a period of three years, after which it would be sold back to the Perdian government for an agreed price of 4,000 million rubbits. Galeplus would supply three years of technical expertise and training for local staff, for an annual fee of 40 million rubbits, after Perdian taxation. Other after tax net cash flows from the investment in Perdia are expected to be negligible during the three year period.

Perdia has only recently become a democracy, and in the last five years has experienced inflation rates of between 25% and 500%. The managers of Galeplus are concerned about the foreign exchange risk of the investment. Perdia has recently adopted economic stability measures suggested by the IMF, and inflation during the next three years is expected to be between 15% per year and 50% per year. Galeplus's bankers have suggested using a currency swap for the purchase price of the factory, with a swap of principal immediately and in three years' time, both swaps at today's spot rate. The bank would charge a fee of 0.75% per year (in sterling) for arranging the swap. Galeplus would take 75% of any net arbitrage benefit from the swap, after deducting bank fees. Relevant borrowing rates are:

	UK	Perdia
Galeplus	6.25%	PIBOR + 2.0%
Perdian counterparty	8.3%1	PIBOR + 1.5%

N.B. PIBOR is the Perdian interbank offered rate, which has tended to be set at approximately the current inflation level. Inflation in the UK is expected to be negligible.

	Exchange rates
Spot	85.4 rubbits/£
3 year forward rate	Not available

Required:

(i) Estimate the potential annual percentage interest saving that Galeplus might make from using a currency swap relative to borrowing directly in Perdia.

(6 marks)

(ii) Assuming the swap takes place as described, provide a reasoned analysis, including relevant calculations, as to whether or not Galeplus should purchase the communications centre. The relevant risk adjusted discount rate may be assumed to be 15% per year. **(8 marks)**

(c) As alternatives to the currency swap the bank has suggested:

(i) A swaption with the same terms as the currency swap, and an upfront premium of £300,000.

(ii) A European style three year currency put option on the total expected net cash flow in year 3 at an exercise price of 160 rubbits/£, and an upfront premium of £1.7 million.

Required:

Discuss and evaluate the relative merits of these suggestions for Galeplus. **(8 marks)**

(Total: 30 marks)

71 MJY PLC

Assume that it is now 31 December. MJY plc is a UK based multinational company that has subsidiaries in two foreign countries. Both subsidiaries trade with other group members and with four third party companies (company 1 – company 4).

Projected trade transactions for three months' time are shown overleaf. All currency amounts are in thousands.

Payments (read down) '000'

Receipts (read across) '000'	Co 1	Co 2	Co 3	Co 4	MJY	Subsidiary 1	Subsidiary 2
MJY	$90	£60	€75	–	–	£40	$50
Subsidiary 1	£50	€85	$40	$20	€72	–	€20
Subsidiary 2	£15	–	€52	$30	£55	€35	–
Company 1	–	–	–	–	–	–	–
Company 2	–	–	–	–	$170	–	–
Company 3	–	–	–	–	$120	€50	–
Company 4	–	–	–	–	–	–	€65

Foreign exchange rates	$/£	€/£
Spot	1.7982 – 1.8010	1.4492 – 1.4523
3 months forward	1.7835 – 1.7861	1.4365 – 1.4390

Currency options. £62,500 contract size. Premium in cents per £

	Calls		Puts	
Strike price	*February*	*May*	*February*	*May*
1.80	1.96	3.00	3.17	5.34
1.78	2.91	3.84	2.12	4.20

Required:

Working from the perspective of a group treasurer, devise a hedging strategy for the MJY group, and calculate the expected outcomes of the hedges using forward markets, and, for the dollar exposure only, currency options. **(15 marks)**

INTEREST RATE RISK

72 INTEREST RATE HEDGE

Assume that it is now mid December.

The finance director of Shawter plc has recently reviewed the company's monthly cash budgets for the next year. As a result of buying new machinery in three months time, the company is expected to require short-term financing of £30 million for a period of two months until the proceeds from a factory disposal become available. The finance director is concerned that, as a result of increasing wage settlements, the Central Bank will increase interest rates in the near future.

LIBOR is currently 6% per annum and Shawter can borrow at LIBOR + 0.9%.

Derivative contracts may be assumed to mature at the end of the month.

Three types of hedge are available:

Three months sterling future (£500,000 contract size, £12.50 tick size)

December	93.870
March	93.790
June	93.680

Options on three months Sterling futures
(£500,000 contract size, premium cost in annual %)

	Calls			Puts		
	December	*March*	*June*	*December*	*March*	*June*
93750	0.120	0.195	0.270	0.020	0.085	0.180
94000	0.015	0.075	0.115	0.165	0.255	0.335
94250	0	0.030	0.085	0.400	0.480	0.555

FRA prices:

3 v 6	7.01 – 6.91
3 v 5	7.08 – 7.00
3 v 8	7.28 – 7.20

Required:

Prepare a report for the finance director, which:

(i)   briefly discusses the relative advantages and disadvantages of the three types of hedge;

(ii) illustrate how the short-term interest risk might be hedged, and the possible results of the alternative hedges, if interest rates increase by 0.5%.

All relevant calculations must be shown.   **(15 marks)**

73   INTEREST RATE SWAP

(a)   Explain the possible benefits to a company of undertaking an interest rate swap.
                                                                            (4 marks)

(b)   The following five-year loan interest rates are available to Stentor, an AA credit rated company, and to Evnor, a BB+ rated company.

	Fixed rate	*Floating rate*
Stentor	8.75%	LIBOR + 0.50%
Evnor	9.50%	LIBOR + 0.90%

A bank is willing to act as an intermediary to facilitate a five year swap, for an upfront fee of £20,000 and an annual fee of 0.05% of the swap value. Both of these fees are payable by EACH of the companies. Taxation may be ignored.

Required:

Evaluate, using an illustrative swap, whether or not an interest rate swap may be arranged that is beneficial to both companies.   **(6 marks)**

                                                                    (Total: 10 marks)

74   CALVOLD

(a)   Discuss how interest rate swaps and currency swaps might be of value to the corporate financial manager.   **(10 marks)**

(b) Calvold plc has a one year contract to construct factories in a South American country. At the end of the year the factories will be paid for by the local government. The price has been fixed at 2,000 million pesos, payable in the South American currency. *[handwritten: payment on 6 mths & 1 yr.]*

In order to fulfil the contract Calvold will need to invest 1,000 million pesos in the project immediately, and a fixed additional sum of 500 million pesos in six months time.

The government of the South American country has offered Calvold a fixed rate-fixed rate currency swap for *one year* for the full 1,500 million pesos at a swap rate of 20 pesos/£1. Net interest of 10% per year would be payable in pesos by Calvold to the government. There is no forward foreign exchange market for the peso against the pound. *[handwritten: No money market]*

Forecasts of inflation rates for the next year are: *[handwritten: PPPT for future spot rate.]*

[handwritten: If something is only happening once ∴ NO need to work out Expected value.]

Probability	UK		South American country
0.25	4%	and	40%
0.50	5%	and	60%
0.25	7%	and	100%

The peso is a freely floating currency which has not recently been subject to major government intervention. *[handwritten: PPPT]*

[handwritten: Now] The current spot rate is 25 pesos/£1. Calvold's opportunity cost of funds is 12% per year in the UK. The company has no access to funds in the South American country. *[handwritten: No money market hedge.]*

Taxation, the risk of default, and discounting to allow for the timing of payments may be ignored.

Required:

Evaluate whether it is likely to be beneficial for Calvold plc to agree to the currency swap. *[handwritten: → With swap → No swap.]*

(15 marks)

(Total: 25 marks)

75 TAYQUER PLC

The directors of Tayquer plc are considering the use of options to protect the current interest yield from their company's £9.75 million short-term money market investments. Having made initial enquiries they have been discouraged by the cost of the option premium. A member of the treasury staff has suggested the use of a collar as this would be cheaper.

Protection is required for the next eight months. Assume that it is now 1 June.

LIFFE interest rate options on three month money market futures
Contract size is £500,000, premium cost is in annual %

	Calls		Puts	
	Dec	March	Dec	March
9100	0.90	1.90	–	0.02
9150	0.56	1.45	0.05	0.06
9200	0.27	1.04	0.17	0.13
9250	0.09	0.68	0.45	0.24
9300	0.01	0.20	0.83	0.32
9350	–	0.05	1.13	0.54

Tick size is 0.01%, and tick value £12.50.

The current interest rate received on Tayquer's short-term money market investments is 7.5% per annum.

Assume that Tayquer can buy or sell options at the above prices. Commission, taxation and margins may be ignored.

Required:

Discuss how, and estimate at what cost, collars may be used to protect against the interest yield risk. Recommend at which exercise price(s) the collar should be arranged. **(10 marks)**

76   DUPLICATE PLC

Duplicate plc has a commitment to borrow £6 million in five months time for a period of four months. A general election is due in four months time, and the managers of Duplicate plc are concerned that interest rates could significantly increase just after the election.

Duplicate can currently borrow at LIBOR + 1%. Three month LIBOR is at 7.5%.

Current LIFFE £500,000 sterling three month futures prices are:

September	92.60
December	92.10

Assume that it is now the end of June and that futures contracts mature at the end of the relevant month.

Required:

(a)   Illustrate how Duplicate plc could use a futures hedge to protect against its potential interest rate risk. The type and number of contracts must be included in your illustration.   **(5 marks)**

(b)   Estimate the basis risk for this hedge both now, and at the time the contract is likely to be closed out. Comment upon the significance of your estimates for Duplicate plc. Illustrate your answer with reference to the impact of a 2% increase in LIBOR.

(5 marks)

(Total: 10 marks)

77   AUTOCRAT PLC   *Interest Rate + Foreign Currency*

cc = £

The CEO of Autocrat plc is reviewing the company's interest rate and currency risk strategies for the next few months. There has recently been considerable political instability with some countries showing signs of moving towards economic recession whilst others are still showing steady growth. Both interest rates and currency rates could become more volatile for many major trading countries.

Autocrat is expected to need to borrow £6,500,000 for a period of six months commencing in six months' time.

The company also needs to make a US$ payment of $4.3 million in three months' time.

margin = 0

Assume that it is now 1 December. Futures and options contracts may be assumed to expire at the end of the relevant month, and the company may be assumed to be able to borrow at the three-month LIBOR rate.

LIFFE futures prices, £500,000 contract size

March	95.56
June	95.29

interest rate futures

LIFFE options on futures prices, £500,000 contract size. Premiums are annual % amounts. *— Interest rate*

	CALLS		PUTS	
	March	June	March	June
95250	0.445	0.545	0.085	0.185
95500	0.280	0.390	0.170	0.280
95750	0.165	0.265	0.305	0.405

Interest rate (handwritten note for 95250–95750)

Three-month LIBOR is currently 4.5% *→ annual rate*

Foreign exchange rates

Forward Hedge

Spot $1.4692 – 1.4735/£1

3 month forward $1.4632 – 1.4668/£1

Currency option prices   *Currency options*

Philadelphia Stock Exchange $/£ options, contract size £31,250, premiums are cents per £1:

	CALLS		PUTS	
	March	April	March	June
1.450	3.12	–	1.56	–
1.460	2.55	2.95	1.99	2.51
1.470	2.14	–	2.51	–

Required:

(a)   Discuss the relevant considerations when deciding between futures and options to hedge the company's interest rate risk.   **(6 marks)**

(b)   Using the above information, illustrate the possible results of hedges with:

(i)   futures, and

(ii)   options

increase interest rates

if interest rates in six months' time increase by 0.75%. Recommend which hedge should be selected and explain why there might be uncertainty as to the results of the hedges.   **(11 marks)**

(c)   Illustrate and discuss the possible outcomes of forward market and currency options hedges if possible currency rates in three months' time are either:

exercise

(i) $1.4350 – $1.4386/£1   *estimate spot on conversion*   *Cash flow*

or (ii) $1.4780 – $1.4820/£1.   **(8 marks)**   *lapse*

(d)   Discuss and illustrate whether or not a currency straddle option with an exercise price of 1.460 might be an appropriate hedging strategy for Autocrat plc. Explain the circumstances in which straddle options could be a profitable strategy.   **(5 marks)**

(Total: 30 marks)

78   HYK COMMUNICATIONS PLC

rate agreed (handwritten note)

The monthly cash budget of HYK Communications plc shows that the company is likely to need £18 million in two months' time for a period of four months. Financial markets have recently been volatile. The finance director of HYK plc fears that short term interest rates could rise by as much as 150 basis points. If few problems occur then short term rates could fall by 50 basis points. LIBOR is currently 6.5% and HYK plc can borrow at LIBOR + 0.75%.

The finance director does not wish to pay more than 7.50%, including option premium costs, but excluding the effect of margin requirements and commissions.

LIFFE £500,000 three month futures prices. The value of one tick is £12.50

December	93.40
March	93.10
June	92.75

LIFFE £500,000 three months options prices (premiums in annual %)

Exercise price	Calls			Puts		
	December	March	June	December	March	June
92.50	0.33	0.88	1.04	–	–	0.08
93.00	0.16	0.52	0.76	–	0.20	0.34
93.50	0.10	0.24	0.42	0.18	0.60	1.93
94.00	–	0.05	0.18	0.36	1.35	1.92

Assume that it is now 1 December and that exchange traded futures and options contracts expire at the end of the month. Margin requirements and default risk may be ignored.

Required:

(a) Estimate the results of undertaking EACH OF an interest rate futures hedge and an interest rate options hedge on the LIFFE exchange, if LIBOR

    (i) increases by 150 basis points AND

    (ii) decreases by 50 basis points.

    Discuss how successful the hedges would have been.

    State clearly any assumptions that you make. **(18 marks)**

(b) Discuss the relative advantages of using exchange traded interest rate options and over-the-counter (OTC) interest rate options. **(6 marks)**

(c) Your finance director has received some quotations for over-the-counter (OTC) interest rate options and wonders whether or not they are too expensive. Outline the main determinants of interest rate option prices, and comment upon whether or not the OTC options are likely to be expensive. **(6 marks)**

(Total: 30 marks)

79 COLLAR HEDGE

(a) Discuss the advantages of hedging with interest rate caps and collars. **(6 marks)**

(b) Current futures prices suggest that interest rates are expected to fall during the next few months. Troder plc expects to have £400 million available for short-term investment for a period of 5 months commencing late October. The company wishes to protect this short-term investment from a fall in interest rates, but is concerned about the premium levels of interest rate options. It would also like to benefit if interest rates were to increase rather than fall. The company's advisers have suggested the use of a collar option.

LIFFE short sterling options (£500,000), points of 100%

Strike price	Calls		Puts	
	Sept	Dec	Sept	Dec
95250	0.040	0.445	0.040	0.085
95500	0	0.280	0.250	0.170
95750	0	0.165	0.500	0.305

LIBOR is currently 5% and the company can invest short-term at LIBOR minus 25 basis points.

Required:

(i)   Assume that it is now early September. The company wishes to receive more than £6,750,000 in interest from its investment after paying any option premium. Illustrate how a collar hedge may be used to achieve this. (**N.B.** It is not necessary to estimate the number of contracts for this illustration).

(7 marks)

(ii)   Estimate the maximum interest that could be received with your selected hedge.

(2 marks)

(Total: 15 marks)

80   LEADING NEWSPAPERS

Assume that the following data were published in a leading financial newspaper on 1 January 1995.

				Yield	
			Interest	Redemption	Price
Exchequer	13.50%	1995	12.50	5.13	108
Treasury	8.75%	1998	7.87	5.56	$111\,^{5}/_{32}$
Treasury	11.50%	2002-5	8.77	6.40	$131\,^{5}/_{32}$
Exchequer	12.00%	2009-14	8.25	7.00	$145\,\frac{1}{2}$

Required:

(a)   Explain what these data indicate about the term structure of interest rates and briefly discuss possible reasons for this term structure. **(6 marks)**

(b)   A financial manager wishes to invest surplus funds in government bonds for a period of one year. If the manager does not expect interest rates to change during the next year, use the following data relating to two bonds of similar risk to recommend how the investment should be undertaken in order to maximise expected yield. Interest is paid annually on the bonds and annual interest has just been paid.

Coupon	Maturity	Price	Redemption yield
$11\,^{3}/_{4}\%$	One year	£103.06	8.43%
$11\,\frac{1}{4}\%$	Two years	£103.94	9.01%

(4 marks)

(Total: 10 marks)

81   FOLTER PLC

Folter plc has short-term equity holdings in a number of companies that it considers might be future take-over targets.

The equity market has recently been very volatile, and the finance director is considering how to protect the equity portfolio from adverse market movements, in case some of the holdings need to be sold, at short notice, by the end of October.

The finance director is particularly concerned about 2 million shares that are currently held in Magterdoor plc. The shares are trading at 535 pence.

Assume that it is now 1 June and that option contracts mature at the month end.

LIFFE Traded options (1,000 shares)

	CALLS			PUTS		
	July	October	January	July	October	January
500	37.5	52.5	60.5	12.0	24.5	35.0
550	16.5	24.0	34.0	21.0	51.0	60.0

Required:

(a) Illustrate how Folter plc might use traded options to protect against a fall in the share price of Magterdoor plc. Assuming that Folter has to sell the shares at the end of October at a price of 485 pence, evaluate the outcome of the hedge(s). **(4 marks)**

(b) Assume that the option delta of Magterdoor is 0.47. Illustrate how a delta neutral hedge might be used to protect against price movements of the shares of Magterdoor. Comment upon any practical problems of using a delta hedge for this purpose.

(4 marks)

(c) Discuss the reasons why the January 550 call option premium is not the same as the intrinsic value of the option. **(4 marks)**

(d) The managing director of Folter suggests increasing its holding in Magterdoor from 2% to 6% of that company's issued shares. Discuss briefly the advantages and disadvantages of this strategy. **(3 marks)**

(Total: 15 marks)

82 INTEREST RATE HEDGES

Assume that it is now 1 June. Your company expects to receive £7.1 million from a large order in five months' time. This will then be invested in high quality commercial paper for a period of four months, after which it will be used to pay part of the company's dividend. The company's treasurer wishes to protect the short-term investment from adverse movements in interest rates, by using futures or forward rate agreements (FRAs).

The current yield on high quality commercial paper is LIBOR + 0.60%.

LIFFE £500,000 three month Sterling futures. £12.50 tick size.
September 96.25
December 96.60

Futures contracts mature at the month end. LIBOR is currently 4%.

FRA prices (%)

4 v 5 3.85 – 3.80
4 v 9 3.58 – 3.53
5 v 9 3.50 – 3.45

Required:

(a) Devise a futures hedge to protect the interest yield of the short-term investment, and estimate the expected lock-in interest rate as a result of the hedge. **(4 marks)**

(b) Ignoring transactions costs, explain whether the futures or FRA hedge would provide the higher expected interest rate from the short-term investment. **(2 marks)**

(c) If LIBOR fell by 0.5% during the next five months show the expected outcomes of each hedge in the cash market, futures market and FRA market as appropriate.

(6 marks)

(d) Explain why the futures market outcome might differ from the outcome in (c) above.

(3 marks)

(Total: 15 marks)

THE GLOBAL ECONOMIC ENVIRONMENT AND GLOBAL FINANCIAL MANAGEMENT

83 IMF

Discuss the role of the IMF and its significance to the activities of multinational companies.

(10 marks)

84 CURRENT ACCOUNT DEFICIT

Discuss how a government might try to reduce a large, persistent, current account deficit on the balance of payments, and illustrate what impact such government action might have on a multinational company operating in the country concerned. Explain the possible role and impact of the International Monetary Fund (IMF) in this process. **(15 marks)**

85 FOREIGN TRADE RISKS

Excluding foreign exchange risks, discuss, with examples, how the risks of foreign trade might be managed. **(10 marks)**

86 POLITICAL RISK

The finance department of Beela Electronics has been criticised by the company's board of directors for not undertaking an assessment of the political risk of the company's potential direct investments in Africa. The board has received an interim report from a consultant that provides assessment of the factors affecting political risk in three African countries. The report assess key variables on a scale of –10 to + 10, with –10 the worst possible score and + 10 the best.

	Country 1	Country 2	Country 3
Economic growth	5	8	4
Political stability	3	-4	5
Risk of nationalism	3	0	4
Cultural compatibility	6	2	4
Inflation	7	-6	6
Currency convertibility	-2	5	-4
Investment incentives	-3	7	3
Labour supply	2	8	-3

The consultant suggests that economic growth and political stability are twice as important as the other factors.

The consultant states in the report that previous clients have not invested in countries with total weighted score of less that 30 out of a maximum possible 100 (with economic growth and political stability double weighted). The consultant therefore recommends that no investment in Africa should be undertaken.

Required:

(a) Discuss whether or not Beela electronics should use the technique suggested by the consultant in order to decide whether or not to invest in Africa. **(8 marks)**

(b) Discuss briefly how Beela might manage political risk if it decides to invest in Africa. **(7 marks)**

(Total: 15 marks)

87   GILTOR PLC

At a luncheon meeting the managing director of Giltor plc has told two of his colleagues, who hold senior executive positions in different companies, that he has recently obtained from his bank forecasts of exchange rates in one year's time. His two colleagues also work for companies that are heavily engaged in international trade, and both agree to obtain their own forecasts. The following week the three again meet for lunch and compare the forecasts made by their banks. These forecasts are shown below:

	$/Euro	£/Euro	Yen/$	$/£
Bank 1	0.76	0.56	120	1.36
Bank 2	0.84	0.64	140	1.31
Bank 3	1.00	0.65	140	1.54
Current spot rates	0.88	0.62	125	1.42
	USA	UK	Euro zone	Japan
Annual inflation rates	3%	2%	3%	(1%)
Annual short-term interest rates	3.25%	4.75%	4.18%	0.01%

The three senior executives are puzzled by this information

Required:

Prepare a report discussing and analysing the above information, and explaining why the banks' forecasts might differ. Your analysis should include calculations based upon inflation rates and interest rates.

Discuss in the report the mechanisms influencing future exchange rates and whether or not it is possible to accurately forecast such future exchange rates, and if so under what circumstances.   **(15 marks)**

88   DEBOIS SA

Debois SA, a French multinational company, has subsidiaries in the United Kingdom and Norway.

The UK subsidiary produces components that are transferred to Norway for final production.

The components are sold by the UK subsidiary to the Norwegian subsidiary for a unit price of €144, with annual sales of 125,000 units. Total production expenses are 80% of the sales price. The finished goods are sold in the Norwegian market for the equivalent of €350, yielding a taxable profit per unit in Norway of the equivalent to €70.

Tax rates are as follows:	France	UK	Norway
Corporate tax on profits	33.3%	25%	40%
Withholding tax on dividends	10%	–	8%

Bilateral double tax treaties exist between each of the countries which allow credit for foreign tax paid against any domestic tax liability.

It is the policy of Debois to annually remit all profit from foreign subsidiaries to the parent company in the form of dividends.

Tutorial note: These tax rates and tax agreements are hypothetical.

Required:

(a)   Illustrate how the tax liability of Debois SA might be reduced by a 20% increase in the transfer price between the UK and Norwegian subsidiaries.   **(6 marks)**

(b)   Discuss briefly the possible practical problems of such a change in transfer price.
                                                                                                                              (4 marks)

                                                                                                              (Total: 10 marks)

89 COUNTRIES

Your company has purchased the following data which provide scores of the political risk for a number of countries in which the company is considering investing in a new subsidiary.

	Total	Economic performance	Debt in default	Credit ratings	Government stability	Remittance restrictions	Access to capital
Weighting	100	25	10	10	25	15	15
Gmala	37	13	4	5	5	10	0
Forland	52	5	10	9	16	8	4
Amapore	36	12	2	3	9	5	5
Covia	30	9	3	2	15	1	0
Sottia	39	15	4	3	11	4	2

Countries have been rated on a scale from 0 up to the maximum weighting for each factor (e.g. 0 – 15 for remittance restrictions). A high score for each factor, as well as overall, reflects low political risk.

A proposal has been put before the company's board of directors that investment should take place in Forland.

Required:

Prepare a brief report for the company's board of directors discussing whether or not the above data should form the basis for:

(a)   the measurement of political risk   **(5 marks)**

(b)   the decision about which country to invest in.   **(5 marks)**

(Total: 10 marks)

90 GROWTH OF MULTINATIONALS

The global turnover of the largest multinational companies is greater than the gross national product of many countries.

Discuss factors that might explain the successful growth of large multinational companies.

(10 marks)

91 TRANSFER PRICING STRATEGIES

(a)   Briefly discuss the possible objectives of transfer pricing strategies used by multinational companies.   **(4 marks)**

(b)   Shegdor plc, a UK based multinational company, has subsidiaries in three countries – Umgaba, Mazila and Bettuna.

–   The subsidiary in Umgaba manufactures specialist components, which may then be assembled and sold in either Mazila or Bettuna.

–   Production and sales volume may each be assumed to be 400,000 units per year no matter where the assembly and sales take place.

–   Manufacturing costs in Umgaba are $16 per unit and fixed costs (for the normal range of production) $1.8 million.

–   Assembly costs in Mazila are $9 per unit, and in Bettuna $7.5 per unit. Fixed costs are $700,000 and $900,000 respectively.

–   The unit sales price in Mazila is $40 and in Bettuna $37.

– Corporate taxes on profits are at the rate of 40% in Umgaba, 25% in Mazila, 32% in Bettuna, and 30% in the UK. No tax credits are available in these three countries for any losses made.

– Tax allowable import duties of 10% are payable on all goods imported into Mazila.

– A withholding tax of 15% is deducted from all dividends remitted from Umgaba.

– Shegdor expects about 60% of profits from each subsidiary to be remitted direct to the UK each year.

– Cost and price data in all countries is shown in US dollars.

Required:

Evaluate and explain:

(i) whether the transfer price from Umgaba should be based on fixed cost plus variable cost, or on fixed cost plus variable cost plus a mark up of 30%;

(ii) whether assembly should take place in Mazila or Bettuna. **(8 marks)**

(c) Comment upon the likely attitude of the governments of each of the four countries towards the transfer price and assembly location selected in b (i) and b (ii) above.

(3 marks)

(Total: 15 marks)

92 HGT

HGT plc is a UK based multinational company with two overseas subsidiaries. The company wishes to minimise its global tax bill, and part of its tax strategy is to try to take advantage of opportunities provided by transfer pricing.

HGT has subsidiaries in Glinland and Rytora.

Taxation	UK	Glinland	Rytora
Corporation tax on profits	30%	40%	25%
Withholding tax on dividends	–	10%	–
Import tariffs on all goods (not tax allowable)	–	–	10%

The subsidiary in Glinland produces 150,000 graphite golf club shafts per year which are then sent to Rytora for the metal heads to be added and the clubs finished off. The shafts have a variable cost in Glinland of £6 each, and annual fixed costs are £140,000. The shafts are sold to the Rytoran subsidiary at variable cost plus 75%.

The Rytoran subsidiary incurs additional unit variable costs of £9, annual fixed costs of £166,000, and sells the finished clubs at £30 each in Rytora.

Bi-lateral tax agreements exist which allow foreign tax paid to be credited against UK tax liability.

All transactions between the companies are in pounds sterling. The Rytoran subsidiary remits all profit after tax to the UK parent company each year, and the Glinland subsidiary remits 50% of its profit after tax.

Required:

The parent company is considering instructing the Glinland subsidiary to sell the shafts to the Rytoran subsidiary at full cost. Evaluate the possible effect of this on tax and tariff payments, and discuss briefly any possible problems with this strategy. **(10 marks)**

93   LDC DEBT

(a)   Outline the main methods that have been suggested to reduce the debt problem of less developed countries (LDCs).   **(6 marks)**

(b)   Explain the potential significance of the LDC debt problem to multinational companies.   **(4 marks)**

(Total: 10 marks)

94   GLOBAL DEBT PROBLEM

(a)   Discuss the reasons for the existence of the 'global debt problem'. Explain briefly what is meant by financial contagion and how financial contagion might affect the global debt problem.   **(7 marks)**

(b)   Explain the main attempts that have been made to resolve the global debt problem and how governments might try to limit financial contagion.   **(8 marks)**

(Total: 15 marks)

95   EXCHANGE RATE SYSTEMS

Discuss the possible foreign exchange risk and economic implications of each of the following types of exchange rate system for multinational companies with subsidiaries located in countries with these systems:

(a)   a managed floating exchange rate;

(b)   a fixed exchange rate linked to a basket of currencies; and

(c)   a fixed exchange rate backed by a currency board system.   **(15 marks)**

96   BOSTER PLC

Boster plc is a multinational company that has investments in several developing countries. It is considering investments in three more developing countries, Ammobia, Flassia and Hracland. All three countries have a history of political instability, but Boster believes that the potential returns from the investments might justify the political risk.

A consultancy report has produced the following assessments of the countries.

	Expected investment return (%)	*Political risk (%)*
Ammobia	21	33
Flassia	18	29
Hracland	28	42

Political risk was measured by investigating key variables in the relevant countries. These were: corruption, changes in government, social conditions, cultural issues, unfair trade and asset security.

Boster will invest in a maximum of two of the countries, with an equal amount invested in each country. The countries are in diverse parts of the world, and the returns from the investments in the three countries are believed to be independent.

Required:

(a)   Calculate the risk, return and coefficient of variation of the possible investment combinations.   **(6 marks)**

(b)   Discuss how useful the information calculated in (a) above might be to Boster in making its investment decisions.   **(5 marks)**

(c)   Briefly discuss other ways by which Boster might attempt to measure the potential political risk of the investments.   **(4 marks)**

(Total: 15 marks)

97   WORLD TRADE ORGANISATION

(a)   Provide examples of how countries might impose protectionist measures to control the volume of imports.   **(5 marks)**

(b)   Discuss the role and main objectives of the World Trade Organisation (WTO), and its potential effect on protectionist measures.   **(6 marks)**

(c)   Briefly discuss the possible effects of the activities of the WTO for a multinational company with foreign direct investment in a developing country that has recently joined the WTO.   **(4 marks)**

(Total: 15 marks)

Section 2

ANSWERS TO PRACTICE QUESTIONS

OBJECTIVES AND CORPORATE GOVERNANCE

1 INFLUENCE ON OBJECTIVES

Non-financial issues, ethical and environmental issues in many cases overlap, and have become of increasing significance to the achievement of primary financial objectives such as the maximisation of shareholder wealth. Most companies have a series of secondary objectives that encompass many of these issues.

Traditional **non-financial issues** affecting companies include:

(i) **Measures that increase the welfare of employees** such as the provision of housing, good and safe working conditions, social and recreational facilities. These might also relate to managers and encompass generous perquisites.

(ii) **Welfare of the local community and society as a whole**. This has become of increasing significance, with companies accepting that they have some responsibility beyond their normal stakeholders in that their actions may impact on the environment and the quality of life of third parties.

(iii) **Provision of, or fulfilment of, a service**. Many organisations, both in the public sector and private sector provide a service, for example to remote communities, which would not be provided on purely economic grounds.

(iv) **Growth of an organisation**, which might bring more power, prestige, and a larger market share, but might adversely affect shareholder wealth.

(v) **Quality**. Many engineering companies have been accused of focusing upon quality rather than cost effective solutions.

(vi) **Survival**. Although to some extent linked to financial objectives, managers might place corporate survival (and hence retaining their jobs) ahead of wealth maximisation. An obvious effect might be to avoid undertaking risky investments.

Ethical issues of companies were brought into sharp focus by the actions of Enron and others. There is a trade-off between applying a high standard of ethics and increasing cash flow or maximisation of shareholder wealth. A company might face ethical dilemmas with respect to the amount and accuracy of information it provides to its stakeholders. An ethical issue attracting much attention is the possible payment of excessive remuneration to senior directors, including very large bonuses and 'golden parachutes'.

Key answer tips

Should bribes be paid in order to facilitate the company's long-term aims? Are wages being paid in some countries below subsistence levels? Should they be? Are working conditions of an acceptable standard? Do the company's activities involve experiments on animals, genetic modifications etc? Should the company deal with or operate in countries that have a poor record of human rights? What is the impact of the company's actions on pollution or other aspects of the local environment?

Environmental issues might have very direct effects on companies. If natural resources become depleted the company may not be able to sustain its activities, weather and climatic factors can influence the achievement of corporate objectives through their impact on crops, the availability of water etc. Extreme environmental disasters such as typhoons, floods, earthquakes, and volcanic eruptions will also impact on companies' cash flow, as will obvious environmental considerations such as the location of mountains, deserts, or communications facilities. Should companies develop new technologies that will improve the environment, such as cleaner petrol or alternative fuels? Such developments might not be the cheapest alternative.

Environmental legislation is a major influence in many countries. This includes limitations on where operations may be located and in what form, and regulations regarding waste products, noise and physical pollutants.

All of these issues have received considerable publicity and attention in recent years. *Environmental pressure groups* are prominent in many countries; companies are now producing social and environmental accounting reports, and/or corporate social responsibility reports. Companies increasingly have multiple objectives that address some or all of these three issues. In the short-term non-financial, ethical and environmental issues might result in a reduction in shareholder wealth; in the longer term it is argued that only companies that address these issues will succeed.

ACCA marking scheme	
	Marks
Examples of non-financial, ethical and environmental issues. Up to 4 marks for each (and up to 5 marks for excellent answers).	12
Discussion of their importance.	3-4
Total	15

2 BONDS AND COVENANTS

(a)   **Bondholders** are concerned that payments of interest and repayments of principal should be made on time and without problems. The willingness of bondholders to provide funds to companies depends on the risks and returns that they face, including the companies' expected cash flows, assets (including available security on assets), and credit ratings for the bonds.

Shareholders, in theory, seek to maximise the value of their shares. This is not necessarily consistent with the interests of bondholders, nor the incentive to maximise the total value of the company (the value of equity plus debt). Shareholders seeking to maximise their wealth might take actions that are detrimental to bondholders. For example shareholders (normally through their agents, the company's managers) might use the finance provide by bondholders to invest in very risky projects, which change the character of the risk that the bondholders face. If the risky projects are successful, then the rewards flow primarily to the shareholders. If the projects fail then much of the cost of failure will fall on the bondholders. If there are no constraints on shareholders, the shareholders might have a natural incentive to take such risks.

Management, acting on behalf of shareholders, might also reduce the wealth, and/or increase the risk of bondholders by:

(i)   selling off assets of the company

(ii)   paying large dividends

(iii)   borrowing additional funds that rank above existing bonds in terms of prior payment upon liquidation.

The incentive for shareholders to take on risks at bondholders' expense is especially strong when the company is in financial difficulties and in danger of failing. In such circumstances the shareholders may believe that they have little to lose by undertaking risky projects. In the case of corporate failure significant 'bankruptcy costs' normally exist. Direct costs of bankruptcy include receivers and lawyers' fees, whilst indirect costs might include loss of cash flow prior to failure through loss of sales, worse credit terms etc. When corporate failure occurs most of the firm's value will be transferred to its debt holders who ultimately bear most of the bankruptcy costs.

(b)   **Bond covenants** might include:

(i)   An **asset covenant**. This would govern the company's acquisition, use and disposal of assets. This could be for specified types of assets, or assets in general.

(ii)   **Financing covenant**. This covenant often defines the type and amount of additional debt that the company can issue, and its ranking and potential claim on assets in case of future default. For example, there could be a covenant whereby the bond issuer undertakes not to issue any bonds in the future that take precedence over the covenanted bonds in the event of a liquidation of the company.

(iii)   **Dividend covenant**. A dividend covenant restricts the amount of dividend that the company is able to pay. Such covenants might also be extended to share repurchases.

(iv)   **Financial ratio covenants**, fixing the limit of key ratios such as the gearing level, interest cover, net working capital, or a minimum ratio of tangible assets to total debt.

(v)   **Merger covenant**, restricting future merger activity of the company.

(vi)   **Investment covenant**, concerned with placing restrictions on the company's future investment policy.

(vii)   **Sinking fund covenant** whereby the company makes payments, typically to the bond trustees, who might gradually repurchase bonds in the open market, or build up a fund to redeem bonds.

There will often also be a 'bonding covenant' that describes the mechanisms by which the above covenants are to be monitored and enforced. This often includes an independent audit and the appointment of a trustee representing the interests of the bondholders. From the company's perspective, the major disadvantage of covenants is that they restrict the freedom of action of the managers, and could prevent viable investments, or mergers from occurring. They also necessitate monitoring and other costs. However, covenants are also of value to companies. Without covenants the company might not be able to raise as much funds in the form of debt, as lenders would not be prepared to take the risk. Even if lenders were to take the risk they would require a higher default premium (higher interest rates) in order to compensate for the risk. The existence of covenants therefore reduces the cost of borrowing for a company.

ACCA marking scheme		
		Marks
(a)	Discussion of reasons 1-2 for each good point	8
(b)	Examples of covenants. 1 mark for each sensible suggestion.	5
	Advantages and disadvantages to companies (not investors)	2-3
Total		15

3   CORPORATE GOVERNANCE

Tutorial note: the suggested answer focuses on the UK Combined Code, as amended in 2003. However, the question does not specifically as about corporate governance in the UK, and a well-prepared answer can refer to the governance rules in any other country. The examiner commented that answers which included comments on how points (i) – (vi) might comply with other corporate governance systems were equally acceptable.

Solution

Many aspects of the extracts in the question would not comply with corporate governance systems such as the UK Combined Code guidelines.

(i)   *Audit fees and auditor independence.* In the UK, it is a requirement of company law that all audit fees and fees for other services provided by auditors should be fully disclosed. Non-audit fees include fees for tax advice, management consultancy and general accountancy services.

It has been argued that the partner(s) responsible for the audit should be regularly changed so that the audit is perceived to be more objective, and there is less chance of missing important anomalies in the audit process. However, there are no provisions about audit partner rotation in the Combined Code. It should be the responsibility of the audit committee to ensure the independence of the auditors, and to review the appointment/re-appointment and make suitable recommendations to the full board.

(ii)   The UK Combined Code states that the remuneration committee should consist of at least three (or two, in the case of smaller companies) members, and these should all be independent non-executive directors. The committee should objectively determine the remuneration and individual packages for each executive director and also the chairman and 'senior management' (but consult with the chairman and/or CEO about the remuneration of the other executive directors).

(iii)   The UK Combined Code states that the roles of chairman and chief executive should not be exercised by the same individual. The division of responsibilities between the chairman and chief executive should also be clearly established, agreed by the board and set out in writing. The chairman should be independent, and the CEO should not go on to become chairman in the same company.

(iv)   The disclosure of whether principles of good corporate governance have been applied is not normally enough; companies should also fully explain how such principles have been applied. The requirements for preparing a corporate governance report (and 'comply or explain' in this report) are contained in the UK Listing Rules for listed companies.

(v)   There is a requirement for directors to meet regularly and to retain full and effective control over the company. In practice, it is doubtful if anyone holding so many Directorships, whether executive or non-executive, could devote sufficient time to each company to effectively fulfil their responsibilities. However, the Combined Code makes no specific reference to the number of directorships any individual may hold. The Code merely states that the letter of appointment of an NED should set out the expected time commitment, and the individual should also make a disclosure to the board, before his appointment, of his other time commitments. There is also a requirement in the Code for individual directors to undergo a performance appraisal annually. Presumably, any director who does not have the time to perform his duties properly will be identified and asked either to commit more time or to resign.

(vi)   This is likely to comply with the Combined Code, although the board should also review risk management generally, not just the system of internal controls. The Combined Code states that the directors should maintain a sound system of internal control and, at least annually, conduct a review of the effectiveness of the group's system of internal controls and they should report to the shareholders that they have done so. The review should cover all material controls. These include not just financial controls, but also operational controls, compliance controls and the risk management system.

Tutorial note: This question – and solution – does not cover every aspect of the UK Combined Code. Similarly, corporate governance codes in other countries will address other issues, in addition to those covered by this question. Perhaps a significant item to remember in the UK is that it is recommended that at least one half of the board of directors in large listed companies (and at least two directors in smaller companies) should be independent non-executive directors. A further item to note for the UK is the introduction of the Directors' Remuneration Disclosure Regulations in 2002, amending the Companies Act 1985 and requiring detailed disclosures about directors' remuneration and remuneration policy.

(b)   **Report on Corporate Governance in the USA, Germany and Japan.**

The broad principles of corporate governance are similar in the UK, the USA and Germany, but there are significant differences in how they are applied. In particular, whereas the UK and Germany have voluntary corporate governance codes, the US system is based on legislation (the Sarbanes-Oxley Act).

USA

There are many similarities between corporate governance in the UK and USA. However, whereas the UK has historically relied upon a system of self-regulation and voluntary codes of best practice, the USA corporate governance structure is more formalised, often with legally enforceable controls. In the US, certain statutory requirements for publicly-traded companies, which are set out in the Sarbanes-Oxley Act. These requirements include the certification of published financial statements by the CEO and the chief financial officer (finance director), faster public disclosures by companies, legal protection for whistleblowers, a requirement for an annual report on internal controls, and requirements relating to the audit committee, auditor conduct and avoiding 'improper' influence of auditors. The Act also requires the Securities and Exchange Commission and the main stock exchanges to introduce further rules, relating to matters such as the disclosure of critical accounting policies, the composition of the board and the number of independent directors. The Act has also established an independent body to oversee the accounting firms. (This is called the Public company Accounting Oversight Board, or 'Peek-a-Boo'). Managers must be careful to comply with regulations to avoid possible legal action against the company or themselves individually.

Germany

As both the UK and Germany are members of the EU, they must both follow EU directives on company law. A major difference that exists in the board structure for companies is that the UK has a unitary board (consisting of executive and non-executive directors together), whereas German companies have a two-tier board of directors. The Supervisory Board of non-executives (Aufsichrat) has responsibility for corporate policy and strategy, and the Management Board of executive directors

(Vorstand) has responsibility primarily for the day to day operations of the company. The supervisory board typically includes representatives from major banks that have historically been large providers of long-term finance to German companies (and are often major shareholders). The supervisory board does not have full access to financial information, is meant to take an unbiased overview of the company, and is the main body responsible for safeguarding the external stakeholders' interests. The presence on the supervisory board of representatives from banks and employees (trade unions) may introduce perspectives that are not present in some UK boards. In particular, many members of the supervisory board would not meet the criteria under UK Combined Code guidelines for being considered independent.

Japan

Although there are signs of change in Japanese corporate governance, much of the system is based upon negotiation or consensual management rather than a legal or even a self-regulatory framework. As in Germany, banks have a significant influence, as have representatives of other external companies as shareholders. It is not uncommon for Japanese companies to have cross holdings of shares with their suppliers, customers, banks etc., all being represented on each others boards. There are often three boards of directors: Policy Boards, responsible for strategy and comprised of directors with no functional responsibility, Functional Boards, responsible for day to day operations, and largely symbolic Monocratic Boards. The interests of the company as a whole should dictate the actions of the boards. This is in contrast to the UK or US systems where, at least in theory, the board should act primarily in the best interests of the shareholders, the owners of the company.

The consensual management style should be respected even though at times decision-making might seem slow.

ACCA marking scheme		
		Marks
(a)	Correct comment on each point	9
(b)	Contrasts between UK and each country (do not give extra marks for comparison with all three countries) Implications for managers	4–5 max 6
Total		15

STRATEGY FORMULATION INCLUDING VALUATION OF SECURITIES

4 FINANCING MIX

(a) Short-term financial planning is usually considered to be planning for up to a year in duration, often broken down into monthly data. It typically focuses on operational planning and liquidity management. Short-term plans should:

(i) Link directly to longer term strategic and tactical plans, and should facilitate the implementation of such plans.

(ii) Provide detailed information for each segment of the business. Information within short-term plans would normally include projected profit and loss accounts, balance sheets and cash flow data, and clearly identify how any expected cash flow deficits are to be financed.

(iii) Clearly show the underlying assumptions of the plans, for example relating to interest rates and exchange rates, inflation and industry conditions.

(iv)   Be consistent with other elements of the planning process, for example manpower planning, and capacity constraints.

(v)   Include some form of contingency or flexible planning should results deviate from the expected plan.

(vi)   Incorporate detailed monitoring and control mechanisms.

(b)   A downward sloping yield curve indicates long-term funds are currently cheaper than short-term, and that short-term interest rates are expected to fall in the future. The managing director has suggested that the majority of assets, which are predominantly short-term assets, should be financed from medium to long-term sources. This would appear to be sensible, as it offers secure finance at a relatively low cost.

However, there are possible disadvantages with long-term borrowing:

(i)   If the yield curve returns to the more normal upward sloping shape, the short-term interest rate may move to below the longer-term rate that the company has locked into (e.g. with a bond issue). The company may not be able to redeem the long-term borrowing at an early date without penalty charges.

(ii)   As working capital needs tend to fluctuate, there may be periods when surplus cash exists, which, depending upon the spread between investment and borrowing rates, might only be invested at interest rates that are below the cost of the long-term borrowing.

(iii)   A longer-term loan does not have the flexibility of other forms of financing such as an overdraft, which can be increased or reduced as cash flow varies.

   Tutorial note: However, the fact that overdraft facilities are not committed, and can be withdrawn by a bank without notice, makes them fairly unattractive to large companies.)

(iv)   Longer-term finance might need to be secured on the company's assets; such security would then not be available to be pledged against other loans.

ACCA marking scheme		
		Marks
(a)	One mark for each good point	5
(b)	Reward understanding of the yield curve, risk and the flexibility offered by different types of financing in this situation	_5_
Total		<u>10</u>

5   CORPORATE FAILURE

Examiner's comment

This question requires analysis and understanding of techniques that might be used to attempt to forecast corporate failure, how to estimate free cash flow, and what actions should be taken, if any, as a result of information provided and calculated regarding a company's financial health. Part (e) examines understanding of factors that might influence the expenditure of £100,000 on a report, including the possible effect of market efficiency on this decision.

Briefing document for Snowwell plc:

(a)   The **current S_0 score** may be estimated as follows.

			Weighted score	*See working:*
S_1	$3.5 \times (43/348)$	=	0.432	W1
S_2	$1.8 \times (193 - 215)/436$	=	(0.091)	W2
S_3	$0.25 \times (348/267)$	=	0.326	W1, W3
S_4	$0.69 \times (336/620)$	=	<u>0.374</u>	W4
Total S_0 score			**1.041**	

Workings

(W1) *Total market value of equity*

232 pence × 150 million shares = £348 million.

(W2) *Medium and long-term capital employed (assumed to be book values)*

	£m
Shareholders funds	192
14% loan stock	150
Floating rate bank loans	94
	436

(W3) *Market value of debt*

The market value of the loan stock is not given in the question. Given a current redemption yield of 8%, the market value of 14% loan stock with three years remaining to maturity and redemption is estimated to be:

Years		Cash flow	Discount factor at 8%	Present value
		£		£
1–3	Interest	14	2.577	36.08
3	Redemption	100	0.794	79.40
				115.48

Tutorial note: The redemption yield is a gross yield, ignoring taxation.

Total market value of loan stock = £150 million nominal value × 1.1548 = £173.22 million.

Total market value of debt is therefore £173.22 million + £94 million = £267.22 million, say £267 million.

(W4) *Present value to infinity of current operating free cash flow*

Current operating free cash flow may be estimated as follows:

	£ million
Profit before tax	23
Add:	
Depreciation	38
After-tax cost of interest (20 × 0.70)	14
	75
Subtract:	
Tax	(7)
Increase in working capital ((22) – (24))	(2)
Replacement investment	(35)
Free cash flow	31

Examiner's comment

Other definitions of free cash flow are possible, including adjustments for the change in loans and disposal of assets.

Weighted average cost of capital:

The pre-tax cost of debt is 8%, therefore the after-tax cost of debt is:

8 (1 – 0.30)% = 5.6%.

	Market value £m		Cost	£m
Equity	348	(W1)	12.0%	41.760
Debt	267	(W3)	5.6%	14.952
	615			56.712

WACC = (56.712/615) = 0.922 or 9.22%.

Present value to infinity of free cash flow

£31 million/0.0922 = £336 million.

(b) **Significance of the S_0 score**

The S_0 model suggests that a score of 1.04 is just above the level of probable failure, and at the low end of the remedial action range. However, this model is unlikely to be useful in predicting the probability of failure of Snowwell plc because:

(1) The model was produced in 20X1 and might not still be relevant in 20X3.

(2) Models predicting corporate failure are usually tailored to specific industries and specific size of companies. This general model might not be applicable to Snowwell.

(3) There is no evidence about the predictive ability of the model.

(4) Models which are based upon accounting ratios suffer the same weaknesses as the accounting systems on which they are based.

(5) No matter what such models predict, managers may be able to take remedial action that will prevent corporate failure.

(c) **Alternative assessment methods**

Other ways by which corporate financial distress or failure might be predicted include:

(1) Alternative models predicting failure such as those of Argenti, Marais and Beaver, or use of profit and logic analysis.

(2) Financial ratios, especially those focusing on liquidity, cash flows, gearing and market values.

(3) Accounting information including levels of debt, liquidity, payment periods, contingent liabilities, and post balance sheet events

(4) Macro events affecting the company, including inflation and foreign exchange rates.

(5) Market information, especially the potential growth of the jewellery sector.

(6) Actions of competitors.

(7) Comment by company directors (e.g. profit warnings), analysts and newspapers.

(8) Audit reports – if accurate!

(9) Credit ratings produced by specialist agencies and banks.

(d) **Recommendations**

Snowwell is not recommended to take any action based upon the S_0 model. Any recommendation would be assisted by additional financial analysis, especially of growth trends and ratios.

Selected ratios and growth trends:

	% growth
Turnover	6.9
Fixed assets	6.3
Stock	22.8
Creditors	18.1
Debtors	(5.9)

	20X3	20X2
Current ratio	0.90	0.87
Quick ratio	0.17	0.20

Gearing (market value of medium- and long-term debt/ market value of equity) = 276/348 = 77%.

Interest cover = 43/20 = 2.15 times.

The current and quick ratios are low, but probably not unusually low for a retailer. Gearing at 77% is significantly higher than the industry average and might be a cause for concern, and interest cover at 2.15 is quite low.

The immediate problem is that stock has increased much more than turnover, leading to a similar increase in creditors. Snowwell's managers should urgently review the company's stock levels. Reducing stock would release cash flow and might allow gearing to be reduced. Consideration might also be given to reducing the level of dividends paid, unless profits are expected to increase in 20X4.

(e) **Purchasing the full report**

The organisation providing the forecast is considered to be reputable and is likely to have tailored the forecast to Snowwell using analysis which has been specifically related to Snowwell's size and industry. If Snowwell could not easily replicate the analysis itself, and if the forecasting company has a good track record of predicting failure it might be worth purchasing the forecast. However, if the market in which Snowwell operates is considered to be efficient, then market analysts will already be aware of the publicly available information used in the model, and this should already have been incorporated in the share price of 232 pence. A price of this level does not suggest that investors feel that the company is likely to fail in the near future.

If the market is not considered to be efficient, and/or the forecasting technique is believed to be superior, and to convey significant new information, then Snowwell might have a reason to purchase. In such circumstances a purchase might be conditional upon the information not being released to any third parties, although if relevant information was then to be withheld by Snowwell's managers this might not be considered to be ethical, and acting in the best interests of all stakeholders.

Examiner's comment

The S_0 model used in the question is a fictitious model.

ACCA marking scheme		
		Marks
(a)	S_1	1
	S_2	1
	S_3	3
	S_4	5 – 6
	Overall S_0 score	1
		11
(b)	Reward sensible criticism – roughly 1 mark per point	4
(c)	0.5 – 1 mark per point, depending on detail	4
(d)	Relevant calculations	3 – 4
	Recommendations regarding actions	3 – 4
	Maximum	7
(e)	Reward sensible discussion, especially if related to the possible effect of the information on price, and to market efficiency discussion	4
Total		30

6 NOIFA LEISURE PLC

Key answer tips

Ensure that you include a thorough analysis of performance and comment on the chairman's statement.

The chairman states in his report that turnover has risen dramatically (by 209%) and that the share price has almost doubled during the last four years. These comments are both accurate. However, he also states that the company's objective is to become the largest hotel group in the United Kingdom. This might suggest that a greater emphasis is being given to sales revenue maximisation rather than profit maximisation. Such a policy may result in a financial position which is not particularly strong. A more detailed analysis is performed below.

(1) **Profitability**

	20X6	20X7	20X8	20X9
Return on turnover	21%	19%	16%	14%
(Profit before tax and interest ÷ turnover)				
Return on capital employed	25%	24%	21%	15%
(Profit before tax and interest ÷ shareholders' funds and debt)				
Return on total assets	17%	16%	13%	10%
(Profit before tax and interest ÷ fixed assets and current assets)				

Each of the profitability ratios calculated above shows a marked decline over the four-year period, indicating that levels of profitability have not kept pace with the rapid expansion.

(2) **Working capital and liquidity**

	20X6	20X7	20X8	20X9
Stock turnover (Turnover ÷ stock)	8.1×	8.2×	7.0×	6.2×
Debtor days (Debtors ÷ average daily sales)	63	51	56	50
Current ratio (Current assets ÷ current liabilities)	0.85	0.73	0.68	0.68
Acid test ratio (Current assets less stock ÷ current liabilities)	0.50	0.40	0.36	0.32

The general trend in the company's collection period from debtors shows an improvement. However, the stock turnover has decreased over the period, perhaps due to less efficient management as expansion has occurred.

The liquidity ratios, on the other hand, are of greater concern since they show a steady deterioration, with the result of an overdraft being necessary for financing working capital from 20X7.

(3) **Gearing**

	20X6	20X7	20X8	20X9
Total debt (including the overdraft) ÷ shareholders' funds	83%	72%	117%	109%
Total debt ÷ total assets	62%	61%	68%	65%
Interest cover (Profit before tax and Interest ÷ interest)	4.8×	4.4×	3.3×	2.6×

Gearing has increased substantially in 20X8 and then reduced slightly in 20X9. However, since 20X9 the company has acquired Beddall Hotels which involves an additional £100 million of debt, thus increasing the total debt: shareholders' funds to

$$\frac{102 + 180 + 68 + 100}{321} = 140\%$$

taking the 20X9 figures.

The interest cover has declined dramatically, partly as a response to the increased gearing, but also due to the lower profitability of the company.

(4) **Market factors**

	20X6	20X7	20X8	20X9
Earnings per share (pence) (Profit after tax and extraordinary item ÷ 500 million shares)	6.0	7.0	7.0	8.2
Price earnings ratio (Share price ÷ earnings per share)	13.7	14.9	17.1	19.4

Both the earnings per share and price earnings ratio have increased over the few years. Given that there have been no new share issues, the earnings per share figures simply represent the modest increase in total profit which has not kept pace with the substantial increase in turnover.

The price earnings ratio appears to show a strong position until it is compared with the equivalent ratio for the leisure industry. In 20X6 Noifa has a P/E ratio in excess of that for the industry (13.7 against 10), but by 20X9 that position has been reversed with Noifa's P/E ratio being 19.4 and that of the industry 25. Similarly the increase in Noifa's share price (to which the chairman makes mention) is not particularly impressive when compared to the share index of the leisure industry. The latter shows an increase over the period of 121% ((394 − 178)/178) whereas the increase in Noifa's share price is only 94% ((159 − 82)/82).

(5)   **Analysis by activity**

In order to perform a meaningful analysis, it is necessary to convert the turnover and profit figures into percentage terms.

	20X6		20X7		20X8		20X9	
	Turnover	*Profit*	*Turnover*	*Profit*	*Turnover*	*Profit*	*Turnover*	*Profit*
Hotels	60.4	73.5	61.3	68.4	64.0	49.3	69.3	49.0
Theme park	4.6	(6.1)	4.9	(3.3)	4.9	4.0	5.0	5.4
Bus company	7.4	12.2	7.6	13.3	7.8	18.7	6.8	19.6
Car hire	13.2	14.3	12.2	13.3	10.6	16.0	9.1	16.3
Zoo	1.5	(2.0)	1.6	(1.7)	1.8	0	1.5	(1.1)
Waxworks	3.1	2.0	3.0	5.0	2.7	5.3	2.1	5.4
Publications	9.8	6.1	9.4	5.0	8.2	6.7	6.3	5.4
	100.0	100.0	100.0	100.0	100.0	100.0	100.0	100.0

Whereas there has been growth in most of the company's activities the most substantial expansion has been in the hotel business with turnover increasing from 60.4% of the total in 20X6 to 69.3% in 20X9. However, despite the increase in the proportion of turnover, the profit contributed has fallen dramatically from 73.5% of the total in 20X6 to 49.0% in 20X9. Therefore it is clearly the hotel expansion which has resulted in the overall decline in relative profitability.

(6)   **Conclusion and recommendation**

The analysis of the different segments of the business above would indicate that it may be preferable for the company to turn its attention away from hotel expansion to a more profitable area, such as the theme park (which has become profitable) or the bus company or the waxworks. This would involve a change in the stated objective of becoming the largest hotel group in the UK, but would probably benefit the shareholders in terms of the wealth maximising criterion.

A second consideration is concerned with the financing and gearing ratio of the company. It has been shown above that the gearing level has increased dramatically over the four-year period and that it has subsequently risen still further as a result of the euro loan to finance the acquisition of Beddall Hotels. Although the company has a large asset base to support the debt (£696 million of tangible fixed assets which will comprise hotel buildings with a high market value) the interest cover is deteriorating. Therefore if the hotel expansion does not become more profitable, the company could have difficulties in meeting its obligations.

An alternative means of financing future acquisitions, including that of Beddall Hotels, would therefore be desirable. Although the euro loan is low risk, it has increased the gearing further and will also introduce foreign currency risk. Therefore an alternative of equity finance via a new issue of shares should be considered to reduce both the financial risk introduced through gearing and the currency risk.

7   COMPANY'S SHARES

Key answer tips

To gain the 'higher skills' marks you need to discuss the validity of the dividend valuation model together with implications of market efficiency.

Report on the valuation of the company's shares

From the data provided, the analyst appears to have used the dividend growth model in the valuation process.

According to the dividend growth model the intrinsic value of the company's shares should be 600 pence, as illustrated below. The actual value is 645 pence, suggesting that the shares are overvalued by approximately 7.5%.

	Dividend per share (pence)	Growth (%)
20X0	19.86	
20X1	21.45	8
20X2	23.17	8
20X3	25.02	8

Using the dividend growth model and assuming dividend growth of 8% every year in perpetuity:

$$\text{Price} = \frac{D_1}{Ke - g} = \frac{25.02(1.08)}{0.125 - 0.08} = 600 \text{ pence}$$

Tutorial note: The same conclusion about the average annual growth rate in dividends could have been obtained by calculating the cube root of (25.02/19.86) and then subtracting 1. The cube root is taken because we have data for growth over three years. The cube root of (25.02/19.86) is 1.0800, so the average annual growth rate in dividends is 0.0800 or 8%.

The belief that a share is undervalued or over-valued, based on the use of only externally available information, implies that the stock market is not semi-strong form efficient. Although markets are not efficient at all times, there is substantial evidence to suggest that semi-strong form efficiency normally exists in most well-developed markets.

Even if market efficiency is expected, the dividend growth model is by no means the only technique that might be used to estimate share value. The discounted value of expected future cash flows is a theoretically superior technique. The dividend growth model makes a number of assumptions including:

(i)   Dividend growth will be constant which is very unlikely. Dividend growth is assumed to result from earnings growth which itself results from new, constant return investments financed only by retained earnings.

(ii)   The company will retain a constant fraction of earnings.

In this example, the growth in earnings per share is much more volatile than the growth in dividend per share, and the company might not be able to sustain a constant 8% growth in dividends.

Estimates of share value based upon the dividend growth model are therefore themselves suspect, and the analyst is probably not justified in suggesting that the share is overvalued based on this evidence only.

8 BNG PLC

Key answer tips

Ensure you apply the correct technique in part (b) (i.e. they are redeemable bonds), and highlight the relationship between interest rates and bond prices in part (c).

(a) The bonds of Magnacorp offer a redemption yield of 7%, 10 year maturity and a credit rating of A –. The closest alternative to this investment is Suprafirm, with a redemption yield of 7.5%, an identical maturity and a similar credit rating (BBB+ against A –). As the yield to redemption is higher for an almost identical bond, BNG might consider switching from the bonds of Magnacorp to the bonds of Suprafirm, as long as the extra yield compensates for the risk difference between the investments and any transactions costs.

Tutorial note: In the Standard & Poor's credit rating system for bonds, a credit rating of AA– is just one 'notch' above a credit rating of BBB+. Both are 'investment grade' ratings. The lowest investment grade credit rating in the S&P system is BBB –.

(b) The expected market price of Grandit with a coupon of 7.8% and redemption yield of 6.0%, assuming annual payments of interest, is:

Year	Item	Cash flow	Discount factor at 6%	PV
1–4	Interest p.a.	7.8	3.465	27.03
4	Redemption	100.0	0.792	79.20
Expected market price				106.23
Actual market price				105.83
Difference				0.40

The current market price is 40 pence lower than would be expected if the actual yield were 6%. The actual yield is therefore higher than 6%.

Tutorial note: At higher yields, bond prices are lower.

(c) A fall in interest rates will lead to an increase in bond prices and the value of a bond portfolio. The greater the fall in interest rates, the greater the rise in bond value. If medium term interest rates are expected to fall by more than long-term rates then it might be worth selling the longer term bonds of Magnacorp and buying the medium-term bonds of Grandit before any fall in interest rates occurred. Additionally low coupon bonds are more sensitive to changes in interest rates than high coupon bonds.

Tutorial note: If the yield curve is already upward-sloping and medium-term rates then fall by more than longer-term rates, the yield curve will still be upward-sloping, but with a steeper slope. The wording of the question in part (c) is unusual and possibly misleading.

9 TOUTPLUT INC

(a) **Economic Value Added is estimated by:**

Net operating profit after tax (NOPAT) – (capital employed × cost of capital).

NOPAT is normally measured in cash flow terms after numerous adjustments to accounting profit. However, economic depreciation is also deducted when estimating NOPAT, as it is considered to be a measure of the economic use of assets during a year. It is assumed that NOPAT can be estimated from the data provided by adding back to after tax profit non-cash expenses (excluding economic depreciation), and net of tax interest. (Adding back net of tax interest results in earnings that would have been reported had all of the company's capital requirements been financed with ordinary shares. Interest and the tax effect of actual gearing are incorporated in the weighted average cost of capital.)

EVA **capital employed** is based on the book economic value of capital at the beginning of the relevant period. As there is no information on full adjustments, the book value of shareholders' funds and medium and long-term debt, plus the value of non-capitalised leases, will be used.

	20X2	*20X3*
NOPAT	56.6 (= 44 + 10 + (4 × 0.65))	68.9 (= 55 + 10 + (6 × 0.65))
Capital employed	233 (= 223 + 10)	260 (= 250 + 10)

The weighted average cost of capital is estimated using target capital structure:

20X2	15% × 0.6 + 9% (1 − 0.35) × 0.4	=	11.34%
20X3	17% × 0.6 + 10% (1 − 0.35) × 0.4	=	12.80%

EVA 20X2	= 56.6 − (233 × 0.1134)	=	$30.18 million
EVA 20X3	= 68.9 − (260 × 0.1280)	=	$35.62 million

Using the EVA measure the company has created significant value in both of the two years, and has apparently performed well.

(b)   If the EVAs for each year of an investment were summed over the entire life of the investment and then discounted, the result, in theory, should equal the net present value of the investment at the time the investment was made.

(c)   **Advantages of EVA include:**

(i)   It measures the value added to an organisation after deducting a charge for the use of capital made by that organisation.

(ii)   It is based on cash flows and is less easy to manipulate than accounting data.

(iii)   EVA may be consistent with the objective of maximising shareholder wealth.

(iv)   EVA can easily be communicated to, and understood by, managers and employees.

(v)   EVA may be used to judge performance by managers, and linked to remuneration schemes which reward the creation of value to the organisation.

Disadvantages include:

(i)   Calculations of EVA are complicated and require many adjustments to accounting information.

(ii)   EVA is normally historic. It does not help decide future investments and strategy.

(iii)   EVA may distort investment by favouring investments with relatively small capital outlays, or relatively short time horizons. Such investments are likely to produce higher EVAs in the near future.

(iv)   EVA comparisons between companies are not directly valid, unless an adjustment is made for the relative size of companies.

(v)   EVA usually relies on CAPM for the estimate of the weighted average cost of capital. CAPM is based upon restrictive assumptions and may not accurately estimate the cost of capital.

(vi)   EVA is not suitable for young companies or financial institutions.

ACCA marking scheme		
		Marks
(a)	EVA definition	1
	NOPAT	2
	Capital employed	1
	Cost of capital	1
	EVAs	1
	Comment	1
		7
(b)	Correct relationship	2
(c)	Advantages	3
	Disadvantages	3
	Look for 2–3 of each for maximum marks	
Total		15

10   WURRALL PLC

(a)   Proforma accounts

Proforma profit and loss account for the years ended March 2005–8

£ million

	2005	2006	2007	2008
Turnover	1,787	1,929	2,064	2,188
Operating costs before deprecation	(1,215)	(1,312)	(1,404)	(1,488)
EBITDA	572	617	660	700
Tax allowable depreciation	(165)	(179)	(191)	(203)
EBIT	407	438	469	497
Net interest payable	(63)	(65)	(66)	(70)
Profit on ordinary activities before tax	344	373	403	427
Tax on ordinary activities	(103)	(112)	(121)	(128)
Dividends	(135)	(146)	(158)	(167)
Amount transferred to reserves	106	115	124	132

Proforma balance sheets 2005–8

£ million

	2005	2006	2007	2008
Fixed assets				
Land and buildings	310	310	350	350
Plant and machinery (net)	1,103	1,191	1,275	1,351
Investments	32	32	32	32
	1,445	1,533	1,657	1,733
Current assets				
Stocks	488	527	564	598
Debtors	615	664	710	753
Cash in hand and short term deposits	22	24	25	27
	1,125	1,215	1,299	1,378

Creditors: amounts falling due within one year:				
Short term loans and overdrafts (balancing fig)	266	287	332	320
Other creditors	514	556	595	630
	(780)	(843)	(927)	(950)
Creditors: amounts falling due after one year:				
Borrowings[1]	(580)	(580)	(580)	(580)
	1,210	1,325	1,449	1,581
Capital and reserves				
Called up share capital (10 pence par)	240	240	240	240
Reserves	970	1,085	1,209	1,341
	1,210	1,325	1,449	1,581

[1]Refinanced with a similar type of loan in 2006

Tutorial note: This is a fairly straightforward forecast of pro-forma accounts and should be a good opportunity to score marks. However, ensure that presentation is both clear and appropriate.

(b) The *pro forma* accounts are based primarily upon the percentage of sales method of forecasting. This provides a simple approach to forecasting, but is based upon assumptions of existing or planned relationships between variables remaining constant, which are highly unlikely. It also does not allow for improvements in efficiency over time.

(i) Accurate forecasts of sales growth are very difficult. Sensitivity or simulation analysis is recommended to investigate the implications of sales differing from the forecast levels. A constant growth rate of 6% forever after four years is most unlikely.

(ii) Cash operating costs are unlikely to increase in direct proportion with sales. The variable elements (wages, materials, distribution costs etc.) could all move at a higher or lower rate than sales, whilst the fixed elements will not change with the value of sales at all in the short run. If the company becomes more efficient then costs as a proportion of sales should reduce.

(iii) Unless tax allowable depreciation from new asset purchases exactly offsets the diminishing allowances on older assets, and effect of the increase in assets with sales growth, this relationship is unlikely to be precise. The government might also change the rates of tax allowable deprecation.

(iv) Assuming a direct relationship between stocks, debtors, cash and other creditors to sales could promote inefficiency. Although a strong correlation between such variables exists, there should be no need to increase stock, debtors and creditors in direct proportion to sales.

(v) Paying dividends as a constant percentage of earnings could lead to quite volatile dividend payouts. Most investors are believed to prefer reasonably constant dividends (allowing for inflation) and might not value a company with volatile dividends as highly as one with relatively stable dividends.

(c) Free cash flow will be estimated by EBIT(1-t) plus depreciation less adjustments for changes in working capital and expenditure on fixed assets. (N.B. other definitions of free cash flow exist)

| | £ million | | | |
	2005	2006	2007	2008
Change in land and buildings	–	–	40	–
Change in plant and machinery	91	88	84	76
Change in working capital	15	27	–	56
Change in assets	106	115	124	132

| | £ million | | | |
	2005	2006	2007	2008
EBIT (1-t)	285	307	328	348
Depreciation	165	179	191	203
Change in assets	(106)	(115)	(124)	(132)
Free cash flow	344	371	395	419

The present value of free cash flow for the company after 2008 may be estimated by

$$\frac{FCF2008(1+g)}{WACC-g} \text{ or } \frac{419(1.06)}{0.11-0.06} = 8{,}883$$

The estimated value of the company at the end of 2008 is £8,883 million. From this must be deducted the value of any loans in order to find the value accruing to shareholders. From the pro forma accounts, loans are expected to total £900 million, leaving a net value of £7,983 million. If the number of issued shares has not changed, the estimated market value per share is $\frac{7{,}983}{2{,}400} = 333$ pence per share, an increase of 58% on the current share price.

Based upon this data the managing director's claim that the share price will double in four years is not likely to occur.

However, the impact of the performance of the economy, and unforeseen significant changes affecting Wurrall plc mean that

Such estimates are subject to a considerable margin of error.

(d)   Ratios

	2005	2006	2007	2008
Gearing (%)	41.1	39.6	38.6	36.3
Current ratio	1.44	1.44	1.40	1.45
Quick ratio	0.82	0.82	0.79	0.82
Return on capital employed[1] (%)	22.7	23.0	23.1	23.0
Asset turnover	1.00	1.01	1.02	1.01
EBIT/Sales (%)	22.8	22.7	22.7	22.7
Debtor collection period (days)	126	126	126	126

[1]EBIT/(shareholders equity plus long term debt). Other definitions are possible

---

Key answer tip

You have a wide choice of ratios in this question. Do not produce a long list of ratios illustrating similar trends. Choose carefully and produce a few key ratios that provide a valuable insight into the business. Equally, there are ratios other than those above that could be used alternatively to provide this insight.

It is difficult to comment upon ratios without comparative data for companies in the same industry. The current gearing level, at 42.3%, breaches the covenant limit of 40%, and it is expected to continue to do so in 2005. Whether or not this breaches the one-year covenant is not clear, but would need to be investigated by the company and action taken to reduce gearing if the covenant was to be breached for too long a period. The debtor collection period appears high at 126 days. It is unlikely that credit would be given for such a long period, and the company might consider improving its credit control procedures to reduce the collection period. If this is successful it could also reduce the overdraft and help reduce the gearing level.

Another ratio that would need investigating is the asset turnover. At around one this is relatively low. Unless the industry is very capital intensive, management should consider if assets could be utilised more efficiently to improve this ratio, and with it the return on capital employed.

As previously mentioned, managers might also review the company's dividend policy. Paying a constant level of earnings could lead to volatile dividend payments which might not be popular with investors, including financial institutions, that rely upon dividends for part of their annual cash flow.

Wurrall proposes to finance any new capital needs with increases in the overdraft. Overdraft finance is not normally considered to be appropriate for long term financing, and the company should consider longer term borrowing or equity issues for its long-term financing requirements.

ACCA marking scheme		Marks
(a) Proforma accounts		
Profit and loss accounts		5–6
Balance sheets		6–7
		12
(b) 1–2 marks for each good point		8
(c) Free cash flow estimate		5
Present value of the company and shares		4
Comment/conclusion re the managing director		1
		10
(d) Ratios or other calculations		5–6
Problems and suggested actions		5–6
		10
Total		40

11 REMUNERATION

(a) The suggestion by the managing director is intuitively attractive in that most companies believe they need to attract the best managers, and high remuneration is necessary to achieve this. Whilst this may be the case the link between a high salary and managerial performance is not proven. Paying more than the current 'going rate' also has the effect of leading to continuing increases in senior management salaries, which might be unpopular with shareholders, employees and other stakeholders. There is also no suggestion of remuneration linked to performance.

Suggestion (ii), linking salary to turnover, is probably the least credible. Although sales growth and market share might be important, this should not be at the expense of cash flow and wealth creation. An extreme example would be that turnover, and hence the managing director's remuneration, could be increased by halving the price of the company's products. This is not, however, very likely to create wealth.

Suggestion (iii) relates to share options, which have been commonly used by companies for many years. They are intended to motivate senior managers to take decisions that will result in share price increases and wealth creation, and goal congruence between shareholders and managers. To some extent they may achieve this, but potential problems are:

(i)   Share price increases may be caused by factors outside of the control of managers, yet they will still be rewarded for such increases

(ii)   The appropriate size of the option package is difficult to determine.

Many large companies have recently been criticised for offering share options deals that are too generous.

Suggestion (iv) relates to EVA®. Economic value added measures the annual wealth creation after taking into account a charge for the amount of capital employed. Remuneration schemes linked to EVA® are intended to reward the creation of value to the organisation. This is a valid objective, but EVA® is not suitable for all types of organisation (e.g. financial services companies), and may be creatively increased by relatively low levels of investment – at least in the short term. If an EVA® based incentive scheme is to be used it might be better to base it on a percentage of the incremental EVA® achieved by the new managing director rather than a percentage of the total EVA®.

(b)   The value of a call option on a share may be estimated using the put-call parity theorem, $P^P = P^C - P^S + Xe^{-rT}$

The option exercise price is 120 pence × 75% or 90 pence, and the put option price is given at 35 pence.

Therefore $35 = P^C - 120 + 90e^{-(0.04)(1)}$

Solving, $P^C = 68.53$ pence

Tutorial note: It is important to thoroughly evaluate the call option.

Call options on 3,000,000 shares would have an approximate value of £2,055,900, which appears to be quite generous to an unproven manager. It would be better to fix the call option exercise price above the current market price rather than below it. The managing director would then be more likely to be rewarded for his own performance if the share price increases, although, as previously mentioned, share price movements are not always the result of good management. The period of the option at only one year is also very short; an option over a three-or five-year period would give more time for the policies of the new managing director to be reflected in the share price.

EVA® estimates require a number of adjustments to profit. In order to estimate NOPAT (net operating profit after tax) advertising is normally removed from the profit and loss account and added to capital employed. Three years will be added, but this is subjective. It is necessary to add back interest paid, as this will be included in the capital charge, the weighted average cost of capital. Additionally taxation will need to be increased by the benefit taken in the profit and loss account from tax relief on interest payments (such tax relief is included in WACC), and the tax relief on the advertising expense.

	£ million	
Turnover	546	
Cost of sales	369	
Depreciation	52	
Taxation	37.8	$(27 + (26 + 10) \times 0.3)$
NOPAT	87.2	

Capital employed should be based upon capital at the start of the year. Adjusting for three years advertising, the capital employed is £450 million.

EVA® is NOPAT – (Capital employed × cost of capital)

EVA® is 87.2 – (450 × 0.095) = £44.45 million.

If the managing director were to receive 1.5% of EVA this would be £666,750, much less than the share option. However, as previously mentioned, it might be better to link a remuneration scheme to incremental EVA® after the manager is in post.

ACCA marking scheme			
			Marks
(a)	Salary 20% more		1–2
	Link to turnover		1
	Share options		2
	EVA		2
		Max	6
(b)	Call option calculation		3
	Comment		1
	EVA calculation		4
	Comment		1
Total			15

PORTFOLIO THEORY AND CAPM

12   PORTFOLIO RISK AND RETURN (MALTEC)

(a)   The **portfolio return** is the weighted average return from the five investments. As the investments are of equal value, the average return ((14 + 16 + 12 + 9 + 22)/5) = 14.6%.

Portfolio diversification offers no enhancements to return, although it does offer the opportunity for improved combinations of risk and return.

As there is believed to be no correlation between any of the investments, and each investment is 0.20 of the total portfolio, portfolio risk may be estimated as:

$$\sqrt{(0.2)^2\,8^2 + (0.2)^2\,10^2 + (0.2)^2\,7^2 + (0.2)^2\,4^2 + (0.2)^2\,16^2}$$

$$= \sqrt{2.56 + 4.0 + 1.96 + 0.64 + 10.24}$$

$$= \sqrt{19.4}$$

$$= 4.4\%$$

Tutorial note: If you are not sure about this calculation, we have to calculate the total portfolio variance, and having found this take the square root to arrive at the standard deviation of portfolio returns.

With a portfolio of only five investments, the benefits of diversification have reduced portfolio risk, measured by the standard deviation of expected returns, to approximately that of the lowest risk individual investment. This portfolio risk reduction is quite large because of the lack of correlation between the investments. The further away the correlation coefficient is from +1, the greater the risk reduction through diversification.

(b)   In theory, a well-diversified investor will not place any extra value on companies that diversify. This is because an investor can diversify himself, by investing in shares and other securities of different companies in different markets and in different geographical areas.

On the contrary, as diversification is expensive, and might move companies away from their core competence, a diversified company might have a relatively low market value. However, not all investors are well diversified, and even well diversified investors might benefit from a diversified company. A diversified company might have a less volatile cash flow pattern, be less likely to default on interest payments, have a higher credit rating and therefore lower cost of capital, leading to higher potential NPVs from investments and a higher market value.

If the diversification is international, the benefits of diversification will depend on whether the countries where the investments take place are part of any integrated international market, or are largely segmented by government restrictions (e.g. exchange controls, tariffs, quotas). If markets are segmented, international diversification might offer the opportunity to reduce both systematic and unsystematic risk. An integrated market would only offer the opportunity to reduce unsystematic risk. Most markets are neither fully integrated nor segmented, meaning that international diversification will lead to some reduction in systematic risk, which would be valued by investors.

It is to be hoped that risk reduction is not the only objective of Maltec: returns and shareholder utility are also important.

ACCA marking scheme		
		Marks
(a)	Portfolio return	1
	Portfolio risk	2–3
	Comment	1–2
	Maximum marks for (a)	5
(b)	Reward understanding, especially comments about the benefits of international diversification	5
Total		10

13 ALPHA VALUES

Key answer tips

Note that you are not being asked for an explanation of alpha values here, but why they might arise and how they may change over time.

(a) The alpha value is any abnormal return that exists relative to the required return from an investment, as estimated by using the capital asset pricing model (CAPM). The beta of the companies' shares may be estimated from:

$$\text{Beta} = \frac{\text{Covariance } R_1, R_M}{\text{Variance } R_M}$$

The market standard deviation is 5%. The market variance is therefore 25%.

Tutorial note: The variance is the standard deviation squared.

The beta estimates are:

Dedton $\frac{32}{25} = 1.28$

Paralot $\frac{19}{25} = 0.76$

Sunout $\dfrac{24}{25} = 0.96$

Rangon $\dfrac{43}{25} = 1.72$

	Forecast returns	*Required returns*		*Alpha*
Dedton	16%	6% + (14.5% – 6%)×1.28 =	16.88%	- 0.88%
Paralot	12%	6% + (14.5% – 6%)×0.76 =	12.46%	- 0.46%
Sunout	14%	6% + (14.5% – 6%)×0.96 =	14.16%	- 0.16%
Rangon	19%	6% + (14.5% – 6%)×1.72 =	20.62%	- 1.62%

A positive alpha value implies that it is possible to make higher than normal return, for the systematic risk taken. A negative alpha implies a lower than normal return.

A financial manager wishing to invest in shares might favour those with a positive alpha, subject to the shares satisfying other selection criteria such as the desired level of risk.

If a positive or negative alpha exists for the shares of the company of the financial manager, and the market is at least semi-strong form efficient, the alpha would be expected to move to zero as the company's share price changes due to arbitrage profit-taking. For example, in theory a company with a positive alpha would expect relatively high demand for its shares, increasing share price and thereby decreasing return until the alpha is zero.

(b) Positive or negative alpha values exist for shares most of the time. If CAPM is a realistic model, alpha values should only be temporary and the same alpha values would not be expected to exist in a year's time.

Alphas may exist due to inaccuracies and/or limitations of the CAPM model including:

(i) The CAPM tends to overstate the required return of high beta securities and to understate the required return of low beta securities. The returns of small companies, returns on certain days of the week or months of the year are observed to differ from those expected from CAPM.

(ii) Data input into the CAPM may be inaccurate. For example it is impossible to accurately calculate the market risk and return.

(iii) Other factors in addition to systematic risk might influence required return. The arbitrage pricing theory (APT) suggests that a multi-factor model is necessary.

(iv) CAPM is also based on a number of unrealistic assumptions.

14 PHANTOM PLC

Key answer tips

Note that it is important in the second part not to over focus on portfolio theory but also to mention the wider strategic motives for corporate acquisition, or alternatives to portfolio theory that might be used such as CAPM.

(a) **Tutorial note:** To answer this question, you need to be able to apply the formula for the standard deviation of returns of a two-asset portfolio, as a measurement of risk of the portfolio. This is given in the formula sheet for the examination. The most efficient portfolio will be the one that gives the highest return and the lowest risk. The expected return of a portfolio is simply the weighted average return of the two assets in the portfolio.

It is assumed that each two-asset portfolio will contain equal amounts by market value of each asset, so that the proportion of each asset in the portfolio is 0.5.

Portfolio risk and return estimates

Mangeit and Altalk

$Risk:$ $\sigma p = \sqrt{(0.5)^2\,17^2 + (0.5)^2\,29^2 + 2(0.5)(0.5)(0)(17)(29)}$

$\qquad = \sqrt{72.25 + 210.25 + 0}$

$\qquad = \sqrt{282.5}$

$\qquad = 16.81$

Expected return: Rp = (0.5)11 + (0.5)20 = 15.5%

Altalk and Legi

$Risk:$ $\sigma p = \sqrt{(0.5)^2 \times 29^2 + (0.5)^2\,21^2 + 2(0.5)(0.5)(0.4)(29)(21)}$

$\qquad = \sqrt{210.25 + 110.25 + 121.80}$

$\qquad = \sqrt{442.30}$

$\qquad = 21.03$

Expected return: Rp = (0.5) 20 + (0.5) 14 = 17%

Mangeit and Legi

$Risk:$ $\sigma p = \sqrt{(0.5)^2\,17^2 + (0.5)^2\,21^2 + 2(0.5)(0.5)(0.62)(17)(21)}$

$\qquad = \sqrt{72.25 + 110.25 + 110.67}$

$\qquad = \sqrt{293.17}$

$\qquad = 17.12$

Expected return: Rp = (0.5)11 + (0.5)14 = 12.5%

Summary	*Mangeit and Altalk*	*Altalk and Legi*	*Mangeit and Legi*
Risk (standard deviation)	16.81	21.03	17.12
Return	15.5	17.0	12.5

The combination of Mangeit and Legi has a lower return but higher risk than Mangeit and Altalk and is therefore an inefficient portfolio. From the data provided it is not possible to ascertain which of Mangeit and Altalk or Altalk and Legi is a more efficient two-asset portfolio. The portfolio of Mangeit and Altalk has a lower risk and a lower return than the portfolio of Altalk and Legi, but it is not clear whether or not this lower risk and return is more efficient than the higher risk and higher return of Altalk and Legi.

(b)   Phantom plc's strategy should **not** be to purchase the most efficient portfolio of two shares. If the shares are intended as the first stage of a possible acquisition, Phantom should establish which of the three companies it would be best to purchase in order to fulfil its strategic plans, and shares in that company or those companies should be purchased. The investment decision should not be based on the normal criteria for financial investment in shares.

Even if the investment was seeking only financial returns, a decision based on the risk/return characteristics of two-asset portfolios is not recommended. If portfolio theory is to be used, which might be the case if Phantom is not a well-diversified company, the portfolio relationships between all of Phantom's investments and activities should be considered, not just these possible new investments. If Phantom is well diversified, the decision should be based upon the expected return related to the systematic risk of the investments, not the total risk as measured by portfolio theory.

15 MUNXAY PLC

(a) The beta values of each of the four projects may be estimated using:

Correlation coefficient of the project and the market multiplied by the standard deviation of the project's returns, and all divided by the standard deviation of returns from the market, i.e.

$$\text{beta} = \frac{\rho_{im} \sigma_i}{\sigma_m}$$

Project 1: $\dfrac{0.55 \times 15}{13} = 0.635$

Project 2: $\dfrac{0.75 \times 20}{13} = 1.154$

Project 3: $\dfrac{0.84 \times 14}{13} = 0.905$

Project 4: $\dfrac{0.62 \times 18}{13} = 0.858$

The **overall company beta** is the weighted average of the project betas, the weighting being by their proportion of total market value.

The beta of Munxay is estimated to be:

$(0.28 \times 0.635) + (0.17 \times 1.154) + (0.31 \times 0.905) + (0.24 \times 0.858) = 0.860.$

Using the capital asset pricing model, the return that might be expected from Munxay may be estimated to be:

$5\% + (14\% - 5\%)\, 0.860 = 12.74\%.$

The return historically (over the last five years) has been:

$(0.28 \times 10\%) + (0.17 \times 18\%) + (0.31 \times 15\%) + (0.24 \times 13\%) = 13.63\%.$

Assuming these historical returns are expected to continue, the share price of Munxay is likely to be undervalued, as the company is yielding a higher return than expected for its systematic risk.

(b) Reasons why the results may not correctly identify whether the share price is overvalued or undervalued include the following:

(i) The data relating to returns, risk and correlation with the market is historical and is unlikely to repeat itself in the future. Betas may change over time, reflecting changes in the risk of the projects. Ideally the capital asset pricing model (CAPM) should use forecasts of data, but these will also be subject to uncertainty and inaccuracy.

(ii) The market may not be totally efficient and may not accurately reflect information available. Alternatively the market may only be semi-strong form efficient and not have knowledge of the full information known internally within the company.

(iii) CAPM, upon which the evaluation is based relies upon a series of restrictive assumptions, and there is evidence that it might overstate or understate the required returns on high beta and low beta securities, small companies, investments with low P/E ratios, and in certain seasons or on certain days of the week. It is only a single period, single factor model, whereas multi-factor models such as the arbitrage pricing theory might be more accurate.

(iv) The market risk premium may not be constant. The difference between the market return and the risk free rate can vary over time.

16   HASDER PLC

Key answer tip

This question requires understanding of the potential benefits of international diversification, and the ability to analyse risk and return data in order to assist investment decision-making.

(a)   *Tutorial note:*

This question was a compulsory question in the June 2003 examination. If you are not familiar with statistics, and the computation of standard deviations for a two-asset portfolio, or correlation coefficients, this question might provide a useful guide to the level of knowledge that you could be required to show.

Solution

It is useful to estimate the return and risk of the two diversification alternatives before examining in detail the views of the directors. The portfolio return is simply the weighted average of the expected returns of the two elements of the portfolio. The portfolio risk may be estimated using the two-asset portfolio theory equation, based upon the expected risk and return of each alternative.

Europe

	Probability	Return (%)	Expected value of return (%)
Low growth	0.3	7	2.1
Average growth	0.5	12	6.0
Rapid growth	0.2	21	4.2
			12.3

East Asia

	Probability	Return (%)	Expected value of return (%)
Low growth	0.3	2	0.6
Average growth	0.5	30	15.0
Rapid growth	0.2	15	3.0
			18.6

UK

	Probability	Return (%)	Expected value of return (%)
Low growth	0.3	6	1.8
Average growth	0.5	13	6.5
Rapid growth	0.2	17	3.4
			11.7

Portfolio returns

Expected return UK/Europe = (0.7) (11.7) + (0.3) (12.3) = 11.88%.

Expected return UK/East Asia = (0.7) (11.7) + (0.3) (18.6) = 13.77%.

Portfolio risk

The **two-asset portfolio equation** measures the total risk of the portfolio. This will include some specific or unsystematic risk:

Portfolio risk UK/Europe

$$\sqrt{(4.03)^2 (0.7)^2 + (4.86)^2 (0.3)^2 + 2(0.7)(0.3)(17.89)}$$

$$\sigma_p = 4.20$$

Portfolio risk UK/East Asia

$$\sqrt{(4.03)^2 \, (0.7)^2 \, + (12.26)^2 \, (0.3)^2 \, + 2(0.7)(0.3)(31.98)}$$

$\sigma_p = 5.91$

Summary: portfolio expected return and risk

	Portfolio return	*Portfolio risk*	*Coefficient of variation*
UK alone	11.70	4.03	0.344
UK/Europe	11.88	4.20	0.354
UK/East Asia	13.77	5.91	0.429

Tutorial note: The coefficient of variation is the ratio of the portfolio risk to the portfolio expected return. For example, for the UK alone, it is (4.03/11.70) = 0.344.

It is not obvious from these results which investment is best. As risk increases, so does the expected return. The coefficient of variation, which shows the amount of risk per pound of expected return, would suggest that continuing only in the UK is the best course of action. However, the risk/return preferences of Hasder plc would need to be considered before a decision was made, as would strategic and other issues discussed below.

Director A

Director A's view has merit in that the company would be sticking to its core market and core competence. However, overseas investments are not always too risky. Some overseas investments are less risky than UK investments. If total risk is considered, then international diversification can produce risk/return combinations that are not available from investing only in the UK. The benefits of international portfolio diversification might reduce overall risk below that available in the UK, and provide better combinations of risk and return for Hasder. This is the view of **Director B** who correctly states that international diversification will open up new opportunities.

Director C produces no evidence that overseas investments are more expensive than UK investments. In many multinational companies, lower labour and materials costs have been key motives for overseas investments. Such investments have therefore been cheaper than similar UK-based investments.

If the company is investing overseas purely to achieve diversification it is fair to say that in most cases shareholders, by investing in international unit trusts or mutual funds (or something similar) could diversify for themselves easily and more cheaply. However, some countries do not permit such portfolio investments, and their markets are largely segmented from major Western markets. Segmented markets could include the developing markets in East Asia. Hasder might be able to offer risk/return combinations that are valued by its shareholders if it invests in countries where they could not easily invest themselves as part of their share portfolios. Investing in segmented markets might also mean that the systematic risk of investments available to Hasder can be reduced, especially if the segmented markets have a low or negative covariance with returns in the UK market.

International diversification might also result in less variability of cash flows for Hasder, as the markets are not perfectly correlated. This reduction in risk, if recognised by providers of finance, might result in lower financing costs, and a lower cost of capital.

Director D

The summary table above shows that investment in East Asia offers a higher potential return than in Europe, but at significantly higher risk. If the coefficient of variation is considered then it is the least-favoured alternative.

Director E suggests a much higher proportion of investment in East Asia. If 50% – 70% was invested in Asia, and assuming market values reflected these proportions:

Expected portfolio returns

50% East Asia – Expected return UK/East Asia = (0.5) (11.7) + (0.5) (18.6) = 15.15%.

70% East Asia – Expected return UK/East Asia = (0.3) (11.7) + (0.7) (18.6) = 16.53%.

Portfolio risk UK/East Asia

If 50% of portfolio invested in East Asia:

$$\sqrt{(4.03)^2 (0.5)^2 + (12.26)^2 (0.5)^2 + 2(0.5)(0.5)(31.98)}$$

$\sigma_p = 7.59$

If 70% of portfolio invested in East Asia:

$$\sqrt{(4.03)^2 (0.3)^2 + (12.26)^2 (0.7)^2 + 2(0.3)(0.7)(31.98)}$$

$\sigma_p = 9.41$

The potential returns increase significantly, but so too does risk. Unless Hasder is seeking very high returns and is prepared to take the extra risk, there is no evidence to support the view that a higher proportion should be invested in East Asia. Such a move would probably mean closing some UK operations with the resultant problems of redundancy, and would be a major strategic change from the company's current position.

The risk and return evidence should only be part of the decision process. The data itself is likely to be subjective and inaccurate. It is impossible to know with any degree of accuracy what future returns will be, and the assignment of probabilities to different economic states is at best speculative.

Other factors that might influence the decision include:

(i)   How do the investments fit with Hasder's strategic plans?

(ii)   Has a full competitor/market analysis been undertaken?

(iii)   Has the company any strategic reason for favouring Europe or East Asia?

(iv)   Has political risk been considered, and its possible effects built into the cash flows?

(v)   Has foreign exchange risk been included?

(vi)   Are there other investment alternatives?

(vii)   What future options could arise from the investments?

(viii) What are the non-financial implications of the investments?

(ix)   Is total risk the best measure of risk? Should systematic risk be used instead?

(b)   *Tutorial note:* If you do not know how to calculate a correlation coefficient for a two-asset portfolio, you will be unable to answer this part of the question. Study the solution carefully, and try to learn and apply the formula if you are not familiar with it.

Solution

The correlation coefficient may be estimated by:

$$\frac{\text{Covariance A and B}}{\text{Standard deviation A} \times \text{standard deviation B}}$$

(i)   UK/Europe: $\dfrac{17.89}{4.03 \times 4.86} = 0.91$

(ii)   UK/ East Asia: $\dfrac{31.98}{4.03 \times 12.26} = 0.65$

Although the returns between the UK and Europe and the UK and East Asia are both positively correlated, the degree of correlation is much higher for the UK and Europe at 0.91. This means that relatively little risk reduction will take place because of the strong positive relationship between the UK and Europe. This is evidenced by the portfolio standard deviation of 4.20, which is little different from the individual standard deviations.

The lower correlation coefficient of 0.65 between the UK and East Asia allows much more risk reduction from international diversification, with the standard deviation of East Asia alone (12.26) reducing to a much safer 5.91 as part of a portfolio with the UK.

(c)   **Using CAPM**

Required return = Risk free rate + [(Market return – Risk-free rate) × Beta]

Europe:

Required return is 5% + (13% – 5%) 0.85 = 11.8%.

The expected return is 12.3%.

The European investment is expected to provide an abnormally good return for its systematic risk, and on that basis would be recommended.

East Asia:

Required return is 8% + (18% – 8%) 1.32 = 21.2%.

The expected return is 18.6%.

The investment is not providing sufficient return for its systematic risk and would not be recommended.

However, strategic and non-financial factors should also play a major role in the decision process.

ACCA marking scheme		Marks
(a) Estimates of risk and return		
UK return		1
Europe/UK risk and return		3
East Asia/UK risk and return		3
Views of directors		
A		2 – 3
B		2
C		2 – 3
D		1
E including additional calculations		3 – 4
Marks may be credited for relevant overlap		
Other factors relevant to the decision 1 mark for each good point, maximum marks		8
Maximum awarded for part (a)		25
(b) Estimates		3
Discussion		3
(c) Estimates of required return		2
Discussion of implication for the diversification decision		2
Total		35

17   WONPAR PLC

Report

To: The board of directors

From: Accountant

Date: xx/xx/xx

Subject: **The proposed portfolio investment**

Investing internationally can offer opportunities that do not exist in national markets. International investment offers a new portfolio set and new risk-return combinations that are not present in a purely domestic market. A diversified international portfolio may offer greater return and less risk than is possible in a single domestic market, and rational investors should take advantage of the opportunities offered by international portfolio investment.

In general the lower the correlation coefficient between market returns, the greater the benefit that may be achieved from diversifying a portfolio internationally. Such diversification reduces the unsystematic risk of the investment.

If the markets in different countries are not fully integrated, i.e. they do not have total freedom of movement of capital and information, it is possible to reduce the systematic risk as well as the unsystematic risk of an investment through international portfolio diversification.

Director 1 has focused on only one country, France. Although France does have a relatively high expected return and low standard deviation of returns, investing only in France is not likely to eliminate all unsystematic risk, and will not offer the diversification benefits of a portfolio of investments that encompasses many countries. In order to achieve the risk-return combination shown, Wonpar would have to invest in a broad range of French securities which have the same expected portfolio risk and return as the French market, or index-tracking French unit trusts. There is no guarantee that historical relationships of risk and return will repeat themselves. The measure of risk used by Director 1, the standard deviation of expected returns, considers total risk. There is no reason why a portfolio of £5 million should not be well diversified, in which case Wonpar should focus upon the systematic risk of the investment and not the total risk.

Director 2 has identified the low correlation between the UK and Singapore markets, which offers good diversification possibilities. However, it would be better not to focus on one country, but instead to have a portfolio of investments that encompasses many different countries. This would provide more opportunity for the reduction of both unsystematic and systematic risk, and a diversified international portfolio would involve less foreign exchange risk or political risk than investing in a single country.

18   DELTA HEDGE (UNIGLOW)

(a)   **Delta** measures the change in the option price (premium) as the value of the underlying share moves by 1%.

$$\text{Delta} = \frac{\text{change in the price of the option}}{\text{change in the price of the underlying share}}$$

It is measured by N(d1) in the Black-Scholes option pricing model.

As the share price falls, delta falls towards zero. Delta may be used to construct a risk-free hedge position, whereby overall wealth will not change with small changes in share price.

Theta measures the change in the option price as the time to expiry increases. The longer the time to expiry of an option, the greater its value. Theta may be used to estimate by how much the value of an option will fall as time to expiry shortens.

Vega measures the change in option price as a result of a 1% change in the share price volatility or variance. As volatility increases, the value of both call and put options increases.

All three are of use to treasury managers when hedging their investments. As their values approach zero the hedged position will become unaffected by changes in these variables (share price, time to expiry and share price volatility).

(b) (i) N(d1) is required in order to determine the delta hedge.

$$d1 = \frac{\ln(200/220) + 0.06(0.25)}{0.5\sqrt{0.25}} + 0.5(0.5)\sqrt{0.25}$$

$$= \frac{-0.09531 + 0.015}{0.25} + 0.125$$

$$= -0.32124 + 0.125$$

$$= -0.19624$$

From normal distribution tables:

N(d1) = 0.5 − 0.0778 = 0.4222

Delta = 0.4222

Tutorial note:

The formula for d1 is given in the formula sheet in the examination, but you need to understand what the variables in the formula are, and how to do the calculation. It starts with the natural logarithm (ln) of (200/220), i.e. the share price divided by the exercise price for the call option. You need a calculator to work out natural logarithms, and ln (200/220) = ln 0.909091 = − 0.09531. Check all the other items in the formula carefully. Remember that T, the time to expiry, is three months = 0.25 years.

You should be able to calculate that d1 = − 0.19624. From the standard normal distribution table, 0.19624 standard deviations is above the 0.19 value (0.0753) but below the 0.20 value (0.0793). Interpolating, we get a value for 1.19624 of: [0.0753 + (624/1000) (0.0793 − 0.0753)] = 0.0778. This is the figure in the answer above.

d1 is less than 0, so subtract 0.0778 from 0.5.

Solution continued

In order to protect against a fall in Uniglow's share price, the easiest hedge would be to write (sell) options on Uniglow's shares. A delta of 0.4222 means that the relevant hedge ratio is:

$$\frac{1}{0.4222} = 2.368$$

In other words, a delta hedge would involve writing 2.368 options for every 1 share in the portfolio.

To hedge 100,000 shares (when option contracts are for 1,000 shares each):

$$\frac{100,000 \times 2.368}{1,000} = 237 \text{ options on Uniglow's shares need to be written.}$$

(ii)   A hedge such is this is only valid for a **small change** in the underlying share price. As the share price alters the option delta will alter and the hedge will need to be periodically rebalanced.

ACCA marking scheme				Marks
(a)	Delta, theta, vega: 1–2 marks for each. 2 only if an excellent answer For maximum marks importance must be discussed Maximum			5
(b)	(i)	N(d1) Delta hedge		4 $\underline{4}$ $\underline{8}$
	(ii)	Relevant comment – especially small movements		$\underline{2}$
Total				$\underline{\underline{15}}$

19   BLACK-SCHOLES (AVT)

(a)   Option prices in the basics Black-Scholes model relating to European options are determined by the following five factors:

(i)   The spot price of the underlying security

(ii)   The exercise price of the option

(iii)   The time until expiry of the option

(iv)   The risk of the option, as normally measured by the historic volatility of the return on the underlying security

(v)   The risk free rate of interest within the economy

A decrease in the value of each of these factors will have the following effect:

(i)   *The spot price.* As the spot price falls the call option will become less valuable as the exercise of the option will result in the purchase of a security of lower value than previously.

(ii)   *The exercise price.* The lower the exercise price, the greater the value of a call option as there is more potential for profit upon exercising the option.

(iii)   *The time until expiry of the option.* A reduction in the time to expiry of the option will reduce the value of the option, as the time value element of the option price is reduced.

(iv)   *The risk of the option.* A reduction in risk will reduce the value of a call option. This is because the decrease in variance reduces the chance that the security price will lie within the tail of the distribution (i.e. above the exercise price) of the share price when the option expires.

(v)   *The risk free rate.* A reduction in the risk free rate will decrease the value of the call option because the money saved by purchasing the call option rather than the underlying security is reduced. If an option is purchased the cash saved could be invested at the risk free rate. A reduction in the risk free rate makes purchasing the call option relatively unattractive and reduces the option price.

(b)   (i)   The existing bonus scheme, based on earnings per share, has the advantage that earnings per share are easily measured. However, this scheme suffers from the problems of all accounting based measures in that it may be influenced by the accounting policies selected, and is not based on the economic cash flows of the company, which are likely to influence the share price. Maximisation of earnings per share is not the same as maximisation of share price and shareholder wealth.

The advantage of the share option scheme is that, in theory, it will motivate managers to improve the share price as they will directly benefit from this. This should achieve goal congruence with shareholders who are also seeking to maximise the share price. However, the extent to which their total remuneration is influenced by the incentive scheme may influence managers' decisions and their motivation to maximise share price. It is also debatable how much middle managers can directly influence the share price, and whether or not they are aware of which of their decisions will have the desired influence. A further problem of share option schemes is that share prices frequently move for reasons that are nothing to do with the actions of managers, (e.g. lower interest rates will normally result in higher share prices). Ideally managers should be rewarded for their contribution to share price increases, but this is very difficult to measure.

(ii)   **Using the Black-Scholes model for European-style call options**:

A dividend payment is due during the option period. The share price, Ps, should therefore be reduced by the present value of this expected dividend. The dividend per share has remained constant for three years. It is assumed that it will be constant in the next year.

The present value of the dividend (discounted at the risk free rate) is:

$$\frac{25}{1.06} = 23.58 \text{ pence}$$

The share price, Ps, is therefore estimated to be $610 - 23.58 = 586.42$ pence.

Using the Black-Scholes model, the call price = Ps N(d1)-Xe-rT N(d2)

$$d_1 = \frac{\ln(586.42 / 500) + 0.06(1)}{0.38\sqrt{1}} + 0.5(0.38)\sqrt{1}$$

$$= \frac{\ln(1.17284) + 0.06}{0.38} + 0.5(0.38)1$$

$$= \frac{0.1594 + 0.06}{0.38} + 0.19$$

$$= 0.7674. \text{ (Round this to 0.77.)}$$

$$d_2 = d_1 - \sigma\sqrt{T} = 0.7674 - 0.38 = 0.3874$$

(Round this to 0.39.)

Tutorial note: You might have had some difficulty with these formulae, which are given in the formula sheet in the examination. Here, Ps = 586.42 and X is the option exercise price of 500. The term 'ln' stands for the natural log of something, which is the log of the constant value. It is therefore sometimes written as log e. To obtain the value of log e (586.42/500), you need a calculator that can do these computations. Here log e of 1.17284 is + 0.1594.

The risk-free interest rate r is 0.06 and the time period of 1 year means that $T = 1$. The standard deviation of the share price, σ, is 0.38. A number to the power 0.5 means the square root of that number.

Having calculated d1, the calculation of d2 is relatively straightforward, using the formula in the formula sheet for the examination.

Solution continued

The next step is to calculate $N(d_1)$ and $N(d_2)$. For 0.77 standard deviations, the probability is 0.2794. For 0.39 standard deviations, the probability is 0.1517. The values of d1 and d2 are both positive, so we add 0.5.

From normal distribution tables:

$$N(d_1) = 0.5 + 0.2794 = 0.7794$$

$$N(d_2) = 0.5 + 0.1517 = 0.6517$$

Inputting this data into the call option price formula $= Ps\, N(d_1) - Xe^{-rT}\, N(d_2)$

$$\text{Call price} = 586.42(0.7794) - \frac{500(0.6517)}{e^{(0.06)(1)}}$$

$$= \quad 457.06 - (325.85/1.062)$$

$$= \quad 457.06 - 306.83 = 150.23 \text{ pence}$$

Tutorial note: The value of e to the minus 0.06 is the same as 1 divided by e to the power of 0.06. You need a calculator to compute this value. e to the power 0.06 is 1.062.

The expected option call price is 150.23 pence per share, giving a current option value of 5,000 x 150.23 pence = £7,511.

Conclusion

The options are currently in the money and are likely to be attractive to managers as they have an expected value in excess of the bonuses that are currently paid. However, the risk to managers of the two schemes differs and this might influence managerial preferences, depending upon individual managers attitudes to risk. The Black-Scholes model assumes that the volatility of the share price over the past year will continue for the coming year. This is very unlikely. A different volatility will greatly influence the value of the option at the expiry date.

(iii) (1) AVT plc should not agree to grant the manager put options. The holder of a put option, which allows a share to be sold at a fixed price, would benefit its holder more the further the price of the share fell below the exercise price of the option. As far as the options are concerned it would be in the manager's interest to take decisions that reduced the company's share price, rather than increased it!

(2) The put option price may be found from the put-call parity equation.

$$Pp = Pc - Ps + X\, e^{-rT}$$

$$e^{-rT} = 1.062 \text{ (calculated earlier in this solution)}$$

$$Pp = 150.23 - 586.42 + 500/1.062$$

$$= 150.23 - 586.42 + 470.81$$

$$= 34.62 \text{ pence}$$

The manager is incorrect. Put options are not more valuable than call options in this situation.

Tutorial note: Your answer may differ slightly due to rounding differences in the calculations.

ACCA marking scheme		
		Marks
(a) One mark for each correct movement of the option price determinants. One extra mark if all determinants are correctly identified.		6
(b) (i) Advantages/problems of:		
Existing bonus scheme		2–3
Share option scheme		3–4
		6
(ii) Adjustment of Ps for the dividend		2–3
Estimate of call price		6–7
Conclusion		2
		11
(iii) 1 Correction conclusion with reason		3
2 Estimate of put price and comment		4
Total		30

20 CHANCIT PLC

(a) Rational investors would normally require increased return when taking increased risk. The expected returns and risks of the two divisions' managers are:

Division 1

Expected NPV	*Risk (σ)*	*Expected return (£m)*
£1,000,000 with certainty	0	1.00
80% chance of £1.3m, 20% chance of £700,000	0.24	1.18
60% chance of £1.8m, 40% chance of £300,000	0.74	1.20
40% chance of £2.5m, 60% chance of £100,000	1.08	1.06
20% chance of £3.0m, 80% chance of (£100,000)	1.24	0.52
10% chance of £4.0m, 90% chance of (£200,000)	1.26	0.22

Division 2

The missing risk for the two probability combinations may be estimated as follows:

Probability	*Return(£m)*	*Expected return*	*(Return deviation)^2 ×probability*
0.35	3.0	1.0551	1.421
0.65	(0.1)	(0.065)	0.765
		0.985	variance = 2.186
			σ = 1.48

Tutorial note: Note that the deviation is the difference between the expected return and the predicted uncertain return.

Probability	*Return(£m)*	*Expected return*	*(Return deviation)^2 ×probability*
0.20	4.0	0.80	2.258
0.80	(0.2)	(0.16)	0.564
		0.64	variance = 2.822
			σ = 1.68

Expected NPV	Risk (6)	Expected return (£m)
£1,000,000 with certainty	0	1.00
85% chance of £1.3m, 15% chance of £700,000	0.21	1.21
75% chance of £1.8m, 25% chance of £300,000	0.65	1.43
50% chance of £2.5m, 50% chance of £100,000	1.20	1.30
35% chance of £3.0m, 65% chance of (£100,000)	1.48	0.99
20% chance of £4.0m, 80% chance of (£200,000)	1.68	0.64

If these data correctly reflect risk/return combinations of equal satisfaction (utility) they show unusual attitudes towards high risk. Initially there is the expected relationship between increased risks and increased returns. However, it appears that the divisions' managers would be willing to take unusually high risks in order to gain the possible opportunity of earning very high returns, even if the chance of achieving such returns is relatively low. There is in fact an inverse relationship between risk and return where possible best case returns are at or above £2,500,000.

If this attitude towards risk and return is reflected in the managers' investment decisions for the company, it could lead to them selecting relatively risky projects in order to try to achieve a very high return. Such projects would not provide the best possible expected NPV for the company.

(b) Possible actions are:

(i) Provide additional training for the managers in capital investment decision-making.

(ii) Take more decisions centrally. Reduce the local autonomy of managers.

(iii) Replace the managers

(iv) Do nothing, as the board may not consider the analysis to be relevant.

(c) The analysis focuses upon the standard deviation as the measure of risk. This is a measure of total risk, whereas it is often argued that the relevant risk in decision-making is the systematic risk of the investment. The analysis might have been improved by trying to measure managers' attitudes to return and systematic risk.

Analyses such as this might be criticised for presenting only hypothetical opportunities and for being removed from the actual pressures of decision-making. Managers might react differently when there is real money at stake.

ACCA marking scheme		Marks
(a)	Expected returns	2
	Missing risk data	3
	Discussion	3
		8
(b)	Possible actions – 1 mark for each sensible suggestion.	3
(c)	Reward especially discussion of relevant risk, and real world effects	4
Total		15

21   PENSION FUND

Key answer tips

Part (a) asks for alpha values to be calculated. This is a standard calculation for shares but you need to follow the instructions carefully to get a result for the bonds.

Part (b) involves calculating a weighted average beta and the corresponding required return. Key here is making the assumption that the Government bonds have a beta of zero.

Part (c) involves the usual criticisms of CAPM.

(a)   A positive abnormal return will exist if the expected return from a security is higher than the required return. For shares this may be established by using the capital asset pricing model (CAPM).

The betas of the individual shares may be found using:

$$\text{Beta} = \frac{\text{correlation coefficient} \times \text{investment standard deviation}}{\text{market standard deviation}}$$

Flitter $\dfrac{0.76 \times 25}{15} = 1.27$

Polgin $\dfrac{0.54 \times 18}{15} = 0.65$

Scruntor $\dfrac{0.63 \times 35}{15} = 1.47$

Using the CAPM, required return = Rf + (Rm – Rf) beta

	Required return		Expected return	Alpha
Flitter	4% + (10.5% – 4%) 1.27 =	12.26%	11%.	(1.26%)
Polgin	4% + (10.5% – 4%) 0.65 =	8.22%	9.5%	1.28%
Scruntor	4% + (10.5% – 4%) 1.47 =	13.56%	13.5%	(0.06%)

For the bonds the relative durations are:

UK Government $\dfrac{1.5}{75} = 0.20$

Supragow $\dfrac{8.6}{7.5} = 1.15$

Teffon $\dfrac{14.2}{7.5} = 1.89$

	Required return	Expected return	Alpha
UK Government	4% + (5.8% – 4%) 0.20 = 4.36%	4.5%	0.14%
Supragow	4% + (5.8% – 4%) 1.15 = 6.07%	5.3%	(0.77)%
Teffon	4% + (5.8% – 4%) 1.89 = 7.40%	7.2%	(0.20)%

If these data are accurate, the shares of Polgin and the UK Government bond offer a positive abnormal return.

(b)   The beta of the revised portfolio is the weighted average of the betas of the components of the portfolio. The UK Government bond is virtually risk free and is assumed to have a beta of 0. As the pension fund wishes to keep the maximum possible investment in shares, £60 million will be invested in the shares of Polgin, and £40 million in bonds.

The new portfolio beta is: $\dfrac{1{,}000(0.62) + 60(0.65) + 40(0)}{1{,}100} = 0.599$

The required portfolio return is 4% + (10.5% – 4%) 0.599 = 7.89%

(c)   The active strategy relies upon the pension fund managers being able to regularly correctly identify underpriced securities. The implication is that the securities markets are not continuously efficient, and that excess returns can be earned by trading in mispriced securities. Markets are certainly not perfectly efficient, but whether or not mispriced securities can be regularly found that will lead to an abnormal return, after any administrative and transactions costs, is debatable.

A policy of selecting only mispriced securities might mean that the portfolio risk and return are not consistent with the objectives of the portfolio or desire of the investment clients.

The strategy is based upon using the capital asset pricing model, and presumes that the model presents an accurate measure of the required returns from securities. The CAPM, however, is based upon a number of unrealistic assumptions, such as a perfect capital market exists, borrowing and lending can take place at the risk free rate, investors have the same expectations about risk and return, investors are well diversified, and all investors consider only the same single time period. It also states that systematic risk is the only relevant measure of risk. It is likely that multi-factor models such as the arbitrage pricing theory offer better explanations of the relation between risk and return. Accurate data input for elements of the CAPM such as the market return and relevant betas are difficult to estimate, and the CAPM has empirical anomalies, for example it appears to overstate the required return on high beta securities and understate the required return on low beta securities.

ACCA marking scheme			
			Marks
(a)	Shares		3–4
	Bonds		3–4
			—
		Maximum	7
(b)	Portfolio beta		2
	Return		1
			—
			3
(c)	Reward sensible discussion of theoretical and practical issues	Maximum	5
			—
Total			15

22   DAYLON PLC

Key answer tips

Once you have identified that you have to value a put option with an exercise price of 342 pence, the application of Black-Scholes and put-call parity is reasonably straightforward.

In part (b) ensure you discuss your points by relating them to the specific circumstances of Daylon.

(a)   The investment bank is offering to sell to Daylon plc an option to sell Mondglobe ordinary shares at a price no worse than 5% below the current market price of 360 pence. This is a put option on Mondglobe shares at a price of 342 pence. The Black-Scholes option pricing model may be used to estimate whether or not the option price is a fair price. The value of a put option may be found by first estimating the value of a call option and then using the put-call parity theorem.

Basic data:

Share price 360 pence

Exercise price 342 pence

Risk free rate 4% (0.04)

Volatility is measured by the standard deviation. The variance is 169% therefore the standard deviation, σ is 13% (0.13)

The relevant period is six months (0.5)

Using call price = $PsN(d_1) - Xe^{-rT} N(d_2)$

$$d_1 = \frac{\ln(360/342 + .04\,(0.5))}{.13\,(0.5)^{.5}} + 0.5\,(0.13)\,(0.5)^{.5}$$

$$= 0.8218$$

$$d_2 = d_1 - \sigma\,(T)^{0.5} = 0.8218 - 0.0919 = 0.7299$$

From normal distribution tables:

$N(d1) = 0.5 + 0.2944 = 0.7944$

$N(d2) = 0.5 + 0.2673 = 0.7673$

Inputting data into call price = $Ps\,N(d1) - Xe^{-rT} N(d_2)$

$$\text{Call price} = 360\,(0.7944) - \frac{342(0.7673)}{e^{(0.4)\,(0.5)}}$$

$$= 285.98 - 257.22 = 28.76 \text{ pence}$$

The value of a put option on a share may be estimated using the put-call parity theorem, $P^P = P^C - P^S + Xe^{-rT}$

The option exercise price is 342 pence, and the call option price has been estimated to be 28.76 pence.

Therefore $P^P = 28.76 - 360 + 342e^{-(0.04)(0.5)}$

Solving, $P^P = 3.99$ pence

Daylon's holding of 5,550,000 shares multiplied by the put option price gives a fair option price according to the Black-Scholes model of £221,445.

If the data is correct then the investment bank is charging £28,555 more than the theoretical fair value for the put option.

(b)   Relevant factors that might influence the decision include:

   (i)   The Black-Scholes model is not a perfect estimator of option prices. For example it relies upon the assumption that the price volatility will continue for the relevant future period. In reality price volatility might be quite different.

   (ii)   The option is for only a six month period. If Daylon wishes to protect against a price fall after that date then further options will be necessary at additional cost.

   (iii)   There may be tax implications if any gains are made from the option.

   (iv)   There might be cheaper alternatives than the over the counter option. For example using stock index futures with the hedge size adjusted for Mondglobe's beta, or the use of a collar option which would reduce the premium costs, but would limit any gains if Mondglobe's share price was to increase.

   (v)   The company might consider hedging the whole portfolio, not just the part represented by Mondglobe's shares.

ACCA marking scheme		Marks
(a)	Estimate of the put option price	
	Call option price	6
	Put option price	3
	Conclusion	1
		___
	Reward technique, and reasonable attempts to estimate the call option first and then use put-call parity	10
(b)	1–2 marks for each point. Look especially for problems of Black-Scholes, alternative hedges, comments about the total portfolio and the limited time horizon.	
	max	5
		___
Total		15
		___

COST OF CAPITAL AND RISK ANALYSIS

23 BENTRAS

(a) *Tutorial note:* The optimal WACC is the minimum WACC achievable. The approach in the solution is to find the cost of equity and then the WACC at different levels of gearing. To calculate the cost of equity at different levels of gearing, we must first calculate the geared beta for that level of gearing, and use the geared beta in the CAPM formula to derive the cost of equity. Having found the cost of equity, and given the cost of debt as stated in the question, we can calculate the WACC at each gearing level.

Assuming all market risk is borne by equity holders (i.e. the beta of debt is zero), the relationship between the beta of geared and ungeared equity is:

$$\text{Geared beta} = \text{Ungeared beta} \times \frac{E + D(1-t)}{E}$$

The cost of equity and weighted average cost of capital may be estimated for various levels of gearing.

The cost of equity is calculated using CAPM, $ke = Rf + (Rm - Rf) \text{ beta}$.

With 100% equity, the cost of equity (= the weighted average cost of capital) is:

$6\% + (14\% - 6\%)\,0.85 = 12.8\%$.

Gearing	Geared beta		Cost of equity
10% debt	$0.85 \times \dfrac{90 + 10\,(1-0.30)}{90}$	$= 0.916$	13.33%
20% debt	$0.85 \times \dfrac{80 + 20\,(1-0.30)}{80}$	$= 0.999$	13.99%
30% debt	$0.85 \times \dfrac{70 + 30\,(1-0.30)}{70}$	$= 1.105$	14.84%
40% debt	$0.85 \times \dfrac{60 + 40\,(1-0.30)}{60}$	$= 1.247$	15.97%
50% debt	$0.85 \times \dfrac{50 + 50\,(1-0.30)}{50}$	$= 1.445$	17.56%

$$\text{WACC} = k_e \frac{E}{E+D} + k_d(1-t)\frac{D}{E+D}$$

$$= 13.33\%(0.9) + 6.5\%(1 - 0.3)(0.1) = 12.45\%$$

This calculation may be repeated to produce the following table:

Gearing (% debt)		WACC
10	13.33%(0.9) + 6.5%(1 – 0.3)(0.1)	12.45%
20	13.99%(0.8) + 7.1%(1 – 0.3)(0.2)	12.19%
30	14.84%(0.7) + 7.8%(1 – 0.3)(0.3)	12.03%
40	15.97%(0.6) + 7.8%(1 – 0.3)(0.4)	11.96%
50	17.56%(0.5) + 7.8%(1 – 0.3)(0.5)	12.28%

(Calculations beyond 50% are not needed, as it is obvious that the minimum cost capital structure is below 50%).

Purely on the basis of these estimates the optimal capital structure for the company is 60% equity, 40% debt.

(b) 60% equity and 40% debt is not necessarily the capital structure that the company should adopt.

The above model does not take account of **significant costs that might exist at high levels of gearing**. These include:

(i) **Direct and indirect bankruptcy costs**. Direct bankruptcy costs refer to the legal and associated costs in reorganising a failed company. Indirect costs occur in financially distressed companies and can have an effect on sales, supplier and employee relationships, and may cause distortions in investment strategies due to conflicts of interest between shareholders and debt holders.

(ii) **Agency costs** involved in monitoring and controlling the actions of managers.

(iii) **Tax exhaustion**. The benefit of tax relief on interest payments will be lost if, at a certain level of gearing, the company no longer has taxable income against which to offset the tax relief.

Additionally:

(i) The financing mix the company uses may affect operating income. This is assumed not to be the case in the model used in part (a).

(ii) 60% equity, 40% debt implies a BBB credit rating, the minimum investment grade rating. Institutional investors, who are likely to be the company's major shareholders, may not like such a low rating, and may sell the company's shares. Some institutional investors will not invest below an A rating.

(iii) Some providers of finance may ration or refuse additional credit when gearing is high.

(iv) Managers may not allow gearing to become high as this might increase the risk of them losing their jobs if the company experiences financial distress.

(v) Companies may choose to follow other theories of capital structure such as the Pecking Order Theory.

ACCA marking scheme		Marks
(a)	Estimates of ke	4
	Estimates of WACC	3
	Conclusion	1
		8
(b)	1-2 marks for each good point. 2 marks only if good explanation is included	7
Total		15

24   NETRA PLC

Key answer tips

The examiner has used the assumptions of the Modligliani and Miller model as a framework for his answer here. This approach can be used whenever you are asked to comment upon the usefulness/limitations/relevance of information produced from a theoretical model.

(a)   Assuming that all earnings are paid out as dividends, the current cost of equity (and overall cost of capital) is total earnings divided by the market value of the company's shares:

	£000
EBIT	2,500
Taxation	825
Earnings = dividends	1,675

The market value of equity is two million shares × 420 pence per share = £8.4 million.

$$Ke = \frac{£1,675,000}{£8,400,000} = 19.94\%$$

If equity is replaced by debt the value of the company will increase.

V geared = V ungeared + Dt (Amount of debt × tax rate)

With £2 million debt

V geared = 8,400 + (2,000 x 0.33) = 9,060.

	£000
Total value of the company	9,060
Market value of debt	2,000
Value of equity	7,060

With £4 million debt

V geared = 8,400 + (4,000 x 0.33) = 9,720

	£000
Total value of the company	9,720
Market value of debt	4,000
Value of equity	5,720

Cost of equity	*£2 million debt*	*£4 million debt*
	£000	£000
EBIT	2,500	2,500
Interest	200	400
	2,300	2,100
Taxation (33%)	759	693
Earnings/dividends	1,541	1,407
Cost of equity Ke =	1,541/7,060	1,407/5,720
	= 21.83%	= 24.60%

WACC

£2 million debt:

$$WACC = 21.83 \times \frac{7,060}{9,060} + 10\,(1 - 0.33)\,\frac{2,000}{9,060}$$

$$= 18.49\%$$

£4 million debt:

$$WACC = 24.60 \times \frac{5,720}{9,720} + 10\,(1-0.33)\,\frac{4,000}{9,720}$$

$$= 17.23\%$$

Alternative method of calculation

Or alternatively using $WACC = Ke_u\left(1-\dfrac{Dt}{E+D}\right)$

£2 million debt:

$$WACC = 19.94\left(1-\frac{2,000 \times 0.33}{7,060+2,000}\right) = 18.49\%$$

£4 million debt:

$$WACC = 19.94\left(1-\frac{4,000 \times 0.33}{5,720+4,000}\right) = 17.23\%$$

The higher the level of gearing, the lower the cost of capital becomes, due to the benefit from tax relief on interest payments.

(b) As debt is introduced into the capital structure it is likely that the cost of capital will initially fall. However, the estimates produced in (a) may not be accurate because:

(i) They rely on the assumptions of the Modigliani-Miller (MM) model, many of which are unrealistic such as the capital market is perfectly efficient, debt is risk free, information is costless and readily available, there are no transactions costs, investors are rational and make the same forecasts about the performance of companies, and investors and companies can borrow at the risk free rate.

(ii) Only corporate taxation is considered and not the impact of other forms of taxation including personal taxation.

(iii) MM assumed that debt is permanent. Netra's debt has a five-year time horizon.

(iv) The estimates ignore possible costs that might be incurred as gearing increases, which would reduce share price and increase the cost of equity (and possibly debt). These include bankruptcy costs, agency costs, and tax exhaustion.

(v) Inaccuracies exist in the measurement of the data required for the model.

25 CONVERTIBLE DEBENTURE

(a) **Share price falls to 470**

If interest rates do not change the lowest value that the convertible debenture is likely to have during the next two months is its value as straight debt. Any value above this will be value attributed to the conversion option that exists, and will give a higher conversion price per share.

The expected value as straight debt is

$£8 \times 3.240^1 =$	25.92
$£100 \times 0.708 =$	70.80
	96.72

[1]3.240 is the present value of an annuity of £1 for four years at 9%, the company's cost of straight debt.

This would give a conversion price per share of $\dfrac{£96.72}{20} = 484$ pence.

If the market falls to 470 pence, no conversion will be expected, and the market value of the debentures will be £20 million (nominal) × 0.9672 = £19.344 million.

Assuming the cost of equity remains unchanged, as the equity has the same systematic risk as the market, the cost of equity is estimated to be 15%. The market value of equity would fall to $£180m \times \dfrac{470}{520} = £162.69m$

The existing market value of debt is:

	£m
Convertible debenture (£20 million × 1.10)	22.0
Other debt	23.0
	45.0

If conversion does not occur the value of the convertible debentures will fall and the new value of debt is then expected to be:

£23m + £19.344m = £42.344m.

The value of the company, equity + debt (in £ million), will be.

162.69 + 42.344 = 205.034.

The after-tax weighted average cost of capital is then estimated to be:

$$\dfrac{162.69}{205.034} \times 15\% + \dfrac{42.344}{205.034} \times 9\% \,(1-0.3) = 13.20\%$$

(b) **Share price rises to 570**

If the market price in two months is 570 pence then conversion is likely. At the current price of debt of £110, the conversion price would be £110/20 shares = 550 pence.

If conversion occurs, $\dfrac{£20,000,000}{£100}$ or 200,000 £100 debentures will be converted.

This will lead to the issue of 200,000 × 20 or 4 million new shares, with an assumed market value of 4m × 570 pence or £22.8 million. (In reality the conversion may lead to a dilution in earnings per share and the price of the shares could fall to lower than 570 pence.)

The total value of equity is then expected to be $\dfrac{570}{520} \times £180m + £22.8m = £220.11m.$

The market value of debt will then be the value of the remaining debt, which is £23 million.

The total market value of the company, equity + debt, will be (220.11 + 23.0) £243.11 million.

With conversion, the after tax weighted average cost of capital is estimated to be:

$$\dfrac{220.11}{243.11} \times 15\% + \dfrac{23}{243.11} \times 9\%(1-0.3) = 14.18\%$$

The weighted average cost of capital is expected to increase because of the higher proportion of relatively expensive equity in the capital structure. The cost of equity and cost of debt have been assumed to remain unchanged. Even if the share price changes the cost of equity might remain unchanged, the price changes being caused directly by general market movements and the beta remaining at one. However, the change in gearing upon conversion could influence both the cost of debt and cost of equity as the risk to both shareholders and bondholders is likely to be reduced with a lower level of gearing.

26 KULPAR

Key answer tips

This question examines the impact of charging capital structure on a company's cost of capital and value. It is easy to lose your way in the calculations. Try to keep a clearly organised, step-by-step approach.

(a) The company's existing gearing is £458 million equity to £305 million debt, or 60% equity 40% debt.

Cost of equity

A change in gearing will result in a change in the equity beta. Assuming the beta of debt is zero, the equity beta with no gearing may be estimated by:

$$\text{Beta ungeared} = \text{beta geared} \times \frac{E}{E + D(1-t)} \text{ or } 1.4 \times \frac{60}{60 + 40(1-0.3)} = 0.9545$$

If gearing was 80% equity, 20% debt by market values

The 'ungeared' beta may be 'regeared' to find the new equity beta:

$$\text{Beta geared} = \text{beta ungeared} \times \frac{E + D(1-t)}{E} \text{ or } 0.9545 \times \frac{80 + 20(1-0.3)}{80} = 1.122$$

Using CAPM to obtain the *cost of equity*:

$$ke = Rf + (Rm - Rf) \text{ beta or } 5.5\% + (14\% - 5.5\%) \, 1.122 = 15.04\%$$

If gearing was 40% equity, 60% debt by market values

This may be 'regeared' to find the new equity beta:

$$\text{Beta geared} = \text{beta ungeared} \times \frac{E + D(1-t)}{E}$$

$$= 0.9545 \times \frac{40 + 60(1-0.3)}{40} = 1.957$$

Using CAPM to obtain the *cost of equity*:

$$ke = Rf + (Rm - Rf) \text{ beta or } 5.5\% + (14\% - 5.5\%) \, 1.957 = 22.13\%.$$

Cost of debt

The cost of debt depends on interest cover and the credit rating. (The figures below assume that the total market value of the company, equity plus debt, will be approximately (458 + 305) = 763 million, regardless of the gearing level.)

	80%E, 20%D		40%E, 60%D	
Net operating income	110		110	
Depreciation	20		20	
EBIT	90		90	
Interest	12.21	(£152.6m debt)	50.36	(£457.8m debt)
Interest cover	7.37		1.79	
Cost of debt	8.0%	(AA rating)	11.0%	(BB rating)

The interest payable is found by examining different interest rate and interest cover possibilities.

80% equity 20% debt must fall into the AA rating. (If the interest rate was 9%, interest would be £ 13.73 million and cover 6.55 times, still AA rating cover.)

40% equity, 60% debt must fall into the BB rating. (If the interest rate was 9%, interest would be £41.20 million and cover 2.18 times, still BB rating cover.)

Weighted average cost of capital

At 80% equity, 20% debt

WACC = 15.04% × 0.80 + 8.0% (1 – 0.3) 0.20 = 13.15%

At 40% equity, 60% debt

WACC = 22.13% × 0.40 + 11.0% (1 – 0.3) 0.60 = 13.47%.

The existing cost of equity is: 5.5% + (14% – 5.5%) 1.4 = 17.4%

The **existing WACC** is 17.4% × 0.60 + 9% (1 – 0.3) 0.40 = 12.96%.

(*Note:* It is assumed that the existing pre-tax cost of debt is 9% (A credit rating) since the current interest cover is 90/22 = 4.1 times.)

The two alternative capital structures would be expected to increase the cost of capital from its current level.

Corporate value

Using the suggested equation:

Company free cash flow (in £ million) = 90 (1 – 0.3) + 20 – 20 = 63.

The growth rate is unknown. However existing corporate value, company cash flow and weighted average cost of capital are known, allowing the growth rate to be estimated with the dividend growth model.

$$763 = \frac{63\,(1+g)}{0.1296 - g}$$

Solving:

763 (0.1296 – g) = 63 (1 + g)

98.88 – 763g = 63 + 63g

826g = 35.88

g = 0.043 or 4.3%.

Assuming this growth rate remains unchanged, corporate value with different gearing levels is estimated to be:

80% equity, 20% debt: $\dfrac{63(1+0.043)}{0.1315-0.043} = £742m$

40% equity, 60% debt: $\dfrac{63(1+0.043)}{0.1347-0.043} = £717m$

Altering the capital structure to either of the two suggested levels is expected to reduce corporate value from its current level of £763 million. It is recommended that the capital structure is kept at its current level of 60% equity, 40% debt.

(b)   The estimates of corporate value are only approximations and may be incorrect for many reasons including:

(i)   The assumption of constant growth may be incorrect.

(ii)   Corporate value in this model is sensitive to the level of capital spending which might alter considerably from period to period.

(iii) The model ignores the cash flow impact of any changes in working capital.

(iv)   Corporate cash flow would be better estimated by:

(EBIT – depreciation)(1 – t) + depreciation – capital spending + or – change in working capital

(v)   Any change in gearing would involve transactions costs as shares were repurchased or issued, and debt was issued or redeemed.

(vi)   Repurchases of shares might not be possible at the current market price.

(vii)   The corporate tax rate might change.

(viii) Credit rating agencies use other factors in addition to interest cover when deciding a company's rating, such as the quality of the company's management or the volatility of a company's cash flows.

(ix)   Operating cash flow might itself be affected by a change in debt rating.

(x)   The valuation does not take account of any additional costs that might exist at high levels of gearing such as direct and indirect bankruptcy costs.

(xi)   Tax exhaustion might exist at high gearing levels whereby the company can no longer benefit from tax relief on interest paid on incremental debt issues.

(xii)   Corporate debt is not risk free and does not have a beta of zero. A positive beta will alter the cost of capital estimates.

27   BOND PRICES

Tutorial note: Increasingly, the examiner appears to expect examination candidates to show a knowledge and understanding of statistics in financial arithmetic. This question is a good example. Set in June 2003, part (b) requires candidates to calculate the present value of an annuity over 30 time periods, at a cost of capital that is not a whole number. The only reliable way to do this is to apply the formula for the present value of an annuity. This is:

$$\text{Present value} = \frac{A}{r}\left(1 - \frac{1}{(1+r)^n}\right)$$

where A is the annuity (regular cash flow amount

r is the cost of capital

n is the number of cash flows.

If you did not know his formula, try to learn it, and then try using it to answer part (b) of the question.

Solution

(a)   A **yield curve** may be upward-sloping because of:

(i)   **Future expectations**. If future short-term interest rates are expected to increase then the yield curve will be upward sloping. The greater the expected future rise in interest rates, the more steep the upward-slope of the yield curve will be.

(ii)   **Liquidity preference**. It is argued that investors seek extra return for giving up a degree of liquidity with longer-term investments. Other things being equal, the longer the maturity of the investment, the higher the required return, leading to an upward-sloping yield curve.

(iii)   **Preferred habitat/market segmentation**. Different investors are more active in different segments of the yield curve. For example banks would tend to focus on the short-term end of the curve, whilst pension funds are likely to be more concerned with medium- and long-term segments. An upward-sloping curve could in part be the result of a fall in demand in the longer-term segment of the yield curve leading to lower bond prices and higher yields.

(b)   (i)   **Current bond prices**

Zero coupon bond

Zero coupon bond price will be: $\dfrac{£100}{(1.06)^{15}}$ = **£41.73.**

Tutorial note

Alternative method

Year		Cash flow	Discount factor at 6%	Present value
15	Redemption value	100.0	0.417	41.70

This gives an answer that is not quite as accurate, since discount tables are to just three decimal places. However, it should provide an acceptable solution.

12% gilt with a semi-annual coupon

Present value of annuity of £6 for 30 periods at 3% is:

$$\frac{6}{0.03}\left(1-\frac{1}{(1.03)^{30}}\right) = 200\,(1-0.4120) = 117.60$$

This is the present value of the interest receipts to maturity.

	£
Present value of interest payments	117.60
Present value of redemption using $\dfrac{1}{(1+0.03)^{30}} \times £100$	41.20
Bond market value	**158.80**

If interest rates increase by 1% to 7%

Zero coupon bond

Market price = $\dfrac{£100}{(1.07)^{15}}$ = **£36.25**

This would represent a decrease in price of £5.48 or 13.1%.

12% gilt with a semi-annual coupon

Present value of annuity of £6 per period for 30 periods at 3.5% is:

$$\frac{6}{0.035}\left(1-\frac{1}{(1.035)^{30}}\right) = 171.43\,(1-0.3563) = 110.35$$

This is the present value of the interest receipts to maturity.

	£
Present value of interest payments	110.35
Present value of redemption using $\dfrac{1}{(1+0.035)^{30}} \times £100$	35.63
Bond market value	**145.98**

This is a decrease of £12.82 or 8.1%.

If interest rates decrease by 1% to 5%:

Zero coupon bond

Market value $= \dfrac{£100}{(1.05)^{15}} = $ **£48.10**

This is an increase of £6.37 or 15.3%

12% gilt with a semi-annual coupon.

Present value of annuity of £6 per period for 30 periods at 2.5% is:

$$\frac{6}{0.025}\left(1 - \frac{1}{(1.025)^{30}}\right) = 240\,(1 - 0.4767) = 125.59$$

This is the present value of the interest receipts to maturity.

	£
Present value of interest payments	125.59
Present value of redemption using $\dfrac{1}{(1+0.025)^{30}} \times £100$	47.67
Bond market value	**173.26**

This is an increase of £14.46 or 9.1%.

(ii) The price/yield relation is not linear; it has a convex shape. There is a bigger absolute movement in bond prices when interest rates fall than when they rise. The percentage movement is also higher for low coupon bonds than high coupon bonds. Other things being equal, a financial manager would prefer to hold high coupon bonds if interest rates are expected to increase, and low or zero coupon bonds when interest rates are expected to decrease.

(iii) If interest rates are expected to rise, and the gap between yields on short and long dated bonds to widen, the financial manager would not want to hold longer dated bonds as these would suffer a larger fall in price than short dated bonds. Short dated bonds, probably with high coupons, would be preferred.

ACCA marking scheme			
			Marks
(a)	For full marks three reasons are necessary		4
(b)	(i)	current market prices	2
		increase 1%	2
		decrease 1%	2
	(ii)	Reward awareness of different size of movement and its implication	3
	(iii)	Full marks for correct interpretation	2
Total			15

28 CAPITAL STRUCTURE STRATEGY

Key answer tips

This is a broad question and a number of different approaches are possible. While it is important that the answer is underpinned by appropriate theoretical knowledge the approach should be practical and in a format which is appropriate for a briefing document for a Board of Directors.

Briefing document on capital structure strategy

From a corporate perspective there are two vital questions:

Can the value of a company, and hence shareholder wealth, be increased by varying the capital structure?

What effect will capital structure have on risk?

If value can be created by a sensible choice of capital structure then companies should try to achieve an optimal, or almost optimal, capital mix, as long as this mix does not have detrimental effects on other aspects of the company's activities.

Evidence on the importance of capital structure to a company's value is not conclusive. There is general agreement that, as long as a company is in a tax paying position, the use of debt can reduce the overall cost of capital due to the interest on debt being a tax allowable expense in almost all countries. This was suggested by two Nobel prize winning economists, Miller and Modigliani. However, high levels of debt also bring problems, and companies with very high gearing are susceptible to various forms of risk, sometimes known as the costs of financial distress. This might include the loss of cash flows because customers and suppliers are worried about the financial stability and viability of the company and move business elsewhere or impose less favourable trading terms, or even extra costs that would exist (payments to receivers etc.) if the company was to go out of business.

A common perception about capital structure is that as capital gearing is increased the weighted average cost of capital falls at first. However, beyond a certain level of gearing the risk to both providers of debt and equity finance increases, and the return demanded by them to compensate for this risk also increases, leading to an increase in the weighted average cost of capital. There is a trade-off between the value created by additional tax relief on debt and the costs of financial distress. Overall, there is therefore an optimal capital structure, which will vary between companies and will depend upon factors such as the nature of the company's activities, realisable value of assets, business risk etc. According to the theory, companies with many tangible assets should have relatively high gearing, companies with high growth, or that are heavily dependant on R&D or advertising would have relatively low gearing.

The impact of personal taxation on the capital structure decision is less clear, although investors are undoubtedly interested in after tax returns. If personal tax treatment differs on different types of capital, then investors may have a preference for the most tax efficient type of capital.

Not all companies behave as if there is an optimal capital structure, and on average, in countries such as the UK and USA, the average capital gearing is lower than might be expected if companies were trying to achieve an optimal structure. It must however be remembered that moving from one capital structure to another cannot take place overnight. The cost of debt, via interest rates, and the cost of equity, can change quite quickly. It is therefore not surprising that companies do not appear to be at an optimal level.

Where no optimal level appears to be sought by a company, there are several suggested strategies with respect to capital structure. Among the most popular is the pecking order theory, which is based upon information asymmetry, the fact that managers have better information about their company than the company's shareholders. This leads to a company preferring internal finance to external finance, and only using external finance in order to undertake wealth creating (positive NPV) investments. Companies use the safest sources of finance first.

(1)   Internal funds (including selling marketable securities)

(2)   Debt

(3)   Equity

The amount of external finance used depends upon the amount of investment compared with the amount of internal funds, and the resultant capital structure reflects the relative balance of investment and available internal funds.

Another view is that capital structure is strongly influenced by managerial behaviour. There are potential conflicts of objectives between owners and managers (agency problems).

Capital structure will be influenced by senior managers' personal objectives, attitudes to risk, compensation schemes and availability of alternative employment. A risk averse manager seeking security may use relatively little debt. Free cash flow (cash flow available after replacement investment) is sometimes perceived to be used by managers for unwise acquisitions/investments which satisfy their personal objectives, rather than returning it to shareholders. Many such managerial/agency aspects may influence capital structure, and this does not give clear guidance as to capital structure strategy.

No matter what the conclusion about the impact of capital structure on cash flows it is likely that some financing packages may be more highly regarded by investors than others. For example, securities designed to meet the needs of certain types of investor (zero coupon bonds etc), securities that are more liquid, securities with lower transactions costs, and securities which reduce conflict between parties concerned with the company, especially shareholders, managers and the providers of debt.

Conclusion

It is likely that the choice of capital structure can directly affect cash flows and shareholder wealth, but too high a level of gearing will increase risk. The impact on cash flows and corporate value of the capital structure decision is far less than the impact of capital investment decisions.

ACCA marking scheme	
	Marks
Answers to this question could vary considerably. The focus should be upon issues relevant to the real world and practical decision-making. Do not credit theoretical discussion which ignores real world issues e.g. MM without tax. Look for traditional theory – with implications, tax effects (MM or otherwise), awareness of actual capital structures, static trade off, pecking order, behavioural effects etc. Reward format and content that might be appropriate to a board of directors.	
Total	15

29 MCTEE

Key answer tips

Part (a) asks for a list of factors to consider when choosing finance and should be bookwork.

Part (b) then asks you to use these factors in assessing six specific financing packages. It is vital that you calculate amounts and costs as a minimum but that you do not try to calculate so many figures that you fail to reach a conclusion.

(a) Factors that should be considered include:

    (i) *Foreign exchange risk.* As the subsidiary is in the USA and will generate revenues in $US the subsidiary should logically be financed with $US. The interest payments and repayment of principal would be serviced from the $ revenues generated, reducing or eliminating the foreign exchange risk associated with the financing.

    (ii) *Maturity.* The investment is presumably for a long period, certainly more than five years. Finance of at least this duration would normally be used, except for working capital needs, unless there are circumstances (e.g. interest rates are expected to fall) that might favour temporary shorter maturity financing.

(iii)   *Cost.* McTee would favour relatively cheap finance. Included in any costs would be any transactions costs or other fees. However, if the market is efficient the price paid will be the correct price for McTee's risk.

(iv)   *Flexibility.* Financing that can be adjusted, repaid or swapped without significant cost penalties would be more attractive.

(v)   *Speed.* As McTee is proposing to purchase an existing company the finance used would need to be available quickly. Alternatively some short-term borrowing could be arranged to cover the initial purchase, with this refinanced when feasible with longer term funds from the capital market.

(vi)   *Risk.* What effect will the sources of finance have on risk as measured by capital gearing, interest cover etc.?

(vii)   *The effect on future financing.* How will the finance raised now affect the company's ability to raise various forms of finance in the future?

(viii)   *Tax.* What will be the effect on the company's tax situation, both in the UK and internationally? How tax efficient are the financing alternatives?

(ix)   *Expectations about future interest rate.* What is the shape of the yield curve? Will some form of fixed or floating rate finance be more suitable?

(x)   Will specific forms of finance such as deep discount or zero coupon bonds, convertibles or bonds with warrants be attractive to investors?

(xi)   Will the form of finance have any impact on the restrictive covenant?

(xii)   What security, if any, is required?

(xiii)   What is the state of the financial markets? Is the equity market in a bull or bear phase? In theory, if markets are efficient this should not matter, but in reality companies seem reluctant to issue shares in a falling market.

(b)   The suggested answer is only one of many alternative solutions. Candidates will be rewarded for other relevant discussion and recommendations.

Report on financing alternatives for the proposed US subsidiary

The subsidiary would only sell in the US market and would generate dollar cash flows. It would therefore be logical to finance the acquisition in dollars, to achieve a 'natural' foreign exchange hedge. Any interest payments and repayment of principal would be made from dollar cash flows generated by the subsidiary.

A total of $80 million is required, $72 million for fixed assets and $8 million for working capital. At the current spot exchange rate, the financing need is equivalent to:

$$\frac{\$8m}{1.7985} = £44.48 \text{ million}$$

As the bulk of the finance relates to long-term fixed asset purchases, it would be unusual to finance these with short-term funds. Any use of short-term finance, such as dollar commercial paper, would normally be associated with financing the working capital requirement.

The ratio of the book value of total debt finance to total assets, if the subsidiary is entirely financed by debt is:

$$\frac{38 + 30 + 18 + 44.48}{117.8 + 8.1 + 98.1 + 44.48} \times 100\% = 48.6\%$$

The US subsidiary could be entirely financed by debt without breeching the covenant, however this would increase gearing, and would impact upon the company's ability to raise additional debt finance. It is often argued that companies should increase gearing until they have reached an optimal capital structure. It is not possible to establish an optimal gearing for McTee, but if the overall cost of capital could be reduced by using debt rather than equity, it would be advantageous to do so.

Rights issue

An equity issue would provide long-term capital which could be converted into dollars and used for the US venture. From a group perspective, paying dividends in pounds on additional equity does not create foreign exchange exposure. However, the fact that the subsidiary's cash inflows are in dollars does create exposure, and this exposure would not be partially offset by any dollar cash outflows to service this type of financing.

Equity is a relatively expensive form of financing, as it involves more risk for investors than interest bearing securities, and offers no tax relief to the company on dividend payments.

The current cost of equity may be estimated using the dividend valuation model:

$$k_e = \frac{D_1}{p} + g \text{ or } \frac{22.2(1.04)}{302} + 0.04 = 0.1164 \text{ or } 11.64\%$$

This cost could increase a little as a result of the rights issue, as the rights issue price is below the current market price.

The proposed one for four rights issue would mean issuing 20 million new shares at 280 pence each, a total of £56 million. After 5% issue costs of £2.8 million this is a net £53.2 million. Unless McTee has need for additional finance for its UK operations only approximately 17 million new shares would need to be issued to finance the US subsidiary.

Cost, currency risk, and the relatively long lead time required for a rights issue are detrimental factors to the rights issue, but it is a possible source of finance.

Fixed rate loan

The 7% Sterling fixed rate loan could provide all of the necessary finance. With an initial fee of 1%, in order to provide usable finance of the dollar equivalent of £44.48 million, approximately $\frac{£44.48m}{0.99}$ = £44.93m would need to be issued.

The after tax Sterling cost of this may be estimated by solving:

$$44.93 = 0.4493 + \frac{3.145(1-0.3)}{1+kd} + \frac{3.145(1-03)}{(1+kd)^2} \dots + \frac{3.145(1-0.3)}{(1+kd)^5} + \frac{44.93}{(1+kd)^5}$$

By trial and error:

		£m
5% interest:		
PV annuity	$2.202 \times 4.329 =$	9.532
PV	$44.93 \times 0.784 =$	35.225
Fee		0.449
		45.206

The after tax Sterling cost of debt is just above 5% per year.

However, this loan would leave the company exposed to foreign exchange risk in the same way as the rights issue, and for this reason is not recommended.

Commercial paper

Dollar commercial paper is short-term financing. Unless interest rates are expected to fall, it is suggested that this is only used to finance the $8 million working capital element of the proposed acquisition. The annual dollar cost is currently $LIBOR of 3% + 1.5% + 0.5%, a total of 5%. After tax relief this is 5%(1 – 0.3) = 3.5%. No issue costs are given, but some are likely, which would increase this cost. The interest rate looks quite low, but it is a floating rate and is susceptible to interest rate changes. If dollar interest rates are expected to increase, commercial paper will become less attractive when renewed.

McTee might consider using more than $8 million from this source, but if the financing was to be used to support longer term operations there would be a maturity mismatch.

Swiss Franc loan

The 2.5% Swiss franc loan has a low Swiss franc interest rate. However, like any foreign currency loan the foreign exchange risk implications must be considered. Swapping the loan into a dollar loan is possible, and the overall annual headline cost looks relatively cheap at 4.8%. However, a swap would fix the medium term Swiss franc exchange rate against the dollar, leaving McTee exposed to unknown movements in the pound against the Swiss franc.

The after tax cost of a Swiss Franc loan and swap is:

$$80.00 = 2.40 \text{ (fee)} + \frac{3.84(1-0.3)}{1+kd} + \frac{3.84(1-0.3)}{(1+kd)^2} \dots + \frac{3.84(1-0.3)}{(1+kd)^5} + \frac{80.00}{(1+kd)^5}$$

By trial and error:

4% interest:		£m
PV annuity	$2.688 \times 4.452 =$	11.967
PV	$2.680 \times 0.822 =$	65.760
Fee		2.400
		80.127

The after tax cost is a little over 4%.

The maximum loan net of fees would be SF77.6m, or approximately $60.71m

(SF77.6m/1.278 = $60.71m where 1.278 is the cross rate for converting SF into $), which would be insufficient to finance the entire US venture.

Unless some form of long-term hedge against foreign exchange risk could be arranged this loan is not recommended. If a long-term £/Swiss Franc hedge is possible, the cost of this hedge must be added to the above cost to find an overall cost to compare with the alternatives.

Eurobond

The 6.85% Eurobond would be denominated in Sterling, presumably because McTee has a relative price advantage in issuing a Sterling denominated bond. The bond could then be swapped into dollars, and could provide all of the longer term financing necessary for the acquisition. £42 million less total upfront costs of 3.7% gives a net £40.446 million or $72.74 million, which is not enough to finance the entire investment. The bond is for a ten-year period, which could provide longer term financing for McTee. It is not secured, which would allow assets to be used as security against future loans.

The after tax cost is:

$$42.00 = 1.554 \text{ (fees)} + \frac{2.08(1-0.3)}{1+kd} + \frac{2.08(1-0.3)}{(1+kd)^2} \dots + \frac{2.08(1-0.3)}{(1+kd)^{10}} + \frac{2.08(1-0.3)}{(1+kd)^{10}}$$

By trial and error:

4% interest:		£m
PV annuity	$1.455 \times 8.111 =$	11.802
PV	$1.942 \times 0.676 =$	28.392
Fees		1.554

41.748

The after tax cost of the Eurobond issue plus swap is a little less than 4%.

Floating rate term loan

The term loan can only provide $40 million. Its initial cost is $ LIBOR plus 3.0%, or 6.0%. Net of tax relief this is 4.2%. It has the advantage of providing direct dollar finance, but requires security, and is relatively expensive.

Summary of available funding

	Maximum net amount ($m)	Cost (%)	Currency	Comments
Rights issue	95.68	11.64 +	£	Possible – Expensive
Fixed rate loan	89.03	5 +	£	FOREX risk
Commercial paper	15.00	3.5 floating	$	Possible
Swiss Franc loan	60.71	4 +	$	No – unless hedged
Eurobond	72.74	4 –	$	Possible
Floating rate term loan	40.00	4.2 floating	$	Possible

Recommendation

Although all the financing sources could potentially be used, a combination of the Eurobond loan swapped into dollars, and dollar commercial paper would provide a cost effective and tax efficient financing mix, relevant to the subsidiary's asset structure. The rights issue might be used for some or all of the financing if the company does not wish to increase capital gearing.

ACCA marking scheme		
This question requires analysis and understanding of factors that influence the selection of finance for an overseas direct investment, and the ability to analyse and select between specific sources of finance taking into account their foreign exchange and other risks.		
		Marks
(a) 1 mark for each valid point. Look for brief discussion rather than one word answers. 2 marks for very well explained points	Maximum	10
(b) General comments about the mix and maturity of the finance, and foreign exchange risk		2
Covenant		1
Rights issue		3–4
5 year Sterling loan		2–3
Commercial paper		2–3
Swiss franc loan		3–4
Eurobond		3–4
Floating rate loan		2
Reasoned recommendation		2
	Maximum	20
Allow for overlap between the financing sources		
Total		30

30   SEMER PLC

Key answer tips

Part (a) is tricky as it is easy to accept the mistakes when presented with them. The best approach is to plan your own calculations first and then assess the ones given.

In part (b) there is no need to calculate the change in the cost of equity to reflect the higher gearing. This part is tricky enough already, particularly when calculating the new level of dividends, the revised free cash flow and hence be able to estimate market value.

Part (c) should be a fairly routine discussion of the impact of higher gearing but make sure you also discuss the accuracy of the estimates produced in part (b)

(a)   Revised estimates of the current cost of capital and value

The cost of equity has been correctly estimated using the capital asset pricing model to be 11.8%.

The cost of debt should be the current cost of debt, not the historic cost of debt of 8% when the debenture was issued. It should also be estimated on an after tax basis as interest on debt is a tax allowable expense.

The current cost of debt may be estimated from the redemption yield of the existing debenture. The debenture matures in five years time. The redemption yield may be estimated by solving the following equation for kd.

$$112 = \frac{8(1-0.3)}{1+kd} + \frac{8(1-0.3)}{(1+kd)^2} \ldots\ldots + \frac{8(1-0.3)}{(1+kd)^5} + \frac{100}{(1+kd)^5}$$

By trial and error:

At 5% interest:

PV annuity 5.6 × 4.329	=	24.24
PV 100 × 0.784	=	78.40
		102.64

At 3% interest:

PV annuity 5.6 × 4.580	=	25.65
PV 100 × 0.863	=	86.30
		111.95

The after tax cost of debt is approximately 3%

The weighted average cost of capital (WACC) should be estimated using the market values of equity and debt, not book values.

The market value of equity is 160 million × 410 pence = £656m

The market value of debt is £119m + (£50m × 1.12) = £175m

$$WACC = 11.8\% \times \frac{656}{831} + 3\% \times \frac{175}{831} = 9.95\%$$

As free cash flow is expected to grow by 3% per year, the present value of the company's free cash flows may be estimated by using the equation for a growth perpetuity:

$$PV = \frac{FCF(1+g)}{WACC-g} \text{ or } \frac{60(1.03)}{0.0995 - 0.03} = £889 \text{ million}$$

(b)   Estimated new cost of capital:

If equity is repurchased such that the gearing becomes 50% equity, 50% debt, the new estimated weighted average cost of capital is:

$$11.8\% \times \frac{415.5}{831} + 3\% \times \frac{415.5}{831} = 7.40\%$$

Impact on the value of the company:

The free cash flow to the company will not change when equity is replaced by debt.

Expected new value

$$\frac{60\,(1.03)}{0.074 \quad 0.03} = £1,404.5 \text{ million}$$

This is a very large potential increase in value.

(c)   **Report on the proposed adjustment of gearing through the repurchase of ordinary shares**

The effect of capital structure on the value of a company is not fully understood.

Increasing the proportion of debt in the capital structure may reduce the overall cost of capital due to the interest on debt being a tax allowable expense. Even if a company is in a non-tax paying position, mixing additional low cost debt with relatively expensive equity might reduce the weighted average cost of capital. In such circumstances the proposed strategy to increase gearing would have some validity. However, increasing gearing can also bring problems. Risk to investors, and therefore the required returns on equity and debt, will increase as gearing increases. Very high levels of gearing might lead to direct and indirect bankruptcy costs, with a detrimental effect on cash flow and corporate value. Any benefits from increasing the proportion of debt in the capital structure will be to some extent offset as a result of increased risk with high gearing.

The revised estimates of the effect on the cost of capital and value of Semer are not likely to be accurate. Reasons for this include:

(i)   The company will not be able to repurchase the necessary shares at their current market value. Approximately £240 million value of equity would need to be repurchased, or more than one third of the existing market value of equity. As repurchases take place it is likely that the share price will significantly increase.

(ii)   The cost of debt is unlikely to remain constant. As more debt is issued lenders will demand a higher interest rate to compensate for the extra risk resulting from higher gearing levels. The cost of equity will also increase with higher gearing. These effects will increase the weighted average cost of capital to a higher level than that estimated.

(iii) The precise market values of debt and equity after the repurchase are unknown, and again will reflect the market attitude to the new risk of the higher gearing.

The value of the company is likely to be much lower than that estimated, as the weighted average cost of capital is likely to be underestimated.

ACCA marking scheme	
	Marks
This question requires understanding of how the cost of capital and value of a company might be estimated, and of the possible affect on a company's market value when capital gearing is increased.	

(a)	Existing cost of capital For full marks brief reasons for adjustments must be given	
	Cost of equity correct	1
	Revised after tax cost of debt	6–7
	Market value of equity (1 for an attempt at MV that ignores reserves)	2
	Market value of debt	2
	Revised weighted average cost of capital	2
	Free cash flow value including growth	2
		───
	max	15
(b)	New weighted average cost of capital	2
	New value	3
		───
		5
(c)	Discussion of the effect of increasing gearing	5–6
	Reasons why the estimates might not be accurate	5–6
	max	10
		───
Total		30
		───

INVESTMENT DECISIONS: DECISION-MAKING TECHNIQUES

31 DARON

Key answer tips

The question clearly states that nearly 40% of the marks for part (a) are for the discussion – make sure you pay sufficient attention to the written aspects as opposed to the computational aspects of the problem.

(a) **Report for the managers of Daron**

Offer to purchase the company

Any recommendation regarding the sale of the company to a competitor for $20 million should be made in the best interests of the shareholders. An offer of $20 million is an 8.7% premium over the current share price (which is quite low).

Estimates of the present values of future cash flows from internal data suggest that no matter which party wins the election the company's value will be in excess of $20 million; $21 million if party B wins, and $30.3 million if party A wins.

However, these estimates are by no means precise. Inaccuracy could exist due to:

(i)   Incorrect inflation estimates.

(ii) Errors in sales volume and cost projections.

(iii) Inaccurate discount rate estimates.

(iv) The assumption of a constant 30% corporate tax rate.

Sensitivity analysis is recommended to analyse the significance of changes in key variables. The cash flow estimates do not incorporate any value for options relating to opportunities that might exist between now and 2013 if operations continue. Nor is there data on the expected realisable value of the company in 2013 (which is the last year for which cash flow data is available). Even if further investment was not undertaken at that time, the present value of the realisable value of land, buildings and cash flow released from working capital needs to be considered. This would increase the above present value estimates. On financial grounds the informal offer of $20 million is not high enough to be recommended. Additionally, selling to a competitor might have other implications such as redundancies, closure of part of the existing operations and a detrimental impact on the local community.

Investing in the purchase of a hotel

Appendix 2 shows the financial estimates of the hotel purchase. An APV of $0.56 million suggests that the hotel investment is financially viable. However, this estimate is also subject to many of the possible inaccuracies noted above. The base case NPV is heavily influenced by the realisable value of $10 million in 2008. Future hotel values could vary substantially from this estimate.

Investment in the hotel industry is a strategic departure from the company's core competence. If the objective is primarily to diversify activities to reduce risk this may not be in the shareholders' best interest as they can easily achieve diversification of their investment portfolios, through unit trusts or similar investments. As the company is in a declining industry, in the long term diversification may be essential for survival. A medium to long term strategic plan should be formulated examining alternative strategies, and alternative investments which may offer better financial returns than the hotel investment, and/or be closer to the company's existing core competence.

Appendix 1

Valuation of business cash flows

Present value estimates:

Political party A wins the election

$ million

	2004	2005	2006	2007	2008	2009-2013
Sales	28.0	29.0	26.0	22.0	19.0	19.0
Variable costs	17.0	18.0	16.0	14.0	12.0	12.0
Fixed costs	3.0	3.0	3.0	3.0	3.0	3.0
Depreciation	4.0	3.0	3.0	2.0	1.0	-
	24.0	24.0	22.0	19.0	16.0	15.0
Taxable profit	4.0	5.0	4.0	3.0	3.0	4.0
Taxation (30%)	1.2	1.5	1.2	0.9	0.9	1.2
	2.8	3.5	2.8	2.1	2.1	2.8
Add back depreciation	4.0	3.0	3.0	2.0	1.0	-
Working capital	-	1.0	2.0	3.0	3.0	-
Net cash flow	6.8	7.5	7.8	7.1	6.1	2.8
Discount factors at 13%	0.885	0.783	0.693	0.613	0.543	1.910
Present values	6.0	5.9	5.4	4.4	3.3	5.3

Expected total present value, up to year 2013 = $30.3 million.

Tutorial note: The discount factor for years 2009 – 2013, which are years 6 – 10 (five years) is calculated by taking the cumulative discount factor at 13% for years 1 – 5. This (from tables) is 3.517. However, applying this discount factor to the annual cash flows would give a value as at the end of year 5. To obtain a present value (year 0 value) we must discount further by the year 5 factor at 13%, which is 0.543.

The cumulative discount factor for annual cash flows at 13% for years 6 – 10 is therefore 3.517 × 0.543 = 1.910.

Political party B wins the election

$ million

	2004	2005	2006	2007	2008	2009–2013
Sales	30.0	26.0	24.0	20.0	16.0	16.0
Variable costs	18.0	16.0	15.0	12.0	11.0	11.0
Fixed costs	3.0	3.0	4.0	4.0	4.0	4.0
Depreciation	4.0	3.0	3.0	2.0	1.0	-
	25.0	22.0	22.0	18.0	16.0	15.0
Taxable profit	5.0	4.0	2.0	2.0	0.0	1.0
Taxation (30%)	1.5	1.2	0.6	0.6	-	0.3
	3.5	2.8	1.4	1.4	0.0	0.7
Add back depreciation	4.0	3.0	3.0	2.0	1.0	-
Working capital	(1.0)	2.0	2.0	3.0	3.0	-
Net cash flow	6.5	7.8	6.4	6.4	4.0	0.7
Discount factors at 18%	0.847	0.718	0.609	0.516	0.437	1.366
Present values	5.5	5.6	3.9	3.3	1.7	1.0

Expected total present value, up to year 2013 = $21 million

Tutorial note: The discount factor for years 2009 – 2013, which are years 6 – 10 (five years) is calculated by taking the cumulative discount factor at 18% for years 1 – 5. This (from tables) is 3.127. However, applying this discount factor to the annual cash flows would give a value as at the end of year 5. To obtain a present value (year 0 value) we must discount further by the year 5 factor at 18%, which is 0.437.

The cumulative discount factor for annual cash flows at 13% for years 6 – 10 is therefore 3.127 × 0.437 = 1.366.

Notes

(1) The use of expected values is not recommended as it does not reflect a situation that is likely to occur in reality.

(2) **Discount rate, political party A wins**

	$m
Market value of equity 20m shares at 92c =	18.4
Debt	14.0
	32.4

The risk free rate *including inflation*, given expected inflation of 5% each year, is:

(1.04) (1.05) =1.092 or 9.2%.

The market return including inflation at 5% per annum is:

(1.10) (1.05) = 1.155 or 15.5%

Using CAPM, the cost of equity $K_e = R_F + (R_m - R_F) \beta_e$

$$K_e = 9.2\% + (15.5\% - 9.2\%)\, 1.25 = 17.075\%$$

$$\text{WACC} = 17.075\% \times \frac{18.4}{32.4} + 10\%\,(1 - .3)\,\frac{14}{32.4} = 12.72\% \text{ or}$$

approximately 13%.

(3)   **Discount rate, political party B wins**

The risk free rate including inflation, given expected inflation of 10% each year, is:

$$(1.04)(1.10) = 1.144 \text{ or } 14.4\%$$

The market return including inflation at 10% per annum is:

$$(1.10)(1.10) = 1.21 \text{ or } 21\%$$

Using CAPM, the cost of equity $K_e = 14.4\% + (21\% - 14.4\%)\,1.25 = 22.65\%$

$$WACC = 22.65\% \times \frac{18.4}{32.4} + 15.5\%\,(1 - .3)\,\frac{14}{32.4} = 17.6\% \text{ or}$$

approximately 18%.

Note: This is only a rough estimate of the cost of capital, as the share price is likely to fall with higher inflation, leading to higher gearing and a change in risk for the providers of the debt finance.

Both K_e and K_d could alter because of these factors.

The use of the current share price in both WACC estimates is problematic. In an efficient market this price will reflect the present uncertainty about the forthcoming election. Once this uncertainty is resolved the share price is likely to change, leading to new market weighted gearing levels. Fortunately the investment decision is not highly sensitive to marginal changes in the discount rate.

Appendix 2

Base case NPV

For APV the base case NPV is required, which is estimated from the ungeared cost of equity. This is estimated from the ungeared cost of equity, as follows.

Assuming corporate debt is risk free:

$$\beta e \text{ ungeared} = \beta e \text{ geared } \frac{E}{E + D(1-t)}$$

$$= 1.25 \times \frac{18.4}{18.4 + 14(1 - 0.3)} = 0.82$$

Ke ungeared = 9.2% + (15.5% − 9.2%) 0.82 = 14.4% or approximately 14%.

A discount rate of 14% has therefore been used to calculate the base case NPV.

Cash flows, possible hotel purchase
$ million

	2004	2005	2006	2007	2008
Turnover	9.0	10.0	11.0	12.0	13.0
Variable costs	6.0	6.0	7.0	7.0	8.0
Fixed costs	2.0	2.0	2.0	2.0	2.0
	8.0	8.0	9.0	9.0	10.0
Taxable profit	1.0	2.0	2.0	3.0	3.0
Taxation (30%)	0.3	0.6	0.6	0.9	0.9
	0.7	1.4	1.4	2.1	2.1
Realisable value					10.0
Working capital	(1.0)	-	-	(1.0)	-
Net cash flows	(0.3)	1.4	1.4	1.1	12.1
Discount factors at 14%	0.877	0.769	0.675	0.592	0.519
Present values	(0.3)	1.1	0.9	0.7	6.3

Base case NPV = ($9.0)m + $8.7m = $(0.3)m

Financing side effects for the five year period:

Including issue costs, the gross sum of finance to be raised will be $\dfrac{9m}{0.98}$ = $9,184,000.

Issue costs are therefore $184,000.

Interest is at 10%, so this will give **annual tax savings** of:

$9.18m × 10% × 30% = $275,520 per year.

Discounted at 10%, this gives a present value of 3.791 × $275,520 = $1,044,000

Note: This assumes that an extra $9,184 million debt capacity is created by the hotel investment. If less debt capacity is created the present value of the tax shield attributable to the investment will be reduced.

The 10% coupon is assumed to reflect correctly the risk of the convertible, and is used as the discount rate for the tax savings.

The estimated APV is the base case NPV plus the financing side effects.

	$m
Base case NPV	(0.30)
Issue costs	(0.18)
PV of tax saving	1.04
APV	0.56

(b) Daron's current gearing, measured by the *book value* of medium and long term loans to the *book value* of equity is: 14/22 or 63.6%

No information is provided about short-term loans which would increase this gearing figure further. A $9 million convertible debenture issue would initially increase gearing to 23/22 = 104.5%.

Such a high level of gearing involves 'high' financial risk, especially for a company in a declining industry. The coupon rate of 10%, or $918,400 interest per year would have to be paid for five years or more. Convertible debentures normally carry lower coupon rates than straight debt. Daron can borrow long term from its bank at 10% per year, and the 10% coupon on the convertible appears to be expensive. However, this could be explained by the market seeking a relatively high return because of the size of the loan.

If conversion takes place the gearing level will fall, but this is will not occur for at least five years. At the $100 issue price the effective conversion price is $100/60 or 167 centos per share

This represents an average share price increase of 12.7% per year over five years, which is possible if market prices in general increase, but is by no means guaranteed.

The existence of the call and put options has potentially significant implications for Daron plc. The call option allows the company to limit the potential gains made by debenture holders. If the share price reaches 200 centos between 1 January 2009 and 31 December 2011 the company can force the debenture holders to convert, giving maximum capital gains on conversion of 33 centos per share (relative to the $100 issue price). This is a small gain and may not be popular with investors. If the share price falls below 100 centos between the same dates, the debenture holders can ask the company to redeem the debentures at par, forcing the company to find $9 million for repayment of the debentures. If the market price of the shares has only moved by a maximum of eight centos over five years, the company might experience difficulty refinancing the $9 million, leading to severe problems in finding the cash for redemption.

32   TOVELL PLC

(a)   *Tutorial note:* Your answer should show understanding of the theoretical and practical arguments relating to corporate diversification into several industries.

Tovell has a strategy of diversifying into many industries in order to reduce risk for the company's shareholders. Rational shareholders should already be well-diversified, in order to eliminate unsystematic risk. If shareholders are not well diversified this may be achieved quickly and cheaply through the purchase of such investments as general unit trusts. The expense of the company undertaking diversification is likely to be much greater than that of individual investors in the company diversifying themselves, and therefore a sub-optimal strategy from the investors' viewpoint. As the primary objective of companies is usually assumed to be the maximisation of shareholder wealth the strategy would not normally be recommended.

However, diversification might have beneficial effects for shareholders including:

(i)   Less volatile internal cash flows, making servicing existing debt less risky, and therefore increasing the debt capacity of the company. Greater use of debt with no extra risk could reduce the overall cost of capital, and increase shareholder wealth.

(ii)   If diversification is into foreign markets where exchange controls or other barriers prevent or restrict shareholders directly investing (i.e., segmented markets), it might be possible for shareholders to reduce their systematic risk through Tovell investing in such markets which have risk-return combinations which would not otherwise be available to shareholders.

(iii) If a company fails there are many 'bankruptcy' costs including receiver's fees and the possibility of assets being sold cheaply in a 'forced-sale'. Such costs may significantly reduce wealth of shareholders. A diversified company may have a lower risk of corporate failure because of reduced *total* risk of the company (measured by variance of returns). Shareholders may be willing to accept the costs of diversification if the probability of corporate failure is reduced.

(b)   *Tutorial note:* In your solution, you should select an appropriate investment evaluation technique (hopefully APV) for a diversification, where gearing levels have changed, to show understanding of its limitations, and to prepare a report supported by the financial evaluation of given data.

Report on the financial viability of the fast food investment

The proposed investment is in an industry where the company has no existing activities, and differs in risk to the company's existing activities, as is evidenced by the equity betas of the company and the industry. The investment is to be financed by £800,000 of debt and £1,578,947 of equity. This gives a gearing level of approximately 0.5 to 1, which is significantly different from the company's current market weighted gearing of 0.4 to 1.

As the investment results in a change in capital structure, is not marginal relative to the size of the company, and does not have the same level of systematic risk as the company, the current weighted average cost of capital should not be used as the discount rate.

There is no easy way to adjust the weighted average cost to take into account these changes. It is recommended that the fast food investment is evaluated using the **adjusted present value (APV) technique**. This approach examines directly the effects of the financing methods that are being used, which, for this investment, relate to tax relief on interest payments, the benefit of a subsidised loan, and issue costs associated with the rights issue.

The estimated APV of the investment is negative, (£113,608), which suggests that the investment is not financially viable. However, this ignores the potentially valuable option to continue operations after the initial five year period by further investment in equipment. Any final decision should include consideration of the financial effects of this option, and any other opportunities that might arise as a result of diversifying into the fast food industry.

Limitations of APV

APV offers an opportunity to evaluate investments where gearing and risk differ from the company's existing operation. However, it has its limitations including:

(i)   The equation for asset betas in a taxed world assumes that cash flows are perpetuities. The cash flows for this investment are not perpetuities.

(ii)   APV requires the identification of all financing side effects and their discount at a rate reflecting their risk. In a complex investment situation, especially an overseas investment, it might be difficult to identify relevant financing side effects, and their appropriate discount rates.

Appendix

APV = Base case NPV + Present value of financing side effects.

Base case NPV

This may be estimated by discounting net cash flows by the discount rate applicable to the risk associated with an ungeared investment. As the investment is in the fast food industry, the base case NPV should be estimated using data from this industry.

Cost of equity ungeared

$$\beta \text{ asset } (= \beta \text{ equity ungeared}) = \beta e \frac{E}{E + D(1-t)} + \beta d \frac{D(1-t)}{E + D(1-t)}$$

$$\beta \text{ asset} = 1.4 \frac{1}{1 + 1(1-0.3)} + 0.25 \frac{1(1-0.3)}{1 + 1(1-0.3)}$$

$$= 0.823 \quad + \quad 0.103$$

$$= 0.926$$

Using CAPM

$$Ke \text{ ungeared} = R_F + (R_M - R_F) \beta \text{ equity ungeared}$$

$$5\% + (12.5\% - 5\%)\, 0.926 = 11.945\%.$$

A discount rate of 11.945% will therefore be used to calculate a base case NPV.

Year	0	1	2	3	4	5	6
	£000	£000	£000	£000	£000	£000	£000
Operating flows (+ 5% pa)		420	441	463	486	511	
Taxation (1 year in arrears)			(126)	(132)	(139)	(146)	(153)
Initial outlay	(2,300)						
Realisable value						1,250	
Tax saved by capital allowance (see note)	–	–	79	59	44	33	100
Net flows	(2,300)	420	394	390	391	1,648	(53)
Discount factors at 11.945%	1.000	0.893	0.798	0.713	0.637	0.569	0.508
Present values	(2,300)	375	314	278	249	938	(27)

Base case NPV = (£173,000)

Note: Tax saved by capital allowance

Year	Written down value	Allowance (25%)	Tax saving (at 30%)	Year available
	£000	£000	£000	£000
1	1,050	262	79	2
2	788	197	59	3
3	591	148	44	4
4	443	111	33	5
5	332	83	25	6
Balancing	249	249	75	6

(It might be argued that the tax saving is a relatively safe cash flow and should be discounted at a rate lower than the ungeared cost of equity. If so the resultant base case NPV would be slightly larger.)

Financing side effects

(i) ***Tax relief on interest payments*** *(assumed available years 2 – 6)*

The benefit from the investment in terms of increased debt capacity is £1 million. Although only £800,000 is being borrowed, the APV should be based upon theoretical benefits of the debt capacity as these are available to the company and may be used through debt issues for other investments (these too must be evaluated on their *own* impact on debt capacity). The tax shield benefit is therefore based upon £1 million of debt, £800,000 at 6% and the remaining £200,000 at the normal market rate of 9%.

Annual interest		Tax relief
	£	£
£800,000 × 6% =	48,000	× 0.3 = 14,400
£200,000 × 9% =	18,000	× 0.3 = 5,400
		19,800

The discount rate used will be a rate reflecting the risk of the debt, in this case the pre-tax cost of debt, 9%.

PV of an annuity at 9% for five years, from years 2 – 6,

$$= 3.890 \times 19,800 \times \frac{1}{1.09} = £70,662$$

Tutorial note: The present value of an annuity at 9% for five years = 3.890. Here, the annual cash flows start in year 2, so a discount factor of 3.890 will give a discounted value as at the end of year 1. To convert this to a year 0 present value, we have to discount from year 1 values, using a discount factor 1/1.09.

The PV of tax relief, commencing year 2, is £70,662.

(ii) ***Subsidised loan***

Tovell is receiving £800,000 at 3% less than normal market rates because of its financing choice.

This produces an after tax saving (with a one year lag in tax) of:

Years 1 – 5 £800,000 × (0.09 – 0.06) per year = £24,000

Years 2 – 6 tax of £800,000 × (0.09 – 0.06) × 0.3 = (£7,200)

The PV of this saving, discounted at 9% representing the market risk of debt is:

	£
3.890 × £24,000	93,360
3.890 × 0.917 × (£7,200)	(25,683)
	67,677

(iii) *Issue costs*

The cost of the investment after issue costs (it is assumed that none exist on the loan) is £2.3 million. Net proceeds of the rights issue are the cost of the investment minus the amount to be raised in debt capital = £2.3m – £0.8m = £1.5m.

With issue costs of 5% gross proceeds of the rights issue are £1.5 million/0.95 = £1,578,947. **Issue costs are therefore £78,947.**

The **expected APV of the investment** is:

	£
Base case NPV	(173,000)
Tax relief on interest	70,662
Benefit from subsidised loan	67,677
Issue costs	(78,947)
APV	(113,608)

33 WICKERN

(a) In the following NPV calculation, the cash inflows each year are the original remittable cash flows to the UK.

Year		Item	Cash flow (note (1)) £m	Discount factor at 16% (note (2))	Present value £m
2000	1	Remittable to the UK	1.72	0.862	1.48
2001	2	Remittable to the UK	2.12	0.743	1.58
2002	3	Remittable to the UK	2.04	0.641	1.31
2003	4	Remittable to the UK	2.15	0.552	1.19
2004	5	Remittable to the UK	2.47	0.476	1.18
2005	6	Remittable to the UK	2.39	0.410	0.98
2006	7	Remittable to the UK	2.49	0.354	0.88
2007	8	Remittable to the UK	2.60	0.305	0.79
					9.39
	0	Initial investment			(8.00)
	8	PV of realisable value (note (3))			3.20
		Expected project NPV			4.59

Notes:

(1) As corporate taxation in Movania was expected to be higher than in the UK, no further UK tax liability was expected to arise.

(2) The discount rate may be estimated using CAPM, $ko = Rf + (Rm – Rf)$ beta.

The original estimate is $7\% + (15\% – 7\%)1.125 = 16\%$.

(3) PV of realisable value in 2007:

€12 million = 78.71 million MF = £10.5 m at MF7.5/£1, the rate used in cash flow estimates.

£10.5 million × 0.305 = £3.2 million.

Actual present values for the first four years were:

Year		Item	Cash flow	Discount factor at 16%	Present value
			£m		£m
2000	1	Remittable to the UK	0.44	0.862	0.38
2001	2	Remittable to the UK	0.56	0.743	0.42
2002	3	Remittable to the UK	0.41	0.641	0.26
2003	4	Remittable to the UK	0.68	0.552	0.38
		Total actual present values –2000-2003			1.44
		Forecast present values 2000 2003			5.56
		Adverse variance			(4.12)

During the first four years of the investment's life the actual performance was £4.12 million worse in present value terms than expected. This is almost enough to eliminate the entire expected NPV for the full eight years of the investment.

This adverse performance may be attributed to several factors:

(i) The estimates of UK cash flows were based upon an assumption that the exchange rate between the Movanian franc and the pound would remain constant at MF7.5/£1. In reality the franc weakened from MF7.5/£1 to more than MF11/£1 during the four-year period.

(ii) Cash inflows from public skating were significantly below projections and have not increased at all since 2000. Any future projections should be based upon actual cash flows between 2000 and 2003, or additional advertising undertaken to try to stimulate additional public skating.

(iii) Cash flows from ice-hockey matches were only 60-70% of expectations. Advertising might help here, but to some extent such receipts will be dependent upon how well the ice hockey team(s) are performing.

(iv) Except in 2003 concert receipts were also below expectations, and cash outflows on concerts at least double the original forecasts. Analysis of these outflows should be undertaken to see why they occurred and if they can be reduced. This also relates to general overheads that were higher than forecast, even though cash revenues were much lower than expected.

(b) **Report**

To: Board of directors

From: Accountant

Date: xx/xx/xx

Subject: **The retention or disposal of the ice-skating rink.**

From a financial perspective, the decision about whether to retain or dispose of the rink should be based on the relative present values of expected incremental cash flows from the three options from 2004 onwards. The option with the highest present value should be selected. However, there may be strategic or other non-financial influences that outweigh the findings of the financial analysis.

Given the inflation differential between the UK and the eurozone, using the purchasing power parity theory, the euro will be expected to fall in value relative to the pound by:

$$\frac{0.05 - 0.02}{1.02} = 0.0294 \text{ or } 2.94\% \text{ per year}$$

Exchange rate forecasts		euros/£1
2003	Spot	1.690
2004		1.740
2005		1.791
2006		1.843
2007		1.898

These exchange rate forecasts may be used to determine the sterling cash flows for the next four years. However, if the UK joins the eurozone during this period the pound will become fixed against the euro at an as yet unknown rate, which would influence the present value projections.

Tutorial note: Although you might have doubts about the validity of the assumptions about the future movement in the exchange rate, the question gives you the information to apply the purchasing power parity formula to predict exchange rates.

1   **Option of disposal in 2007**

Forecast remittable cash flows to the UK are:

	€million			
	2004	*2005*	*2006*	*2007*
Remittable (note (i))	1.6	1.6	1.6	1.6

Cash flows	£ million			
	204	*2005*	*2006*	*2007*
Remittable	0.920	0.893	0.868	0.843
Additional UK tax (1.5%) (note (ii))	0.006	0.006	0.006	0.006
Net cash flows	0.914	0.887	0.862	0.837
Discount factor at 13% (see note (iii))	0.885	0.783	0.693	0.613
Present value	0.809	0.695	0.597	0.513

Notes:

(i)   Remittable cash flows, in euros:

	€ m
Taxable net cash flow	0.7
Tax	(0.2)
Add back depreciation	1.1
Remittable cash flow	1.6

(ii)   Tax rate in Movania 28.5%. Tax rate in UK 30%. Tax rate is higher in the UK, therefore additional tax will be charged on remittances to the UK. Additional tax on remittances to UK = 30% – 28.5% = 1.5%.

(iii) The new discount rate is: 6% + (13.5% – 6%) 0.95 = 13.125% or 13%.

Assuming no significant additional outlays, the expected NPV for the next four years is:

	£ million	
PV of UK cash flows	2.614	
PV of realisable value in 2005	3.876	€12million/1.898 × 0.613
	6.490	

2   **Option of disposal now**

If the land and building was sold now it would sell for:

$$\frac{\text{€15 million}}{1.69} = £8.876 \text{ million}$$

3   **Option of retention beyond 2007**

If the new investment occurs in 2007 the cost will be €50 million.

It is assumed that the UK will join the eurozone in 2007, and that foreign exchange fluctuations are therefore not relevant.

(i)   If the incremental cash flow is €7.5 million each year, assuming this is constant for the next ten years, the net present value at a discount rate of 13% is:

Year	Cash flow €m	DF at 13%	PV €m
0	(50.0)	1.000	(50.000)
1 – 10	7.5	5.426	40.695
			(9.305)

(ii)   If the incremental cash flow is €10 million each year then the present value is:

Year	Cash flow €m	DF at 13%	PV €m
0	(50.0)	1.000	(50.00)
1 – 10	10.0	5.426	54.26
			4.26

Thus with a €7.5 million per annum cash flow there is a negative net present value from 2007 onwards of €9.305 million, or with a €10 million per annum cash flow there is a positive NPV of €4.26 million. These are NPV values in terms of present values as at the end of 2007.

If these are put in terms of values at the end of 2003 (by multiplying by a discount factor of 0.613), the values arc €(5.70) million and €2.61 million. Using the forecast exchange rate for 2007 of €1.898/£1 gives £ values of (£3.003) and £1.375 million.

Summary:		*NPV*
	£ million	£ million
(1) Immediate disposal		8.876
(2) Disposal in 2007		6.490
(3) Retention beyond 2007:		
(i) €7.5 million incremental cash flow		
NPV to 2005	2.614	
NPV from 2005 for 10 years	(3.003)	
Total NPV		(0.389)
(ii) €10 million incremental cash flow		
NPV to 2007	2.614	
NPV from 2007 for 10 years	1.375	
Total NPV		3.989

Based upon this data it appears better for the company to sell the ice-rink now.

However, the realisable values are based upon the value of the site and buildings and not the business as a going concern, which could be much higher. The data also assumes no cash flows beyond 2017 or no realisable value in 2017, and that cash flows between 2007 and 2017 are constant. Any growth in cash flows, or extension of the period, would increase the expected NPV from the new investment. all the time

real options?
risk analysis
also review

(c)   Factors that should be considered in order to assist the decision include:

(i)   Estimates should be produced of a range of NPVs based upon different assumptions. Sensitivity analysis or simulation analysis might be useful in this process.

risk

(ii)   The accuracy of the cash flow estimates should be investigated in more depth. Previous experience shows that the company's estimates were relatively inaccurate.

accuracy

(iii) Is the rink being used to full capacity? Could it be opened cost effectively for longer hours? It is possible to hold more concerts and to generate additional cash flow by varying the use of the rink. Are there other possible uses such as exhibitions and conferences that have not yet been tried?

(iv)   Can capacity be enlarged to attract bigger 'stars' to the concerts, or a larger audience to ice hockey matches?

(v)   Are cash flows in real or nominal terms? As the discount rates are nominal all cash flows should be in money terms.

(vi)   Are there alternative uses for the site that could yield a higher expected NPV?

(vii) What is the local/ regional competition from similar rinks, both now and in the foreseeable future?

(viii) What are national trends in the popularity of ice-skating and ice hockey?

(xi)   What future options will exist for the company if it retains the site that will not be possible if the site is sold, i.e. what is the opportunity cost of selling the rink?

xii) Economic risk – Hedge ??

ACCA marking scheme		
		Marks
(a)	*Original cash flow projections*:	
	Discount rate	2
	Present values of operating cash flows	1
	Present value of realisable value	2
	Expected NPV	1
	Actual cash flows:	
	Present values of operating cash flows	1
	Variance	1
	Comment on UK tax liability	1
	Discussion of reasons for the variance:	
	Exchange rates	3
	Cash flow variances	2
	Suggestions for actions	3
Total		15

34   JETTER PLC

(a)   CAPM may be used to estimate whether or not the projects are expected to yield a high enough return relative to their systematic risk.

$$\text{Beta} = \frac{\text{Correlation coefficient} \times \text{Project standard deviation}}{\text{Market standard deviation}}$$

Project	1	2	3
	$\dfrac{0.76 \times 8.4}{6.9}$	$\dfrac{0.63 \times 4.6}{6.9}$	$\dfrac{0.58 \times 14.3}{6.9}$
Beta =	0.93	0.42	1.20

Using CAPM, required return = Rf + (Rm – Rf) beta

Project	1	2	3
Required return (%)	14.37	9.78	16.80
Expected return (%)	15.00	11.00	17.00
Abnormal return (%)	0.63	1.22	0.20

All three projects are expected to generate satisfactory returns relative to their systematic risk. Other things being equal, the project with the highest expected NPV should be selected. However, NPVs cannot be estimated from this data. It is recommended that investment 2 is selected as it is the largest investment in terms of initial outlay, and also has the largest expected abnormal return.

The investment of any surplus funds in the money market is irrelevant as such investment has an expected NPV of zero (assuming the money market is efficient).

(b)   A profitability index of 1.3 on an investment of £40 million implies a present value of cash inflows of £52 million (£40m x 1.3), and a NPV of £12 million ((£40m x 1.3) – £40m).

The discount rate that will produce a present value of £52 million may be found by solving:

$$£52m = \frac{16}{1+r} + \frac{16}{(1+r)^2} + \frac{16}{(1+r)^3} + \frac{16}{(1+r)^4}$$

$$\frac{52}{16} = 3.25$$

Tutorial note: 3.25 is the cumulative discount factor for years 1 – 4 at a discount rate of r.

Using PV of annuity tables, the discount factor for four years giving a PV annuity value of 3.25 is slightly below 9%.

The beta required to produce a discount rate of 9% is approximately 0.33. The estimated beta is too high.

Tutorial note:

Rf + β (Rm – Rf)	=	9
6 + β (15 – 6)	=	9
9 β	=	3
β	=	0.33

(c)   The current gearing using market values is:

Equity:

200 million shares x £2.20 = £440 million.

The cost of equity is estimated to be: 6% + (15% – 6%) 1.25 = 17.25%.

Debt:

The market price of debt is:

$$\frac{£71m \times £105.50}{£100} = £74.91 \text{ million}$$

The cost of debt may be estimated from the redemption yield of existing long-term debt.

$$£105.5m = \frac{12(1-0.3)}{1+kd} + \frac{12(1-0.3)}{(1+kd)^2} + \frac{12(1-0.3)}{(1+kd)^3} + \frac{12(1-0.3)}{(1+kd)^4} + \frac{100}{(1+kd)^4}$$

By trial and error:

At 8%

8.4×3.312	=	27.82	
100×0.735	=	73.50	
		101.32	

At 6%

8.4×3.465	=	29.11	
100×0.792	=	79.20	
		108.31	

Interpolating:

$$6\% \ + \frac{2.81}{2.81 + 4.18} \times 2\% \ = 6.8\%$$

The cost of debt is approximately 6.8%

Weighted average cost of capital

$$WACC = \ ke \times \ \frac{E}{E+D} + kd\,(1-t)\ \frac{D}{E+D}$$

$$= \ 17.25\% \times \ \frac{440}{440+74.91} + 6.8\%\ \frac{74.91}{440+74.91}$$

Jetter's cost of capital is 15.73%

The new investment is not likely to alter the gearing of the company significantly, as the investment is financed by internal funds, which, in theory, does not alter gearing but only changes the nature of the company's assets. The £12m NPV is likely to accrue primarily to the shareholders and might reduce gearing slightly as the value of equity increases. The risk of the new project appears to be very low (asset beta of 0.33; given the company's gearing, the equity beta would only be a little higher than this), which will reduce the overall equity beta of the company, and the cost of equity. The overall effect is likely to be a small decrease in the weighted average cost of capital.

(d) (i) Betas estimated from standard regression techniques may not provide the best estimate of a company's true beta. High betas are argued to be overestimated, and low betas to be underestimated. Additionally estimation errors are likely to be greater in small companies than in large companies. Adjusted betas have been suggested to try to reduce estimation errors and produce a more accurate beta. The suggested adjustment lowers betas of more than 1 and increases betas of less than 1.

Tutorial note: If you are not sure about this point, work out some examples. For example, an unadjusted beta of 0.9 (less than 1) would be adjusted upwards by the formula to 0.933, whereas an unadjusted beta of 1.2 (above 1) would be adjusted downwards to 1.13.

(ii)

Project	1	2	3
Unadjusted beta	0.93	0.42	1.20
Adjusted beta	0.95	0.61	1.13

Using CAPM, required return = Rf + (Rm – Rf) β

Project	1	2	3
New required return (%)	14.55	11.49	16.17
Expected return (%)	15.00	11.00	17.00
Abnormal return (%)	0.45	(0.49)	0.83

Project 2 would not have a high enough expected return, and would no longer be the project selected.

(e)   CAPM suggests that a simple linear relation exists between beta and expected return. It may be used to estimate the cost of equity (hence the required rate of return) to be used as part of the discount rate of capital investments. However, CAPM is based upon a series of restrictive assumptions including:

(i)   Investors are only interested in the mean and variance of their expected returns.

(ii)   Investors have the same beliefs about the mean and standard deviations of portfolios.

(iii) Investors have the same one period time horizon.

(iv)   There are no taxes or transactions costs.

(v)   Investors can borrow or lend at the risk free rate.

(vi)   No individual investor can influence the market price of a security.

Additionally CAPM is an ex-ante model, but the data used in the model are normally ex-post. Empirical tests of CAPM suggest that company size, market to book value ratios, price earnings ratios, dividend yields and long-term contrarian strategies are to some extent related to expected returns, not just beta. However, there is debate (e.g. by Roll) about whether CAPM can actually be tested.

Another view is that returns are influenced by behavioural bias by investors e.g. bias against companies with low market to book value ratios. Despite its theoretical limitations, CAPM is relatively easy to apply and is widely used in capital investment decisions.

APT is a multi-factor model that assumes that returns on investments are generated by a number of industry and market factors, rather than just within a mean-variance framework. It relies upon less restrictive assumptions than CAPM and allows for the possibility that investors may hold different types of risky portfolios. Unfortunately there is little agreement on what the factors are that explain returns, hence the model is difficult to apply to capital investment decisions.

ACCA marking scheme		Marks
This question requires the use of appropriate techniques to select between investment opportunities, and an understanding of the use and limitations of CAPM and APT.		
(a)	Decision criteria/technique used	1
	Project betas	2
	Required/expected/abnormal returns	3
	Choice of project/conclusion	2
		8
(b)	Total PV	1
	Discount rate calculations	3
	Required beta/conclusion	1
		5
(c)	Cost of equity	1
	Cost of debt	3
	WACC (including gearing)	2
	Discussion of the effect on the cost of capital	2–3
	Maximum	8
(d) (i)	Reward comments about inaccuracy and examples	3
(ii)	Calculations	2
	Conclusion	1
		6
(e)	CAPM	4–5
	APT	3–4
	Maximum	8
Total		35

35   STRAYER PLC

(a)   Assuming the risk of companies in the printing industry is similar to that of Strayer's new investment, the beta of the printing industry will be used to estimate the discount rate for the base case NPV.

Ungearing the beta of the printing industry:

$$\text{Asset beta} = \text{Equity beta} \times \frac{E}{E + D(1-t)} = 1.2 \times \frac{50}{50 + 50(1 - 0.30)} = 0.706$$

Using the capital asset pricing model:

K_e ungeared = 5.5% + (12% − 5.5%) 0.706 = 10.09% or approximately 10%.

Annual after tax cash flows = £5 million (1 − 0.3) = £3,500,000.

From annuity tables with a 10% discount rate:

			£
Present value of annual cash flows	3,500,000 × 6.145	=	21,507,500
Present value of the residual value	5,000,000 × 0.386	=	1,930,000
			23,437,500
Less initial investment			25,000,000
Base case NPV			(1,562,500)

Financing side effects relate to the tax shield on interest payments, the subsidised loan, and issue costs associated with external financing.

Tax relief:

£5 million 8% loan. Interest payable is £400,000 per year, tax relief is £400,000 × 0.3 = £120,000 per year.

£4 million subsidised loan. Interest is £240,000 per year, tax relief £72,000 per year.

Total annual tax relief £192,000 per year. The present value of this tax relief, discounted at the risk free rate of 5.5% per year is: £192,000 × 7.541 = £1,447,872.

(The tax relief on interest payments allowed by government is assumed to be risk free. The mid-point between 5% and 6% in annuity tables is used. N.B. discounting at a rate higher than the risk free rate could be argued, especially if the company might be in a non taxpaying position in some years.)

Subsidy:

The company saves 2% per year on £4,000,000 or £80,000, or £80,000 × (1 − 0.30) = £56,000 after tax.

As this is a government subsidy it is assumed to be risk free and will be discounted at 5.5% per year.

£56,000 × 7.541 = £422,296.

Issue costs:		£
Debt: £5 million × 1%	=	50,000
Equity: £10 million × 4%	=	400,000
		450,000

Tutorial note: To calculate the adjusted NPV, we have to allow for the value of the tax relief and the subsidy, but deduct the issue costs for the finance.

The adjusted present value is estimated to be:

(£1,562,500) + £1,447,872 + £422,296 − £450,000 = (£142,332)

Based upon these estimates the project is not financially viable.

(b)   APV may be a better technique to use than NPV when:

(i)   There is a significant change in capital structure as a result of the investment.

(ii)   The investment involves complex tax payments and tax allowances, and/or has periods when taxation is not paid.

(iii)   Subsidised loans, grants or issue costs exist.

(iv)   Financing side effects exist (e.g. the subsidised loan) which require discounting at a different rate than that applied to the mainstream project.

ACCA marking scheme		
		Marks
(a)	Base case NPV	5
	Tax relief	3
	Subsidy	2
	Issue costs	1
	APV/conclusion	1
		12
(b)	One mark for each relevant point, maximum	3
Total		15

36   AVTO

Examiner's comment

This question requires analysis of the viability of an overseas investment taking into account all relevant financial and non-financial effects, including possible blockage of remittances from the country.

Appraisal of the proposed investment in Terrania

The investment will be evaluated using both financial and non-financial criteria, including the possible political risk involved with investing in Terrania. However, international direct investment is sometimes undertaken for strategic reasons, which, at least in the short term, might outweigh financial considerations.

(a)   **Financial appraisal**

Projected cash flows:

Terranian francs (million)

Year	0	1	2	3	4	5
Sales (W2)		659	735	785	838	
Labour (W3)		228	262	288	317	
Local components (W4)		90	104	114	125	
German components (W5)		41	47	52	57	
Distribution (W6)		20	23	25	28	
Fixed costs (W6)		50	58	63	70	
Total costs		(429)	(494)	(542)	(597)	

			230	241	243	241	
Taxable cash flows			230	241	243	241	
Tax on cash flows at 20%			(46)	(48)	(49)	(48)	
Tax saved from depreciation (W7)			29	22	16	12	
Equipment		(580)					
Working capital (W8)		(170)	(34)	(31)	(23)	(26)	284
Remittable to the UK		(750)	179	184	187	329	284

UK cash flows (£ million)

Year	0	1	2	3	4	5
Remittable to the UK (W9)	(20.35)	4.13	3.80	3.62	5.96	4.82
Additional 10% UK tax on Terranian cash flow (W10)		(0.20)	(0.27)	(0.31)	(0.33)	
	(20.35)	3.93	3.53	3.31	5.63	4.82
Discount factors at 15% (W11)	1.000	0.870	0.756	0.658	0.572	0.497
Present values	(20.35)	3.42	2.67	2.18	3.22	2.40

Net present value = (£6.46 million)

Workings

(W1) *Exchange rates*

Exchange rates are assumed to change in line with changes in inflation rates, in accordance with the Purchasing Power Parity theory.

Year	*0*	*1*	*2*	*3*	*4*	*5*
Change factor		× (1.20/1.02)	× (1.15/1.03)	× (1.10/1.03)	× (1.10/1.03)	× (1.10/1.03)
T franc/£1	36.85	43.35	48.40	51.69	55.20	58.96
T franc/€1	23.32	27.44	30.63	32.71	34.94	

(W2) *Sales*

Year	*1*	*2*	*3*	*4*
Sales (units)	50,000	50,000	50,000	50,000
Sales price (€)	€480	€480	€480	€480
Revenue (€m)	24.0	24.0	24.0	24.0
Exchange rate (W1)	27.44	30.63	32.71	34.94
Revenue (T francs m)	659	735	785	838

(W3) *Labour*

Labour cost has been increased by a factor of 1.20 to reflect the use of 300 workers in order to gain use of the rent-free factory. The cost of 50 extra workers in Year 1 is $(50/250) \times (3{,}800 \text{ T francs} \times 50{,}000) = 38$ million francs. The annual after-tax costing of renting the factory would be 75 million $\times (1 - 0.20) = 60$ million francs. Avto would select the rent-free factory as the cost is lower.

The cost of 300 workers in Year 1 is (in T francs millions):

$(3{,}800 \times 50{,}000) + 38.0 = 228.$

This will rise due to inflation by 15% in Year 2, 10% in Year 3 and 10% in Year 4.

(W4) *Local components*

Cost in Year 1 = 50,000 units × 1,800 T francs = 90 million T francs. This will rise with inflation by 15% in Year 2, 105 in Year 3 and 10% in Year 4.

(W5) *German components*

Cost in Year 1 = 50,000 units × €30 = €1,500,000. This cost will rise with inflation by 3% each year from Year 2 onwards.

Year	1	2	3	4
Cost (€000)	1,500	1,545	1,591	1,639
Exchange rate (W1)	27.44	30.63	32.71	34.94
Cost in T francs (m)	41	47	52	57

(W6) *Distribution costs, fixed costs and feasibility study costs*

The sales and distribution costs in Year 1 will be 50,000 × 400 T francs = 20 million T francs. These costs will rise with inflation, by 15% in Year 2, 10% in year 3 and 10% in Year 4.

The fixed costs in Year 1 will be 50 million T francs. These costs will rise with inflation, by 15% in Year 2, 10% in year 3 and 10% in Year 4.

The cost of the feasibility study is irrelevant, because it is a sunk cost.

(W7) *Tax saved from depreciation*

In T francs millions	Year 1	Year 2	Year 3	Year 4
Written down value at start of year	580	435	326	244
Tax-allowable depreciation (25%)	145	109	82	61
Tax saving (20%)	29	22	16	12

(W8) *Working capital*

Working capital is assumed to increase each year in line with inflation in Terrania, and to be released at the end of Year 5.

In TF millions	Year 0	Year 1	Year 2	Year 3	Year 4	Year 5
Working capital requirement	170	204	235	258	284	0
Cash flow in year	(170)	(34)	(31)	(23)	(26)	284

Tutorial note on working capital assumption

The solution here gives the examiner's preferred approach to calculating the working capital cash flows. This assumes that working capital builds up into Year 4 and the investment in working capital is not recovered until Year 5. An alternative approach would be to assume that the working capital is recovered early in Year 5, i.e. at the end of Year 4 rather than at the end of Year 5. If you prefer this assumption, the cash flow in Year 4 would be + 258 rather than – 26, and there would be no cash flow at all in Year 5.

This alternative solution would have been fully acceptable, but the calculations of the cash flows and project NPV, and the analysis, would then be different.

(W9) *Funds remittable to the UK*

	Year 0	Year 1	Year 2	Year 3	Year 4	Year 5
In TF millions	(750)	179	184	187	329	284
Exchange rate (W1)	36.85	43.35	48.40	51.69	55.20	58.96
In £ millions	(20.35)	4.13	3.80	3.62	5.96	4.82

(W10) *Additional UK tax on Terranian cash flow*

Since a bilateral tax treaty exists between the UK and Terrania, and tax in Terrania is lower than tax in the UK by 10% (30% – 20%), an additional 10% taxation will be levied on Terranian cash flows in the UK.

In T francs millions	Year 1	Year 2	Year 3	Year 4
Taxable cash flows	230	241	243	241
Tax-allowable depreciation (25%)	145	109	82	61
Taxable in Terrania	85	132	161	180
Extra 10% tax	8.5	13.2	16.1	18.0
Exchange rate	43.35	48.40	51.69	55.20
Extra tax in £ millions	£0.20m	£0.27m	£0.31m	£0.33m

(W11) *Discount rate, Terranian investment*

Cost of capital = 4.5% + 1.5 (11.5 – 4.5)% = 15%.

(W12) *Discount rate, UK investment*

Cost of capital = 4.5% + 1.1 (11.5 – 4.5)% = 12.2%, say 12%.

(W13) *Net cost of closure in Year 0*

	£m
Closure costs	(35.0)
Tax saving (30%)	10.5
Proceeds from asset disposals	20.0
Net cash flow	(4.5)

(W14) *Net cost of downsizing in Year 0*

	£m
Closure costs	(20.0)
Tax saving (30%)	6.0
Proceeds from asset disposals	10.0
Net cash flow	(4.0)

Analysis

The expected NPV is: (£6.46) million. The expected investment in Terrania if viewed alone does not appear to be financially viable. However, the closure or downsizing of UK operations should also be considered.

Closure would have a Year 0 net cost, after tax, of at least £4.5 million (see W13). The cost could be more if the full existing market in the EU cannot be supplied from Terrania, and closure might have other adverse effects on the local community that have not been quantified, and on the government in terms of extra support for redundant workers and their families.

Downsizing would still have some of these effects, but would also offer the opportunity of selling to a larger market that could not otherwise have been supplied from Terrania alone. If the UK operation is downsized, the Year 0 net cost, after tax, of downsizing is £4 million (see W14). Expected annual net cash flows are (£4 million, less tax at 30%) £2.8 million at Year 0 values. Increasing these net cash flows by UK inflation, we can calculate a present value of the cash flows from downsizing, as follows:

4m × 0.7 ← 2·8

In £ millions	Year 0	Year 1	Year 2	Year 3	Year 4
Cash flow	(4.0)	2.86	2.94	3.03	3.12
Discount factor at 12% (W12)	1.000	0.893	0.797	0.712	0.636
Present value of cash flow	(4.0)	2.55	2.34	2.16	1.98

Net present value = £5.03m

The total present value of cash flows from downsizing is £5.03 million over the four-year period. Downsizing results in a much more favourable outcome than total closure. If a period of longer than four years were considered the expected present value from downsizing would be even larger.

Overall the investment in Terrania plus downsizing does not appear to be financially viable, with an expected NPV of (£1.43) million (= £5.03m – £6.46m). However, one major problem with the cash flow estimates is the realisable value used for the Terranian assets in year 4. If the Terranian investment is to continue beyond four years, which is implied in the information provided, then the present value of cash flows beyond four years should be considered, not the realisable value of assets. This present value is likely to be substantially higher. For example, even ignoring growth, the value of the operating cash flows (179 million Terranian francs in year 4) for an additional ten years at a discount rate of 15% would be TF 898 million (179 million × 5.019). This is much more than the TF 150 million estimated realisable value of assets used above in the DCF analysis.

(b) **Wider commercial considerations**

Aspects of the cash flows that would need to be investigated further before a decision was made include:

(i)   What rent would be payable for the factory after year 4?

(ii) How accurate are the forecasts of sales, costs, tax rates etc? Sensitivity analysis or simulation analysis might be used to investigate the effect of changes in key cash flows.

(iii) Will the investment lead to other opportunities (future options)? If so an attempt should be made to value such options.

(iii) The strategic importance of the investment to the company.

(v)   The political risk of Terrania. The fact that the country has had twelve changes of government in the last ten years does not necessarily mean that there is substantial political risk. Countries such as Italy have also experienced frequent changes of government. However, the degree of international indebtedness and potential lack of support from the IMF could affect the future prospects of the country. It would be useful to know the ability of Terrania to service its debt, given the problems with the banana crop and competition from neighbouring countries.

(vi) The existence of better opportunities elsewhere. For example would it be possible to produce the DVD players in neighbouring countries where labour costs are even lower?

(c) **The impact of blocked remittances**

Avto should investigate how likely are further restrictions on remittances from Terrania. If remittance restrictions are introduced Avto could partially mitigate their effects by investing in the Terranian money market, but the effect of the restrictions would still reduce the present value of expected cash flows by approximately £1.83 million (see below) unless increased direct investment in Terrania was planned. Remittance restrictions might be avoided by increasing transfer prices paid by the foreign subsidiary to the parent company, or by trying to move cash out of Terrania by means of other forms of payment such as royalties, payment for patents, or management fees. It is likely that the Terranian government would try to prevent many of these measures being used.

If remittances were blocked for four years and the funds invested in the Terranian money market.

	Cash flow		*End of Year 4 value*
	TF millions		TF millions
Year 1	179	(× 1.15 × 1.10 × 1.10)	249
Year 2	184	(× 1.10 × 1.10)	223
Year 3	187	(× 1.10)	206
Year 4	329		329
End-of-Year 4 remittable value			1,007
Expected exchange rate, end of Year 4			55.20
£m equivalent at end of Year 4			18.24
Discount factor at 15%			0.572
Present value			**10.43**

The present value of remittable funds (without additional UK tax) if no blockage exists is £12.26 million. The blockage would therefore reduce the expected present value of cash flows by approximately £1.83 million.

Any final decision regarding investment in Terrania must also take into account other non-financial factors such as the nature of the country's legal system, bureaucracy, efficiency of internal processes, cultural and religious differences, and local business practices and ethics.

ACCA marking scheme	
	Marks
Criteria for making the decision	1
Estimates of future exchange rates	3
Terranian cash flows:	
Sales	1
Labour (including 300 workers) – with reason	2–3
Local components	1
Fixed costs	1
German components	1
Capital allowances/savings	3
Taxation	1
Equipment plus realisable value	1
Working capital	2
Feasibility study = sunk cost	1
UK cash flows:	
Remittable	1
Additional tax	2
Discount rates, UK and Terrania	2
NPV and conclusion	1
	24
Reward technique even if calculation errors exist	
Net cost of closure	1
Impact of downsizing	3
Comment on accuracy of cash flows – especially reward comments about what happens after year 4	4–5
Blocked remittances:	
Calculations	2
Discussion	2–3
Other information/analysis that would be useful	4–5
Total	40

37 FUELIT PLC

Key answer tips

This question involves identifying two sets of cash flows and two discount rates. Time is likely to be the main problem. Try to cover as much of the answer as possible even if no one aspect is completed. To facilitate discussion, make assumptions where necessary. With such long time scales you must work in real terms. Remember to adjust the WACC calculated discount rate to a real rate. The conclusions reached by this solution might seem unrealistic, given the financial problems of the nuclear power industry!

(a) **Financial evaluation of the alternative power stations**

Alternative 1: Gas fuelled power station

Cash flows at current prices (£ million)

	Years 4 – 13 (annual)	Years 14 – 28 (annual)
Revenue	<u>800.0</u>	<u>800.0</u>
Labour	75.0	75.0
Fuel purchases	500.0	500.0
Sales and marketing	40.0	40.0
Customer relations	5.0	5.0
Other	5.0	5.0
Tax allowable depreciation (10% of 600, yrs 4 – 13)	<u>60.0</u>	<u>-</u>
	685.0	625.0
Taxable profit	115.0	175.0
Tax at 30%	(34.5)	(52.5)
	80.5	122.5
Add back depreciation	<u>60.0</u>	<u>-</u>
Annual net operating cash flows	<u>140.5</u>	<u>122.5</u>

Tutorial note: interest costs are included in the discount rate and should not be in the cash flow table as a cash flow item.

Cost of capital, gas

Cost of equity using CAPM is $4.5\% + (14\% - 4.5\%)\,0.7 = 11.15\%$

WACC $= 11.15\% \times 0.65 + 8.5\% \,(1 - 0.3) \times 0.35 = 9.33\%$

However, this is the nominal cost of capital which includes inflation. The cash flow projections exclude inflation and must be discounted at a real cost of capital. given the assumption of annual inflation of 3% per annum, the real cost of capital is:

$$\frac{1.0933}{1.03} = 1.061$$

6% will be used as the real discount rate for gas.

NPV calculation, gas

Discount factors at 6%

Cumulative discount factor, years $1 - 10 = 7.360$

Cumulative discount factor, years $4 - 13$ (10 years) at year 3 value $= 7.360$.

Present value of cumulative discount factor, years $4 - 13 = 7.360 \times$ discount factor for year $3 = 7.360 \times 0.840 = 6.182$.

Cumulative discount factor, years 1 – 15 = 9.712.

Cumulative discount factor, years 14 – 28 (15 years) at year 13 value = 9.712.

Present value of cumulative discount factor, years 14 – 28 = 7.360 x discount factor for year 13 = 9.712 × 0.469 = 4.555.

Discount factor year 28 = discount factor year 15 x discount factor year 13 (since 15 + 13 = 28) = 0.417 × 0.469 = 0.196.

Year	Item	Cash flow	Discount factor at 6%	PV
		£ million		£ million
1	Capital outlay	(300.0)	0.943	(282.9)
2	Capital outlay	(300.0)	0.890	(267.0)
3	Decommissioning cost	(10.0)	0.840	(8.40)
28	Decommissioning cost	(25.0)	0.196	(4.90)
4	Redundancy costs	(4.0)	0.792	(3.17)
4- 13	Operating cash flows	140.5	6.182	868.6
14 – 28	Operating cash flows	122.5	4.555	558.0
	Project NPV			860.23

The NPV of an investment in a gas-fuelled power station is + £860.23 million.

Alternative 2: Nuclear-fuelled power station

Cash flows at current prices (£ million)

	Years 4 – 13 (annual)	Years 14 – 28 (annual)
Revenue	800.0	800.0
Labour	20.0	20.0
Fuel purchases	10.0	10.0
Sales and marketing	40.0	40.0
Customer relations	20.0	20.0
Other	25.0	25.0
Tax allowable depreciation (10% of 3,300, yrs 4 – 13)	330.0	-
	445.0	115.0
Taxable profit	355.0	685.0
Tax at 30%	(106.5)	(205.5)
	248.5	479.5
Add back depreciation	330.0	-
Annual net operating cash flows	578.5	479.5

Cost of capital, nuclear power

Cost of equity using CAPM is 4.5% + (14% – 4.5%) 1.4 = 17.8%

WACC = 17.8 × 0.40 + 10%(1 –0.3) × 0.60 = 11.32%

The real cost of capital is $\frac{1.1132}{1.03}$ = 1.081

8% will be used as the real discount rate for nuclear power.

Estimates of the discount rates assume that the value of the pound will not change relative to the euro, or alternatively that the UK will join the eurozone in the near future. If this does not occur and inflation differentials between the UK and eurozone remain similar the cost of debt should be slightly less as the euro is expected to fall in value relative to the pound (since inflation in the eurozone is estimated at 5% and in the UK at only 3%).

NPV calculation, nuclear power

Discount factors at 8%

Cumulative discount factor, years 1 – 10 = 6.710

Cumulative discount factor, years 4 – 13 (10 years) at year 3 value = 6.710.

Present value of cumulative discount factor, years 4 – 13 = 6.710 × discount factor for year 3 = 6.710 × 0.794 = 5.328.

Cumulative discount factor, years 1 – 15 = 8.559.

Cumulative discount factor, years 14 – 28 (15 years) at year 13 value = 8.559.

Present value of cumulative discount factor, years 14 – 28 = 8.559 × discount factor for year 13 = 8.559 × 0.368 = 3,150.

Discount factor year 28 = discount factor year 15 x discount factor year 13 (since 15 + 13 = 28) = 0.315 × 0.368 = 0.116.

Year	Item	Cash flow	Discount factor at 8%	PV
		£ million		£ million
1	Capital outlay	(1,650)	0.926	(1,527.90)
2	Capital outlay	(1,650)	0.857	(1,414.05)
3	Decommissioning cost	(10.0)	0.794	(7.94)
28	Decommissioning cost	(1,000.0)	0.116	(116.00)
4	Redundancy costs	(36.0)	0.735	(26.50)
4- 13	Operating cash flows	578.5	5.328	3,082.25
14 – 28	Operating cash flows	479.5	3.150	1,510.40
	Project NPV			1,500.26

The NPV of an investment in a nuclear power station is + £1,500.26 million.

If decommissioning in year 28 costs only £500 million, the expected NPV will be higher by £500 million × 0.116 = £58 million. The NPV will therefore be £1,558 million.

Conclusion

On the basis of these figures, the **nuclear energy option would produce a higher NPV**.

(b)   Information that might assist the decision process includes:

(i)   How accurate are the projected cash flows? Are the various revenues and costs likely to be subject to the same price level changes?

(ii)   Is the risk of the project correctly measured by the beta estimates?

(iii)   What is the chance of significant changes in tax rates or tax allowable depreciation?

(iv)   Are there likely to be delays in construction?

(v)   How accurate is the estimate of the working life of the power stations? What happens if technology changes?

(vi) Is the technology well tested, especially for the nuclear alternative?

Sensitivity and/or simulation analysis to investigate outcomes under different assumptions is strongly recommended.

(vii) What will be the impact of the alternative levels of gearing on other activities of the company and on the company's share price?

(viii) What real options might exist with the alternative projects?

(ix) How significant are non financial factors? In the light of nuclear accidents in Russia and Japan how safe is the nuclear alternative? How environmentally or politically acceptable would this alternative be? Even if the nuclear alternative is the better choice financially this might be outweighed by non-financial considerations.

(c) The external advisor has suggested adjusting the discount rate as the decommissioning costs are not known with any certainty. As these cash flows are relatively risky an adjustment to the discount rate might be justified. The decommissioning costs are cash outflows. In order to reflect the higher risk the discount rate of these cash flows should be reduced to result in a higher negative present value.

(d) Capital investment decisions are often based upon the present value of expected future cash flows, discounted at a rate that reflects the risk of the project. However this ignores any actions that can be taken after the project has commenced to alter the cash flows, or any future opportunities that might arise as a direct result of having undertaken the project. Opportunities to respond to changing future circumstances are known as options. When such options relate to capital investments they are commonly known as real options. The existence of real options can significantly add to the value of an investment. If investments are judged only on their expected NPV, and the value embedded in the options is ignored, then an incorrect investment decision might result. Unfortunately the valuation of real options is extremely difficult.

In the context of the power station investment a number of options might exist including:

(i) The option to abandon the project. This is likely to be easier and more valuable with the gas project than the nuclear project because of the lower cost, and much fewer decommissioning problems of the gas project.

(ii) The option to expand production. This is also likely to be more valuable with the gas project as much lower investment is required in new plant to expand.

(iii) The option to adjust the nature of production, for example the fuel used. This is far easier for the gas project which could probably switch to oil or other fuels at a much lower cost than the nuclear project.

(iv) The option to take advantage of new technology. Once again there is likely to be more flexibility in the gas project.

In conclusion there are likely to be more valuable real options associated with the gas fuelled power station project.

38 UTOPIA HOTEL GROUP

Key answer tips

While getting carried away with the cost of capital and NPV calculations you may have lost sight of the actual requirement – to produce a breakeven occupancy rate – so do not assume one in your answer.

(a) The new hotel will be financially viable if it produces an expected net present value of at least zero. The Utopia group would obviously prefer the NPV to be as high as possible, but the financial viability may be assessed against the zero NPV requirement.

All revenues, costs and values are given at current prices. No details of how price changes will affect these are given, therefore the real NPV, ignoring inflation, will be estimated. This involves discounting real cash flows with a real discount rate.

As the investment is not expected to significantly affect the business risk or the financial risk of the group, the group's current real weighted average cost of capital may be used as the discount rate.

The cost of debt

The gross yield of a new issue of long dated debentures may be estimated from the redemption yield of the current debentures, which have 13 years to redemption.

By trial and error

The coupon rate is 12% and the tax rate is 33%, and for perpetual debt this would give an after tax cost of (12% × 67%) = 8.04% if the debt traded at par. The market value of the debt is above par, indicating that the redemption yield will be lower than 8.04%. Here, an 8% cost of debt will be tested first. After tax annual cash flows are 100 × 12% × (1 – 0.33) = 8.04.

Year		Cash flow	Try 8% Discount factor at 8%	PV	Try 6% Discount factor at 6%	PV
1 – 13	Interest	8.04	7.904	63.55	8.853	71.18
13	Redemption	100	0.368	36.80	0.469	46.90
				100.35		118.08
0	Current MV	114	1.000	114.00	1.000	114.00
				(13.65)		4.08

Interpolating, the after tax cost of debt is approximately:

$$6\% + \frac{4.08}{4.08 + 13.65} \times 2\% = 6.46\%$$

This is assumed to be cost of the debenture and of the floating rate term loan, although in reality the term loan could have a slightly different cost.

Cost of equity

Using CAPM, ke = Rf + (Rm – Rf) betae

ke = 7% + (15% – 7%) 0.8

= 13.4%

Weighted average cost of capital

	£m
The market value of equity is 480 million shares × 3.45 =	1,656
The market value of debt is: term loans	150
debentures (200 million × 1.14)	228
	2,034

$$\text{WACC} = 13.4\% \times \frac{1,656}{2,034} + 6.46\% \times \frac{378}{2,034} = 12.11\%$$

However, this is weighted average cost of capital using market rates (nominal rates) which include inflation. In order to find the real discount rate, the effect of inflation must be removed. The annual inflation rate is expected to be 3.8%

The real discount rate is therefore estimated to be: $\frac{1.1211}{1.038} - 1$

= 0.08 or 8%.

Present value calculations

Using the estimated real discount rate of 8% per year, the present values of the expected cash flows of the new hotel (£000) over a 15 year operating period are as follows.

Workings (in £000)

1   Non-residential income = 1,000, less tax each year, years 3–17:
     1,000 (1 – 0.33) = 670.

2   Annual outlays net of tax, years 3 – 17 = 6,200 (1 – 0.33) = 4,154.

3   Refurbishment net of tax = 10,000 (1 – 0.33) = 6,700 in both Year 7 and
     Year 12.

4   *Tax allowable depreciation.* It is assumed that the first tax allowance will
     reduce tax payments in Year 1.

Year	1	2	3 – 17
Total capital cost	5,000	30,000	50,000
Allowance (2.5% of cost)	125	750	1,250
Tax saved (33%)	41	247	412

5   *Discount factors at 8%*

Years 3 – 17 is a period of 15 years.

The present value of £1 per annum for years 1 – 15 at 8% = 8.559.

This is the present value from the start of year 3, i.e. at the end of year 2, of £1 per annum for years 3 – 17.

To convert a year 2 discount factor to a present value, multiply by the discount factor for year 2 at 8%, which is 0.857.

PV of £1 per annum, years 3 – 17, at 8% = 8.559 × 0.857 = 7.335.

The discount factor for year 17 can be calculated by multiplying the year 15 discount factor by the year 2 discount factor (since 15 + 2 = 17).

Discount factor at 8%, year 17 = 0.857 × 0.315 = 0.270.

Year		Cash flow	Discount factor at 8%	PV
		£000		£000
0	Capital expenditure	(5,000)	1.000	(5,000)
1	Capital expenditure	(25,000)	0.926	(23,150)
2	Capital expenditure	(20,000)	0.857	(17,140)
17	Value of business	60,000	0.270	16,200
1	Tax allowable depreciation	41	0.926	38
2	Tax allowable depreciation	247	0.857	212
3 – 17	Tax allowable depreciation	412	7.335	3,022

3 – 17	Non-residential guest income	670	7.335	4,914
3 – 17	Annual outlays	(4,154)	7.335	(30,470)
7	Refurbishment cost	(6,700)	0.583	(3,906)
12	Refurbishment cost	(6,700)	0.397	(2,660)
2	Working capital invested	(1,500)	0.857	(1,286)
17	Working capital recovery	1,500	0.270	405
	Net PV of costs			(55,821)

These net costs exclude the PV of contribution from guests.

If S is the occupancy rate, and is between 0 and 1 (1 being 100% occupancy), then cash flows from years 3-17 that are directly linked to the occupancy rate are:

£000

Annual cash flow from room sales (less tax) is

$(100 \times 365 \times 300S)(1 - 0.33)/1,000 =$ 7,337S

Contribution from food and drink

$(40 \times 0.4 \times 1.4 \times 365 \times 300S)(1 - 0.33)/1,000 =$ 1,643S

Contribution from other facilities

$(15 \times 0.3 \times 1.4 \times 365 \times 300S)(1 - 0.33)/1,000 =$ 462S

9,442S

This is the expected cash inflow, directly linked to the occupancy rate, between years 3 and 17.

The present value of this inflow will be:

$9,442S \times 7.335 = 69,257S$

The zero NPV position will be where the present value of the cash flows that are not related to occupancy (a net outflow) equals the present value of those that are related to occupancy.

i.e. where $69,257S = 58,821$

S = 0.849 or 84.9%.

This means that the hotel must achieve an occupancy rate of almost 85% over a period of 15 years. This is a level that most hotel groups would not expect to achieve, suggesting that the hotel is not expected to be financially viable.

(b)   The above estimate of occupancy rate is not likely to be accurate as it is based upon imprecise estimates of future cash flows. At the very least sensitivity analysis of the major components of cash flows should be undertaken in order to estimate a possible range of occupancy rates that could occur. Significant errors might include:

(i)   Many of the cash flow projections may not be accurate. For example will an average of 1.4 persons per night use a room? Is the room charge and the additional per capita spend accurate? Are annual outlay estimates accurate? Outlays are assumed to be fixed, but electricity, staff costs etc. will vary with the number of guests. How has the residual value of £60 million in 17 years time been established and what margin of error is there?

(ii)   The cost of capital estimate may not be accurate.

(iii)   The analysis has been undertaken in real terms, with the implicit assumption that all cash inflows and outflows are affected by changing prices in the same way. If, as is likely, cash flows are affected by changing price to differing degrees this will result in a different required occupancy rate.

(iv)   Corporate tax rates and tax allowances may change during a 17 year period.

(v)   The risk of the group may alter during the period, influencing the required return of investors and the cost of capital.

(c)   The director is correct that **many of the assumptions of CAPM are unrealistic**. These include:

(i)   CAPM assumes that investors are fully diversified. Many investors do not hold well diversified portfolios.

(ii)   The company is assumed to make decisions purely on behalf of its shareholders. Decisions may be influenced by other stakeholders including directors, employees, the government and the local community.

(iii)   CAPM is a single period model, whilst investment projects are normally multi-period.

(iv)   CAPM is based upon largely perfect market assumptions many of which are not observed in real world conditions.

Additionally, as well as problems with underlying assumptions, the data required to input into CAPM may be difficult to obtain, especially the beta and the expected market return. Historic data is mostly used in CAPM, but the model is ex-ante. Use of historic data assumes that historic relationships will continue into the future.

There is evidence that CAPM does not correctly express risk return relationships in some circumstances such as for small companies, low beta companies, certain days of the week or months of the year.

The **arbitrage pricing theory (APT)** does not assume that the expected return is only influenced by a single measure of risk, beta, it assumes that expected return is influenced by several independent factors (e.g. inflation, interest rate, the level of industrial production) and that the sensitivity of individual companies to these individual factors will vary. APT has less constraining assumptions than CAPM, for example it is not a single period model and does not require some of the perfect market assumptions of CAPM. However, the major weakness of APT is that it is extremely difficult to identify the relevant factors and the appropriate sensitivities of such factors for individual companies, and hence it is difficult to use as a practical decision-making tool.

Although CAPM has its weaknesses, it is relatively simple to use and, until APT is developed further, it is recommended that CAPM is used rather than APT.

39   MOVER PLC

Key answer tips

Use your own knowledge and common sense to question the realism of cash flows. Note that the question concerns investment in Mover's shares and not directly in the tunnel project.

The risk of the project is unknown, but experience of other tunnel projects such as the channel tunnel suggests that the risk could be high. If inflation is expected to be about 4%, the risk free rate is likely to be higher than this, possibly 7% to 8%. Historically the market risk premium over the risk free rate has been approximately 8% to 9%, giving an expected market return of 15% to 17%. A high-risk investment would probably require a return in excess of this level. The cash flows are in real terms, excluding inflation, and must therefore be discounted at a real rate. Even if the project is only of a similar risk to the market this would require a real discount rate in the range 11% to 13%.

The most favourable financial position of the tunnel project will be shown when the net cash flows are discounted to infinity. In reality the life of a tunnel is finite!

At discount rates of 11% or 13 % the expected NPV of the investment with an infinite life may be estimated to be:

£ million

Year	Cash flows	Discount factor (11%)	Present value	Discount factor (13%)	Present value
2005	– 450	0.901	– 405	0.885	– 398
2006	– 500	0.812	– 406	0.783	– 392
2007	– 550	0.731	– 402	0.693	– 381
2008	– 650	0.659	– 428	0.613	– 398
2009	– 200	0.593	– 119	0.543	– 109
2010	200	0.535	107	0.480	96
2011	300	0.482	145	0.425	128
2012	320	0.434	139	0.376	120
2013	340	0.391	133	0.333	113
2014	360	0.352	127	0.295	106
2015	400	0.317	127	0.261	104
After 2015[1]	400/0.11	0.317	1,153	0.261	803
			NPV = 171		NPV = (208)

Note on the PV of cash flows after 2015

Assuming annual cash flows of 400 each year in perpetuity from 2016 onwards, the discounted value of the post-2015 cash flows, in terms of Year 2015 'present' values, is:

(i)   *At a discount rate of 11%*: 400/0.11 = 3,636.4.

(ii)   *At a discount rate of 13%*: 400/0.13 = 3,076.9.

These should be discounted from Year 2015 (Year 11) values to present values:

(i)   *Discount rate 11%*: PV = 3,636.4 × 0.317 = 1,153.

(ii)   *Discount rate 13%*: PV = 3,076.9 × 0.261 = 803.

The **internal rate of return**, in real terms, is about:

11% + [171/(171 + 208)] × (13 – 11%) = 11.9%.

Although tunnels may have an expected life of 50 years or more, discounting the net cash flows for any period less than infinity is likely to result in negative NPV estimates. Even at a market discount rate the project may not be financially viable.

These NPV estimates assume that the cash flow projections are accurate. Cost overruns are common in large construction projects, and the cash flows from usage of the tunnel are difficult to forecast. Any construction delays will also have an adverse effect on the financial viability of the tunnel. Eventually the tunnel will need substantial maintenance, repairs and possible upgrading, none of which are evident in the cash flow forecasts.

If the tunnel project is a large part of Mover's activities preliminary estimates suggest that the project will probably have an adverse effect on the company's financial health. Unless the company's other activities are expected to produce large positive NPVs which offset the potential weakness of the tunnel project, further analysis is not recommended, nor is investment by the pension fund in Mover plc.

Tutorial note: The examiner commented that students failed to mention whether discount rates were 'real' or 'nominal'. The project's IRR is about 12% ignoring the relevant, project specific, inflation rate of 4%. This means that the discount rate that, when applied to the **cash flows** of the project, will give an NPV of zero is (1.12 × 1.04) –1 or 16½ %.

Interpretation of internal rates of return and discount rates is often confused because cash flows of projects increase at one rate (here 4%). A country's general rate of inflation may well be different (the UK's currently either 1½% or 2½% depending upon what measure is used) and shareholders expected growth in dividends is another figure.

40 WACC

(a) The weighted average cost of capital (WACC) is the effective after tax cost of the different sources of finance used by a company. The costs of the different sources are normally weighted by their market values. WACC is often used to discount the incremental cash flows of an investment in order to estimate the NPV (net present value), the expected change in corporate value resulting from the investment. In order to add value for shareholders it is necessary for the return from an investment to exceed the WACC. WACC is therefore a very useful tool to assist in project evaluation and the measurement of wealth creation. However, it has some problems and limitations. It is sometimes not clear about whether or not to include short-term finance such as overdrafts in the estimate of the weighted average cost of capital and in theory WACC should not be used when:

(i) There is a significant change in the capital structure of the company as a result of the investment.

(ii) The operating risk of the company changes as a result of the investment.

(iii) The investment has complex tax payments and tax allowances, and/or periods when tax is not paid.

(iv) There are subsidised loans or other benefits associated explicitly with an individual project.

In such circumstances the adjusted present value (APV) may be a better technique to analyse investments than the WACC with NPV. APV requires the estimation of the base case NPV of operating cash flows (discounted at the ungeared cost of equity), and, separately, the present value of any financing side effects. It allows more complex financing situations to be dealt with, and the different types of cash flow, with different risks, to be discounted at a rate specific to the individual risk. However, APV also has theoretical and practical problems.

In order to estimate the APV it is necessary to correctly identify all of the financing side effects, and the risk of each individual side effect. This is not an easy task, especially for international investments. APV also relies on some of the unrealistic assumptions of the Modigliani and Miller model (with tax), for example the equation for asset betas used in most APV estimates assumes that cash flows are perpetuities, which is normally not the case.

(b) **Report on the proposed Internet auction investment**.

Key answer tips

Note the importance of using both financial and non financial indicators in assessing the investment – the latter to encompass a discussion of real options in year 6.

The investment will be assessed using both financial and non-financial indicators. It is also important to consider the strategic fit of such an investment, and whether the investment will move the company too far from its core competence.

As the IT infrastructure will require major new investment after six years, the period of the financial evaluation will be six years.

The adjusted present value technique (APV) requires the estimation of the base case NPV of operating cash flows, and, separately, the present value of any financing side effects. Revised financial data:

Internet auctions project

S$000

Year	0	1	2	3	4	5	6
Auction fees		4,300	6,620	8,100	8,200	8,364	8,531
Outflows:							
IT maintenance costs		1,210	1,850	1,920	2,125	2,168	2,211
Telephone costs		1,215	1,910	2,230	2,420	2,468	2,518
Wages		1,460	1,520	1,680	1,730	1,765	1,800
Salaries		400	550	600	650	663	676
Allocated head office overhead		50	55	60	65	66	68
Marketing	500	420	200	200	–	–	–
Royalty payments for use of technology	680	500	300	200	200	200	200
Lost contribution		80	80	80	–	–	–
Rental of premises		280	290	300	310	316	323
Tax allowable depreciation		540	432	432	432	432	432
Total outflows	1,180	6,155	7,187	7,702	7,932	8,078	8,228
Profit before tax	(1,180)	(1,855)	(567)	398	268	286	303
Tax (24.5%)	289	454	139	(98)	(66)	(70)	(74)
	(891)	(1,401)	(428)	300	202	216	229
Add back depreciation		540	432	432	432	432	432
Other outflows							
IT infrastructure	(2,700)						
Working capital	(400)	(24)	(24)	(25)	(26)	(10)	509
Net flows	(3,991)	(885)	(20)	707	608	638	1,170
Discount factors (10%)		0.909	0.826	0.751	0.683	0.621	0.564
Present values	(3,991)	(804)	(17)	531	415	396	660

The expected base case NPV is ($2,810,000)

Notes:

(i) The discount rate for the base case NPV should be the ungeared cost of equity, taking into account the risk of the investment. In order to reflect the risk of the investment, the ungeared equity beta of the Internet auction sector will be used. Assuming corporate debt to be virtually risk free:

$$\text{Beta ungeared} = \text{Beta equity} \times \frac{E}{E + D(1-t)}$$

$$\text{Beta ungeared} = 1.42 \times \frac{67}{67 = 33(1-0.245)} = 1.035$$

Using CAPM

Keug = Rf + (Rm – Rf) beta

Keug = 4% + (9.5% – 4%) 1.035 = 9.69%

10% will be used as the discount rate to estimate the base case NPV.

(ii)   The market research is a sunk cost.

(iii)   Working capital is assumed to be released at the end of year 6. Working capital in year 5 is assumed to increase by the 2% inflation rate in Singapore.

The financing side effects of the investment are the tax relief on interest payments, the issue costs and the benefit from the government subsidy.

Tax relief on interest payments

The benefit from the tax shield will be estimated based upon the debt used for the investment, although it could be argued that this should be based upon the percentage debt capacity of the company.

Total borrowing for the investment is $3,100,000

Annual tax relief on borrowing $3,100,000 × 4.5% (net of the subsidy) × .245 = $34,177.

The discount rate used will be the risk free rate as the tax relief is offered by a highly stable government in Singapore.

The present value of tax relief for 6 years is:

$34,177 × 5.242 = $179,158

Government subsidy

The benefit from the government subsidy is an interest saving of 1% per year.

$3,100,000 × 1% = $31,000

The present value for six years, discounted at the risk free rate, is $31,000 × 5.242 = $162,502

Issue costs

Issues costs are $3,100,000 × 1.5% = $46,500

The estimated present value of the financial side effects is:

$179,158 + $162,502 − $46,500 = $295,160

The estimated APV of the investment is ($2,810,000) − $295,160 = ($2,514,840)

From a financial perspective this appears to be a very poor investment.

However, there are a number of other factors to consider. The data contains no information about what happens after four years, or in the case of the revised estimates, six years.

Although major new investment would be needed after six years there is likely to be a realisable value or going concern value at that time which could be substantial. Several real options could exist at year six, including the option to reinvest and possibly expand operations, or perhaps to use the existing Internet auction clientele for other purposes such as Internet marketing. The initial investment decision should ideally take into account the expected present value from real call options such as these, although even if sophisticated option pricing models are used, real options are very difficult to accurately value. It would also be useful to investigate the effect on cash flow of the option to abandon the project part way through its expected life (effectively a put option).

Other important factors might be:

(i)   The accuracy of data. How confident is Trosoft that the forecast sales and costs will occur?

(ii)   Sensitivity and/or simulation analysis would be useful to investigate the impact of different assumptions on net cash flows.

(iii) Has the risk of the venture been accurately assessed? The discount rate of the operating cash flows is based on CAPM, and is subject to its theoretical and practical problems.

(iv) Are there new technologies involved in the investment which are not yet fully developed and proven?

(v) What will be the reaction of other Internet auction providers? Will they cut auction listing costs?

(vi) Are there alternative investments that would provide a better strategic fit for Trosoft?

(vii) Are there existing or possible future government regulations that would affect the investment?

ACCA marking scheme		
		Marks
This question requires analysis of an investment decision where a company is diversifying into a new sector. It also requires understanding of the weighted average cost of capital and adjusted present value, and the circumstances in which such techniques might be used.		
(a) WACC		4–5
Adjusted present value		4–5
		———
	Max	8
(b) Use of six year time horizon		1
Adjusted overhead		1
Lost contribution		1
Ignoring market research		1
Other pre tax cash flows (1 mark if only four years used)		2
Tax allowable depreciation		2
Add back depreciation (or use of equivalent tax savings)		1
Working capital – including final inflow		1
Reasonable technique to estimate base case NPV		1
		———
		11
		———
Discount rate for base case NPV 4		4
Financing side effects:		
Tax relief		3
Subsidy		3
Issue costs		1
Overall APV estimate		1
Other factors:		
Real option discussion		3
Other discussion. Look for strategic fit, alternatives, realisable value.		
Non-financial factors accuracy of data, risk etc.		6
		———
Total		40
		———

41 TAX RULES

(a) Tax haven holding companies might be used for:

(i) Reducing the total tax paid by a multinational company by allowing better use to be made of credits from foreign tax payments by overseas subsidiaries against a domestic tax liability. This is typically due to the taxable income from overseas subsidiaries, if channelled via a tax haven holding company, being treated as coming from one source rather than several separate sources. This may allow more overseas tax credits to be fully utilised.

(ii) Reduction of capital gains tax when taxable gains are made in foreign subsidiaries. Such gains may escape tax if they are deemed to accrue in the tax haven.

(iii) A reduction in withholding tax. Diverting income through tax havens may reduce the withholding tax liability relative to making distributions direct from a subsidiary to a parent company.

(iv) Holding companies may be tax efficient refinancing centres, which allow the efficient redistribution within the group of cash generated by overseas subsidiaries, without the cash being distributed via the parent company.

(b) (i)

	£000		
	Annovia	*Cardenda*	*Sporoon*
Taxable income	100	100	100
Local corporate income tax	40	25	20
Available for distribution	60	75	80
Amount paid as dividend to UK before withholding tax	42	30	64
Withholding tax on dividend	4.2	–	3.2
Distribution to UK gross of withholding tax	42	30	64
Grossed up for UK tax (x 100/(100 – local tax rate))	70	40	80
UK tax liability (30%)	21	12	24
Foreign tax credit	21	10	19.2
UK tax payable	–	2	4.8

Overseas taxation is 92.4 (40 + 25 + 20 +4.2 +3.2). Total taxation is 99.2 (overseas tax plus UK tax).

If the UK government taxes gross income:

	£000		
	Annovia	*Cardenda*	*Sporoon*
Income	100	100	100
Local corporate income tax	40	25	20
Available for distribution	60	75	80
Amount paid as dividend to UK before withholding tax	42	30	64
Withholding tax on dividend	4.2	–	3.2
Income for UK tax purposes	100	100	100
UK tax liability (30%)	30	30	30
Foreign tax credit	30	25	23.2
UK tax payable	–	5	6.8

Total taxation is 104.2, an increase of 5.0.

(ii)   Using a tax haven holding company

	£000 Current situation	Proposed new tax
Gross distribution to UK from holding company (net of overseas corporate tax)	136	
Grossed up for UK tax	190	300
UK tax liability	57	90
Foreign tax credit	57	90
UK tax payable	–	–
Total taxation	92.4	92.4

In both cases using what is sometimes known as a dividend mixer company in a tax haven will reduce the total tax payable, by reducing the UK tax payable. This is because Boxless can make more use of the credits available in the UK from foreign tax that has been paid, especially in the relatively high tax country of Annovia. In the case of the proposed new tax rule, Boxless has paid sufficient foreign tax to save 11.8 in UK tax relative to not using the tax haven holding company.

ACCA marking scheme			
			Marks
(a)		1 mark for each valid point. 2 if very well explained (Max 4)	4
(b)	(i)	Current tax position	4
		Tax if new rule is introduced	3
			———
			7
			———
	(ii)	Benefits from using holding company	4
Total			———
			15
			———

42   NOVOROAST PLC

(a)   **Report**

The proposed investment in the South American country by Novoroast plc

Novoroast should assess the expected financial viability of the proposed investment using the net present value of expected sterling cash flows. However, international direct investment is sometimes undertaken for strategic reasons, which, at least in the short term, might outweigh financial considerations.

Estimates of future cash flows require forecasts of exchange rates. Based on purchasing power parity the expected peso exchange rate is as follows.

		Peso/£1
Spot		13.421
Year 1	$13.421 \times (1.20/1.03)$	15.636
Year 2	$15.636 \times (1.15/1.04)$	17.290
Year 3	$17.290 \times (1.15/1.04)$	19.119
Year 4	$19.119 \times (1.15/1.04)$	21.141
Year 5	$21.141 \times (1.15/1.04)$	23.377

Tutorial note: Since inflation is higher in the South American country than in the UK, the peso will fall in value against sterling.

Workings

Year	1	2	3	4	5
Sales (000 units)	8	60	120	120	120
Unit price (pesos) (plus 10% p.a.)	1,450	1,595	1,754.5	1,930	2,123
Local variable cost per unit (pesos)	600	720	828	952	1,095
Chips: cost in £000	64	480	960	960	960
Exchange rate	15.636	17.290	19.119	21.141	23.377
Cost in pesos (millions)	1,000	8,300	18,400	20,300	22,400

Working capital needed Start of:	*Increase in working capital* (000 pesos)	*Total working capital* (000 pesos)	*Explanation*
Year 1	20,000		
Year 2	29,000	49,000	(20,000 × 20%) + 25,000
Year 3	9,800	58,800	(49,000 × 20%)
Year 4	8,800	67,600	(58,800 × 20%)
Year 5	10,100	77,700	(67,600 × 20%)

Land and buildings:

Value at end of Year 5 = (in millions pesos) $50 \times 1.20 \times 1.15 \times 1.15 \times 1.15 \times 1.15 = 104.9$.

Projected cash flows of the South American subsidiary are:

South American cash flows (million pesos)

Year	0	1	2	3	4	5
Sales		11.6	95.7	210.5	231.6	254.7
Local variable costs		4.8	43.2	99.4	114.3	131.4
Fixed costs		12.0	14.4	16.6	19.0	21.9
Chips		1.0	8.3	18.4	20.3	22.4
Depreciation (on full cost of 60)		12.0	12.0	12.0	12.0	12.0
		29.8	77.9	146.4	165.6	187.7
Taxable net cash flow		(18.2)	17.8	64.1	66.0	67.0
Taxation (25%)		tax holiday			16.5	16.8
		(18.2)	17.8	64.1	49.5	50.2
Add back depreciation		12.0	12.0	12.0	12.0	12.0
		(6.2)	29.8	76.1	61.5	62.2
Land and buildings	(50)					104.9
Plant and machinery (less grant)	(54)					
Working capital	(20)	(29.0)	(9.8)	(8.8)	(10.1)	77.7
Remittable to the UK	(124)	(35.2)	20.0	67.3	51.4	244.8
Exchange rate	13.421	15.636	17.290	19.119	21.141	23.377

UK cash flows (£ million)

Year	0	1	2	3	4	5
Remittable	(9.24)	(2.25)	1.16	3.52	2.43	10.47
Earnings from chips (£3 per unit)		0.02	0.18	0.36	0.36	0.36
Tax on chips (at 30%)		(0.01)	(0.05)	(0.11)	(0.11)	(0.11)
Additional tax on SA cash flow (5%)	-	-	-	-	(0.16)	(0.14)
	(9.24)	(2.24)	1.29	3.77	2.52	10.58
Discount factor at 14%	1.000	0.877	0.769	0.675	0.592	0.519
Present value	(9.24)	(1.96)	0.99	2.54	1.49	5.49

The expected NPV is negative: (£690,000)

Notes:

(1) The lost UK cash flows are not relevant as they would have occurred anyway because of the imposition of the tariff.

(2) Working capital is assumed to be released at the end of year 5.

(3) No tax is assumed to be payable on the increase in value of land and buildings.

(4) Discount rate

Market value of equity = 200 million × 410p = (in £m) 820.

Market value of bonds = 180 × 0.80 = (in £m) 144.

Cost of equity: Ke = 6% + (14% – 6%) 1.25 = 16%

Cost of debt: Kd = 6% + (14% – 6%) 0.225 = 7.8%

$$\text{WACC} = 16 \times \frac{820}{964} + 7.8\% \ (1-0.3) \ \frac{144}{964} = 14.42\%$$

14% will be used as the discount rate.

(5) Additional tax on SA cash flow:

	Taxable net cash flow	Exchange rate	Taxable net cash flow	Extra tax at 5%
	(million pesos)		£ million	£ million
Year 4	66.0	21.141	3.122	0.16
Year 5	67.0	23.377	2.866	0.14

Conclusion

The expected NPV of the investment is negative. The investment does not appear to be financially viable.

The financial projections are, however, subject to considerable inaccuracy. This relates in particular to:

(i) Estimates of future exchange rates based upon forecast inflation levels.

(ii) Sales forecasts.

(iii) Price and cost changes may differ from those forecast.

(iv) Tax rates are subject to change

(v) The realisable values in year five are very difficult to estimate.

(vi) The discount rate may not correctly reflect the systematic risk of the South American investment.

Sensitivity analysis or simulation analysis should be used in order to ascertain the impact of changes in sales and other key cash flows. It would be better to undertake several financial projections, based upon different assumptions of sales, exchange rates etc in order to estimate a range of possible net present values, rather than use a single point value.

A crucial question is what happens to cash flows beyond the company's five-year planning horizon. The year five residual values have been based upon the realisable value of assets, not cash flows beyond year five. The latter could produce a much higher expected NPV.

If the investment has the potential to lead to future opportunities/investments, the value of such options should be estimated.

The strategic importance of the venture to Novoroast must also be investigated, as this may heavily influence the final decision.

Any final decision must encompass all relevant non-financial factors of which little detail has been provided. Novoroast must, in particular, be satisfied that there is an acceptable level of political risk, and that there will be no problems with exchange controls and the remittance of funds. The expected period that the import tariff will continue for is important to the decision.

(b)   **Blocked remittances might be avoided** by means of:

(i)   Increasing transfer prices paid by the foreign subsidiary to the parent company.

(ii)   Lending the equivalent of the dividend to the parent company.

(iii)   Making payments to the parent company in the form of royalties, payment for patents, or management fees.

(iv)   Charging the subsidiary additional head office overhead

(v)   Parallel loans, whereby the subsidiary in the South American country lends cash to the subsidiary of another a company requiring funds in the South American country. In return the parent company would receive the loan of an equivalent amount of cash in the UK from the other subsidiary's parent company.

The government of the South American country might try to prevent many of these measures being used.

(c)   Multinational companies may engage in activities which, whilst not illegal, are questionable ethically, and may have detrimental long-term effects on the company's reputation. **Ethical considerations** include:

(i)   Would the investment cause pollution or other environmental damage in the South American country?

(ii)   Does the investment involve experiments on animals, genetic modifications etc?

(iii)   Should the investment be undertaken if the country has a poor record on human rights?

(iv)   If local officials ask for 'inducements' to facilitate the investment process, should these be paid?

(v)   Would the investment in any way assist trading in drugs or arms?

(vi)   Are wages to be paid in the South American country below subsistence level? Are working conditions of an acceptable standard?

43 SLEEPON HOTELS PLC

Key answer tips

An excellent investment appraisal question, but be careful regarding the following:

- You need to calculate a cost of capital that reflects the risks and finance of the project – the existing WACC of the company is no use. You need to de-gear and re-gear the beta of Thrillall.

- You need to make assumptions about the timing of asset purchases, as this will affect the timing of capital allowances.

- Only £250 million of the investment will attract capital allowances – this is assumed to be split equally between the two payments.

- Be careful identifying relevant cash flows, particularly with respect to interest, overheads and the 'savings' in advertising costs.

- Incorporating inflation – most (but not all!) figures are in current terms. The question is not clear regarding the working capital as strictly speaking the outflow at t=1 is not a cost. The examiner's answer inflates the working capital requirement and hence has annual increments.

- Ensure all working capital is released at the end of the project.

- Using a worst-case estimate for the realisable value of assets.

A clear answer layout and systematic approach that gets the easier marks first will help tremendously.

Report on the proposed theme park investment

The decision to invest in a major project must be evaluated using both financial and non-financial information. From a financial perspective the estimated net present value of the investment will provide an indicator of whether or not the project will create wealth. Non-financial considerations will include the strategic fit of the investment with the company and its future plans.

Financial evaluation

Cash flow forecasts (£ million)

Year	0	1	2	3	4	5	6
Cash receipts:							
Adult admission			41.25	42.49	43.76	45.07	
Child admission			34.37	35.40	36.47	37.56	
Food (incremental cash flow)			13.75	14.16	14.59	15.02	
Gifts (incremental cash flow)			11.46	11.80	12.16	12.52	
Total receipts			100.83	103.85	106.98	110.17	
Expenses:							
Labour			42.44	43.70	45.02	46.37	
Maintenance			15.00	19.00	23.00	27.00	
Insurance			2.12	2.19	2.25	2.32	
Capital allowances			62.50	46.88	35.16	26.37	
Total expenses			122.06	111.77	105.43	102.06	
Taxable			(21.23)	(7.92)	1.55	8.11	
Taxation (30%)			6.37	2.38	(0.47)	(2.43)	
			(14.86)	(5.54)	1.08	5.68	
Add back capital allowances			62.50	46.88	35.16	26.37	
Initial cost	(200)	(200)					

Year	0	1	2	3	4	5	6
Realisable value						250.00	
Working capital		(51.5)	(1.55)	(1.59)	(1.64)	(1.69)	57.97
Net cash flow	(200)	(251.50)	46.09	39.75	34.60	280.36	57.97
Discount factors (11%)		0.901	0.812	0.731	0.659	0.593	0.535
Present values	(200)	(226.60)	37.43	29.06	22.80	166.25	31.01

The estimated net present value is (£140.05 million.

Even if the higher realisable value estimate is used, the expected net present value is still significantly negative.

Notes:

(i) Receipts year 2

Adult admission $(6,000)(360)(18)(1.03)^2$ = 41.25 million

Child admission $(9,000)(360)(10)(1.03)^2$ = 34.37 million

Food $(15,000)(360)(8)(0.3)(1.03)^2$ = 13.75 million

Gifts $(15,000)(360)(5)(0.4)(1.03)^2$ = 11.46 million

(ii) Capital allowances:

It is assumed that allowances are available with a one year lag.

Year	Written down value	Capital allowance (25%)	Year available
0 + 1	205	62.50	2
2	187.50	46.88	3
3	140.62	35.16	4
4	105.47	26.37	5

No balancing allowances or charges have been estimated as the year 5 realisable value of fixed assets has been estimated on an after tax basis.

As the hotel business is successful, it is assumed that allowances may be used as soon as they are available against other taxable cash flows of Sleepon plc.

(iii) Interest is not a relevant cash flow. All financing costs are included in the discount rate.

(iv) The market research is a sunk cost.

(v) Apportioned overhead is not a relevant cash flow.

(vi) Although the company will save money by advertising in its existing hotels, this is not a change in cash flow as a result of the project and is not included in cash flows. (In effect the benefit from the savings is present as there is no cash outflow for advertising).

(vii) Discount rate

The current weighted average cost of capital should not be used. The discount rate should reflect the risk of the investment being undertaken; theme parks are likely to have very different risk to hotels. The cost of capital will be estimated using the risk (beta) of Thrillall plc, as Thrillall operates in the theme park sector.

The market weighted capital gearing of Thrillall is:

Equity $400 \times 3.86 = £1,544$ m (78.3%)

Debt $460 \times 0.93 = £428$ m (21.7%)

As the gearing of Thrillall is much less than that of Sleepon, the beta used to estimate the relevant cost of equity will need to be adjusted to reflect this difference in gearing.

Assuming corporate debt is virtually risk free:

Ungearing Thrillall's equity beta:

$$\text{Beta asset} = \text{Beta equity} \times \frac{E}{E + D(1 - t)} \text{ or } 1.45 \times \frac{1,544}{1,544 + 428\,(1 - 0.3)} = 1.214$$

Regearing to take into account the gearing of Sleepon:

$$\text{Beta equity} = \text{Beta asset} \times \frac{E + D\,(1 - t)}{E} \text{ or } 1.214 \times \frac{61.4 + 38.6\,(1 - 0.3)}{61.4} = 1.748$$

The cost of equity may be estimated using the capital asset pricing model.

$$Ke = Rf + (Rm - Rf) \text{ beta equity}$$

$$Ke = 3.5\% + (10\% - 3.5\%)\, 1.748 = 14.86\%$$

Kd is 7.5%, the cost of the new debt used for the project.

The weighted average cost of capital relevant to the new investment is estimated to be:

$$14.86\%\,(0.614) + 7.5\%\,(1 - 0.3)\,(0.386) = 11.15\%$$

11% will be used as the discount rate for the investment.

Other relevant information

The financial projections used in the estimated net present value are subject of considerable inaccuracy. It would be useful to know:

(i)   The accuracy of estimates of attendance levels and spending in the theme park.

(ii)   The accuracy of price and cost changes.

(iii)   Whether or not tax rates are subject to change.

(iv)   The accuracy of the estimate of realisable value in year four.

(v)   The accuracy of the discount rate estimate. The activities of Thrillall are not likely to be of exactly the same risk as the theme park project.

For a major investment it is unwise to rely on a single estimate of expected net present value. Sensitivity analysis or simulation analysis should be used in order to ascertain the impact on the expected NPV of changes in attendance and other key cash flows. It would be better to undertake simulation analysis, based upon different possible attendance levels, costs, risk, tax rates etc. in order to estimate a range of possible net present values, rather than use a single point value.

A crucial question is what happens to cash flows beyond the company's four year planning horizon. The year five realisable values are asset values, not the value of the theme park as a going concern. The value as a going concern could be very different from the asset values, and have a major influence on the investment decision.

Will the theme park investment lead to future opportunities/investments (real options), for example in other theme parks or leisure activities? If so the value of such options should be estimated, and should form part of the investment decision.

Strategic and other issues

The strategic importance of the venture to Sleepon must also be investigated, as this may heavily influence the final decision. Sleepon currently runs a successful hotel chain. It might be better to keep to its core competence in hotels rather than diversify into another sector. If new investments are sought are there better opportunities within the hotel sector?

Any final decision must encompass all relevant non-financial factors of which little detail has been provided. Sleepon must be satisfied that it can recruit an appropriately skilled labour force for the theme park, and should thoroughly investigate the competition in the theme park sector, and the likely reaction of competitors if it enters this new market.

ACCA marking scheme	
	Marks
This question requires the detailed analysis of a potential capital investment in a new industry, including the identification of relevant cash flows, and the risk of the investment. It also involves discussion of strategic and non-financial factors that might affect the investment decision.	
Criterion (a) for the decision	1
Financial evaluation	
Cash admission receipts	3
Food	1
Gifts	1
Expenses	
Labour	1
Maintenance	1
Insurance	1
Capital allowance. For full marks capital allowance must be added back	4
Allow also tax savings estimated directly. (Different timing is allowable)	
Tax	1
Ignoring interest in the analysis	1
Ignoring advertising	1
Ignoring market research and apportioned overhead	1
Initial cost and realisable value	1
Working capital (WC could be recovered in year 5 or year 6)	2
Discount rate estimates. Maximum 3 marks if no ungearing/regearing	7
Correct use of discount factors	1
Estimated NPV with comment	1
	___
max	28
Other relevant information	
1–2 marks for each relevant point. Look for accuracy of data, strategic considerations, suggested improvements in the analysis, what happens after four years, going concern value etc. max	12
	___
Total	40
	___

EXPANSION STRATEGIES AND CORPORATE REORGANISATION

44   SYNERGIES

Briefing Memo: Mergers and acquisitions

(a)   The motive for many mergers and acquisitions is to create incremental value through the existence of synergy when two entities are combined. Synergy means that the value of the new whole is greater than the sum of the previous values of the component parts. Synergy may exist for several reasons:

Operating synergy

Operating synergies arise from improved productivity, or from cost cutting as a result of the merger. Economies of scale or scope might exist in the larger merged entity. Such economies may relate to production, marketing or finance, the latter including access to capital markets on improved terms. There might also be increased market power, allowing some advantage to be taken of an oligopolistic position.

If the victim company was relatively badly managed it might be possible to eliminate inefficiencies that previously existed. Alternatively better use may be made of talented managers who were not previously utilised to their full potential. Where a victim company is 'cash rich' more efficient use might be made of such cash.

Gains may occur from horizontal mergers where competitors are purchased. Gains occur through rationalisation of research and development, sales and distribution, duplicated facilities and sales outlets, computer facilities etc. Vertical mergers between customers and suppliers can create value by eliminating various co-ordination, security of supply and bargaining problems.

Synergy may exist though the greater ability to transfer resources from one division to another.

Financial synergy

Financial synergy may exist after a merger as the new entity may be more diversified. Diversification reduces the risk of cash flows, making the company more attractive to investors and reducing the company's cost of capital.

There may also be tax synergies, whereby the combined entity is able to fully utilise tax allowances or tax losses that could not previously be utilised.

(b)   Evidence suggests that many mergers and acquisitions do not achieve the forecast synergies, and that shareholders in the target firm reap most benefits from any additional value created.

Reasons for not achieving expected synergy include:

(i)   The acquisition decision is based upon incomplete or incorrect information.

(ii)   Synergies are difficult to value.

(iii) Unexpected costs and problems exist when combining two organisations with different organisational structures, cultures and managerial styles.

(iv)   Managers are not given suitable incentives to achieve maximum synergies.

(c)   Mergers purely for diversification may be beneficial as they may reduce the cost of capital as explained above. Other possible benefits from diversification are:

(i)   The flexibility of the company may be enhanced.

(ii)   Debt capacity is normally increased.

(iii) The risk of corporate failure is often reduced.

(iv)   Competitors may find it more difficult to access relevant information about a diversified company, as it is not immediately clear how individual sections of the company are performing, and what is their strategy.

However, it is usually considered that investors can diversify far more efficiently through their portfolios than can company managers.

ACCA marking scheme		
		Marks
(a)	Examples of synergies, operational, financial etc.	7
(b)	Discussion of their potential problems of achievement	4
(c)	Possible benefits of diversification	3 – 4
	Overall conclusion	1
	Maximum	4
Total		15

45   LACETO PLC

(a)   ***Tutorial note:*** This question was set in June 2001, but does not allow for the collapse of the 'dot.com' bubble that happened before then.

Laceto will wish to pay the minimum price that will attract the majority of Omnigen's shareholders to sell. The current market price of 410 pence per share, or a total market value of £123 million, is likely to be the lowest that shareholders of Omnigen would accept, and unless there is an expectation that Omnigen's shares will fall further in value in the near future, a premium over the current market price will normally be payable.

If industry P/E ratios are used to value Omnigen, the range of values would be £182 million to £210 million. (Omnigen's total earnings after tax of £14 million, multiplied by the P/Es of 13:1 and 15:1). However, Omnigen's current P/E ratio is 8.78:1, given a value of £123 million. Even if the share price had not fallen it would only have been just over 13:1, or a value of £184 million. Unless there is an expectation that Omnigen's share price will soon return to a higher level the use of a forecast P/E or comparative P/Es of companies which might have very different characteristics to Omnigen is not recommended.

The realisable value of assets, £82 million, is substantially below the estimates based upon P/E ratios, probably because Omnigen is a profitable company which is planned to continue trading after the potential acquisition. The realisable value of assets is not the recommended valuation method unless it produces a value higher than the value as a going concern.

A better method of estimating the value of Omnigen is to use the cash flow projections to find the present value of Omnigen to Laceto. This will be based upon the free cash flow after replacement expenditure and expenditure required to achieve the forecast growth levels.

A discount rate of 14% is used. See the note below for an explanation of this choice of rate.

Financial year	*20X2*	*20X3*	*20X4*	*20X5*
Net sales	230.0	261.0	281.0	298.0
Cost of goods sold (50%)	115.0	131.0	141.0	149.0
Selling and administrative expenses	32.0	34.0	36.0	38.0
Capital allowances	40.0	42.0	42.0	42.0
	187.0	207.0	219.0	229.0
Taxable	43.0	54.0	62.0	69.0
Taxation (30%)	12.9	16.2	18.6	20.7
	30.1	37.8	43.4	48.3

Add back capital allowances	40.0	42.0	42.0	42.0
Less cash flow needed for asset replacement and forecast growth	(50.0)	(52.0)	(55.0)	(58.0)
Net cash flow = free cash flow	20.1	27.8	30.4	32.3
Discount factors (14%)	0.877	0.769	0.675	0.592
Present values	17.6	21.4	20.5	19.1
Total PV, 20X2 – 20X5	= 78.6			

Assuming 3% growth per annum beyond 20X5 in perpetuity, the present value of the post-20X5 cash flows, in terms of 20X5 values, will be (in £ million):

$$\frac{32.3\,(1.03)}{(0.14 - 0.03)} = £302.4$$

Discount factor at 14% to convert to PV = 0.592.

Present value of post 20X5 cash flows = 302.4×0.592 = £179.0 million.

The total present value is (78.6 + 179.0) £257.6 million. This value is the value of the entire entity, i.e. equity plus debt. The value of debt will depend upon the final gearing, and will vary between approximately £46 million and £59 million (18% – 23% gearing), giving a value of equity between £199 million and £212 million.

If annual growth beyond 20X5 is 5% in perpetuity, the present value of the post-20X5 cash flows, in terms of 20X5 values, will be (in £ million):

$$\frac{32.3\,(1.05)}{(0.14 - 0.05)} = £376.8$$

Discount factor at 14% to convert to PV = 0.592.

Present value of post 20X5 cash flows = 376.8×0.592 = £223.1 million. The present value of the entity would be (78.6 + 223.1) £301.7 million, and the value of equity between (77% – 82%) £232 million and £247 million.

These estimates use a present value to infinity estimate beyond 20X5. If a shorter time horizon was used, for example ten years, the estimates would be considerably reduced.

Assuming these cash flow projections are reasonably accurate (which itself must be subject to serious doubt, e.g. can the imbalance after year five between capital allowances and replacement capital expenditure continue indefinitely), it is worth Laceto offering a premium over the current market price for the shares of Omnigen. In theory, using present values to infinity, it could afford to offer a some premium above the current market price. In order to increase its own value it would offer the lowest price that would attract more than 50% of the shareholders of Omnigen. It is not possible to know what this price would be. An initial bid might offer a 20% premium above the current price, or (20% of 30 million shares × 410p) about £25 million. This would give an offer price of £148 million. If that bid was refused then there could be scope for increasing it up to a maximum of the estimated equity present values discussed above.

It must be stressed that all of the above estimates are subject to significant margins of error, and that valuation for takeovers is not a precise science.

1   *Discount rate:*

Using the capital asset pricing model, the cost of equity of Omnigen would be (allowing for a 0.1 increase in the beta factor):

ke = 6% + (14% – 6%)1.3 = 16.4%.

Omnigen's cost of equity after the acquisition is used as this is likely to reflect the systematic risk of the activities of Omnigen within Laceto. As the range of expected gearing levels is quite small (18% – 23%), and gearing is relatively low, it is assumed that the cost of equity will not significantly change over this range of gearing, other than the change already reflected in the increase in the equity beta by 0.1.

The cost of debt is not given but may be estimated from the data regarding Laceto's debenture. As Omnigen currently has a lower gearing than Laceto, it is assumed increasing Omnigen's gearing should not have a significant effect on Laceto's cost of debt, even if the overall gearing increases to 23%.

The cost of debt, by trial and error is:

At 6% interest

At 6% interest			At 5% interest		
Cash flow	*Discount factor*	*PV*	*Cash flow*	*Discount factor*	*PV*
12 (1 – 0.3)	2.673	22.45	12 (1 – 0.3)	2.723	22.87
100	0.840	84.00	100	0.864	86.40
		106.45			109.27
Value	1.000	(108.80)	Value	1.000	(108.80)
NPV		(2.35)			0.47

By interpolation:

$$5\% + \frac{0.47}{(0.47 + 2.35)} \times 1\% = 5.17\%$$

The weighted average cost of capital may be estimated for the full range of expected gearing:

At 18% gearing:

The weighted average cost of capital is $(16.4 \times 0.82) + (5.17\% \times 0.18) = 14.38\%$

At 23% gearing:

The weighted average cost of capital is $(16.4 \times 0.77) + (5.17\% \times 0.23) = 13.82\%$.

The estimated WACC does not change dramatically over the possible range in gearing.

14% will be used as the discount rate.

(b) **Report on possible defences against a bid by Agressa.com**

Defences against a bid will differ according to whether or not the bid has yet been made.

If no bid has been made Laceto can attempt to make itself unattractive to any potential bidder. Laceto might establish 'poison pills' such as granting the right to alternative shareholders to purchase its shares at a deep discount, or dispose of some of its key activities ('crown jewels') to make it less attractive to Agressa. The company might also introduce 'golden parachutes' for key staff, expensive severance contracts which come into effect if executive jobs are lost as a result of an acquisition. The articles of association could be amended to require a high percentage of shareholders to approve a merger or acquisition, for example 75% plus. Strategic acquisitions are also possible, whereby companies are acquired by Laceto which would be unattractive to a bidder, but are developed to be an integral part of Laceto's activities.

Laceto should also ensure that the financial press and the company's shareholders are kept fully informed about the company's financial strengths and future strategy, with particular focus on key institutional shareholders which are likely to determine the success or failure of any bid. Assets should be regularly revalued to ensure that shareholders are aware of 'current' values.

If Laceto has significant free cash flow it might consider the repurchase of shares in the expectation that the share price will increase and make a takeover more expensive to a potential bidder such as Agressa.

Financial summaries of the two companies are:

| | £ million | |
	Agressa.com	Laceto
Turnover	190	420
Profit before tax	8	41
Taxation	2	12
Market capitalisation of shares	397.5	304
Price/earnings ratio	66:1	10.5:1

Despite its smaller turnover and net assets Agressa.com has a higher market capitalisation, which is manifested in the P/E ratio of 66 times. This probably reflects its position as a 'dot.com' company rather than a traditional retailer.

Once a bid has been made, probably the most important defence against the bid is to persuade shareholders that Agressa.com is currently overvalued. It has relatively small earnings, but a P/E of 66 suggests that the market expects the company to experience rapid future growth. In the limited period of their existence, dot.com companies have experienced great volatility in their share price, many have yet to exhibit sustained growth, and many have failed. Laceto might highlight the history of dot.com companies and their relative risk. It could also criticise the logic behind the acquisition, and the strategic fit of the two companies, although the latter might be difficult as there is an overlap in existing activities.

It might also be argued that the shares of Laceto are undervalued. The company is earning more than £40 million before tax, and its P/E ratio at 10.5 is lower than other companies in the electrical sector. Unless the P/E and prospects of the company are being strongly pulled down by the clothing activities, Laceto should release forecasts (with supporting assumptions) of future earnings and dividends in order to support the argument that it is undervalued.

Laceto might consider making a counter bid for Agressa.com, although this could be contrary to the strategic plans of the company, and might be difficult to achieve given the P/E difference of the companies.

If the combined market share of the two companies is large enough the bid might be referred to regulatory authorities such as the Competition Commission in the UK. Given the size of the companies this is not likely in this case.

A further possibility is to approach a 'white knight', a preferred alternative bidder for the company, but this, if successful, would also result in the company being taken over.

(c)   Payment may be made in ordinary shares, preference shares, some form of debt, often with a conversion or warrant option attached, cash, or some combination of these. From an investor's perspective cash provides a known, precise sum, and might be favoured for this reason. However, in some countries payment in cash might lead to an immediate capital gains tax liability for the investor. Preference shares and debt are rarely favoured by investors as they alter the characteristic and risk of the investment. Payment with ordinary shares offers a continuation in ownership of the entity, albeit as part of the successful bidder. However, relative share prices will change during the period of the bid, and the owner of shares in the potential victim company will not know the precise post-acquisition value of the bid.

Neither of the potential bids in (a) or (b) could be financed entirely in cash without significant new external borrowing, with its resultant impact on gearing. In part (b) the volatility of dot.com shares might make payment in shares unattractive to investors. Sometimes investors are given a choice in the method of payment, with the logic that different forms of payment might be attractive to different types of investor. This could influence the success or failure of both bids, but is problematic for the bidder in that the cash needs and number of shares to be issued are not known, and the company's capital structure may alter in an unplanned manner. Ideally a bidder would like to tailor the form of the bid to that favoured by major investors in the potential victim company.

	ACCA marking scheme	
		Marks
(a)	Minimum price objective	1
	P/E ratios:	
	Calculations	2
	Comment	2
	Discussion of the use of realisable values	1–2
	Cash flow estimates:	
	No interest included	1
	Taxation	1
	Add back capital allowance	1
	Free cash flow adjustment	2
	Discount factor:	
	Cost of equity	2
	Cost of debt	3
	WACC(s)	1–2
	Present values beyond 20X5	2
	Overall value(s)	1–2
	Reward sensible technique even if calculation errors exist	
	Conclusion as to bid price(s) and other relevant discussion.	
	Look for adjustment of debt values for the equity bid price.	
	Reward minimum and sensible ranges. These may differ from the suggested solution.	4–5
		25
(b)	Pre-bid defencs	4–5
	Post-bid defences	4–5
	For very high marks, must use financial data in the report	8
(c)	Advantages and disadvantages of alternative forms of payment from an investor perspective. One mark for each good point.	
	For 6–7 marks, discussion must include all major alternative forms of payment.	7
Total		40

46 OBERBERG AG

(a) (i) **Organic growth** is internal growth, achieved by expansion of existing business or investment in new projects. An advantage of organic growth is that any investment can be planned exactly to the needs of the organisation. A further advantage is that organic growth tends to be in a related area of business, thus overcoming the risks arising from diversification into non-core areas. (Diversification into non-core areas substantially increases the risk of failure.) Organic growth also avoids the payment of a considerable purchase premium over the existing market price that would often required with growth through an acquisition. This premium is not always justified by expected savings/synergies.

(ii) **Acquisitions** have the following potential advantages:

– Growth, market penetration, access to new markets or productive capacity may be achieved at a much quicker rate by buying existing operations.

– High start-up costs are avoided.

– Barriers to entry in an industry or country may be avoided.

– The acquisition may remove an actual or potential competitor from the market.

– The bidder acquires an instant market share, probable expertise of local markets, and an existing 'reputation' of the acquired company. In a foreign country with different language, culture, business practices and accounting, tax and legal systems such expertise is essential.

– They may offer advantages that do not exist with organic growth. These include possible synergy, asset stripping, acquisition of skilled managers or labour, brands, patents and trademarks, acquisition of 'surplus' cash or tax losses.

The **relative risk of acquisitions and organic growth** is important. This is not always easy to quantify, but an acquisition in a foreign country would normally be less risky than an organic start-up in a foreign country, due to the lack of local knowledge, the lack of recognition in the local market, the non-existence of management control systems at a local level, and so on.

(b) **Report on the possible acquisition of Oberberg AG**

In financial terms, Oberberg should be purchased if the expected **adjusted present value (APV)** of the acquisition is positive, in other words if the present value of the incremental cash flows exceeds the price to be paid. However, it is important that the acquisition fits well with the strategic plans of Intergrand, and strategic issues or other non-financial considerations might outweigh the financial findings.

Discount rate for the operational free cash flows

The free cash flows of Oberberg should be discounted at a rate reflecting the risk of Oberberg. Assuming corporate debt to be virtually risk free, the ungeared beta of Oberberg may be estimated using:

$$\text{Beta asset} = \text{Beta equity} \times \frac{E}{E+D(1-t)}$$

E, the market value of equity is 150,000 shares x €300 per share = €45 million.

D, the market value of debt is (€18 million x 1.230) + €30 million = €52.14 million.

$$\text{Beta asset} = 1.4 \times \frac{45}{45+52.14(1-0.25)} = 0.749, \text{ say } 0.75.$$

Using the capital asset pricing model, the cost of equity for Oberberg without gearing is therefore:

4% + (11% − 4%) 0.75 = 9.25%.

A cost of capital of 9% will therefore be used as the discount rate for operating cash flows.

Present value of the operational free cash flows

Based upon the data provided by Oberberg's managers the expected operating cash flows of Oberberg are:

Year	20X3 Year 1 €m	20X4 Year 2 €m	20X5 Year 3 €m	20X6 Year 4 €m
Sales	38.2	41.2	44.0	49.0
Savings from synergies	-	2.0	2.0	2.0
	38.2	43.2	46.0	51.0
Labour	11.0	12.1	13.0	14.1
Materials	8.3	8.7	9.0	9.4
Overheads3.2	3.2	3.2	3.3	3.4
Tax-allowable depreciation	6.3	5.8	5.6	5.2
	28.8	29.8	30.9	32.1
Taxable profit	9.4	13.4	15.1	18.9
Taxation in Germany (25%)	(2.4)	(3.4)	(3.8)	(4.7)
	7.0	10.0	11.3	14.2
Add back depreciation	6.3	5.8	5.6	5.2
Incremental operating working capital	(0.7)	(0.9)	(1.0)	(2.0)
Replacement investment	(4.2)	(4.2)	(4.2)	(4.2)
Operating free cash flows	8.4	10.7	11.7	13.2
Discount factor at 9%	0.917	0.842	0.772	0.708
Present value	7.7	9.0	9.0	9.3

Tutorial notes:

1   The tax-allowable depreciation is first deducted in order to establish the taxable profits and the tax payable on those profits. The depreciation is then added back because it is not a cash flow. The operating cash flows are therefore profits after tax + depreciation.

2   To calculate the present value of the cash flows from Year 5 onwards, which grow by a constant annual percentage amount each year in perpetuity, we can use the dividend growth model formula, which is based on the same arithmetical concept.

Cash flows from 20X6 onwards in perpetuity

Cash flows after 20X6 (year 5 onwards) are expected to grow at 2% per year. The Year 4 'present value' of these cash flows is:

$$\frac{€13.2m\,(1.02)}{(0.09-0.02)} = €192.3 \text{ million.}$$

Converting this Year 4 'present value' to a Year 0 value, we must discount at the Year 4 discount rate at 9%:

Present value of operational free cash flows from Year 5 in perpetuity = €192.3 million × 0.708 = €136.2 million.

The **total present value of operating free cash flows** is:

	€m
Year 1	7.7
Year 2	9.0
Year 3	9.0
Year 4	9.3
Years 5 onwards	136.2
	171.2

Present values of other relevant cash flows:

Tutorial note:

There will be other cash flows arising as a consequence of the decision, and we need to calculate the present value of these, using an appropriate discount rate. These are set out in the table below, and explained in the workings that follow.

	Workings	€ million
Additional UK taxation	(W1)	(10.5)
Publicity benefit	(W2)	7.0
Lost exports	(W3)	(4.3)
Sale of assets	Assume Year 0	8.0
Redundancy cost	Year 0	(5.0)
Investment for expansion	(W4)	(6.8)
Tax relief benefits from debt	(W5)	12.0
Total		0.4

Workings

(W1) *PV of extra taxation in the UK*

As the tax rate in the UK is 5% higher than in Germany, an extra tax liability would arise after acquisition. This extra tax is 5% of the taxable profits calculated earlier. A discount rate of 10%, the cost of Intergrand, will be used to calculate the present value of this tax cost.

Year	2003	2004	2005	2006
	Year 1	*Year 2*	*Year 3*	*Year 4*
	€m	€m	€m	€m
Taxable profit	9.4	13.4	15.1	18.9
Extra tax (5%)	(0.47)	(0.67)	(0.76)	(0.95)
Discount factor	0.909	0.826	0.751	0.683
Present value of extra tax	(0.43)	(0.55)	(0.57)	(0.65)

Extra tax after 20X6 (Year 5 onwards) is assumed to grow at 2% per year. Using the growth model to calculate the present value of cash flows in perpetuity, when there is a constant annual growth rate, the Year 4 'present value' of these cash flows is:

Based upon the present value to infinity such cash flows are valued at

$$\frac{€0.95m\,(1.02)}{0.10 - 0.02} = €12.11 \text{ million.}$$

The Year 0 present value of this Year 4 value, discounting at 10%, is:

€12.11 million × 0.683 = €8.27 million.

The total present value of the extra tax payments is:

	€m
Year 1	0.43
Year 2	0.55
Year 3	0.57
Year 4	0.65
Years 5 onwards	8.27
	10.47

This is rounded in the summary table above to €10.5 million.

(W2) *PV of the benefit of extra publicity*

The benefit of extra publicity is €1 million per year, less tax relief (as the cost of advertising to Intergrand would have been net of tax relief). The tax rate is 30% (25% in Germany and 5% in the UK).

Using Intergrand's discount rate of 10%, the present value to infinity of this annual benefit is $\frac{€0.7m}{0.10}$ = **€7.0 million**.

(W3) *PV of lost export cash flows*

The investment should be charged with the lost export cash flows. After tax, these are £800,000 × 0.5 × (1 – 0.3) = £280,000 per year.

However, using purchasing power parity theory sterling is expected to fall in value by $\frac{1.04}{1.02}$ = 1.0196 or 1.96% per year against the euro.

Year	20X3	20X4	20X5	20X6
	Year 1	Year 2	Year 3	Year 4
Euro/£1 (÷ 0.1.0196 each year)	1.594	1.563	1.533	1.504
£280,000 in €	€446,320	€437,640	€429,240	€421,120
Discount factor at 10%	0.909	0.826	0.751	0.683
Present value in €	€405,705	€361,491	€322,359	€287,625

The Year 4 'present value' of the export losses after 20X6 (Year 5 onwards) is approximately $\frac{€421,120}{0.10}$ = €4,211,200.

This assumes a constant rate between the euro and the pound sterling after 20X6, for example as a result of the UK joining the eurozone.

The Year 0 present value of these export losses is €4,211,200 × 0.683 = €2,876,250.

The **total expected PV of lost exports** is:

	€
Year 1	405,705
Year 2	361,491
Year 3	322,359
Year 4	287,625
Years 5 onwards	2,876,250
	4,253,430

This will be rounded to €4.3 million.

(W4) *PV of investment for expansion*

The investment for expansion of €9 million in 20X5 (Year 3) is included in the evaluation because its effects have been included in the subsequent cash flows for 20X6 onwards.

The present value of this investment, using Intergrand's discount rate of 10%, is:

€9 million × 0.751 = **€6.8 million**.

(W5) *PV of tax relief from the use of debt*

The analysis has so far ignored the interest costs of Oberberg. This is because interest costs are reflected in the cost of capital/discount rate, not in the cash flows themselves, in DCF analysis. however, in this situation, Intergrand would be acquiring the tax relief on the interest costs of Oberberg's €48 million of debt, and the benefits of this tax relief should be included in the analysis.

Loans are assumed to be available to infinity, being re-financed as necessary. From the 20X2 pro forma P&L account, medium- and long-term loans may be estimated to cost approximately 7.1% per year (3.4/48 x 100%).

The PV to infinity of tax relief at a cost of debt of 7.1% is:

$$\frac{€48m \times 0.071 \times 0.25}{0.071} = €12 \text{ million}.$$

This has been discounted at the cost of debt to reflect the risk of debt.

Examiner's comment

As tax relief is allowed by the government and is almost certain, it might be argued that the discount rate should be the risk-free rate.

(W6) *Cash spent on researching acquisition targets is a sunk cost, and therefore irrelevant to the decision.*

The **expected adjusted present value (APV)** of the acquisition is:

	€m
Operating free cash flows	171.2
Other incremental cash flows	0.4
Total APV	**171.6**

However, in order to estimate the price to be paid for Oberberg's shares the value of any outstanding loans should be subtracted. For Oberberg these total €48 million.

The **maximum price to offer for Oberberg's shares** based on estimated cash flows to infinity is €171.6m – €48m = **€122.3 million**.

This is only slightly above the asking price of €115 million, and is subject to a **considerable margin of error**.

Factors that Intergrand should consider prior to making a final decision include:

(i) Cash flows to infinity are used. The present value of cash flows beyond 20X6 constitutes the majority of Oberberg's value. If a shorter time horizon were used the present values would be much less.

(ii) The results are based on forecasts by the managers of Oberberg. The assumptions behind these forecasts need to be examined to assess the likely validity of the forecasts.

(iii) A single estimate of the APV is of limited value. Sensitivity analysis or simulation analysis should be undertaken to examine the impact of cash flows differing from those projected.

(iv) The data does not take into account any future embedded options that might arise from the purchase of Oberberg. Such options could increase the expected APV.

(v) The risk of the investment might be inaccurately estimated, and this risk could change over time.

(vi) Tax rates and tax allowance rules might alter.

(vii) Intergrand is an UK company that is primarily concerned with cash flows that are available in pounds sterling. If the euro continues to appreciate in value, the economic value of the investment in sterling might increase, although economic exposure such as this is difficult to quantify. Additionally, it is not known whether or not the UK will join the eurozone, and if so when this will occur.

(viii) There is no certainty that the lost exports can be diverted to an alternative market.

(ix) There is no information on the size of Intergrand, and how important the acquisition is relative to the total activities of Intergrand. If it is of major importance much more research needs to be undertaken into the proposed acquisition in terms of how integration would occur, including organisational structures, cultures and human resource policies.

(x) Do alternative investments exist that would be a better strategic fit for Intergrand, or have a higher expected NPV/APV?

(xi) Will the two organisations integrate successfully? Are there significant differences in organisational cultures?

(xii) Will key staff of Oberberg stay on after the acquisition?

(xiii) What will be the effect on morale within Oberberg of the redundancies and asset disposals?

(xiv) Would Intergrand need to make any additional investment in Oberberg?

ACCA marking scheme		Marks
(a)	Advantages of organic growth	4-5
	Advantages of acquisitions	4-5
(b)	Operating cash flows:	
	Savings from synergies	1
	Ignoring interest	1
	Revised taxation	1
	Add back depreciation (or equivalent)	1
	Inclusion of replacement investment and WC	1
	Cash flows after 2006	2
	Asset beta	2
	Discount rate	1
	PV of operating cash flows	
	Other cash flows:	3
	Additional taxation	1
	Advertising benefit	3
	Lost exports	1
	Sale of assets and redundancy	1
	Investment for expansion	2
	Tax relief from debt	1
	APV	1
	Conclusion from the data	1
	Discussion. 1 mark for each relevant factor. 2 if very detailed.	9
Total (maximum marks awarded)		40

47 ROMAGE PLC

Key answer tips

Despite the requirements of (a), (b) and (c) this question is effectively testing investment appraisal techniques. Pay particular attention to the calculation of the discount rates – don't get bogged down – if short of time ensure you answer (c) where mark accumulation is easier.

(a)   There are several advantages that are common to both a sell-off and a demerger. Both offer a way to restructure a company. Restructuring may be to dismantle a conglomerate enterprise in order to focus upon a core competence, to react to a change in the strategic focus of the company, or to sell off unwanted assets (for example after an acquisition such as when Granada plc sold off part of the assets acquired in the take-over of Forte plc).

Both forms of restructuring may result in 'reverse synergy', where the separated elements of the business are worth more than the value of the old combined business.

The main difference between a sell-off and a demerger is that the sell-off involves the sale of part of the company to a third party, for cash or some other consideration. Thus control of these assets is lost. However, funds are raised which can be used to develop other parts of the business, or to make acquisitions.

A demerger need not involve a change in ownership. One or more new companies are created and the assets of the old company are transferred to these new companies.

The key question for Romage plc is whether or not it wishes to maintain control of all of its assets. If it does then a demerger is a more appropriate form of restructuring than a sell-off.

(b)   Expected cash flows in real terms (i.e. excluding inflationary increases): (£million)

Manufacturing

Year	1	2	3	4	5	6 onwards
Net operating cash flow	45.0	48.0	50.0	52.0	57.0	60.0
Central costs (cash flows)	6.0	6.0	.0	6.0	6.0	6.0
Tax allowable depreciation	10.0	8.0	7.0	8.0	8.0	8.0
	29.0	34.0	37.0	38.0	43.0	46.0
Taxation (31%)	(9.0)	(10.5)	(11.5)	(11.8)	(13.3)	(14.3)
One-off cost (50% of 16)	(8.0)					
Add back depreciation	10.0	8.0	7.0	8.0	8.0	8.0
Overall cash flow	22.0	31.5	32.5	34.2	37.7	39.7
Discount factor at 10% (see below)	0.909	0.826	0.751	0.683	0.621	*note*
Present values	20.0	26.0	24.4	23.4	23.4	246.5

Total PV = £363.7 million

Note: The present value of £1 in perpetuity at 10% from year 1 onwards is £1/0.10 = 10.0.

The present value of £1 in perpetuity at 10% from year 6 onwards is £1/0.10, discounted from its year 5 value = 10.0 x discount factor at 10% Year 5 = (£1/0.10) × 0.621 = 6.21.

PV of £39.7 per annum from year 6 onwards = 39.7 × 6.21 = 246.5.

The expected NPV to infinity is £363.7 million.

If a 15-year time horizon is used, the present value of the annual cash flows from year 6 onwards will be:

$39.7 \times$ cumulative discount factor at 10%, years 6 – 15 (10 years)

$= 39.7 \times$ cumulative discount factor, years 1- 10 $\times$ discount factor year 5

$= 3.97 \times 6.145 \times 0.621 = £151.5$ million.

This is £95 million less than the value calculated to infinity, and the NPV would therefore be £95 million less, at £268.7 million.

Property sales

Year	1	2	3	4	5	6 onwards
Net operating cash flow	32.0	40.0	42.0	44.0	46.0	50.0
Central costs (cash flows)	6.0	6.0	6.0	6.0	6.0	6.0
Tax allowable depreciation	5.0	5.0	5.0	5.0	5.0	5.0
	21.0	29.0	31.0	33.0	35.0	39.0
Taxation (31%)	(6.5)	(9.0)	(9.6)	(10.2)	(10.9)	(12.1)
One-off cost (50% of 16)	(8.0)					
Add back depreciation	5.0	5.0	5.0	5.0	5.0	5.0
Overall cash flow	11.5	25.0	26.4	27.8	29.1	31.9
Discount factor at 8% (see below)	0.926	0.857	0.794	0.735	0.681	note
Present values	10.6	21.4	21.0	20.4	19.8	271.5

Total PV = £364.7 million

Note: The present value of £1 in perpetuity at 8% from year 1 onwards is £1/0.08 = 12.5.

The present value of £1 in perpetuity at 10% from year 6 onwards is £1/0.08, discounted from its year 5 value = 12.5 $\times$ discount factor at 8% Year 5 = (£1/0.08) $\times$ 0.681 = 8.51.

PV of £31.9 per annum from year 6 onwards = 31.9 $\times$ 8.51 = 271.5.

The expected NPV to infinity is £364.7 million

If a 15-year time horizon is used, the present value of the annual cash flows from year 6 onwards will be:

$31.9 \times$ cumulative discount factor at 8%, years 6 – 15 (10 years)

$= 31.9 \times$ cumulative discount factor, years 1 – 10 $\times$ discount factor year 5

$= 31.9 \times 6.710 \times 0.681 = £145.8$ million.

This is £125.7 million less than the value calculated to infinity, and the NPV would therefore be £125.7 million less, at £239.0 million.

The total of the two divisions to infinity is £363.7m + £364.7m = £728.4 million

The total using a 15 year time horizon is: £268.7m + £239.0m = £507.7 million

The current market value of Romage is £592 million equity plus £125.5 million debt.

From these estimates it appears that, if the market is efficient, the value of the two divisions floated separately should marginally exceed the current value of Romage plc if present values to infinity are used, but will be less than the current value using a 15 year time horizon. Given only a marginal potential benefit with the present value to infinity, and the fact that no replacement capital expenditure has been incorporated into the above cash flows, it does not appear to be financially advantageous for Romage plc to separately float the two divisions.

Supporting calculations: Discount factors:

The two divisions will have their own systematic risk, and it is not acceptable to use Romage's discount rate. Separate rates will be estimated for each division.

Manufacturing division:

It is assumed that the systematic risk of the division may be estimated using the manufacturing beta.

Gearing by market values	Equity		Debt	Total	Equity	Debt
	£m		£m	£m	%	%
Romage	592.0		125.5		82.5	17.5
Manufacturing (55%)	325.6	(term loan)	60.0	385.6	84.4	15.6
Property sales (45%)	266.4	(debentures)	65.5	331.9	80.3	19.7

As the gearing of the manufacturing division differs from that of the comparator industry it is necessary to ungear the industry beta, and to regear the resultant asset beta to take into account the capital structure of the manufacturing division.

Cost of equity

Assuming corporate debt to be risk free

$$\text{Asset beta} = \text{equity beta} \times \frac{E}{E + D(1-t)}$$

$$\text{Asset beta} = 1.3 \times \frac{70}{70 + 30(1-0.31)} = 1.00$$

$$\text{Re-gearing equity beta} = \text{asset beta} \times \frac{E + D(1-t)}{E}$$

$$\text{Equity beta} = 1.00 \times \frac{84.4 + 15.6(1-0.31)}{84.4} = 1.128$$

Cost of equity = Rf + (Rm − Rf) beta

= 5.5% + (14% − 5.5%) 1.128 = 15.09%

The *cost of debt* may be estimated from the redemption yield on the debenture.

Tutorial note: The redemption yield is calculated by trial and error. To select a discount rate to start with, start by calculating the after-tax cash flow for £100 of debentures. Here, this is 13 less tax at 31%, i.e. 8.97. The after-tax cost of irredeemable debt would be 8.97% if the debentures were valued at par. Here, we have redeemable debentures. Also, the market value at 131 is a long way above par, indicating that the yield will be well below 8.97%. A starting point for calculating the redemption yield might therefore be 6%.

Year		Cash flow	Try 6% Discount factor at 6%	PV	Try 5% Discount factor at 5%	PV
1 − 15	Interest	8.97	9.712	87.12	10.380	93.11
15	Redemption	100	0.417	41.70	0.481	48.10
				128.82		141.21
0	Current MV	131	1.000	131.00	1.000	131.00
				(2.18)		10.21

Interpolating:

$$5\% + \frac{10.21}{10.21 + 2.18} \times (6 - 5)\% = 5.82\%$$

The weighted average cost of capital is:

$$\text{ke}\frac{E}{E + D} + \text{kd}(1 - t)\frac{D}{E + D} = 15.09\% \times \frac{325.6}{385.6} + 5.82\% \times \frac{60}{385.6} = 13.65\%$$

However this is the money or nominal weighted average cost of capital. As real cash flows have been used the discount rate should also be real. The expected annual rate of inflation is 3%.

The real discount rate for the manufacturing division is therefore:

$$\frac{1.1365}{1.03} \times 100\% = 10.3\%$$

A discount rate of 10% will be used.

Property sales division:

As the gearing of the property sales division is almost identical to that of the property sales industry the industry beta may be used without ungearing and re-gearing.

Cost of equity:

$$\text{ke} = 5.5\% + (14\% - 5.5\%)\,0.9 = 13.15\%$$

The cost of debt kd has been estimated at 5.82%

The weighted average cost of capital for the property sales division is:

$$13.15\% \times \frac{266.4}{331.9} + 5.82\% \times \frac{65.5}{331.9} = 11.70\%$$

The real discount rate, given expected inflation of 3% per annum, is:

$$\frac{1.117}{1.03} \times 100\% = 8.4\%$$

A discount rate of 8% will be used.

(c) Additional information and analysis might include:

(i) Information on the accuracy of the projected cash flows.

(ii) Estimates of future price changes in individual elements of the cash flows. Different costs and revenues might be subject to different levels of price change. This would allow an estimate of expected NPV using nominal rather than real cash flows.

(iii) Better estimates of the risk of the two divisions. The industry comparisons might not accurately reflect divisional risk.

(iv) More accurate estimates of the gearing of the two divisions.

(v) Sensitivity analysis, best/worst NPV estimates, or estimates using Monte Carlo or other simulation techniques in order to see possible outcomes using different assumptions of cash flows and discount rates.

(vi) Valuation using alternative techniques. It is often argued that valuation should be based upon corporate free cash flow rather than total cash flow, or upon other measures such as EVA (economic value added).

(vii)   NPV analysis does not take account of future options that might arise. It would be useful to know what different options might exist as a result of the separate floats.

(viii) A demerger might result in adverse effects, such as greater difficulty raising capital for the smaller companies, or greater vulnerability to takeover bids. Such effects might not have been taken into account.

(ix)   The views of existing shareholders would be important, especially major institutional shareholders.

48 PEDER AND TULEN

If the companies merge:

	Recession	Slow growth	Rapid growth	Expected value
Total value	105	135	195	142.50
Of which:				
Equity	50	80	140	87.50
Debt	55	55	55	55.55
Without a merger				
Peden				
Total value	42	55	75	57.05
Of which:				
Equity	0	10	30	12.50
Debt	42	45	45	44.55
Tulen				
Total value	63	80	120	85.45
Of which:				
Equity	53	70	110	75.45
Debt	10	10	10	10.00

In the case of recession the shares of Peden are expected to be worthless, and the value of the company insufficient to repay all of the debt. The merger will eliminate the risk that full repayment to the debt holders will not be made, through what is known as the coinsurance effect. In the absence of any operational synergy the total value of the companies remains unchanged, but the wealth of the debt holders of Peden will increase by £0.45 million at the expense of the shareholders of the two companies.

The merger might also result in a gain for shareholders and bondholders if the merged company's cash flows are perceived to be less risky. This might lead to small reductions in both the cost of debt and cost of equity, and make it easier for the company to raise new external finance.

49 OAKTON PLC

(a)   Synergy might exist for several reasons, including:

Economic efficiency gains

Gains might relate to economies of scale or scope. Economies of scale occur through such factors as fixed operating costs being spread over a larger production volume, equipment being used more efficiently with higher volumes of production, or bulk purchasing reducing costs. Economies of scope may arise from reduced advertising and distribution costs when companies have complementary resources. Economies of scale and scope relate mainly to horizontal acquisitions and mergers. Economic efficiency gains may also occur with backward or forward vertical integration which might reduce production costs as the 'middle man' is eliminated, improve control of essential raw materials or other resources that are needed for production, or avoid disputes with what were previously suppliers or customers.

Economic efficiency gains might also result from replacing inefficient management as the result of a merger/takeover.

Financial synergy

Financial synergy might involve a reduction in the cost of capital and risk. The variability (standard deviation) of returns of a combined entity is usually less than the weighted average of the risk of the individual companies. This is a reduction in total risk, but does not affect systematic risk, and hence might not be regarded as a form of synergy by shareholders. However, reduced variability of returns might improve a company's credit rating making it easier and/or cheaper to obtain a loan. Another possible financial synergy exists when one company in an acquisition or merger is able to use tax shields, or accumulated tax losses, which would otherwise have been unavailable to the other company.

Market power

A large organisation, particularly one which has acquired competitors, might have sufficient market power to increase its profits through price leadership or other monopolistic or oligopolistic means.

(b)   (i)   **Comparative P/E ratios**

As Mallard is in a different industry, comparison will be with average P/E ratios in Mallard's industry.

Using the average P/E for recent takeovers of 7:1, and Mallard's earnings per share of 71.04 pence (the market price of 370 pence multiplied by the earnings yield of 19.2%) this would result in a price per share of $7 \times 71.04 = 497$ pence, and a total value of shares of £24.85 million. (An adjusted EPS for Mallard which takes into account the expected effects of the acquisition could be used.)

The use of comparative P/E ratios has a number of weaknesses. There is no guarantee that the companies being compared to Mallard are of similar size, risk, growth rates, or activity to Mallard. Additionally the figure of 7:1 is merely an average for companies which have been recently taken over, and an average might hide a wide variation in the actual P/Es of the companies. P/E ratios are in part based upon historic accounting information (the EPS), and do not consider the impact of the merger or acquisition on future cash flows, and any synergy that might occur. These weaknesses make the use of comparative P/Es of limited value.

(ii)   **Dividend valuation model**

The intrinsic value of Mallard may be estimated using $P = \dfrac{D_1}{Ke - g}$

where g is the growth rate in dividends of 8% or 0.08.

Ke is the cost of equity. Using CAPM this may be estimated to be:

$6\% + (14\% - 6\%)\,0.8 = 12.4\%$

D1 is the expected next dividend per share. The current dividend per share is:

$\dfrac{842}{5,000} = 16.84$ pence

P is estimated to be: $\dfrac{16.84(1.08)}{0.124 - 0.08}$

= 413 pence per share or a total of £20.65 million.

The dividend valuation model assumes a constant growth in dividends, which is not observed for most companies. The growth rate used is for Mallard. This growth rate differs from that of Oakton, and might not continue in the future. If the AIM is an efficient market, the current share price will reflect the correct value of Mallard, not the dividend valuation model, although this price could change once the possible benefits of any synergy are known to the market.

(iii) **Present value of operating cash flows**

	£000
Current pre-tax operating cash flow	5,300
Ongoing adjustments as a result of the acquisition:	
Wage savings	750
Advertising savings	150
	——
	6,200
Tax (33%)	2,046
	——
	4,154
Other cash flows:	
Land and buildings	800
Directors' fees per year for three years (after tax)	(201)
Redundancy costs	(1,200)

The discount rate should reflect the systematic risk of Mallard's industry and will be estimated based upon data for Mallard. (This rate could change after the takeover as Oakton is of a different size and is quoted on a different market.)

Using WACC: $k_e \dfrac{E}{E+D} + k_d (1-t) \dfrac{D}{E+D}$

This discount rate is a market rate which includes inflation. The cash flows, with the exception of the directors' consultancy fees, exclude any future inflation. The cash flows should either be increased by the expected rate of inflation and the market (nominal) discount rate used, or, if the cash flows are not adjusted, the discount rate should be the real discount rate which excludes the effect of inflation. In this case use of the real discount rate is easier, although in reality this may not be as accurate as using nominal cash flows because different types of cash flow might be affected by different levels of price changes. If the real discount rate is used, the payments to the directors should be deflated by the inflation rate in order to maintain comparability with all other cash flows.

The real discount rate is: $\dfrac{1.116}{1.024} = 8.98\%$ or 9%.

Present values (at 9% discount rate)

Year	Item	Cash flow	Discount factor at 9%	PV
		£000		£000
0	Sale of land and buildings	800		800
0	Redundancy costs	(1,200)		(1,200)
1 – 10	Operating cash flows	4,154	6.418	26,660
1	Deflated value of directors' fees	(196)	0.917	(178)
2	Deflated value of directors' fees	(192)	0.842	(162)
3	Deflated value of directors' fees	(187)	0.772	(144)
	Net present value			25,776

Note: Deflated value of directors' fees

The directors will be taking fixed annual fees of £100,000 each or £300,000 in total for three years. The cash flows are being discounted at a real cost of capital, and in real terms, these fees will fall in value each year. The annual cash flows should therefore be deflated to allow for their fall in real value.

For convenience, the tax saving each year is assumed to occur in the same year as the fees are paid.

Given an annual inflation rate of 2.4%, the after-tax deflated value of the fees each year are:

Year 1 £300,000 × (1 − 0.33)/(1.024) = (in £000) 196.

Year 2 £300,000 × (1 − 0.33)/(1.024) (1.024) = (in £000) 192.

Year 3 £300,000 × (1 − 0.33)/(1.024) (1.024) (1.024) = (in £000) 187.

The present value of expected cash flows is theoretically the best of the three suggested valuation methods, but even this relies upon accurate estimates of both cash flows and the discount rate, and does not consider the possible effect of any opportunities (options) that might occur as a result of the acquisition. The expected present value of cash flows over a 10-year time horizon is considerably in excess of the proposed sale price of £22 million. This is without any estimate of the value of any cash flows that occur after 10 years (effectively the realisable value at the end of 10 years). If the purchase of Mallard fits the strategic plans of Oakton, an offer of £22 million is recommended.

(c)　Oakton, in theory, will wish to make payment in whatever form (cash, shares, bonds or some combination of these) that allows a successful purchase at the minimum cost, maintains a desired level of gearing, and does not result in future cash flow problems. However, the company might not wish to use almost all of its money market deposits for one acquisition.

The form of payment for an acquisition is also likely to be influenced by the attitude of the shareholders of the 'victim' company. In this case a major influence could be whether or not the three directors are happy to receive a payment in the form of cash, as a cash payment might lead to immediate capital gains tax liabilities for the directors.

50   DRICOM PLC

Key answer tips

Only show the parts of the balance sheet that are relevant to the report – a full pro forma balance sheet was specifically not required and would have wasted time.

Report for the board of directors of Dricom plc on the proposed reconstruction

The scheme of reconstruction is likely to be successful if:

(i)   It leaves all providers of finance in at least as good a position as they would have been had the reconstruction not taken place.

(ii)   It treats all parties fairly.

(iii)   Adequate finance is provided for the company's needs.

(iv)   As a result of the reconstruction the company is expected to be financially viable.

If the reconstruction does not take place it is possible that the company will be forced into receivership during the next year or soon afterwards as losses are likely to continue without the new investment. Even if the company survives 2004, the £1 million repayment of the convertible debenture in 2005 is likely to pose a major cash flow problem.

The following analysis assumes 30 September 2003 values, but the situation could have deteriorated since that time.

Receivership

If the company was to go into receivership, the expected realisable value of assets would be:

	£000
Land and buildings	1,200
Plant and machinery	1,600
Stocks	670
Debtors	1,090
Cash	35
	4,595
Existing creditors are:	
Secured	
9% debenture	500
8% convertible debenture	1,000
Bank term loan	800
	2,300
Redundancy payments	1,000
Unsecured	
10% loan stock	500
Overdraft	620
Other creditors	940
	2,060

The secured creditors are likely to be fully repaid, and the redundancy payments made, but the unsecured creditors will only receive approximately 63 pence in the pound, assuming all rank equally.

Ordinary shareholders would receive nothing.

Reconstruction

The cash flows associated with the reconstruction are:

Outflows:	£000
Purchase of new machinery and equipment	2,250
Redundancy payments	500
Payment to ordinary shareholders	280
	3,030
Inflows:	
Venture capital company	1,000
BXT bank (incremental loan)	1,200
Directors and employees	750
Sale of surplus machinery	300
	3,250

There is also £35,000 of existing cash. The financing provision looks adequate (assuming the overdraft remains unchanged), but no allowance has been made for possible incremental working capital that will be required in conjunction with a likely increase in sales. It is assumed that the cash resources will be adequate to finance this, but a more detailed evaluation of working capital requirements is recommended.

The **estimated realisable value of assets immediately after the reconstruction**, before any significant change in working capital requirements is forecast to be:

	£000
Land and buildings	1,200
Old plant and machinery	1,300
New machinery and equipment*	2,250
Stocks	670
Debtors	1,090
Cash	255
	6,765

*The realisable value of new machinery and equipment is likely to be less than the purchase price of £2.25 million.

New creditors would be:

Secured		Annual interest
9% debenture	500	45
Bank term loan	2,000	260
Overdraft	620	62
	3,120	367
Unsecured		
10% loan stock	500	50
Other creditors	940	-
	1,440	50
Total creditors	4,560	417

As long as the realisable value of the new machinery and equipment is not significantly less than its book value, the position of creditors has improved, and, on the basis of this data, full repayment should be made in the event of liquidation.

The reaction of the various providers of finance is likely to be as follows.

Ordinary shareholders

The offer of 28 pence per share is a premium of almost 22% over the current share price and unless the shareholders believe that there is some other way that the company can be returned to profitability it is likely to be accepted. However, some shareholders might wish to continue to own shares in the company, and might prefer an offer of new shares to a cash redemption. The company might consider this alternative, which would also reduce the need for financing.

BXT bank

If the company fails BXT bank will receive full repayment of the £800,000 term loan and an expected 63% repayment of the overdraft.

Dricom would request an extra £1.2 million term loan at an additional 1% interest rate, and would offer security on the overdraft.

New secured creditors would be:

	£000
9% debenture	500
Bank term loan	2,000
Overdraft	620
	3,120

Unless the realisable value of the new machinery and equipment is less than £620,000, there now appears to be ample security for all of the bank's loans.

Interest cover from 2004-05 is forecast to be:

£000

$$\frac{\text{Profit before tax and interest}}{\text{Interest}} \quad \frac{750+}{417} = 1.8:1$$

This is relatively low interest cover and might not be satisfactory to the bank. The attitude of the bank to a larger term loan is likely to depend upon convincing the bank that a minimum of the forecast profit figure can be achieved.

Straight debenture holders

The position of the debenture holders remains unchanged. In either situation they are likely to receive full repayment. They may require some form of incentive, for example the addition of warrants to the debenture, in order to agree to the reconstruction.

Loan stock holders

The loan stock holders, who are unsecured, stand a much better chance of full repayment of their loan after the reconstruction and are likely to agree to the reconstruction.

Convertible debenture holders

This is potentially the most difficult group of creditors. As secured creditors they are likely to receive full repayment in a liquidation. They are being asked to exchange certain repayment for new, risky ordinary shares at an effective price of £94/60, or 157 pence per share. The directors and employees are being offered shares at 150 pence per share, and the venture capital organisation at £1 million/700,000 or 143 pence per share. Even if the convertible debenture holders were willing to exchange their debentures for ordinary shares, which is unlikely due to the risk, they would not be willing to pay more for the shares than other groups.

The validity of a new share price of around 150 pence per share must be questioned. Without full information on expected future cash flows detailed analysis cannot be undertaken. However, the expected P/E ratio of Dricom may be compared with the industry average.

Dricom

	No tax £000	With tax £000
Earnings before interest and tax	750 +	750+
Interest	417	417
Taxable income	333	333
Taxation	–	110
	333	223
Earnings per share	$\frac{333}{1,800}$ = 18.5 pence	$\frac{223}{1,800}$ = 12.4 pence
Expected PE ratio (based on 150 pence per share)	8:1	12:1

The with-tax scenario represents the normal situation, giving a P/E ratio of approximately the industry average. Given the company's relatively poor interest cover, and recent history it is doubtful whether investors would be willing to pay 150 pence for new shares as part of the reconstruction. It may be necessary to issue a larger number of shares at a lower share price in order to make the offer attractive, and to raise the required amount of finance.

In order to secure the agreement of the convertible debenture holders Dricom may have to offer them redemption of the debentures, with the associated impact on financing requirements.

The venture capital organisation

The venture capital provider would bear a major risk, as it would hold only equity. The price of 143 pence per share might be regarded as too high by a venture capital provider. Under the proposed reconstruction a total of 1.8 million new 25 pence par value shares would be issued, of which the venture capital organisation would own 700,000 or almost 39% (directors and employees 28%, convertible debenture holders 33%), probably giving it effective control of the company. Almost certainly a venture capital company would require significant board representation. It might also require fixed price options on future share issues or other 'sweeteners' which would provide potential capital gains. Many venture capital organisations would not be willing to take such a high equity stake in a company.

Other creditors

Other creditors are in a similar position to the unsecured loan stock holders, and would stand a much better chance of full repayment of their loan after the reconstruction. Other creditors are likely to agree to the reconstruction.

Directors and employees

Although the company's directors have presumably agreed to participate in the purchase of the shares the attitude of the company's employees is unknown. They may not wish to, or be able to, subscribe to the amount of shares on offer. The success of the proposed reconstruction will partly depend upon finance being agreed by the company's employees.

Conclusion

The reconstruction as currently proposed is unlikely to succeed. The company should consider altering the proposed terms that are to be offered, especially to the existing ordinary shareholders, the convertible debenture holders and to the venture capital provider. The price at which new ordinary shares are to be offered should be reviewed, and a lower price may be necessary.

51 RAYSWOOD PLC

Assumptions:

(1) Share price is the present value of future cash flows i.e. the economic model.

(2) The stock market is weak and semi strong efficient most of the time therefore once new information is communicated to the market it is rapidly reflected in the share price.

(3) In an efficient market shares are fairly priced i.e. a zero NPV transaction. They give investors the exact return to compensate them for the perceived level of systematic risk of the shares.

(4) If shares are a zero NPV transactions, takeovers / mergers cold only be successful due to value created as a result of the merger i.e. the synergies.

(5) Therefore it is absolutely essential that one undertakes an exhaustive review to identify all the synergies. In this question no synergies have been identified, therefore before any final advice would be given to the client one would request an immediate review of all synergies.

(6) The question will therefore have to be answered on the basis of the unrealistic assumption that there are no synergies.

Post acquisition share price:

The Economic Value/Cash Approach:		
Market values:	£m	
Rayswood – 40×3.2 =	128.0	
Pondhill – $150 \times .45$ =	67.5	
PV of the synergies	**0.0**	**Immediate review required**
Value of combined company	195.5	
*No of shares:	65m	
Share price of the combined company	**3.01**	

*No of shares:

Rayswood buys Pondhill in a 1 for 6 shares for share exchange.

Rayswood already has 40m shares and buys Pondhill for $(150 \times 1/6) = 25m$ shares, thus 65m shares in total.

Tutorial note: In fact the takeover has been a wealth decreasing decision in relation to the shareholders of Rayswoods. The new share price of £3.01 is lower than current market price of £3.20. Which reflects the fact that premium payment to Pondhill's shareholders has reduced the wealth of Rayswood's shareholders.

Calculation of the acquisition premium – Value per one share of Pondhill:

Pondhill shareholders get 1 share in Rayswood (£3.01) for every 6 shares of Pondhill.

$$\frac{1 \times 3.01}{6} = £0.50 \qquad \frac{0.50 - 0.45}{0.45} = 11.11\%$$

Therefore before an acquisition premium is paid consideration should be given to ensure that it does not exceed the synergistic effects of the acquisition.

Director's comments:

'As a result of this takeover we will diversify our operations and our earnings per share will rise by 13%, bringing great benefits to our shareholders.'

Risk diversification

One of the primary reasons put forward for all mergers is that the income of the combined entity will be less volatile (less risky) as its cash flows come from a wide variety of products and markets. However this is a reduction in total risk, but has little or no affect on the systematic risk.

Will this benefit the shareholders?

Basic answer: No

Shareholders should diversify for themselves, because a shareholder can more easily and cheaply eliminate unsystematic risk by purchasing an international unit trust. As the majority of investors in PLCs have well diversified portfolios they are only exposed to systematic risk. Thus the reduction of total risk by the more expensive company diversification option is generally not recommended. The Director's comment is incorrect.

Earnings per share will rise by 13%.

Calculation of EPS:

	Rayswood	Pondhill	Enlarged Rayswood
Profit available to ordinary shareholders	7.8m	6.5m	14.3
No of shares	40m	150m	65m*
	19.5p	4.33p	22p

* see working above

% increase in the Earnings per share: $\dfrac{22 - 19.5}{19.5} \times 100 = 13\%$

An increasing EPS does not automatically result in an increase share price, as the P/E ratio may fall to reflect the lower growth potential of the enlarged company.

The P/E ratios:

	Rayswood	Pondhill	Enlarged Rayswood
Share price	320	45	301
EPS	19.5	4.33	22
	16.41	10.39	13.68

In the absence of synergy from the acquisition, purchasing Pondhill, with relatively low growth expectations, will depress the growth of the enlarged Rayswood's post acquisition and thus the post acquisition P/E ratio falls.

Tutorial note:

		Pre Acq	Post Acq
EPS	↑	19.5p	22p
P/E ratio	↓	16.41	13.68
Share price		£3.20	£3.01

P/E counters EPS, rendering it a dubious measure of acquisitions merits at best.

The Director's comment is incorrect, the increasing earnings per shares does not bring great benefits to the shareholders, in fact it masks a potential decrease in the share price.

Non-executive comments:

"The share price of Rayswood will rapidly increase to £3.61 following the announcement of the bid."

Bootstrapping:

A company is able to increase its EPS by merging with a company on a lower P/E ratio than its own. The bootstrapping argument states that the

Share price of the enlarged Rayswood = Post acq EPS × Pre acq P/E ratio of Rayswood.

£3.61	=	22 p	×	16.41 times

It contends that the market may believe that when that merger is completed that the management team of Rayswood can increase growth potential of Pondhill earnings to the same level as Rayswood earnings. It may then assign the Rayswood's higher P/E ratio to the combined earnings of both companies (i.e. the post acq EPS).

There has been some well documented cases of bootstrapping occurring in the 50s and 60s in America however as the stock markets have become more and more efficient it much less likely to occur today.

The investors would request a detail analysis of the synergies so they could calculate the present value of future cash flows.

If there are no synergies identified the higher post acq EPS simply results in a lower post acq P/E multiple as we have seen. Therefore the non-executive is also incorrect in his views.

52 PRICUT PLC

Key answer tips

When you have a volume of information available to you, you must be very focused to avoid carrying out irrelevant and time consuming calculations. The principle aim of the shareholders will be to increase their wealth so look at this first.

(a)   The bid will only be accepted by shareholders of Verlot plc if the value of the bid is at a premium over the current share price. The premium required for acceptance will differ between shareholders.

At current market prices the bid of four Pricut plc shares for three Verlot plc shares values Verlot shares at 309 pence, a premium of 14 pence or 4.7 per cent above the current market price. This is only a small premium (Note: in the UK a premium of 30% would be more usual), and unless acceptance of the bid is recommended by Verlot plc's directors, is unlikely to be attractive to many of Verlot plc's shareholders.

Factors that might influence the decision include:

(i)   Verlot plc currently has higher growth in dividends and earnings per share than Pricut plc. Similarly, the price/earnings ratio of Verlot is 14.75, and of Pricut 13.9 indicating the market expectations of Verlot plc continuing to have slightly better prospects.

(ii)   Using the dividend valuation model $P = \dfrac{D1}{Ke - g}$, the intrinsic value of Verlot's shares may be estimated at $\dfrac{12.5(1.08)}{0.13 - 0.08} = 270$ pence, where 12.5 pence is the current dividend per share.

This would suggest that Verlot plc shares are currently overvalued, and might encourage shareholders to sell. Such a conclusion would imply that the market is inefficient, and is not correctly pricing Verlot plc's shares. Most evidence suggests that the market is semi-strong form efficient (although not at all times).

(iii)   If the shareholders are considering keeping Pricut plc's shares after the acquisition they may be concerned that Pricut plc is much more highly geared than Verlot plc.

Measured by long-term loans to shareholders' funds, gearing levels are:

	Book value	*Market value*
Pricut plc	$\dfrac{314}{222} = 141\%$	$\dfrac{364}{696} = 52\%$
Verlot plc	$\dfrac{17.5}{54.7} = 32\%$	$\dfrac{17.5}{118} = 14.8\%$

Verlot plc's shareholders may be reluctant to accept the extra financial risk. Naturally, they would have the opportunity to sell Pricut shares if they accepted the offer, but this would involve transactions costs and would be at an unknown price.

(iv)   The difference in dividend policy may be important to some shareholders. Dividend yield for Pricut is 3.4% for Verlot it is 4.2%.

Pricut plc's shareholders are likely to welcome the bid if it increases the value of their shares. The estimated effect on share price of the bid is:

	£ million
Total earnings available to shareholders 50 + 8 =	58
Number of shares 300 million + 53.333 million	353.33 million
Expected earnings per share	16.42 pence
Expected P/E ratio (market weighted average of Pricut plc and Verlot plc P/E ratios)	14.02
Estimated price (P/E × EPS)	230 pence

This is a slight fall in share price.

However, when the effects of the rationalisation are announced the impact on expected NPV will be at least £6.8m − £9.0m + £2.70m × 3.605 = £7.53m.

This will add approximately $\dfrac{£7.53m}{353.33m}$ = 2.1 pence to the value of Pricut plc's shares, restoring the value to approximately 232 pence.

Tutorial note: an alternative approach to the above would be as follows:

Market capitalisation		**£m**
Pricut	75m / .25 × 2.32 =	696
Verlot	20m / .50 × 2.95 =	118
PV of the synergy		
Warehouse		6.8
Redundancy	(based on the WACC of Pricut)	(9.0)
Wage savings	2.7 × 3.605	9.73
Total value post merger		**821.53**
No of shares		
Pricut		300.00
Verlot	40 x 4/3 =	53.33
Total number of shares		**353.33**
Value per share – post merger		**2.33**

In terms of the effect on share value Pricut plc's shareholders are likely to be neutral. If, however, there are other synergies or growth opportunities as a result of the acquisition, for example if employing some of Verlot plc's more able managers can improve the cash flows and growth of Pricut plc, then Pricut plc's shareholders are likely to welcome the bid.

Tutorial note: The list of synergies in the question does not appear exhaustive - indeed one would expect economies of scale in purchasing, distribution and marketing functions. Therefore, if additional synergies occur this would be create additional value for both sets of the shareholders.

(b) The financial attraction of the zero coupon debenture can be assessed by estimating the redemption yield and/or likely immediate capital gain. At the current price of 295 pence, a zero coupon debenture is being offered for the equivalent to 295 pence × 10 = £29.50.

This is redeemable at £100 in 10 years time. The gross redemption yield on the debenture may be estimated by solving $£29.50 = \dfrac{£100}{(1+r)^{10}}$.

The required discount factor is 0.295 in ten years. This is found from present value tables to give an interest rate of 13%. A redemption yield of 13% is significantly higher than the current 10% yield on new ten year loan stock, and might be attractive to Verlot's shareholders.

Assuming the zero coupon debenture and new ten year loan stock have the same risk, the expected market price of the zero coupon debenture upon issue may be estimated as:

$$\text{Price} = \frac{£100}{(1+.1)^{10}} = £38.55$$

This is an expected premium, per Verlot plc share, of $\dfrac{£38.55 - £29.50}{10} = £0.905$ or almost 31%. As this would be available as an immediate capital gain it might be attractive to Verlot plc's shareholders. (In practice risk is likely to differ slightly as the securities have a different duration.

Tutorial note: *Duration* is a measure of the relative volatility of bonds caused by/due to changes in prevailing interest rates. It differs from the maturity of the bond by considering the impact of cash flows within the life of the bond. The greater the impact of cash flows within the life of the bond then the shorter is the duration and the less volatile is the bond. (Only in the case of a zero coupon bond is the duration equal to the maturity.) Although the debentures would increase Pricut plc's relatively high level of gearing, there would be no immediate adverse cash flow effects, unless a sinking fund was created to meet the redemption payment in 10 years time.

A cash offer of 325 pence per share is a 10% premium above the current market price, which is better than the initial share offer but significantly worse than the expected premium with the zero coupon bond. Verlot plc's shareholders will know exactly how much they will receive, which is not the case if they are paid in securities, but might be liable to taxation on capital gains that they have made since purchasing the share. No immediate capital gains tax liability would exist if payment was made in shares or debentures.

(c) Any defences against a bid must be legal, and fall within the City Code on Takeovers and Mergers. Some of the directors' suggestions would not be permitted.

After a bid had been made Verlot plc would be prohibited from altering its articles of association to require 75% of shareholders to approve the acquisition.

Section 151 of the Companies Act 1985 prohibits a third party, for a fee, purchasing the company's shares. This suggestion is likely to be viewed as the company effectively purchasing its own shares and would be illegal.

It is possible to announce that profits are likely to double next year, but the assumptions underlying such a statement would need to be clearly specified in order that shareholders could make their own judgement as to its validity.

Verlot plc could mount an advertising campaign criticising the management of Pricut plc, but any statements about performance must be supported by relevant data.

Fixed assets could be revalued by an independent external valuer. Whether or not this has any effect on the perceived market value of Verlot plc would depend upon market efficiency. If the market is efficient the current value of fixed assets would already be known and would form part of the existing market price. In such circumstances a professional revaluation would not result in shareholders placing a higher value on the company.

ACCA marking scheme			Marks
(a)	Discussion of current bid and its premium over share price		2
	Valuation using DVM and comment		3-4
	Dividend policy, dividend growth and EPS growth		2-3
	Gearing differences and risk		2
	Estimates of expected EPS and share price		4-5
	Other discussion		2
		Max	**15**
(b)	Zero coupon yield and value		4-5
	Cash offer and implications		2-3
		Max	**7**
(c)	1-2 marks for correct comment.		
	2 if a full answer is given		
		Max	**8**
Total			**30**

53 PERFORMANCE ASSESSMENT

Key answer tips

This is a very broad question and there are a number of ways in which it could be answered. Make sure that you make use of all the information given in the question, particularly in relation to share prices, share price indices, equity betas and risk free rates.

(a) **Performance report for companies in Asertia and Knowland**

The performance of the companies may be measured against indicators from the relevant economies. A simple measure is to compare growth trends over the four year period.

Asertia

	Indexed trends				*% growth*		
	2000	2001	2002	2003	2000–1	2001–2	2002–3
Turnover	100	131.2	160.4	187.5	31.2	22.2	16.9
Profit	100	138.2	185.5	229.1	38.2	34.2	23.5
RPI	100	135.5	171.7	205.2	35.5	26.7	19.5
Share price	100	125.7	153.1	189.1	25.7	21.8	23.5
Stock market	100	119.9	148.9	189.2	19.9	24.1	27.1

Knowland

	Indexed trends				*% growth*		
	2000	2001	2002	2003	2000–1	2001–2	2002–3
Turnover	100	103.6	109.2	121.4	3.6	5.4	11.2
Profit	100	108.9	126.1	138.0	8.9	15.8	9.5
RPI	100	104.3	107.1	110.8	4.3	2.7	3.5
Share price	100	81.4	86.4	97.0	(18.6)	6.2	12.3
Stock market	100	87.2	91.3	92.7	(12.8)	4.8	1.5

The average investment returns, measured by share price change, are:

Asertia 23.7%

Asertian market 23.7%

Knowland (1.0%)

Knowland market (2.4%)

Indicators for the Asertian company are mixed. Growth in turnover has lagged behind a broad measure of inflation, the retail price index, yet profit after tax has performed relatively well. Despite this profit performance the company's share price has only increased by a similar amount to the general stock market index.

The performance of the company in Knowland appears to be better, with turnover, profit and share price all growing faster than the relevant country indices.

However, comparisons such as this ignore the risk of the two companies. The company in Asertia appears to be much more risky, as evidenced by its relatively high beta. Performance measures incorporating risk would be much more useful.

A possible performance measure is the historic alpha coefficient associated with the investment, the actual return less the required return for the risk of the investment.

Using CAPM, the required return for Asertia was:
19% + (23.7% – 19%) 1.55 = 26.3%

The actual return was 23.7%. The investment has performed worse than would be expected over the period.

For Knowland the required return was: 4% + (–2.4% – 4%) 0.98 = (2.3%)

Actual return was (1.0%). Although the company's share price return was negative, it was still better than might have been expected given the general poor performance of the Knowland stock market. However, historic alphas are unlikely to persist in the future, and negative expected market returns over a long period make little economic sense.

Possible alternative performance measures include excess return to beta, which is useful for a well-diversified investor, and is measured by:

$$\frac{\text{investment return - risk free rate}}{\text{investment beta}}$$

For an investor who is not well diversified, a measure using total risk (the standard deviation of returns) is more appropriate.

$$\frac{\text{investment return - risk free rate}}{\text{standard deviation of returns}}$$

Based upon the available data, the company in Knowland appears to have been the more successful during the last four years.

(b) Other useful information might include:

(i) A benchmark with which to draw comparisons, preferably data for companies in the same industries as the two companies in Asertia and Knowland.

(ii) The objectives and risk aversion of the client.

(iii) Information about whether or not profits, RPI and other data are calculated in the same way in the two countries.

(iv) Total returns from the relevant stock markets and for investors in the companies. The data provided only shows the return from share price movements, and excludes the dividend yield, which might be significant.

(v) Exchange rate movements between the two countries and the UK. The client is likely to be interested in returns in sterling, not in foreign currencies.

(vi) Any tax implications of investing in the two countries.

(vii) Information about the future prospects of the companies. Historic returns do not provide an accurate guide to future performance. What are the future strategies of the two companies, what are their strengths and weaknesses, what is their competition?

(viii) Macro economic information about the two countries and their prospects. Asertia is a relatively high inflation country. Is the government likely to bring this under control? What are key economic indicators and trends?

(ix) How stable are the governments in the two countries and would there be significant political risk with the investments?

ACCA marking scheme			Marks
(a)	Growth rate estimates or index estimates		4
	Discussion and calculation regarding risk		4–5
	Other discussion about performance		2
			___
		Max	10
(b)	One mark for each valid point	Max	5
			___
Total			15
			___

54 PAXIS

Key answer tips

Part (a) involves a lengthy set of discounted cash flow calculations. It is vital that you follow the requirements exactly, set out clear workings and state assumptions as you go along.

Part (b) is a more straightforward discussion of limitations of estimates. Don't just state that a particular figure may be wrong – try to justify why by reference to the underlying assumptions highlighted in part (a).

Part (c) asks for a discussion of the factors that might affect the bid's acceptance. The danger here is that you overrun your time allocation here as it is only worth 4 marks.

Part (d) relies on you having obtained an answer to part (a). If that is not the case, then a pass can still be achieved by evaluating the current bid and discussing non-financial aspects not incorporated into part (a).

Part (e) looks at defences against the bid. The key here is to apply the different approaches to the scenario, rather than just giving an exhaustive list.

(a) The amount of expected synergy created may be estimated by comparing the sum of the pre-acquisition values of the individual companies with the expected post-acquisition value of the combined company.

Paxis

Free cash flow:

Cost of equity using CAPM:

Ke = 4% + (11% – 4%) 1.18 = 12.26%

Weighted average cost of capital:

$$WACC = k_e \frac{E}{E+D} + k_d(1-t) \frac{D}{E+D} = 12.26\% \,(0.7) + 6\% \,(1-0.3)\,(0.3) = 9.84\%$$

(N.B. rounded discount rates, for example 10%, are also acceptable in the solution)

	Paxis £000			
	1	*2*	*3*	*4*
Sales revenue	14,000	14,700	15,435	16,206
Operating costs	(10,640)	(11,172)	(11,730)	(12,317)
EBIT	3,360	3,528	3,705	3,889
Tax (30%)	(1,008)	(1,058)	(1,112)	(1,167)
Add back depreciation	1,523	1,599	1,679	1,762
Replacement investment	(1,680)	(1,764)	(1,852)	(1,945)
Free cash flow	2,195	2,305	2,420	2,539
Discount factors (9.84%)	0.910	0.829	0.755	0.687
Present values	1,997	1,911	1,827	1,744

Value beyond year four is estimated to be: $\dfrac{2,539(1.04)}{0.0984 - 0.04} \times 0.687 = 31,063$

The estimated value of Paxis is £38,542,000

Note: Interest is ignored as financing costs, and their associated tax effects, are included in the company's discount rate.

Wragger

Cost of equity using CAPM:

Ke = 4% + (11% – 4%) 1.38 = 13.66%

Weighted average cost of capital:

WACC = 13.66% (0.45) + 7.5% (1 – 0.3) (0.55) = 9.03%

	Wragger £000			
	1	*2*	*3*	*4*
Sales revenue	10,011	10,662	11,355	12,093
Operating costs	(6,976)	(7,429)	(7,912)	(8,426)
EBIT	3,035	3,233	3,443	3,667
Tax (30%)	(911)	(970)	(1,033)	(1,100)
Add back depreciation	1,172	1,248	1,329	1,415
Replacement investment	(1,321)	(1,406)	(1,498)	(1,595)
Free cash flow	1,975	2,105	2,241	2,387
Discount factors (9.03%)	0.917	0.841	0.772	0.708
Present values	1,811	1,770	1,730	1,690

Value beyond year four is estimated to be: $\dfrac{2,387(1.05)}{0.0903 - 0.05} \times 0.708 = 44,082$

The estimated value of Wragger is £51,033,000

Combined company

		£ million
Market value of equity		
Paxis	7 million x 298 pence =	20.86
Wragger	8 million x (4 x 298)/5 =	19.07 (reflecting the bid value)
Market value of debt		
Paxis	20.86/0.7 x 0.3 =	8.94
Wragger	(8 million x 192 pence)/0.45 x 0.55 =	18.77
		67.64

Weighted average cost of capital:

$$WACC = 12.26\% \ \frac{20.86}{67.64} + 13.66\% \ \frac{19.07}{67.64} + 6\% \ (1-0.3)\frac{8.94}{67.64} + 7.5\%(1-0.3)\frac{18.77}{67.64}$$

WACC = 9.64%

Combined company £000

	1	2	3	4
Sales revenue	24,097	25,543	27,075	28,700
Operating costs (70%)	(16,868)	(17,880)	(18,953)	(20,090)
EBIT	7,229	7,663	8,122	8,610
Tax (30%)	(2,169)	(2,299)	(2,437)	(2,583)
Add back depreciation	2,703	2,865	3,037	3,219
Replacement investment	(3,010)	(3,191)	(3,382)	(3,585)
Free cash flow	4,753	5,038	5,340	5,661
Discount factors (9.64%)	0.912	0.832	0.759	0.692
Present values	4,335	4,192	4,053	3,917

Value beyond year four is estimated to be: $\dfrac{5.661(1.05)}{0.64 - 0.05} \times 0.692 = 88,648$

The estimated value of the combined company is: £105,145,000

The sum of the individual companies is: £38,542,000 + £51,033,000 = £89,575,000

The expected synergy is £15,570,000.

(b) The estimates are based upon unrealistic assumptions and are subject to a considerable margin of error. Possible limitations include:

(i) Sales, operating costs, replacement investments, and dividends are unlikely to increase by the same amount.

(ii) Forecasts of future growth rates may not be accurate. Paxis is unlikely to have access to enough internal information about the activities of Wragger to make accurate projections.

(iii) The expected reduction in operating costs might not be achieved.

(iv) The estimates are based upon present values to infinity of expected free cash flows. A shorter time horizon might be more realistic.

(v) The cost of capital for the combined company could differ from that estimated, depending how the market evaluates the risk of the combined entity.

(vi) The analysis is based upon the assumption that the initial offer price is accepted.

(vii) There is no information about the fees and other costs associated with the proposed acquisition. In many cases these are substantial, and must be included in the analysis.

(viii) The post acquisition integration of organisations often involves unforeseen costs which would reduce the benefit of any potential synergy.

(c) The type of payment might influence the success of the bid. Paxis is proposing a share for share exchange which offers a continuation in ownership of the entity, albeit as part of the successful bidder. However, relative share prices will change during the period of the bid, and the owner of shares in the potential victim company will not know the precise post-acquisition value of the bid. An alternative might be cash payments which provides a known, precise sum, and might be favoured for this reason. However, in some countries payment in cash might lead to an immediate capital gains tax liability for the investor.

The effective price offered would of course be a major influence. Paxis would need to offer a premium over the existing share price, but the size of the premium that would be acceptable is unknown. Informal discussions with major shareholders of Wragger might assist in determining this (subject to such discussions being permitted by the regulatory authorities).

(d) The current bid values the shares of Wragger at £19.07 million, compared to the current market value of £15.36 million, a premium of £3.71 million. The expected synergy is £15,570,000. If these data are accurate the bid could be substantially increased without the shareholders of Paxis suffering a fall in their expected wealth. In theory, the bid could be increased by an additional £11,860,000, or 148 pence for each existing Wragger share.

There might also be strategic reasons for undertaking the bid, and the acquisition of Wragger might lead to future options that are not valued by the above analysis.

The proposed acquisition is expected to result in substantial synergy, and to create wealth for the shareholders of both companies. The directors are recommended to proceed with the bid.

(e) Possible defences against a bid:

Once a bid has been made, probably the most important defence against the bid is for Wragger to persuade its shareholders that Paxis is currently overvalued. It could also criticise the past performance of Paxis, including its relatively low growth, the logic behind the acquisition, and the strategic fit of the two companies. Similarly Wragger might argue that its own shares are undervalued. Wragger could revalue its assets, and produce forecasts (with supporting assumptions) of future earnings and dividends in order to support the argument that it is undervalued. It could also present a clear future strategy to its shareholders to encourage them not to sell.

As the total market value of Wragger is larger than that of Paxis, and Wragger has a higher growth rate, the directors of Wragger might consider making a counter bid for Paxis.

If the combined market share of the two companies is large enough the bid might be referred to regulatory authorities such as the Competition Commission in the UK. Given the size of the companies this is not likely in this case.

A possible last resort strategy is for Wragger to approach a 'white knight', a preferred alternative bidder for the company.

ACCA marking scheme

This question requires estimates of corporate value using free cash flows, and critical analysis of the potential synergy created from an acquisition. It also requires knowledge and understanding of merger offer terms and defenses.

			Marks
(a)	Method of estimating synergy		1
	Ignoring interest in the analysis		1
	Paxis		
	Cost of capital		2
	Year 1–4 free cash flow		2–3
	Value beyond year 4		1
	Wragger		
	Cost of capital		2
	Year 1–4 free cash flow		2–3
	Value beyond year 4		1
	Combined company		
	Market values of equity and debt		2
	Cost of capital		2
	Year 1–4 free cash flow		2–3
	Value beyond year 4		1
	Reward technique in the above calculations		
	Synergy		1
		Maximum	20
(b)	One mark for each valid point	Maximum	6
(c)	Type of payment		1–2
	Price offered		1–2
	One mark each for other relevant reasons	Maximum	2
		Maximum	4
(d)	Estimate of increase in bid		3
	Discussion		2
			5
(e)	Discussion of:		
	Undervalued Wragger		1–2
	Overvalued Paxis		1–2
	Reverse bid		1
	Other relevant points 1 each	Maximum	2
		Maximum	5
		Total	40

55 REFLATOR PLC

Key answer tips

In part (a) it is easier to discuss the advantages of MBOs by looking at the different stakeholders involved.

For part (b) you need to construct an income statement for each year. The trickiest part is separating the interest and capital elements with the "mortgage style" subordinated loan.

In part (c) look at the implications of the warrant scheme on ultimate shareholdings and control.

(a)   The advantages of a buy-out may be viewed from the perspectives of each of the parties involved.

The selling company may regard a buy-out as preferable to the liquidation of a loss making division. A buy-out might result in a higher disposal price, and has the social effect of protecting jobs. Selling part of the organisation might allow the company to focus on its core competence.

The current managers, with their existing expertise of the markets, relationships with clients etc may have a better chance of successfully operating the company. They are also likely to be highly motivated through their significant equity holdings, and by the potential for large capital gains if the company succeeds.

A venture capitalist or other type of investor normally takes a high risk, in the hope of high returns mainly through capital gains. Most investors would seek some form of exit route for their investment after several years, possible through a listing on the AIM or other relevant market. In some countries investing in buy-outs may offer tax advantages.

(b)   The increase in the value of equity may be estimated from the expected retained earnings over the four year period. The maximum 15% dividend payment is assumed.

Year 0		1	2	3	4
Earnings before interest and tax		320,000	410,000	500,000	540,000
Interest 8.5%		170,000	170,000	170,000	170,000
Interest 9% loan[1]		27,000	23,411	19,499	15,236
Earnings before tax		123,000	216,589	310,501	354,764
Taxation (30%)		36,900	64,977	93,150	106,429
Earnings after tax		86,100	151,612	217,351	248,335
Dividend (15%)		12,915	22,742	32,603	37,250
Retained earnings		73,185	128,870	184,748	211,085
Book value of equity	800,000	873,185	1,002,055	1,186,803	1,397,888

Growth in the book value of equity from 800,000 to 1,397,888 over four years is a compound growth rate of 14.97%. This is considerably less than the 20% growth rate claimed by the managers.

It should be noted that this is a book value of equity. The market value of equity is much more relevant to a potential investor, and is likely to be very different from this book value.

Note:

[1]Interest on the 9% loan

The equal annual payment comprising interest and capital that is necessary to pay off a £300,000 loan over six years is:

$$\frac{300,000}{4.486} = £66,875 \text{ (4.486 is the PV annuity factor for six years at 9%)}$$

Year	Remaining value	Interest	Repayment of capital
1	300,000	27,000	39,875
2	260,125	23,411	43,464
3	216,661	19,499	47,376
4	169,285	15,236	51,639

(c)   At the start of the buy-out, the equity holding would be 1,000,000 shares by the managers, and 600,000 by the venture capital organisation. The initial warrant proposal would allow the venture capital organisation to purchase 300,000 new shares after four years, a total of 900,000. The revised suggestion would allow 450,000 new shares to be purchased which would give majority ownership and control of the company to the venture capital organisation. This is likely to be unacceptable to the managers, unless they also will have further opportunities to increase their share ownership, for example through other forms of option.

ACCA marking scheme		
		Marks
(a)	1 mark for each valid point. Look for advantages to the various parties involved in the buy-out max	5
(b)	Interest payments	3–4
	Other elements in retained earnings estimate	2
	Book value of equity and growth rate estimate	2
	max	7
	Bonus mark if comment is made about book value estimates not being very useful (subject to 15 max for the question)	
(c)	Calculations and discussion of the effect on ownership	3
Total		15

TREASURY MANAGEMENT

56   TYR PLC

(a)   Estimates of earnings and dividend per share, and their growth rates are shown below:

	Post-tax earnings per share (pence)	Growth (%)	Dividend per share (pence)	Growth (%)	Inflation (%)
20X1	47.9	–	19.2	–	
20X2	51.3	7.1	20.1	4.7	5
20X3	55.2	7.6	20.9	4.0	4
20X4	55.9	1.3	21.5	2.9	3
20X5	61.9	10.7	22.2	3.3	3
Average annual compound growth		6.6	3.7		

Notes

1   Earnings per share 20X1 = 86.2/180 = 47.9 pence, and so on for other years.

2   Dividend per share 20X1 = 34.5/180 = 19.2 pence, and so on for other years.

3   Average annual growth in dividends per share $= \sqrt[4]{\dfrac{22.2}{19.2}} - 1$

$$= 1.037 - 1$$

$$= 0.037 \text{ or } 3.7\%$$

Current dividend policy

From the above data TYR appears to be following a policy of paying a constant dividend per share, adjusted for the current year's level of inflation.

Success of this policy

The only possible indication from the data of whether or not the dividend policy has been successful is the relative performance of TYR's share price in comparison to the market index. This, however, would rely upon the assumption that the choice of dividend policy influences the share price.

	FT all-share index	Growth (%)	Share price (pence)	Growth (%)
20X1	2895	–	360	–
20X2	3300	14.0	410	13.9
20X3	2845	(13.8)	345	(15.9)
20X4	2610	(8.3)	459	33.0
20X5	2305	(11.7)	448	(2.4)
Average annual compound (decline)/growth		(5.5)		5.6

Notes

4   Average annual change in all-share index $= \sqrt[4]{\dfrac{2{,}305}{2{,}895}} - 1$

$$= 0.945 - 1$$

$$= \text{-0.055, or an average annual decline of 5.5\%.}$$

5   Average annual growth in TYR plc share price $= \sqrt[4]{\dfrac{448}{360}} - 1$

$$= 1.056 - 1$$

$$= 0.056 \text{ or } 5.6\%.$$

TYR's share price has increased over the four-year period by an annual compound rate of 5.6%, much better than the average annual decline of 5.5% suffered by the all-share index. This does not prove that the dividend policy has been successful. The share price might be influenced by many other factors, especially the potential long-term cash flow expectations of the shareholders. Additionally comparison with the all-share index does not measure the performance of TYR relative to companies in its own industry/sector.

(b)   **Additional information** might include:

    (i)   Direct feedback from shareholders, especially institutional shareholders, stating whether or not they are happy with the current dividend policy.

    (ii)   Full details of the registered shareholders, and size of holdings. TYR plc might have a desired spread of shareholders, which could be influenced by the dividend policy adopted.

(iii)   Knowledge of the impact of taxation of dividends on shareholders' attitudes, and specifically on their preferences between dividends and capital gains.

(iv)   The amount of capital investment the company wishes to undertake. The use of retained earnings and other internally generated funds avoids issue costs and the information asymmetry problems of external financing. The level of dividends paid affects the amount of internal funds that are available for investment.

(v)   The impact of dividend payments on corporate liquidity.

(vi)   The signals provided by dividend payments about the future financial health of the company. For example, would the fact the dividend growth is lagging behind earnings growth be considered a positive or negative signal?

(c)   Using the Dividend Growth Model market price $= \dfrac{D_1}{ke - g}$

where D1 is the expected next dividend, ke is the cost of capital and g the growth rate in dividends. Using the average compound growth of 3.7%:

$$\frac{D_1}{ke - g} = \frac{22.2(1.037)}{0.11 - 0.037} = 315 \text{ pence}$$

The actual share price at the end of 20X5 appears to be overvalued relative to the dividend growth model.

This does not prove that the actual market price is overvalued. The dividend growth model relies on restrictive assumptions, such as constant growth in dividends per share in perpetuity, which is unlikely to occur. There are also several factors that influence share prices that are not included within the model. Growth in earnings per share has increased more than growth in dividend per share, and it might be better to use the earnings growth rate in the model as this might more accurately reflect the financial health of the company.

ACCA marking scheme		
		Marks
(a)	Relevant calculations, e.g. EPS, DPS, growth rates	2-3
	Current dividend policy	1-2
	Sensible comment about evidence of success	1-2
(b)	One mark for each relevant point	max 4
(c)	Calculation(s) of value and conclusion	3
	Discussion of validity	2
Total		15

57   DISCOS PLC

(a)   **Trade insurance and forward contract**

The use of trade insurance limits the effect of possible payment/default, although Discos would still have to bear some of the risk.

Discos will want to sell the peso receipts in exchange for sterling.

The spot equivalent of 55 million pesos is:

$$\frac{55}{32.89} = £1,672,241$$

By agreeing to give credit, it is assumed that Discos will incur an interest cost for three months on £1,672,241 at a rate of 6.5%.

The three-month forward rate is 34.55.

If the customer pays on time, receipts in sterling will therefore be: $\frac{55m}{34.55} = £1,591,896$

This is much less favourable than the spot rate, but has the advantage of fixing the expected cash flow from the export deal (i.e. it provides a hedge against a risk of a fall in the value of the peso over the next three months).

If payment is received in three months:

	£	
Receipts from payment	1,591,896	
Interest cost	(27,174)	$(1,672,241 \times 6.5\% \times {}^3/_{12})$
Insurance cost	(20,903)	$(1,672,241 \times 1.25\%)$
Net receipts	1,543,819	

If payment is not made in three months:

The forward contract will have to be fulfilled, or rolled over at an unknown cost. The late payment/default is assumed not to be the result of government action. It is also assumed that the eventual receipts will be exchangeable into sterling at a rate of 35.90 (the current six-month forward rate) although this is very unlikely:

Net receipts would be, after six months:

	£	
From the insurer	1,378,830	(90% of 55 million)/35.90
Interest cost	(54,348)	$(1,672,241 \times 6.5\% \times {}^6/_{12})$
Insurance cost	(20,903)	$(1,672,241 \times 1.25\%)$
Net receipts	1,303,579	

If the estimated 5% risk of late payment or default is accurate, the expected return is:

Outcome	Probability	Net receipts	EV of net receipts
		£	£
Customer pays	0.95	1,543,819	1,466,628
Non-payment: insurer pays	0.05	1,303,579	65,179
			1,531,807

(b) **Export factor**

The use of an export factor eliminates foreign exchange risk as payment will be made in sterling. As the factor is non-recourse, the factor bears the risk if the customer pays late/defaults, except for the reduced sterling payment in six months that would be made to Discos. The factor will also take responsibility for the debt collection process.

The factor will pay less than the spot sterling equivalent of 55 million pesos. The spot value of 55 million pesos is £1,672,241. The maximum amount that the factor will pay is £1,590,000. The difference in these amounts is £82,241. If the factor pays only £1,530,000, the difference will be £88,241. This has a financial consequence for Discos. It is estimated below as an interest cost, for a three-month or six-month period, at 6.5% on £82,241. (*Tutorial note*: Other assumptions might be made.)

If the customer pays in three months:

	£	
From the factor	1,590,000	
Interest cost on factor finance	(20,034)	$(80\% \text{ of } 1,590,000 \times 6.3\% \times {}^3/_{12})$
Other interest costs	(6,504)	$[(20\% \text{ of } 1,590,000) + 82,241] \times 6.5\% \times {}^3/_{12}$
Factor fee	(39,750)	$(1,590,000 \times 2.5\%)$
Net receipts	1,523,712	

If the customer pays late/defaults:

	£	
From the factor	1,530,000	
Interest cost on factor finance	(40,068)	(80% of 1,590,000 × 6.3% × $^6/_{12}$)
Other interest costs	(13,008)	[(20% of 1,590,000) + 88,241] × 6.5% × $^6/_{12}$
Factor fee	(39,750)	(1,590,000 × 2.5%)
Net receipts	1,437,174	

If the estimated 5% risk of late payment or default is accurate, the expected return is:

Outcome	Probability	Net receipts	EV of net receipts
		£	£
Customer pays	0.95	1,523,712	1,447,526
Non-payment	0.05	1,437,174	71,859
			1,519,385

Other issues:

1   Will the factor be prepared to undertake a 'one off' deal, or will further business be required?

2   Will the use of the factor improve the chance of payment? Most factors are subsidiaries of major banks, and might have more market power to achieve payment.

3   Will Discos save administrative/labour costs if the factoring company undertakes the debt collection process? If so such savings would need to be included in any financial assessment.

(c)   **Documentary letter of credit**

The use of a documentary letter of credit should ensure that Discos receives the due payment. The letter of credit is confirmed and irrevocable, which means that as long as Discos correctly presents all the agreed documents to the importer's bank (normally via the exporter's bank), both an accepting bank and a confirming bank guarantee to make payment to the exporter (or to the third party holding the discounted bill of exchange). Thus in the case of late payment/default the guaranteeing banks will bear the risk. Letters of credit are very useful for high value exports, and when dealing with customers whose creditworthiness is uncertain, as is the case here.

Tutorial note: The accepting bank accepts a bill of exchange drawn on the bank by the exporter. This bank is likely to be in the customer's country. A confirming bank adds its guarantee of payment. This bank is likely to be in the exporter's country. Two banks therefore provide an undertaking to pay the bill when it becomes due for payment, provided the exporter presents all the agreed documents within the time limits specified.

The bill of exchange for 55 million pesos will be discounted at 25%. This will provide income for Discos of:

55 million × [1 – (0.25 × 3/12)]

=   55 million × 0.9375 = 51,562,500 pesos.

When the bill is discounted, this sum can be exchanged into sterling at the spot rate (32.89) to obtain £1,567,726.

	£
Discounted receipts from payment	1,567,726
Arrangement cost	(30,000)
Net receipts	1,537,726

The banks guaranteeing the bill will be liable for payment on the bill. Discos plc will immediately discount the bill in Xeridia and convert the net proceeds into sterling at the spot rate, in order to raise the necessary finance. Discos will face no further foreign exchange risk or commercial risk.

Recommendation:

Unless Discos could make substantial administrative savings from option (a) or option (b), the use of a confirmed letter of credit results in the highest expected receipts and is the recommended alternative (assuming that the decision rule is to choose the course of action providing the highest expected value of net receipts).

ACCA marking scheme	
	Marks
Insurance plus forward market	5
Non- recourse factor	5 – 6
Documentary letter of credit plus discounting	4
Conclusion	1
Reward technique	
Total	15

58 NTC PLC

(a) **Centralised treasury management** is normally recommended for multinational companies because:

(i) It allows centralised knowledge of the financial dealings of the entire group, better judgement of risk and exposure management, and the netting of inter-group currency requirements.

(ii) A central treasury can ensure that financial actions are taken that are in line with the objectives of the group as a whole, rather than individual subsidiaries.

(iii) It may perform a watchdog function to ensure that there are no problems in subsidiaries with the use of derivatives.

(iv) It allows greater control over inter-company receipts.

(v) A central treasury function may reduce the cost of borrowing for subsidiaries by lending necessary funds at rates lower than could be obtained by the subsidiaries in local markets. Such funds might be surplus funds from other subsidiaries, which would be offered favourable interest on the surplus, effectively eliminating the interest spread of banks.

(vi) A centralised treasury may have access to international markets, such as the Euromarkets, which are not directly accessible by individual subsidiaries. Such markets may offer more favourable interest rates. Combining the needs of various subsidiaries means that larger amounts will be invested and borrowed, which again may give access to more favourable rates.

(vii) It will be cheaper to develop treasury management and hedging expertise in one central function rather than in each subsidiary.

The main disadvantages of centralised treasury management are:

(i) It potentially removes decision-making and responsibility from the subsidiaries, and may affect motivation and initiative within subsidiaries.

(ii) It relies heavily on the timely provision of information.

(iii) Performance evaluation of staff in subsidiaries may be distorted if actions are taken centrally that are detrimental to the subsidiaries, although in the long-term interest of the group as a whole.

(iv)   The volume of treasury decisions within a multinational may be too large to handle in one central function.

(b)   **Tutorial note:** The table of payments and receipts might be difficult to understand on first reading it. It shows, for example, that the UK division will (in 000s) pay £100 to the Spain division and receive €210 from Spain in the same period. Similarly, Spain will pay €210 to the UK and €120 to the USA, and receive €80 from Hong Kong.

(i)   Receipts and payments in sterling at spot mid-rates:

| Payments (read down) | | | £000 | | |
Receipts (read across)	*UK*	*Spain*	*Hong Kong*	*USA*	*Total receipts*
UK	–	128.96	64.27	76.59	269.82
Spain	100.00	–	49.13	–	149.13
Hong Kong	35.71	–	–	–	35.71
USA	299.40	73.69	26.78	–	399.87
Total payments	(435.11)	(202.65)	(140.18)	(76.59)	854.53
Net	(165.29)	(53.52)	(104.47)	323.28	

Tutorial notes

(1)   Spot mid rates are US$1.4362/£1, €1.62835/£1 and HK$11.20185/£1.

(2)   The receipts minus payments figures are calculated simply by subtracting the payments total for each currency from the receipts total shown in the right hand column of the table.

As a result of multilateral netting the number of transactions may be reduced from nine to three, with the UK parent, the Spanish and Hong Kong subsidiaries each making one payment to the US subsidiary.

(ii)   Forward contracts, money market hedging and currency options will be illustrated.

In order to minimise transaction costs, netting of trade will be used where possible. As the Hong Kong dollar is pegged against the US dollar, the exposure risk of the Hong Kong dollar will be hedged using US dollars. This involves a slight risk, as the Hong Kong dollar might discontinue its pegged position. As interest rates are less than 1% different between the USA and Hong Kong, the economic pressure for the Hong Kong dollar to devalue is not likely to be strong at present.

UK parent net exposures (in 000s):

Payments	Receipts	Net for hedging, ( ) is payment
£100	–	n.a.
–	€210	€210
HK$400	HK$720	$HK320 = $US41.03 (at cross rate of $HK7.800/$US)
US$430	US$110	(US$320). So net = (US$320) – US$41.03 = (US$278.97)

Only two exposures need to be hedged, receipts of €210,000 and payments of US$278,970.

Forward markets:

Euro $\dfrac{€210,000}{1.6166}$ = £129,902 receipt

US$ $\dfrac{$278,970}{1.4285}$ = £195,289 payment

Money markets:

Euro hedge:

Borrow Euro at 5.3% for three months:

$$\frac{€210,000}{1.01325} \text{ or } 207,254 \text{ to repay Euro 210,000 in three months time.}$$

Convert Euro 207,254 at spot of E1.6292/£ to give £127,212.

Invest £127,212 for three months at 6.0% to yield £127,212 × 1.015 = £129,120.

US dollar hedge:

Borrow £191,708 at 6.9% for three months, total cost £195,015.

Convert £191,708 to dollars at the spot of $1.4358/£ to give $275,254.

Invest $275,254 for three months at 5.4% to yield $278,970.

Options:

September put options on £ are required as a payment in US dollars is due.

Exercise price 1.42:

Number of contracts $\dfrac{\$278,970}{1.42}$ = £196,458, $\dfrac{£196,458}{£31,250}$ = 6.29 contracts

£31,250 × 6 × 1.42 = $266,250 is hedged, the remaining $12,720 will be bought forward at $1.4285/£ or a cost of £8,904.

Exercise price 1.43:

Number of contracts $\dfrac{\$278,970}{1.43}$ = £195,084, $\dfrac{£195,084}{£31,250}$ = 6.24 contracts

£31,250 × 6 × 1.43 = $268,125 is hedged, the remaining $10,845 will be bought forward at $1.4285/£ or a cost of £7,592.

Exercise price 1.44:

Number of contracts $\dfrac{\$278,970}{1.44}$ = £193,729, $\dfrac{£193,729}{£31,250}$ = 6.20 contracts

£31,250 × 6 × 1.44 = $270,000 is hedged, the remaining $8,970 will be bought forward at $1.4285/£ or a cost of £6,279.

Premium costs (including three months financing at 6.9% per annum)

Exercise price:

1.42   £187,500 × 2.15c = $4,031 @ $1.4358/£ = £2,808 × 1.01725 = £2,856
1.43   £187,500 × 3.12c = $5,850 @ $1.4358/£ = £4,074 × 1.01725 = £4,145
1.44   £187,500 × 4.35c = $8,156 @ $1.4358/£ = £5,680 × 1.01725 = £5,778

Total cost if the option is exercised:

1.42   £187,500 + £2,856 + £8,904 = £199,260
1.43   £187,500 + £4,145 + £7,592 = £199,237
1.44   £187,500 + £5,778 + £6,279 = £199,557

Note: If the option is sold to include time value, rather than exercised, these costs would be slightly reduced.

In order for the option to be preferred to the best alternative, the money market hedge, which has a cost of £195,015, the total cost of using the option must be less than the cost of the money market hedge. The necessary costs of the option component of the hedge are estimated below, along with the spot rates that would produce this result.

	Money market	*– (Forward*	*+ Premium)*	*= Required option cost*	*Spot rate*
1.42	£195,015	£8,904	£2,856	£183,255	266,250/183,255
1.43	£195,015	£7,592	£4,145	£183,278	268,125/183,278
1.44	£195,015	£6,279	£5,778	£182,958	270,000/182,958

The required spot rates for the option to be the preferred hedge are rates where the dollar is weaker than:

1.42	$1.4529/£
1.43	$1.4629/£
1.44	$1.4757/£

Conclusion:

A forward market hedge is recommended for the Euro transaction.

For the $US payment a money market hedge, or alternatively a currency option hedge with an exercise price of 1.42 is recommended. The 1.42 exercise price is chosen as this has a similar cost to the 1.43 option if it is exercised, but requires the dollar to depreciate less before the option hedge is the preferred alternative to the money market hedge.

(c) As the Russian currency is not convertible, if NTC wishes to export to Russia, payment through countertrade may be the only way in which the deal may be arranged. There may also be restrictions in Russia in the use of convertible foreign currency reserves for the purchase of imports, and limited access to bank credits. Without countertrade there may be no trade in these circumstances.

Problems of countertrade include:

(i) It requires considerable time and effort to organise, and often has high administrative costs.

(ii) It may be difficult and expensive to establish a fair exchange ratio for goods to be countertraded.

(iii) The price for wheat that NTC will receive may be unknown, although a futures market exists in wheat.

(iv) The quality of the wheat is not known with certainty.

(v) One party has to bear transportation costs of the wheat.

(vi) Bank guarantees and other forms of security that exist in foreign trade through documentary letters of credit, bills of exchange etc. are unlikely to exist, possibly increasing the risk of trade for NTC.

Advantages of countertrade include:

(i) Allowing NTC to become known in the Russian market, which may generate future business.

(ii) Eliminating the risks concerned with foreign exchange rate movements.

Tutorial note:

Countertrade involves the sale of goods (or services) to a customer in another country, usually a country whose currency is not freely convertible, and the receipt of payment from the customer in other goods rather than money. These goods are then sold on to another customer or distributor in a country with a freely-convertible currency. For example, a Swiss exporter of optical equipment to a South American country might agree to take payment in other goods, say coffee beans, which could then be sold in the European markets for cash.

ACCA marking scheme			
			Marks
This question requires understanding of the advantages and disadvantages of centralised treasury management and of countertrade, and the ability to evaluate alternative hedging techniques for foreign trade transactions.			
(a)		Advantages	5–6
		Disadvantages	2–3
		Maximum	8
	(i)	Sterling values	2
		Net receipts and payments	3
		Number of transactions	1
			6
(b)	(ii)	Use of net exposures	1
		(2 if includes $HK and $US with comment)	
		Forward markets	2
		Money markets	3
		Options:	
		Use of September puts	1
		Option outcomes at different exercise prices	4–5
		Conditions for options to be the best alternative	
		(reward reasonable attempts)	3
		Conclusion	1–2
		Maximum	15
(c)		Advantages of countertrade	3–4
		Disadvantages of countertrade	2–3
		Maximum	6
Total			35

59 ELECTRONICS COMPANY

(a) There is considerable debate as to whether dividend policy can influence corporate value. Much of the debate concerns the question of whether it is the dividend that affects share value, or the information implied by the payment of the dividend. Dividends may provide, in the cheapest and most efficient manner, unambiguous signals about a company's future prospects and management performance. Managers have an incentive to send truthful signals via dividends, as any changes in dividends that are not likely to be accompanied by changes in cash flows will not fool a market that is at least semi-strong form efficient. Dividends therefore may be a valuable communication medium.

There are a number of possible practical influences on dividend policy including:

(i) Dividends are to be discouraged as they may lead to issue costs associated with raising additional external finance.

(ii) Corporate growth. The faster a company is growing the lower the dividend payment is likely to be.

(iii) Liquidity. Cash is needed to pay dividends. The level of corporate liquidity might influence dividend payouts.

(iv) The volatility of corporate cash flows. Companies may be reluctant to increase dividends unless they believe that future cash flows will be large enough to sustain the increased dividend payment.

(v) Legal restrictions, for example, government constraints, limitations on payments from reserves, and covenants on debt that restrict dividends.

(vi) The rate of inflation. Many shareholders like dividends to increase by at least as much as inflation.

(vii) The desires and tax position of the shareholder clientele. However, most companies have a broad spread of shareholders with different needs and tax positions.

(b) The company's dividend per share has increased, in real terms, by between 6.6% and 12.53% per year during the last five years. Although no comparative industry data is available this appears to be a good performance. The payout ratio has reduced from 38% in 1998 to 30.5% in 2002, which may be why the institutional shareholder has made the criticism. However, there is little point the company paying out large dividends if it has positive NPV investments which can be financed partially by dividend retention. Although there is by no means a perfect correlation between NPV and earnings per share, the fact that earnings per share have consistently increased over the period suggests that the company's investments are financially viable. The company has consistently had high net capital expenditure relative to earnings, and in such circumstances it is not unusual for dividend payments to be relatively low.

The company's share price has not increased by as much as earnings per share, but without information on stock market trends and the relative risk of the company it is not clear whether or not the company's share price is under performing. Unless the institutional shareholder could invest any dividends received to earn a higher yield (adjusted for any differences in risk) there is little evidence to support the validity of the criticism.

Statistical data:	*1998*	*1999*	*2000*	*2001*	*2002*
Earnings per share (pence)	25.6	32.5	39.2	42.4	50.8
Retained earnings (£m)	80	129	172	198	328
Payout ratio (%)	38.1	33.8	32.5	33.0	30.5
Dividends (£m)	49.5	66.0	82.9	97.3	144.1
Real growth in dividend per share (%)		8.48	12.53	6.60	7.49

Tutorial note: Dividend cover is simply the reciprocal of the payout ratio, therefore 1 ÷ 0.381 = 2.6 × for 1998. The other four years figures being 3.0×; 3.1×; 3.0×; 3.3×. The link between retained earnings and net capital investment is as important as these relative measures.

60 TOUTEN PLC

Key answer tips

Do not spend too much time discussing the problems themselves – a brief outline followed by possible ways to minimise them is required.

The answer presented below is indicative of the type of solution required. Other forms of memo are equally acceptable.

Memo

To: All directors of foreign subsidiaries

From: Group Finance Director

It is proposed that the group will shortly centralise its treasury functions. Centralisation of group treasury management functions means that decisions regarding currency management, short-term investment and borrowing and financial risk management will be taken centrally rather than at subsidiary level. This will permit significant efficiency improvements and cost savings. The major effects will be that:

(i) Decisions will be taken in line with the tactical and strategic objectives of the group as a whole, rather than by individual subsidiaries which might from time to time have different objectives.

(ii) A central treasury can better appreciate the total foreign exchange exposure position of the group. Netting and matching of receivables and payables in different currencies will be possible, allowing transactions cost savings as only the net amounts need be hedged or transmitted.

(iii) Better knowledge will exist of total debts and cleared bank balances. This will facilitate interest rate hedging. Surplus cash from one subsidiary will be lent to other subsidiaries at relatively favourable rates, at the very least eliminating a bank lending-borrowing spread.

(iv) Cash may be aggregated together and invested at better rates, and borrowing may be possible at favourable rates, including from international markets to which individual subsidiaries would not have direct access.

(v) It is expensive to establish a high quality specialist treasury management team and supporting technical infrastructure. It is not financially prudent to set up high cost expert teams for each subsidiary.

(vi) A centralised treasury will collect and analyse relevant economic and financial information, and supply such information to subsidiaries to aid in their decision-making.

(vii) Transfer prices will be centrally set to try to minimise the group global tax bill.

(viii) A centralised treasury function, with effective internal controls, will be able to prevent the possibility of major financial losses such as occurred with the collapse of Barings.

The main effect of any form of centralisation is of course that some decision-making will be removed from senior managers of the subsidiaries. The centralisation is intended to increase the efficiency of subsidiaries. I would be pleased to receive any comments and suggestions that you have on the implementation process, and can assure you that at all times you will be fully consulted.

From time to time centralised treasury decisions, taken in the interests of the group, might distort reported cash flows and/or profitability of subsidiaries. Any such distortions will be removed from data used for the performance evaluation of the subsidiaries, and managers of subsidiaries will only be evaluated on the results of actions over which they have full control.

It is important that information flows to the central treasury from subsidiaries are quick and accurate. Full computer support and links will be provided. If you have specialist knowledge of any local conditions that you feel that the central team needs to be aware of, or if you have any specific questions regarding this new policy please contact me at your earliest convenience.

61 SHARE BUY-BACKS AND STOCK SPLITS

Share repurchases are a way for companies to distribute earnings to shareholders other than by a cash dividend. They are also a means of altering a target capital structure; supporting the share price during periods of weakness; and deterring unwelcome take-over bids. Companies typically repurchase shares either by making a tender offer for a block of shares, or by buying the shares in the open market. In the absence of taxation and transactions costs share repurchase and the payment of dividends should have the same effect on share value. However, the different treatment of taxation on dividends and capital gains in many countries may lead to a preference for share repurchases by investors.

If the repurchase of shares is by means of a tender offer, this will often be at a price in excess of the current market value, and may have a different effect on overall company value.

An important question for share value is what information a share repurchase conveys to the market about the company and its futures prospects.

Managers should take decisions that maximise the intrinsic value of the firm. This, in theory, involves undertaking the optimum amount of positive NPV investments. The use of share repurchases, and the payment of dividends, will therefore be influenced by the amount of investment that the company undertakes. When a company does not have sufficient investments to fully utilise available cash flow, the payment of dividends or share repurchases are more likely.

Analysts are believed to normally consider an increase in dividends or share repurchases as good news, as they suggest that the company has more cash, and possibly greater earnings potential, than previously believed. However, if this subsequently proves not to be so, share prices will adjust downwards.

Share repurchases in themselves do not create value for the company, but the market may see the information or signals that they provide as significant new information that will affect the share price.

Share splits are the issue of additional shares at no cost to existing shareholders in proportion to the current holdings, but with lower par value. Share splits have no effect on corporate cash flows and, in theory, should not affect the value of the company. The share motives for share splits include:

(i)   A company wises to keep its share price within a given trading range, e.g. below £10 per share. It is sometimes argues that investors might be deterred by a high share price, and that lower share prices would ensure a broader spread of share ownership. Shareholders could actually lose from lower prices, as the bid-offer spread (the difference between buying and selling prices) is often higher as a percentage of share price for lower priced shares.

(ii)   Companies hope that the market will regard a share split as good news, and that the share price will increase (relative to the expected price) as a result of the announcement. Evidence suggests that even if such reaction occurs it is short-lived unless the company improves cash flows, increases dividends etc. in subsequent periods.

ACCA marking scheme	
	Marks
Share repurchases	4–5
Share splits	3–4
Discussion of effects on share price	6–7
Total	15

FOREIGN EXCHANGE RISK

62   VERTID LTD

Key answer tips

Note the way in which the specific data on inflation, exchange rates and interest rates in the question has been used to illustrate the answer. It is important to consider ALL the risks associated with overseas trade and how these may be managed.

(a)   **Werland franc**

The sales manager believes that there will be substantial foreign exchange risk in trading with Werland. Payment is due in Werland francs (WF) in three months time.

The current sterling equivalent of the payment of 3 million Werland francs is £10,344.83 (WF3 million divided by WF290/£1).

Purchasing power parity theory can be used to estimate future exchange rates, although this theory does not by any means provide a perfect estimate of future currency prices, especially in the short term.

Assuming that current currency relationships are in equilibrium, the expected annual change in the value of the Werland franc relative to sterling is:

$$\frac{1.12-1.03}{1.03} = 0.0874 \text{ or an 8.74\% devaluation of the Werland franc.}$$

In a three-month period this is approximately 2.18% (= 8.74% × 3/12).

The current spot rate for the purchase of Werland francs is WF290/£1

The expected spot rate in three months time (X), given a devaluation of the franc by 2.18% in that time, is found from $\frac{X-290}{290} = 0.0218$

X = 296.32.

Tutorial note: Alternatively, the expected rate = 290 × 1.0218 = 296.32.

At this expected rate, the sterling payment would be $\frac{3,000,000}{296.32} = £10,124.19$.

Although exchange rate risk certainly exists for the Werland transaction, the likely movement in exchange rates is beneficial to Vertid Ltd and will result in less sterling being paid than at the current spot rate. This is by no means certain, because the actual spot rate in three months time could differ significantly from the expected spot rate.

Thodian peso

The sales manager expects little exchange risk in trading with Thodia as the Thodian peso is linked to the US$. Some exchange risk will exist even if the rate of the Thodian peso moves directly with the dollar. Using purchasing power parity the dollar is expected to depreciate annually by:

$$\frac{1.06-1.03}{1.03} = 0.0291 \text{ or 2.91\% relative to sterling.}$$

In six months this is a depreciation of approximately 1.46% (= 2.91% × 6/12), leading to a rate for the sale of dollars in six months of $1.4904/£1 (= 1.4690 × 1.0146). The depreciation in the value of the US dollar and so the peso makes the expected receipts from Vertid a little less in sterling terms.

A greater danger is that the Thodian currency might sever its link with the dollar or devalue against the dollar. There is a significant chance of this as inflation is 20% in Thodia and only 6% in the USA, making it very difficult for the Thodian currency to maintain the existing currency exchange rate relative to the dollar. What is not known is whether any significant change in the Thodian peso/US$ relationship will occur within the next six months.

The sales manager is not correct. Despite the current link with the US$, the transaction with Thodia exposes Vertid Ltd to significant foreign exchange risk.

(b)   **Report for Vertid Ltd on the management of foreign trade risks**

Your company is likely to face three types of risk in connection with its foreign trade. These are:

(i)   foreign exchange risk

(ii)   commercial risk

(iii)   political risk.

(i)   **Management of the foreign exchange risk**

The Werland franc transaction

If you wish to protect against the risk of the deal with Werland you may use either a money market hedge or the currency options market. These are illustrated below. A lead payment is a further alternative, but this will be more expensive than the money market hedge unless a discount for early payment can be negotiated with the company's supplier in Werland. In future deals foreign exchange risk may be avoided by trading only in sterling, but this may put you at a competitive disadvantage in attracting export orders, as the foreign exchange risk will be shifted to your customer.

Money market hedge

A money market hedge would involve borrowing in sterling now (if this is possible, given the current attitude of the bank), converting the proceeds at spot into Werland francs, investing the francs for three months and using the proceeds to make payment for the goods. The process is as follows.

Tutorial note: Payment of WF 3 million is due in three months. With a money market hedge, the company could borrow sterling now and exchange it into francs at the spot rate. It could then invest the francs for three months to earn WF3 million with interest at the end of that time.

Investing francs for three months would earn interest at 12.5% per annum, which is 3.125% over three months.

The amount of francs needed for investment now to earn WF3 million at the end of three months is therefore (WF3 million/1.03125) = WF2,909,091.

To obtain WF2,909,091, the company must buy them spot at 290, at a cost of (2,909,091/290) £10,031.35. It is assumed that the sterling will have to be borrowed for the period of the hedge, which is three months.

These transactions are set out in the solution below.

1   Borrow £10,031.35 at 10% per year for three months.

2   Convert at spot WF290/£ to WF2,909,091.

3   Invest in Werland 2,909,091 francs at 12.5% per year for three months to yield 3,000,000 francs.

4   Use the total proceeds from the investment to make the payment of WF3,000,000.

The interest cost on the sterling loan is £10,031.35 × 10% × 3/12 = £250.78. The total cost of the hedge is £10,282 including interest (£10,031.35 + £250.78).

Ignoring transactions costs, this is less than the current spot price of:

$$\frac{3,000,000}{290} = £10,344.83$$

Foreign currency option

A foreign currency option contract offers protection against unfavourable currency movements, whilst giving you the opportunity to benefit from favourable movements. The price of this flexibility is the payment of an upfront premium for the option. In this situation the option will only be exercised (used) if the spot price of Werland francs in three months time is less than the exercise price. For example a spot price of WF295/£1 would lead to the option being exercised. With a spot price of WF330/£1 the contract would not be exercised, and the WF3 million would be purchased in the spot market.

The use of foreign currency options appears expensive, as is illustrated below for a number of possible spot rates in three months time.

Call options on WF3,000,000 with a 300 exercise price

3 months (WF/£1)	Exercise	Spot rate in Option cost	Currency cost	Total cost
		£	£	£
280	Yes	862	10,000	10,862
290	Yes	862	10,000	10,862
300	Yes	862	10,000	10,862
310	No	862	9,677	10,539
320	No	862	9,375	10,237
330	No	862	9,091	9,953
340	No	862	8,824	9,686

Notes

(1) The option cost is payable upfront and is (3,000,000/300) × 25 cents = WF250,000. At the current spot rate of 290, the sterling cost is £862.

(2) At a spot rate below 300, the options will be exercised. At a spot rate of 300 the contract is likely to be exercised as this would save transactions costs in the spot market.

Unless the spot price in three months time moves to almost WF320/£1, foreign currency options will be more expensive than a money market hedge. An estimate of the exchange rate in three months time using the purchasing power parity theory suggests that the spot rate in three months is expected to be less than WF300/£1.

It might be possible to arrange an OTC option at a lower exercise price and with a lower premium that would be more attractive to your company.

The Thodian peso transaction

Based on the information provided, no available hedge would totally remove the foreign exchange risk of the Thodian deal. There is no forward market and Vertid cannot borrow in Thodian pesos to undertake a money market hedge.

One possibility is to hedge by selling US$ six months forward, as the peso is linked to the dollar. This hedge involves considerable risk if the peso depreciates relative to the dollar, or severs its link with the dollar, which it could easily do.

Using the spot rate of 228 pesos/US$ for selling pesos, the equivalent of (3,500,000/228) $15,350.88 would be received if payment were at spot. The dollar is quoted forward at a discount to sterling, the relevant six month forward rate is (1.4690 + 0.0186 discount) US$1.4876/£1. The hedge using dollars would therefore yield:

$$\frac{\$15,350.88}{1.4876} = £10,319.23 \text{ but only if the existing link of the peso and}$$
dollar still exists.

(ii) and (iii) **Management of commercial and political risk**

Commercial risk includes both the physical risk that goods in transit may be lost, stolen or destroyed, as well as the risk that the buyer will not make payment for the goods according to the terms of the sale. Where the actions of a foreign government prevent or delay payment being made, political risk is said to be involved. Government action can take many forms, ranging from bureaucratic delays to war with the country of the exporter.

A simple way to protect against these forms of risk is insurance. Physical risks of goods in transit may be covered through normal commercial insurance. The risk of non-payment or delayed payment may be insured through specialist providers of export credit insurance. In the UK the largest provider of short-term export credit insurance is NCM Holdings. Protection against commercial risk might also be possible by using an export factoring company, but the size of your company's export activities is not currently large enough to use a factor.

Commercial risk may be reduced by careful credit screening of any overseas customers prior to signing the contract, and by the way that the terms of the foreign trade are arranged. For example, if you arranged for your exports to be linked to a confirmed irrevocable letter of credit, this means that payment to you is guaranteed by at least one bank, making the risk of not receiving payment very low. Such an arrangement will, however, incur extra costs.

(c)   Vertid is effectively receiving a form of financing through the three month credit period on the purchase of goods from Werland. If the company needs finance to make payment for these goods in three months time, or to finance the granting of six months credit to the Thodian customer, there are several possible alternatives, although the number of alternatives is limited for small companies such as Vertid:

(i)   Overdrafts and short-term bank loans. The indication is that Vertid is unlikely to obtain further finance from its bank, although other banks or finance houses may be willing to lend the company money, probably at a relatively high rate of interest.

(ii)   The export transaction could be linked to a bill of exchange. If this bill was accepted (guaranteed) by the bank it could be discounted (sold for less than its face value) to provide immediate finance, rather than wait until the customer made payment in six months time.

(iii)   The export transaction might be arranged via an export merchant, which would buy the goods outright from Vertid, or a confirming house acting as an agent for the foreign buyer which would normally arrange for payment to be made to Vertid upon evidence of shipment of the goods, eliminating the need for external financing.

Other forms of export finance such as factoring, invoice discounting, and the use of acceptance credits are not likely to be available for a company the size of Vertid.

63 SOMAX PLC

Key answer tips

It is important in this question NOT to focus on foreign exchange risk which is largely irrelevant as the loan can be arranged in the same currency in most domestic banking systems and the Euromarkets.

(a) *Tutorial note:* The rates in this question might seem unusual, but you should answer the question on the basis of the data provided.

SFr260 million is approximately £110 million. This is a large sum to borrow from an individual bank. The largest domestic Swiss banks could handle individual loans of this size, but it is possible that the loan would be arranged through several Swiss banks, which spreads the default risk between them. Domestic banking systems are normally subject to more regulation and reserve requirements than the Euromarkets, leading to wider spreads between borrowing and lending rates. The cost of borrowing on domestic markets is often slightly more expensive than the Euromarkets, and may involve fixed or floating charges on corporate assets as security for loans. Few Euromarket loans require security. Domestic market loans may be either fixed or floating rate, but bank loans are more likely to be at a floating rate.

If Euromarkets are used the main choices are:

(i) Eurocurrency loans from the international banking system.

(ii) The issue of securities direct to the market by Somax.

A five year loan is quite long for the Eurocurrency market, which specialises in short to medium-term loans. Large loans can be raised quickly at little issue cost, often through investment syndicates of banks. However, medium-term to long-term international bank loans may be arranged by individual banks or syndicates of banks. Interest on these types of loan is normally floating rate, at SFr LIBOR plus a percentage dependent upon Somax's credit rating. Draw-down dates are often flexible, but commitment fees may be payable if the full amount of the loan is not drawn down immediately, and early redemption penalties are normal.

An argument in favour of using the banking system, whether domestic or international is that banks are specialists in analysing and monitoring debts. If large loans are agreed by banks this is a sign of good credit standing, and may facilitate access to cheaper funds on other capital markets.

Somax has a number of choices of issuing securities on the Euromarket. The Euronote market involves short to medium-term issue of paper such as Euro-commercial paper and Euro-medium term notes. Banks, for a fee, will arrange such issues and may underwrite their success.

Eurobonds (international bonds) are medium to long-term bonds sold in countries other than the country of the currency in which the issue is denominated. Both the eurobond and euronote market provide the opportunity to borrow either fixed or floating rate finance, depending upon which financial instrument is selected although most bond and note issues are at a fixed coupon. Some eurobonds may be convertible or have warrants attached which can offer attractions to both issuers and investors. A disadvantage of the eurobond market is that issue costs are higher than the eurocurrency market, and it takes longer to arrange a eurobond issue. In addition, only very large companies with a good credit rating are likely to issue bonds successfully in the European market. The main advantage of issuing bonds, notes or commercial paper on the euromarket is that funds may normally be raised at a lower interest cost than borrowing from the domestic or international banking system.

(b) The discount rate should be a weighted average cost of capital, which takes into account the systematic risk of the new investment.

Somax proposes to establish a new production plant in Switzerland. As this involves diversifying into a new industry, the company's existing equity beta is unlikely to reflect the systematic risk of the new investment. The project systematic risk may be estimated using the equity beta of the main Swiss competitor after allowing for differences in capital structure (financial risk) between the two companies.

Ungearing the equity beta of the Swiss competitor (using market values):

$$\beta a = \beta e \ \frac{E}{E + D(1-t)}$$

$$\beta a = 1.5 \ \frac{60}{60 + 40(1 - 0.33)} = 1.037$$

The asset beta must be re-geared to reflect the capital structure of Somax. Using market values:

		£m
Equity:	450 million shares at 376 pence	1,692.00
Debt:	Bank loans (210 – 75)	135.00
	14% bonds (£75 million × 1.195)	89.63
		224.63

$$\beta e = \beta a \ \frac{E + D(1-t)}{E}$$

$$\beta e = 1.037 \ \frac{1,692 + 224.63(1 - 0.33)}{1,692} = 1.129$$

Using CAPM, the cost of equity is:

$$Ke = R_F + (R_M - R_F) \ \beta e$$

$$Ke = 7.75\% + (14.5\% - 7.75\%) \ 1.129 \ = 15.37\%.$$

Somax is considering the use of two alternative forms of SFr floating rate financing which involved differing interest costs, varying from 5.75% to 6%. Issuing securities on the Euromarket would normally be slightly cheaper than borrowing directly from international banks. It is assumed that the 5.75% rate refers to Euromarket borrowing.

If the interest rate parity theorem holds, the difference in interest rates between the UK and Switzerland will be the same as the annual percentage difference between spot and forward rates of the pound and Swiss franc.

Using mid rate exchange rates, the difference is:

$$\frac{2.2982 - 2.3273}{2.3273} \times \frac{12}{6} = -0.025 \text{ or } 2.5\%$$

$$\therefore \ \frac{I_G - I_{UK}}{1 + I_{UK}} = -0.025$$

The Swiss franc is at a premium, which means that UK interest rates will be 2.5% higher. The effective interest rates, in sterling terms, are expected to be 8.25% or 8.5% depending upon which form of SFr borrowing is used. Note that gearing levels are not expected to change the estimated weighted average cost of capital is:

$$15.37\% \times \frac{1,692}{1,692 + 224.63} + 8.25\%(1 - 0.33) \ \frac{224.63}{1,692 + 224.63}$$

$$= 14.24\% \text{ or } (14.22\% \text{ using the } 8.46\% \text{ cost of debt})$$

(c) (i) The proposed swap is based on Somax issuing a five year sterling fixed rate bond. The cost of such a bond is not given, and must be estimated. The best estimate is provided by the yield to redemption of this existing fixed rate bond which has five years to maturity. The existing pre-tax yield to redemption is found by solving the following equation:

$$119.5 = \frac{14}{1+Kd} + \frac{14}{(1+Kd)^2} + \frac{14}{(1+Kd)^3} + \frac{14}{(1+Kd)^4} + \frac{14}{(1+Kd)^5} + \frac{100}{(1+Kd)^5}$$

Tutorial note: The redemption yield is found by trial and error. The coupon rate on the debt is 14%, but the market price is 19.5 above par. For a bond redeemable in five years, this is a large premium, showing that the redemption yield will be a lot lower than the coupon yield of 14%. As a starting point, we can try 14% – (19.5/4)% = about 10%.

By trial and error, using present value and annuity tables:

Year	Item	Cash flow	Discount factor at 10%	PV	Discount factor at 9%	PV
1 – 4	Interest	14.0	3.791	53.07	3.890	54.46
4	Redemption	100.0	0.621	62.10	0.650	65.00
				115.17		119.46
0	Market value	119.5	1.000	(119.50)		(119.50)
				(4.33)		(0.05)

The cost of the five year fixed rate bond is approximately 9%. Somax can borrow directly floating rate SFr at 5.75%, or 0.75% above SFr LIBOR. The Swiss company can borrow fixed rate sterling directly at 10.5%.

Swap transactions:

	Somax %	Swiss company %
Actual borrowing	(9.0)	(SFr LIBOR + 1.5)
Swap payments		
Somax to Swiss company	(SFr LIBOR + 1.0)	SFr LIBOR + 1.0
Swiss company to Somax	9.5	(9.5)
Overall cost with the swap	(SFr LIBOR + 0.5)	(10.00)
Cost of direct borrowing	(SFr LIBOR + 0.75)	(10.50)
Gain compared with direct borrowing	0.25	0.50
Less bank fees	0.20	0.20
Overall gain	0.05	0.30

Note: Somax can borrow at a floating rate of 5.75%, and since LIBOR is currently 5%, this means that it can borrow at LIBOR + 0.75%.

The swap would benefit both parties, although most of the arbitrage gains are enjoyed by the bank and the Swiss company. The actual savings from the swap will slightly differ from the above figures as the SFr is strengthening relative to the pound. Any percentage receipts/payments in pounds will not be as large as the same percentage receipts/payments in Swiss francs. If the Swiss franc continues to strengthen, the overall gain to Somax could be eliminated.

(ii) The **benefits of swaps** include:

– Access to markets in which it might be impossible to borrow directly because of an inadequate credit rating. This particularly relates to some fixed rate markets.

– The opportunity to alter the proportion of debt on which fixed and floating rate interest is paid, without physically redeeming debt or issuing new debt.

–   Long-term hedges against both interest rate risk and currency risk. In this case Somax and the Swiss company are protected against currency risk for the full five years of the swap. The main benefit for the bank is the fees from the swap.

The **main risks of swaps** are:

–   Credit risk or default risk if the counterparty to the swaps default.

–   Position risk or market risk. This relates to the gain or loss from movements in interest rates and exchange rates relative to the position if the swap had not been undertaken.

–   Spread risk. If a bank temporarily 'warehouses' a swap with two companies, spread risk exists as interest rates may change during this time lag. There may also be a mismatch in the size and desired duration of the swap between companies, which would expose banks to further risk and necessitate the bank arranging offsetting hedges.

64   ITALIAN GLASS

Key answer tips

This question is not an excuse to write all you know about Forex management. You must consider the particular circumstances outlined and focus your answer accordingly. Ignore the lack of realism in the forecast inflation rates, and try to answer the question with technical accuracy.

The order is not yet definite. If the glass manufacturer wishes to protect against foreign exchange risk at the tender stage, an over the counter option from a commercial bank is suggested. If the tender is not successful the option would not be exercised, and the total cost would be the option premium. An option to sell Kuwait dinar (buy a put option on dinar) could be taken for either:

(i)   the full 18-month period until payment is due

(ii)   the period until the result of the tender is known, and then a further hedge taken for the remainder of the period if the tender is successful. For a short maturity option during the tender period the premium would be low. The further hedge could be another option contract, or a money market hedge involving borrowing Kuwait dinar and converting to euros at the current spot rate. The sum to be borrowed, plus interest at 9% per year, would total the amount of the dinar receipts in 18 months time. The funds converted to euros at spot would be immediately available in Italy.

Estimates of future exchange rates may be made using either the purchasing power parity theorem (PPP) or interest rate parity theorem. Applying PPP suggests that there will be:

$$\frac{0.03 - 0.09}{1.09} = -0.055 \text{ or } 5.5\% \text{ per year discount on the euro.}$$

The euro will weaken against the dinar because of its higher inflation rate.

In 18 months the discount is expected to be $(1 + 0.055) \ (\sqrt{1 + .055}) = 8.362\%$

Using the purchase price of euros, a rate of dinars 3.3000/€1 the expected spot rate in 18 months is 3.3000/1.0862 = 3.0453 dinars/€1.

(This assumes that exchange rates are currently in equilibrium.)

Interest rate differentials between the euro and the dinar are 5% and 5.5% for borrowing and lending rates respectively. These could be used to estimate future spot rate, but evidence suggests that interest rate parity is not as accurate a predictor as purchasing power parity.

The glass manufacturer's normal price would be €350,000 × 1.25 = €437,500.

At spot (using the purchase price of euros, because the company will sell its dinar income and buy euros in exchange) this suggests a tender price of 437,500 × 3.3000 = 1,443,750 dinars.

In order to make a competitive tender the glass manufacturer could use the expected spot rate in 18 months' time as the basis for the tender, giving a tender price of:

€350,000 × dinars 3.0453/€1 = 1,332,319 dinars.

Any tender lower than this would involve less than 25% mark-up.

If an option hedge is used the tender price could be increased by the amount of the option premium. The recommended tender price is not less than 1,332,319 dinars, plus any option premium.

65   VTW PLC

Key answer tips

If you obtain a calculated answer which seems unlikely, make a note of it for the benefit of the examiner – it is more likely to impress than if you carry on regardless!

(a)   The presumption in this question is that if dividend payments out of the country are blocked for three years, the peso income will be invested locally to earn interest, and at the end of the three years, the pesos plus interest will be converted into sterling at the spot rate and remitted to the UK.

If there are no blocked funds, the present value in sterling expected from dividend remittances is:

Year	1	2	3
Peso remittance (million pesos)	180	180	180
Exchange rate	22/£1	24.2/£	26.62/£
Sterling (£ million)	8.182	7.438	6.762
Discount factors (at 20%)	0.833	694	0.579
Present values (£ million)	6.816	5.162	3.915

Total present value is £15.893 million

If the investment is no longer to be financially viable, the NPV of the investment would have to fall by at least £2 million (its expected NPV), or the present value of cash flows from remittances would have to fall to less than £13.893 million.

If dividend remittances are blocked, and peso income is invested at x%, the cash flows will be as follows.

Year	Income	Interest rate	Income plus interest, end of year 3
	million pesos		million pesos
1	180	×	$180(1+x)^2$
2	180	×	$180(1+x)$
3	180	×	180

The interest rate that will yield at least £13.893 million may be estimated by solving for x, where x is the interest rate in decimal format:

$$\frac{0.579(180(1+x)^2 +180(1+x)+180)}{26.62} = £13.893 \text{ million}$$

This may be solved using mathematical formulae, but can be estimated by trial and error.

If x = 0.15

$$\frac{0.579(180(1.15)^2 + 180(1.15) + 180)}{26.62} = £13.595 \text{ million}$$

15% is too low

If x = 0.18

$$\frac{0.579(180(1.18)^2 + 180(1.18) + 180)}{26.62} = £13.986 \text{ million}$$

At an 18% interest rate the investment will just remain financially viable.

(b) Blocked remittances might be avoided by means of:

(i) Increasing transfer prices paid by the foreign subsidiary to the parent company.

(ii) Lending the equivalent of the dividend to the parent company.

(iii) Making payments to the parent company in the form of royalties, payment for patents, or management fees.

(iv) Charging the subsidiary additional head office overhead.

(v) Parallel loans, whereby the subsidiary of VTW in the South American country lends cash to the subsidiary of another company requiring funds in the South American country. In return VTW would receive the loan of an equivalent amount of cash in the UK from the other subsidiary's parent company.

The government of the South American country might try to prevent many of these measures being used.

66 HERLER PLC

(a) Forecast exchange rates using purchasing power parity:

$$12 \text{ months: } 2,400 \times \frac{1 + 2.5}{1 + 0.05} = 8,000$$

If rates change evenly during the year, the rate in six months is expected to be

$$2,400 + \frac{8,000 - 2,400}{2} = 5,200$$

$$24 \text{ months: } 8,000 \times \frac{1 + 2.5}{1 + 0.05} = 26,667$$

The rate in 18 months is expected to be $8,000 + \frac{26,667 - 8,000}{2} = 17,333$.

The *discount rate* for the investment evaluation is 12% per annum. Cash flows are six monthly, and the discount rate is calculated as the square root of (1.12) minus 1. This is 0.058 or 5.8%.

Receipts due:	Receipts	Exch rate	Receipts	Vble costs	Net cash flow	Disc factor	PV
	SF m		£m	£m	£m	12% p.a.	£m
Now	2,000	2,400	833,333	416,667	416,667	1.000	416,667
In 6 months	2,000	5,200	384,615	416,667	(32,052)	0.945	(30,289)
In 12 months	1,200	8,000	150,000	250,000	(100,000)	0.893	(89,300)
In 18 months	2,800	17,333	161,542	583,333	(421,791)	0.844	(355,992)
							(58,914)

The net present value of expected cash flows is negative, (£58,914)

If inflation continues at the rate of 250% per year, in present value terms the construction project is not expected to be financially viable.

(b)   As no forward market or money market hedge is possible, and presumably no hedge using derivative products, the alternatives open to Herler are limited, but might include:

(i)   Arrange a currency swap with an organisation in Surkaya which requires Sterling now. The swap would probably be arranged using a bank as intermediary, and need not be at the current spot rate. The swap could be reversed at an agreed fixed exchange rate either at six monthly intervals, or on completion of the project. This would fix the foreign exchange rates for Herler at known levels.

(ii)   Agree a different payment schedule with more cash paid early. It would be worthwhile for Herler to reduce the overall project price if a larger proportion of the payment was made early in the project.

(iii)   Use a countertrade agreement for all or part of the payment. Payment would then be made using some agreed product or commodity which has a ready resale value in the western world (e.g. oil, minerals, foodstuffs). The goods received would be much more likely to maintain their value in terms of the pound than the Surkayan currency.

Workings for part (a)

Variable costs (in sterling) now are 50% of sterling receipts. Subsequent costs are found by pro-rating this figure according to the value of receipts in Surkayan francs.

Now = 50% of 833,333 = 416,667

In 6 months = 416,667 × 2,000/2,000 = 416,667

In 12 months = 416,667 × 1,200/2,000 = 250,000

Final cost = £416,667 × 2,800/2,000 = 583,333.

67   KYT INC

Key answer tips

Watch out for part questions like (c) which have two requirements, calculate and discuss, under a single heading.

(a)   KYT needs to purchase yen on the spot market in two months time. To protect against the risk of the yen strengthening against the US$, KYT should buy yen futures contracts, hoping to sell at a higher price if the yen strengthens. This is intended to offset any loss relative to the current spot rate when the yen are purchased in the spot market in two months time.

The most suitable contract will be the contract that matures at the nearest date after 1 September. This is the September contract. To protect 140 million yen, 11 contracts will need to be bought (140/12.5 = 11.2 contracts). This will leave 2.5 million yen unhedged (11 contracts x 12.5 million = 137.5 million yen hedge.)

(b)   Basis risk is the difference between the current spot price and the futures price, in this case (128.15 – 125.23) = 2.92 yen.

(c)   Basis risk will be zero at the maturity date of the futures contract, 30 September. If it reduces in a linear manner over the three months to the contract maturity, the expected basis risk on 1 September, when there is still one month to maturity, is $\dfrac{2.92 \times 1}{3}$ = 0.973 yen.

The expected futures price on 1 September is therefore 0.973 yen below the spot price of 120 yen/$1. This is Y119.027/$1 or $0.008401/yen

Expected result of the hedge:

Spot market		$
30 June spot $ value of 140 m yen	(140m/128.15)	1,092,470
1 Sept spot $ value of 140 m yen	(140m /120)	1,166,667
'Loss' on the spot market		74,197
Futures market		
30 June: Buy 11 contracts at	0.007985	
1 Sept: Sell 11 contracts at	0.008401	
Gain on futures position	0.000416	
Total gain (11 contracts)	× 137,500,000 yen	57,200

Hedge efficiency is $\dfrac{57,200}{74,197} = 77\%$

This result may not occur as basis risk is unlikely to decrease in a linear manner. Depending on the movement in basis the hedge efficiency might be higher or lower than 77%.

68   PARTICIPATING CURRENCY OPTION

Key answer tips

Note that the information needs to be reduced to calls (not puts), and June (not December or March). It then becomes more manageable.

The outcome of any currency option hedge will depend upon what spot rate exists in 6 months time. However it is possible to assess the outcomes at different rates. The company wants a hedge against the risk of a fall in the value of its US dollar receipts, i.e. a fall in the value of the dollar against sterling.

Participating option

The participating option has no premium cost and gives a worst case rate of $1.65/£1. At exchange rates between $1.61/£1 and $1.65/£1 the company would suffer a fall in pound receipts when compared to the current spot rate. At rates of less than $1.61/£1 the option would not be exercised and any gain against current spot that the company made when selling the dollars at spot would be shared with the seller of the participating option.

At the current spot rate receipts would be 1,800,000/1.61 = £1,118,012

Exchange rate:	£ receipts from $1.8m	Change relative to current spot (£)
1.70 Option exercised	1,090,909	(27,103)
1.65 Option exercised	1,090,909	(27,103)
1.60 Option not exercised	1,121,495	3,483
1.55 Option not exercised	1,139,241	21,229

Traded options

June call options are required as other contracts expire before payment is due.

If the company does not wish to pay more than £10,000 in premium, then only the 1.65 and 1.70 options are available. The 1.70 option offers poor protection against a weakening of the dollar.

The 1.65 option will require $\dfrac{1,800,000}{1.65 \times 31,250} = 34.91$ or 35 contracts

The premium cost is 35 × 31,250 × 1.1 cents= $\dfrac{\$12,031}{1.6055} = £7,494$

If exercised these contracts require payment in dollars of: $31,250 \times 35 \times 1.65 = \$1,804,687$.

The receipts are only $1.8 million, and an additional $4,687 will need to be bought at spot to fulfil the contract. These will cost £2,757 at a spot rate of €1.70 and £2,841 at a spot rate of $1.65.

Exchange rate:	£ receipts from $1.8m	Premium	Net receipts £	Change £ (compared with spot rate)
1.70: Option exercised	1,090,909 – 2,757	–7,494	1,080,658	– 37,354
1.65: Option exercised	1,090,909 – 2,841	–7,494	1,080,574	– 37,438
1.60: Option not exercised	1,125,000	–7,494	1,117,506	–506
1.55: Option not exercised	1,161,290	–7,494	1,153,796	35,784

Unless the dollar is expected to strengthen significantly the participating option looks the better alternative.

However, the company might also consider an option collar whereby a call option was purchased and a put option sold in order to reduce the net premium payable. Possibilities include buy June 1.65 calls at 1.1 cents and sell June 1.55 puts at 0.9 cents resulting in a net premium of 0.2 cents. This would result in a worst case (ignoring inexact contract sizes) position of $1.652/£1 and a best case position of $1.552/£1. However, this still involves significant exchange rate risk. A better collar would be to buy 1.60 calls at 5.3 cents and sell 1.60 puts at 4.0 cents, resulting in a net premium of 1.3 cents. This would lock in the exchange rate at $1.613/£1 including premium cost, which is almost identical to the current spot rate exchange rate of $1.61/£1.

69 POLYTOT PLC

(a) Possible currency hedges are a forward market hedge, currency futures hedge or currency options hedge.

Forward market hedge

The forward market hedge locks into a known exchange rate at the time the payment by the customer is made. It is a legally binding obligation.

A forward rate is required for four months' time. This may be estimated by interpolating between the three month and one year forward rates.

$1.5362 - 1.5140 = 0.0222 \times 1/9 = 0.0025$

The four month rate is $1.5362 - 0.0025 = 1.5337$

$1.5398 - 1.5178 = 0.220 \times 1/9 = 0.0024$

The four month rate is $1.5398 - 0.0024 = 1.5374$

60% of the receipts will be in $US, i.e. the equivalent to 405m pesos.

At the official rate $\dfrac{P405m}{98.20} = \$4,124,236$

Selling $ forward, $\dfrac{\$4,124,236}{1.5374} = £2,682,605$

The balance of 270m pesos will be converted at 115% of the official rate

$\dfrac{270}{179.745} = £1,502,128$

Total expected receipts are £4,184,733.

Futures hedge

A futures hedge locks the transaction into an expected exchange rate. In this case December futures will need to be bought as the September contract will have expired by the date of the payment, 1 November.

Basis on the December contract is $1.5510 - 1.5275$, or 2.35 cents. The expected basis on 1 November is 2/6 (the remaining period of the futures contract) $\times$ 2.35 cents, or 0.78 cents. The expected lock-in futures price, no matter what happens to actual spot rates, is $1.5275 + 0.0078 = \$1.5353$.

This is slightly better than the forward market rate.

However, basis on 1 November when the futures contract would be closed out (by buying an identical contract) might not be 0.78 cents, due to the existence of basis risk. A better or worse outcome than the expected lock-in rate is possible. The hedge is for $4,124,236

This will require $\dfrac{4,124,236}{1.5353} = £2,686,274$ or 42.98 £62,500 contracts.

43 contracts would be needed, a slight overhedge.

Futures contracts also require the payment of margin, a security deposit. Profit on futures contracts through favourable currency movement may be taken daily, but any losses will result in daily variation margin calls in order to keep the hedge open. The futures contract looks to offer a slightly better rate than the forward contract, but will involve more risks. The company must choose whether or not the expected extra return would compensate for these risks.

Currency options hedge

Currency options offer an advantage over both forwards and futures in that they not only protect against downside risk, they also allow the buyer of the option to take advantage of favourable currency movements by allowing the option to lapse. The price of this extra benefit is the option premium.

Given that the dollar is strengthening against the pound in the forward market, the currency option rates do not look very favourable. As Polytot wishes to exchange dollars for pounds, it will need to purchase December call options. Probably only the 1·5250 and 1·550 strike prices would be considered, as the other rates are far less favourable than the forward market.

Strike price	$ receipts	£ equivalent	Number of contracts	Number used
1.5250	4,124,236	2,704,417	86.54	86 (or 87)
1.5500	4,124,236	2,660,797	85.15	85

86 contracts is $4,098,438 at 1.5250, leaving $25,798 over which could be sold forward at $1.5374/£ to yield £16,780.

85 contracts is $4,117,188 at 1.5500, leaving $7,048 over which could be sold forward to yield £4,584.

Strike price	Premium ($)	Premium (£ at spot)	£ receipts	£ over	Worst case outcome
1.5250	90,031	(58,179)	2,687,500	16,780	2,646,101
1.5500	59,766	(38,621)	2,656,250	14,584	2,622,213

These outcomes are much worse than the forward or futures hedges, but if the dollar was to strengthen further, the options could be lapsed and the pounds purchased in November in the spot market. For example, in order for the 1.5250 option to become better than the forward market hedge the dollar would have to strengthen at least to approximately 1.5250 – (1.5250 – 1.5374 + 0.0335) or 1.5039/£.

The recommended hedge is either the forward market, (unless Polytot is happy with the extra risks of futures) or currency options at a probable strike price of 1.5250.

(b)   The proposed countertrade needs to be compared with the 40% of expected receipts that are at 15% less than the official rate. Three million kilos at 50–60 pence per kilo gives receipts of between £1.5 and £1.8 million. This compares with £1,502,128 from the foreign exchange transaction. The price for the strawberries would need to be in excess of 50 pence per kilo. Other factors that would need to be considered in any countertrade include:

(i)   How reliable is the supplier of the strawberries? Are they of suitable quality and could such a large quantity be supplied?

(ii)   Strawberries are perishable and require specialised transportation. Who is responsible for the costs of transportation, insurance etc?

(iii) What additional administrative/organisational expense will the countertrade involve?

(iv)   What are the tax implications of a countertrade in strawberries?

(c)   Advantages of the Euromarkets include:

(i)   They are more flexible than many domestic markets and not subject to the same degree of control.

(ii)   The cost of borrowing in the Euromarkets is often slightly less than for the same currency in relevant domestic capital markets.

(iii) Interest is normally payable gross, which is attractive to some investors.

(iv)   Very large sums can be quickly raised, without the queuing process that exists in many domestic capital markets.

(v)   Issue costs are relatively low.

(vi)   There is an active secondary market in many types of Euromarket security.

(vii) Eurobonds, in particular, offer the opportunity to swap interest payments into a more convenient form (e.g. fixed to floating rate), often at lower costs than borrowing directly.

Potential problems include:

(i)   The Grobbian company would either need to be rated highly by one of the international rating agencies in order to be able to access the markets, or it would probably be necessary for the company to offer a guarantee from its government in association with any issue.

(ii)   Any Euromarket borrowing is likely to be in dollars or another hard currency. The company will need to convince the market that it has access to sufficient hard currency to fully service the interest and principal payments.

ACCA marking scheme		
		Marks
(a)	Forward market	
	Comment	1–2
	Calculations	3
	Futures market	
	Comment	2
	Calculations	3–4
	Options market	
	Comment	2
	Calculations	4–5
	Conclusion	1
		────
		17
		────
(b)	Value of strawberries calculation	1
	Factors to be considered 1–2 each. Look for common sense answers	5
		────
		6
		────
(c)	Advantages of Euromarkets	3–4
	Potential problems for the Grobbian company	3–4
		────
		7
		────
Total		30

70   CURRENCY SWAPS

(a)   **Advantages of currency swaps include:**

(i)   They allow companies to undertake foreign currency hedging, often for longer periods than is possible with forwards.

(ii)   They are usually cheaper than long term forwards, where such products exist.

(iii)   Finance may be obtained at a cheaper rate than would be possible by borrowing directly in the relevant market. This occurs by taking advantage of arbitrage if a company has a relative funding advantage in one country.

(iv)   They may provide access to finance in currencies that could not be borrowed directly, e.g. due to government restrictions, or lack of a credit rating in the overseas market.

(v)   Currency swaps offer the opportunity to restructure the company's debt profile without physically redeeming debt or issuing new debt.

(vi) Currency swaps might be used to avoid a country's exchange control restrictions.

Potential problems include:

(i) If the swap is directly with a corporate counterparty the potential default risk of the counterparty must be considered. Swaps arranged with a bank as the direct counterparty tend to be much less risky.

(ii) Political or sovereign risk, the possibility that a government will introduce restrictions that interfere with the performance of the swap.

(iii) Basis risk. With a floating to floating swap basis risk might exist if the two floating rates are not pegged to the same index.

(iv) Exchange rate risk. The swap may result in a worse outcome than would have occurred if no swap had been arranged.

(b) (i) Interest rate differentials:

	Fixed rate	*Floating rate*
Galeplus	6.25%	PIBOR + 2%
Counterparty	8.30%	PIBOR + 1.5%
	(2.05%)	0.5%

The overall arbitrage opportunity from using a currency swap is 2.55% per year. Banks fees are 0.75% per year leaving 1.8%. 75% of 1.8% is 1.35% that would be the benefit per year to Galeplus in terms of interest saving from using a currency swap.

(ii) Assuming inflation rates in Perdia are between 15% and 50% per year, the best and worse case exchange rates are:

	Rubbits/£	
	Best case	*Worst case*
Spot	85.40	85.40
Year 1	98.21	128.10
Year 2	112.94	192.15
Year 3	129.88	288.23

Cash flows (million rubbits)

Year	0	1	2	3
Purchase cost	(2,000)			
Fees		40	40	40
Sale price				4,000
	(2,000)	40	40	4,040
Discount factors (15%)	1	0.870	0.756	0.658
Present values	(2,000)	34.8	30.24	2,658.32

With a currency swap 2,000 million of the year 3 cash flows will be at the current spot rate of 85.40 rubbits/£, with the remainder at the end of year 3 spot rate.

Discounted cash flows (£ million)

Worst case rates	(23.42)	0.27	0.16	20.07
Estimated NPV	(£2.92 million)			
Best case rates	(23.42)	0.35	0.27	25.75
Estimated NPV	£2.95 million			

The financial viability of the investment depends upon exchange rate movements. The greater the depreciation in the value of the rubbit relative to the pound, the worse the outcome of the investment. This is due to the year 3 price of the telecommunications centre remaining constant no matter what the exchange rate is at the time.

These estimates assume that exchange rates remain in the above range. In reality they could be better or worse. Additionally non-financial factors such as political risk would influence the decision. For example given the government's current cash flow position how likely is the payment of 4,000 million rubbits to be made in three years' time? Other factors such as taxation in the UK would also need to be considered.

Unless there are strong strategic reasons for buying the centre, for example possible future cash flow benefits beyond year 3, the investment is not recommended. In order for the investment to take place a better hedge against currency risk would need to be found, or the price to be received in year 3 renegotiated to reflect the impact of adverse exchange rate changes.

(c) (i) A swaption is an option on a swap. It allows the buyer to choose whether or not to undertake the swap, depending upon exchange rates in three years time. The swap rate in this example is the current spot rate of 85.40 rubbits/£. A swaption at this exercise price would offer no benefit to Galeplus relative to the straight swap unless the rubbit were to strengthen relative to 85.40/£, in which case the swap would not be used as the end of year 3 spot rate would be more favourable to Galeplus. Given the relative inflation rates in the UK and Perdia, according to the purchasing power parity theory it is very unlikely that the rubbit will strengthen relative to the pound. The use of a swaption is not recommended.

(ii) The currency put option will limit the downside risk of the year 3 cash flows whilst allowing Galeplus to take advantage of favourable exchange rate movements. Using the worst case exchange rate forecasts, the option would be exercised at the end of year 3.

Discounted cash flows (million rubbits)

Year	0	1	2	3
Present values	(2,000)	34.8	30.24	2,658.32

Discounted cash flows (£ million)

Worst case rates	(23.42)	0.27	0.16	16.61
Less option premium	£1.7 million			
Estimated NPV	(£8.08 million)			

Using the best case exchange rate forecasts, the option would not be exercised at the end of year 3 as the expected spot exchange rate at that time is more favourable.

Discounted cash flows (million rubbits)

Year	0	1	2	3
Present values	(2,000)	34.8	30.24	2,658.32

Discounted cash flows (£ million)

Best case rates	(23.42)	0.35	0.27	20.47
Less option premium	£1.7 million			
Estimated NPV	(£4.03 million)			

In both cases the outcome from the put option is very poor. The end of year 3 exchange rate of the rubbit would have to be much stronger than 160/£ in order for the option to be the preferred hedge. The rate would have to move to approximately 108 rubbits/£, which is unlikely. Unless Galeplus is prepared to take the risk of this happening the use of currency options is not recommended.

ACCA marking scheme			
			Marks
(a)	Advantages		4–5
	Disadvantages		4–5
		Max	8
(b)	(i)	Arbitrage opportunity	3
		Benefit to Galeplus	3
			6
	(ii)	Exchange rate estimates	2
		Best case cash flows	2
		Worst case cash flows	2
		(Other treatments of cash flow are possible)	
		Other issues	2
			8
(c)	(i)	Understanding of swaption	1
		Discussion/calculation of the usefulness of swaption	2–3
	(ii)	Worst case overall NPV with option exercised	2
		Best case overall NPV – with option not exercised	2
		Conclusion	1
		Max	8
Total			30

71 MJY PLC

Key answer tips

A tricky question on hedging. It is vital that you approach this in a logical, systematic manner. First eliminate intra-group cash flows to estimate the foreign currency risk exposure of group. Next examine the possible use of forward contracts. Finally look at the options.

You need to contrast the options with the forward contracts to hedge the £:$ exposure. To do this, you must calculate the worst case scenario cost in sterling of obtaining the dollars with the options, taking into account the premium (given in cents so convert at the spot rate) and the need to convert surplus dollars back into sterling at the forward rate.

From a group perspective a sensible hedging strategy would be to net off as many offsetting currency receipts and payments as possible, and to only hedge the relevant net amounts.

As MJY is a UK based multinational, the payments and receipts in pounds are not exposed to currency risk and should be ignored.

All $ and € receipts and payments within the group and with third party companies are relevant when estimating the group currency exposure. In the case of intragroup trade, a receipt for one company is a payment for another.

From a group view, relevant $ receipts are: 90 + 50 + 40 + 20 + 30 = 230

$ payments are: 170 + 120 + 50 = 340

$110,000 net payments need to be hedged

€ receipts are: 75 + 85 + 72 + 20 + 52 + 35 = 339

€ payments are: 72 + 35+ 50 + 20 + 65 = 242

€97,000 net receipts need to be hedged

Forward market hedges:

Buy $3 months forward: $\dfrac{\$110,000}{1.7835} = £61,676$

Sell €3 months forward: $\dfrac{\$97,000}{1.4390} = £67,408$

Currency options:

It is now 31 December. The time of the transactions is 31 March. As the February options will have expired, May options should be used. Pounds need to be sold to purchase dollars, therefore MJY will need to purchase put options. The dollar payment is $110,000, which is the equivalent of approximately one £62,500 option contract.

Option hedge

Strike price	$ if exercised (at spot 1.7982)	Premium ($)	Premium £ (at forward 1.7861)	Overhedge ($)	Overhedge (£)
1.80	112,500	3,338	1,856	2,500	1,400
1.78	111,250	2,625	1,460	1,250	700

Worse case outcomes using currency options:

1.80:62,500 + 1,856 – 1,400 = £62,956

1.78:62,500 + 1,460 – 700 = £63,260

These are both much worse than the forward hedge, but if the dollar was to weaken to more than the relevant strike price, the option could be lapsed, and the necessary $110,000 purchased in the spot market at a more favourable exchange rate.

For a relatively small hedge of this nature a multinational company would probably use a forward contract as it involves less administrative time and costs, and fixes the payment of £61,676.

ACCA marking scheme	
	Marks
Principle of netting off relevant transactions	1
Ignoring £ cash flows	1
$ net	2
€ net	2
Forward market hedges	2
Options hedge	
Use of May put option	1
Option calculations including over hedge	5
Comment on possible benefit of not exercising the option, small hedge size	1–2
Total	15

INTEREST RATE RISK

72   INTEREST RATE HEDGE

Tutorial note: You need to begin by establishing what the problem is. Here, you are looking at ways of hedging an exposure to rising interest rates, given that you need to borrow £30 million in three months' time for a loan period of two months.

Report on hedging alternatives

The current cost of borrowing for two months is $£30,000,000 \times 6.9\% \times \dfrac{2}{12} = £345,000$

Futures

The company may use futures contracts to attempt to make a gain on the futures market that will offset any potential loss in the cash market.

Futures are market-traded instruments that are only available with fixed contract sizes and maturity dates, and only on a limited selection of financial instruments. Hence it might not be possible to hedge exactly the cash market exposure. Futures also require the deposit of a margin, either in cash or approved securities.

The financing will be needed in three months time, in mid-March. March contracts will be used as they have the closest expiry date after the date the funds are needed.

Examiner's note:

Combinations of two contracts are also possible

As the period at risk is two months, the number of contracts needed may be estimated as:

$$\frac{£30,000,000}{£500,000} \times \frac{2}{3} = 40 \text{ contracts}$$

To protect against an increase in the interest rate, 40 contracts would be sold.

Tutorial note: We must sell interest rate futures to hedge the risk of a rise in interest rates. If interest rates do rise, futures prices will fall, and we can close the position by buying futures, to make a profit between the selling And the buying price.

Basis is the current LIBOR rate of 94.00 less the March futures price, 93.79 = 0.21

This will fall to 0 when the contract expires, and it is assumed that it will fall at an even rate over time. There are three and a half months until the contract expires. The funds are needed in three months. The expected basis at the time of borrowing is therefore:

$$0.21 \times \frac{1}{7} = 0.03.$$

The reduction/change in basis after three months is 0.18.

If the interest rate (LIBOR) does rise by 0.5%, the expected futures price in three months is:

$93.79 - 0.5 + 0.18 = 93.47$

Examiner's comment:

Another way of calculating this figure is to use the new LIBOR of 93.50 less the remaining basis of 0.03 = 93.50 − 0.03 or 93.47.

The expected futures gain if futures are closed out in three months will then be:

Selling price	93.79
Purchase price to close position	93.47
Gain per contract	32
(× 40 contract × £12.50)	£16,000

The overall cost of the loan is expected to be as follows.

	£
Borrow £30 million for 2 months at LIBOR + 0.9% = 7.4%	
Interest cost: £30 million × 7.4% × 2/12	370,000
Gain on futures position	16,000
Net cost	354,000

Note: The futures price at the close-out date might differ from 93.47, as the decline in basis might not be linear.

Options

The option contracts specified are also market traded, with similar limitations to the futures, but it is also possible to obtain OTC (over the counter) interest rate options which are tailored directly to a company's needs.

The obvious disadvantage of options is that a premium is payable, often upfront. However, if interest rates were to fall rather than rise the option would be allowed to lapse, and the company would take advantage of the lower market interest rates. In the case of a futures contract this would not be possible.

Hedge

Buy 40 March put options on sterling futures.

Tutorial note: The hedge is provided by the ability to **sell futures**, so you need to **buy put options** on the futures.

Premium cost:	Strike price
93750	£30,000,000 × 0.085% × 2/12 = £4,250
94000	£30,000,000 × 0.255% × 2/12 = £12,750
94250	£30,000,000 × 0.480% × 2/12 = £24,000

Tutorial note: The premium cost is an annual percentage cost, so multiply by 2/12 because the option is required for just two months.

If the interest rate increases by 0.5%, the options will be exercised and the futures contracts sold at the exercise price.

The profit on options contracts will be the exercise price less the expected futures price multiplied by 100%, the tick value and the number of contracts.

Exercise	Profit
93750	(93.75 – 93.47) × 100 × 40 × £12.5 = £14,000
94000	(94.00 – 93.47) × 100 × 40 × £12.5 = £26,500
94250	(94.25 – 93.47) × 100 × 40 × £12.5 = £39,000

Overall cost

Exercise price	Cost of borrowing at 7.4% for 2 months £	Gain on option postion £	Cost of option £		Net cost £
93750	370,000	– 14,000	+ 4,250	=	360,250
94000	370,000	– 26,500	+ 12,750	=	356,250
94250	370,000	– 39,000	+ 24,000	=	355,000

The 94250 exercise price has an expected overall cost of only £1,000 more than the expected futures cost. It might be worth buying this contract in case interest rates fall, which would allow the company to let the option lapse and take advantage of the lower cash market rates.

A collar option which has lower net premium costs, but which restricts the benefits from a fall in interest rates might also be considered.

FRAs

FRAs are OTC instruments, which allow the rate on borrowing at some future period to be fixed today (similar to a forward contract in the foreign exchange market). As with futures, FRAs do not allow the buyer or seller to take advantage of favourable interest rate movements. Unlike futures, FRAs have no margin requirement.

As the company wishes to borrow funds in three months' time for a period of two months, the appropriate FRA would be the 3 v 5 contract.

To hedge against the risk of a rise in interest rates, the company would buy an FRA covering the amount of £30,000,0000.

The contract effectively locks in the rate to the FRA rate of 7.08%

The overall cost is £30,000,000 × 7.08% × 2/12 = £354,000

The futures hedge and the FRA have the same expected total cost. However, because of basis risk the futures cost is not certain, and the futures contracts require margin payments. For these reasons the FRA might be preferred to futures. If there is believed to be a chance of a fall in interest rates the 94250 option might be selected for the hedge.

ACCA marking scheme	
	Marks
Futures:	
Correct type of hedge, maturity and number of contracts	2
Current basis	1
Expected future basis	2
Overall cost or interest rate	1
Options:	
Premium costs	1
Results at different exercise prices	4
FRA:	
Use of 3 v 5	1
Overall cost	1
Discussion/comment (on all parts)	5
Total	15

73   INTEREST RATE SWAP

(a)   Interest rate swaps may provide several benefits to companies including:

   (i)   The ability to obtain finance at a cheaper cost than would be possible by borrowing directly in the relevant market.

   (ii)   The opportunity to effectively restructure a company's capital profile without physically redeeming debt.

   (iii)   Long-term hedging against interest rate movements as swaps may be arranged for periods of several years.

   (iv)   The ability to access a type of finance which could not be accessed directly, for example because the borrower is relatively unknown in the market or has a relatively low credit rating.

(b)   The worst case position where the swap would be beneficial to both companies is when the arbitrage gains from the swap are shared equally.

The differential between fixed rates is 0.75%. The differential between floating rates is 0.40%. The maximum arbitrage gain is therefore 0.35%, or 0.175% to each company if the gain is shared equally. The following swap has been devised so that the gains are shared equally, but alternative swap payments are possible that would achieve the same result.

	Stentor	*Evnor*
Actual borrowing	(8.75%)	(LIBOR + 0.90%)
Swap payments:		
Stentor pays Evnor	(LIBOR)	LIBOR
Evnor pays Stentor	8.425%	(8.425%)
Total cost	(LIBOR + 0.325%)	9.325%
Cost of borrowing direct at floating/fixed rate	LIBOR + 0.5%	9.500%
Saving relative to direct borrowing	0.175%	0.175%

Whether the swap will be beneficial depends upon the size of the swap. For example a 0.175% annual saving on a swap of £10 million is £17,500. The bank's initial fee is £20,000, and annual fee of 0.05% is £5,000.

A swap could, in theory, be arranged that is beneficial to both companies, although the benefits in this example would only start in year two. In reality, Stentor, the higher credit rated company, is likely to receive the larger share of any arbitrage gain, reducing the benefit of the swap for Evnor.

ACCA marking scheme		
		Marks
(a)	One mark for relevant benefit	4
(b)	Swap calculations	5
	Other swaps are acceptable	
	Comment	1
Total		10

74   CALVOLD

(a)   A swap is the exchange of one stream of future cash flows for another stream of future cash flows with different characteristics.

Interest rate and currency swaps offer many potential benefits to companies including:

(i)   The ability to obtain finance cheaper than would be possible by borrowing directly in the relevant market.

As companies with different credit ratings can borrow at different cost differentials in for example the fixed and floating rate markets, a company that borrows in the market where it has a comparative advantage (or least disadvantage) can, through swaps, reduce its borrowing costs. For example a highly rated company might be able to borrow funds 1.5% cheaper in the fixed rate market than a lower rated company, and 0.80% cheaper in the floating rate market. By using swaps an arbitrage gain of 0.70% (1.5% – 0.80%) can be made and split between the participants in the swap.

(ii)   Hedging against foreign exchange risk. Swaps can be arranged for up to ten years which provide protection against exchange rate movements for much longer periods than the forward foreign exchange market. Currency swaps are especially useful when dealing with countries with exchange controls and/or volatile exchange rates.

(iii)   The opportunity to effectively restructure a company's capital profile by altering the nature of interest commitments, without physically redeeming old debt or issuing new debt. This can save substantial redemption costs and issue costs. Interest commitments can be altered from fixed to floating rate or vice versa, or from one type of floating rate debt to another, or from one currency to another.

(iv)   Access to capital markets in which it is impossible to borrow directly. For example, companies with a relatively low credit rating might not have direct access to some fixed rate markets, but can arrange to pay fixed rate interest by using swaps.

(v)   The availability of many different types of swaps developed to meet a company's specific needs. These include amortising swaps, zero coupon swaps, callable, puttable or extendable swaps and swaptions.

(b)   **Using the swap**

The currency swap will provide some protection against the likely depreciation in the value of the peso. 1,500 million pesos will be swapped, with the swap reversed at the year end at the *same rate*. At a swap rate of 20 pesos/£1 the cost of the swap will be:

$$\frac{1,500m}{20} = \text{£75 million}$$

The opportunity cost of this £75 million is interest for one year at 12% = £9m.

At the year end 1,500 million pesos can be swapped back at the same rate of 20 pesos/£1. Revenue will be 2 million pesos, so 500 million pesos is exposed to currency risk.

The expected level of inflation in the UK is 5.25%, and in the South American country 65%. (UK: $0.25 \times 4\% + 0.5 \times 5\% + 0.25 \times 7\% = 5.25\%$. South America $0.25 \times 40\% + 0.5 \times 60\% + 0.25 \times 100\% = 65\%$.)

Purchasing power parity theory may be used to estimate an expected exchange rate at the end of the year, based on these weighted average inflation rates. However, it is probably more useful to Calvold to see the range of exchange rates that might occur, and evaluate their effects on sterling cash flows.

Possible inflation rates: UK 7%, South America 100%

Using PPP the £ would be expected to strengthen by:

$$\frac{1 - 0.07}{1.07} = 0.8691 \text{ or } 86.91\%$$

The expected year end exchange rate would be 46.73 pesos/£1 (25×1.8691).

Possible inflation rates: UK 5%, South America 60%

$$\frac{0.60 - 0.05}{1.05} = 0.5238 \text{ or } 52.38\%$$

The expected exchange rate would be 38.10 pesos/£1 (25×1.5238).

Possible inflation rates: UK 4%, South America 40%

$$\frac{0.40 - 0.04}{1.04} = 0.3462 \text{ or } 34.62\%$$

The expected exchange rate is 33.65 pesos/£1 (25×1.3462).

The interest cost of the swap is 1,500 million $\times$ 10% = 150 million pesos.

Revenue at the end of the year will be 2 million pesos. Deducting the 150 million pesos interest cost of the swap, and the 1,500 million pesos in the swap leaves 350 million pesos to be remitted at the spot rate at the year end.

Possible exchange rate	Pesos (m)	£m
46.73	350	7.49
38.10	350	9.19
33.65	350	10.40

The sterling value of the remittances could range from £7.49 million to £10.40 million. The opportunity cost of funds is £9 million (calculated above). Calvold would therefore only profit from the contract if inflation in South America does not move to 100%, which is the worst case scenario.

If the swap is not used

If the swap is not used, the full 2,000 million pesos is exposed to currency risk. In six months the sterling cost of 500 million pesos will depend on inflation levels and the exchange rate. A steady fall in value of the peso is assumed over the year.

Inflation:7% UK, 100% S America		Exchange rate	Pesos	Sterling value
			million	£m
Immediate cost		25.00	(1,000)	(40.00)
Cost in 6 months	(25 + 46.73)/2	35.87	(500)	(13.94)
Receipts in 1 year		46.73	2,000	42.80
Net				(11.14)

Inflation:5% UK, 60% S America		Exchange rate	Pesos	Sterling value
			million	£m
Immediate cost		25.00	(1,000)	(40.00)
Cost in 6 months	(25 + 38.10)/2	31.55	(500)	(15.85)
Receipts in 1 year		38.10	2,000	52.49
Net				(3.36)

Inflation:4% UK, 40% S America		Exchange rate	Pesos	Sterling value
			million	£m
Immediate cost		25.00	(1,000)	(40.00)
Cost in 6 months	(25 + 33.65)/2	29.33	(500)	(17.05)
Receipts in 1 year		33.65	2,000	59.44
Net				2.39

However, the opportunity cost of funds in the UK would £40 million at 12% = £4.8m, plus a further cost for the second six months for the finance required for the 50 million pesos expenditure.

Given the expected movements in exchange rates, in no circumstances will the contract be profitable if the swap is not used.

If Calvold is to proceed with this contract the currency swap should be used, but even with the swap there is risk that the contract will not be profitable if the South American country experiences a very high rate of inflation.

75 TAYQUER PLC

Key answer tips

Note that this question requires a very specific understanding of collars and it is not sufficient simply to discuss an interest rate cap.

A collar will involve Tayquer arranging both a floor and a ceiling (lower and upper limits) on its interest yield. This may be achieved by:

(1)   buying a call option on futures and

(2)   selling (or writing) a put option on the same futures contract, but with a different exercise price.

As protection is required for the next eight months, to cover the full period March contracts will be used.

If Tayquer wishes to protect its current interest yield, the company is likely to fix the floor at the current yield, i.e. it will buy call options at 9250, or an interest rate of 7.5% (100 – 92.50).

The option would be exercised if interest rates fall below 7.5% and the futures price rises above 9250.

In order to reduce the net premium cost, the potential gain on the interest from short-term investments if interest rates were to rise may be reduced by selling March put contracts at a lower exercise price than 9250. For example, if the interest rate rose to 9% and the put option had been sold at the 9150 exercise price, the buyer of the put option would exercise the option at any futures price lower than 9150. A 9% interest rate implies a futures price of 9100. The 1.5% gain in interest rate rises would be split 1% to Tayquer and 0.5% to the buyer of the put option. Any further interest rate rises will result in the extra interest earned by Tayquer being equal to the increased loss on the puts. Hence Tayquer will only benefit from the first 1% of interest rate increase but will be protected from any reduction in interest rates. Tayquer, in this example, has fixed minimum interest received at 7.5%, and the maximum at 8.5%.

The net per cent premium payable at various combinations of collar are:

Buy call	Premium paid % p.a.	Sell put	Premium received % p.a.	Net cost % p.a.
9250	0.68	9200	0.13	(0.55)
9250	0.68	9150	0.06	(0.62)
9250	0.68	9100	0.02	(0.66)

To protect £9.75 million for eight months:

$$\frac{£9.75\ million}{£500,000} \times \frac{8}{3} \text{ contracts are required}$$

= 52 contracts (£26 million)

The total premium will be between £26 million × 0.55% × 3/12 and £26 million × 0.66% × 3/12, or between £35,750 and £42,900, depending upon which collar is selected.

(As the contracts are three-month contracts, and the premium cost is in annual percentage, the percentage cost must be divided by four. Alternatively these costs may be estimated using ticks.)

The choice of exercise price at which to sell the put option will depend upon Tayquer's views on how far interest rates could rise, and the potential gains if rates do rise.

Put exercise price	Net premium cost	Gain for Tayquer if interest rates rise	Net possible gain/ (loss)
	% p.a.	% p.a.	% p.a.
9200	(0.55)	0.50	(0.05)
9150	(0.62)	1.00	0.38
9100	(0.66)	1.50	0.84

The best potential gains are from a put option exercise price of 9100, but Tayquer may not be willing to lose the £7,150 premium income relative to a 9200 put option exercise price (£42,900 – £35,750).

In reality trading costs may make any options strategies more expensive than they appear to be from the figures presented.

Tutorial note:

The above answer is the examiner's official version. An alternative approach to this question would be as follows:

The purchased option:

A company buys an option to protect itself against an adverse movement and allow it to take unlimited advantage of a favourable movement. In case of Tayquer plc, as it wishes to hedge a deposit position it would buy a call option at 92.50 to protect the current interest rate of 7.50%.

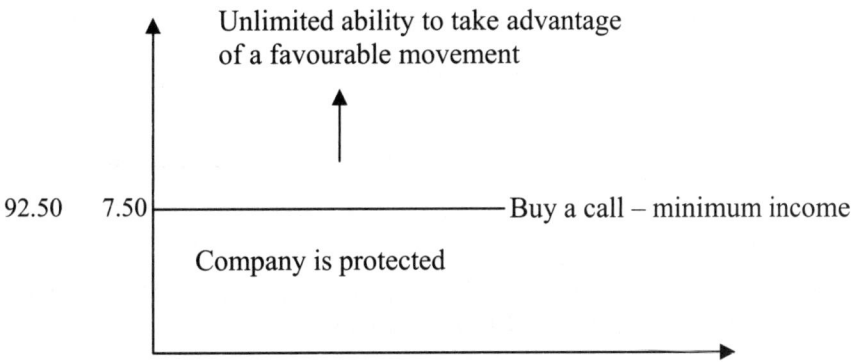

Number of contracts = (£9.75/£0.50) × (8 months/3 months) = 52 contracts

- The question clearly states that protection is required for eight months as it is now the 1 June, protection is required to 1 February therefore March contracts must be used.

The cost/premium of the purchased option can be expensive, hence the use of a collar.

Cost of options: Buy 52 £ March put contacts at an exercise price of 92.50

68 ticks x £12.50 x 52 contracts = (£44,200)

A collar:

- A collar is an option combination. After initially buying an option to protect the position the company then sells an option to reduce the cost of the purchased option.

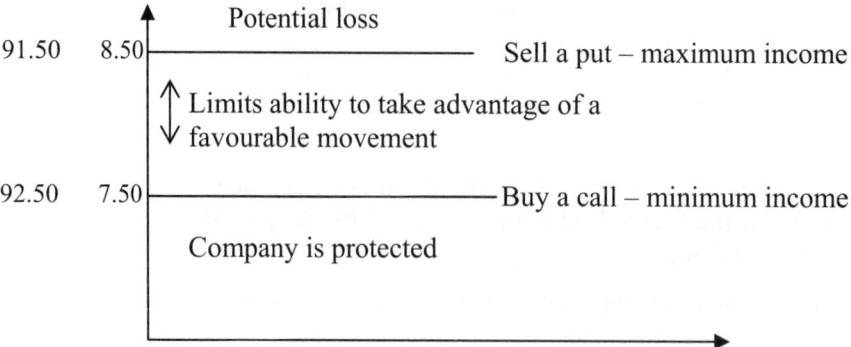

The next question is at what exercise price should Tayquer sell the puts at? The lower the maximum income (ceiling) the greater the receipts from selling the option, however the greater the potential loss if the interest rises above the ceiling.

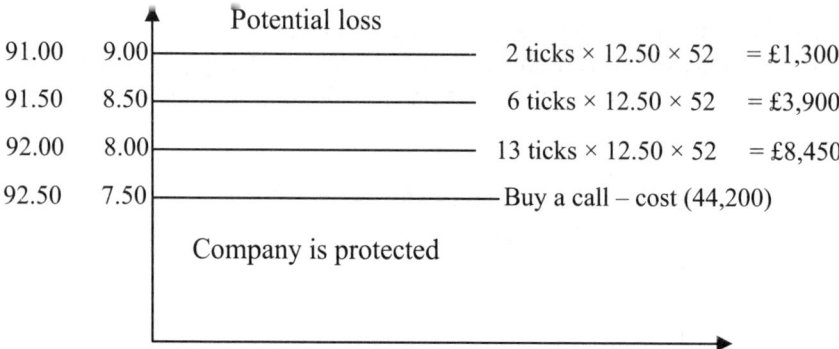

Example of a collar in action:

- Say Tayquer sold put options at 92.00 it would receive £8,450 thus reducing the cost of the hedge to £35,750 i.e. (£44,200 - £8,450).

- However if interest rates rose to 8.50% the company can not take advantage of .50% favourable movement therefore the opportunity cost is 50 ticks x £12.50 x 52 contracts = £32,500.

- The choice of exercise price to sell the put options at will depend upon Tayquer's views on how far interest rates could rise.

76   DUPLICATE PLC

Key answer tips

It is rare that an examiner will ask for computations without analytical comment on their significance and this question is no exception.

(a)   The General Election is due in late October, after the expiry of the September contract. The interest rate risk will, therefore, be hedged using the December contract.

Duplicate plc will hedge a possible increase in interest rates leading to a potential 'cash market' loss by **selling futures contracts** now. If interest rates rise the futures price will fall, and Duplicate plc will make a futures profit by buying back after the interest rate rise the same number, type and maturity of futures contract at a lower price than it sold futures for now.

For a four-month exposure the company would need to sell:

$$\frac{£6,000,000}{£500,000} \times \frac{4}{3} = 16 \text{ December three-month sterling contracts.}$$

(b) Basis risk is the difference between the futures price and the current 'cash market' price of the underlying security.

Basis may be found by comparing the futures price with three month LIBOR.

Current LIBOR (100 – 7.50)	92.50
December futures price	92.10
	0.40 = 0.40% or 40 basis points.

The futures price and cash market price will converge to the same value at the maturity date of the futures contract, i.e. the basis will be zero at the maturity date of the contract at the end of December.

If the basis reduces steadily over the next six months as the maturity date approaches, assuming that the futures contract would be closed out at the end of November when the loan commences, the basis (at the end of November with one month remaining to the maturity of the December contract) is expected to be:

$1/6 \times 40 = 6.67$ or 7 basis points.

Tutorial note: Basis will have fallen over the five months to the end of November by $5/6 \times 40 = 33.33$ points.

On this occasion the expected movement in basis will be disadvantageous to Duplicate plc. If interest rates increase the gain on the futures market is expected to be the movement in interest rates less the 33 basis points change from the time the contract is sold in June to the time it is closed out in November. For example if interest rates increase by 2% to the equivalent of 90.50, the futures price, with seven basis points, is expected to move to 90.43. The loss of 2% in the cash market will be offset by only a 1.67% gain in the futures market, which is an imperfect hedge. There is, however, no guarantee that the basis at the end of November will be seven points. If there are significant movements in yield curves between June and November a lower or higher basis could exist.

77 AUTOCRAT PLC

(a) **A hedge with interest rate futures** offers protection against the downside risk of borrowing or investment (i.e. against the risk of higher borrowing costs or lower investment yields). A futures contract is bought or sold such that, if the underlying 'cash market' rate moves in an adverse direction, there will be a gain on the futures position that largely offsets the 'loss' in the cash market. For example, if futures are used to hedge the risk of a rise in short-term interest rates on a future loan, a rise in interest rates would add to the interest cost on the loan, but this would be offset by a gain on the futures position. On the other hand, if the cash market interest rate moves favourably, there will be an offsetting loss on the futures position.

However, futures prices might not move by exactly the same amount as the cash market, due to **basis risk**, and perfect hedges are rare. Futures also involve the up-front payment of a margin (initial security deposit), and are only available in standard contract sizes and for a limited number of interest rate instruments. If a loss arises on the futures position, there will also be a requirement to pay additional margin (variation margin) to cover the loss. The existence of the margin system and futures clearing houses does, however, offer protection against counterparty default.

Interest rate options offer the right but not the obligation to exercise the right to borrow or lend at a fixed rate, the exercise rate for the option. Options are therefore used in hedging to limit the downside risk. However, if the underlying 'cash market' rate has moved in favour of the buyer of an option, the buyer can let the option(s) lapse and take advantage of the more favourable 'cash market' rate to borrow or invest. Options on interest rate futures are exchange-traded, and they share many of the features of futures such as a limited selection of contracts and standardised contract sizes. Alternatively, interest rate options may be arranged over-the-counter (OTC). OTC interest rate options are mainly offered by banks and can be tailor-made to the specific needs of the buyer. They offer more flexibility in the type, size and maturity of option that is offered. All options involve the **payment of a premium**, often upfront, which is payable whether or not the option is exercised.

Options offer a more flexible hedge than futures, but have a much higher cost.

(b)   (i)   **Futures**

Creating a hedge with futures

Autocrat plc needs to borrow in six months' time, and wishes to protect against an increase in interest rates during the next six months. To do this it will **sell** June futures contracts.

The amount to hedge is £6,500,000. Each futures contract is for £500,000 and three months. As the period at risk is six months, the number of contracts is doubled, i.e. 6/3. The number of contracts required is therefore:

$$\frac{£6,500,000}{£500,000} \times \frac{6}{3} = 26 \text{ contracts}$$

The sale price is 95.29, which represents an interest rate of 4.71% (100 – 95.29).

Basis

The futures price differs from the current 'spot market' interest rate. This difference is 'basis'.

Futures price	95.29
Spot market price (100 – 4.5)	95.50
Basis	0.21

Basis is 21 points or 0.21%, with the futures price lower than the equivalent spot market price.

At the end of June when the contracts mature, basis will be 0 (i.e. the futures price will equal the current spot market price). There are seven months until the maturity date. In six months' time when Autocrat needs to borrow the expected basis is:

$$0.21\% \times \frac{1}{7} = 0.03\%$$

This assumes a linear decline in the basis. It is therefore assumed that in six months' time, the futures price will be 3 basis points lower than the spot market rate at that time.

The effect of the hedge with futures

If the interest rate increases by 0.75%, LIBOR will move from 4.5% to 5.25%. The expected futures price will be:

Spot market price (100 – 5.25)	94.75
Basis	0.03
Expected futures price	94.72

The company will borrow in the cash market at 5.25% (ignoring any additional margin above the LIBOR rate that the bank charges on its loans to Autocrat). The interest cost will be:

£6,500,000 at 5.25% × 6/12 = £170,625.

There will be a gain on the futures position.

Original sale price	95.29
Buy futures to close the position: price	94.72
Gain on each contract	0.57

The value of one basis point is £12.50 (= £500,000 × 0.01% × 3/12). The total gain on 26 contracts will therefore be:

57 basis points × £12.50 x 26 contracts =   £18,525

The effective overall cost of borrowing with the futures hedge is:

	£
Interest on six-month loan	(170,625)
Gain on futures position	18,525
Net cost	**(152,100)**

The effective interest rate on the borrowing is therefore:

(152,100/6,500,000) × 12/6 × 100% = **4.68%.**

The futures contract effectively locks into the futures rate (4.71%), less the expected basis of 0.03%, i.e. an overall interest rate of 4.68%. It does not lock into the current cash market rate when the futures position was established (4.5%). However, this 4.68% rate is not certain, since the futures price in six months' time might not be three basis points different from the cash market rate, because there might not be a linear decline in basis, i.e. **basis risk** might exist. If basis is different from 3 basis points, the effective cost of borrowing will also be different.

(ii) **Options**

Creating a hedge with options on futures

Autocrat plc would need to buy June put options on futures, giving it the right to sell futures if the options are exercised.

The hedge would be to buy 26 June put options.

	Strike price				Premium cost
(i)	95250	£6,500,000 × 0.185% × 6/12	=		£6,012.5
(ii)	95500	£6,500,000 × 0.280% × 6/12	=		£9,100.0
(iii)	95750	£6,500,000 × 0.405% × 6/12	=		£13,162.5

Examiner's comment

Alternatively the premium may be estimated using basis points multiplied by the tick value for the contract and number of contracts, e.g. 18.5 × £12.50 × 26 = £6,012.5).

The effect of the hedge with options

The company will borrow £6,500,000 for six months at 5.25%, and the interest cost will be £170,625.

If interest rates increase by 0.75%:

- The company will borrow £6,500,000 for six months at 5.25%, and the interest cost will be £170,625.

- The options will be exercised (or sold if there is any time value left) and the 26 futures contracts sold at a profit.

This expected profit would be the exercise price at which futures could be sold, less the expected futures price in six months, multiplied by 100%, the tick value and the number of contracts. The expected futures price (see above) is 94.72.

Exercise price			Profit on sale of futures
95250	$(95.25 - 94.72) \times 100 \times 26 \times £12.5$	=	£17,225
95500	$(95.50 - 94.72) \times 100 \times 26 \times £12.5$	=	£25,350
95750	$(95.75 - 94.72) \times 100 \times 26 \times £12.5$	=	£33,475

Exercise price	95250	95500	95750
	£	£	£
Interest on loan	(170,625.0)	(170,625)	(170,625.0)
Profit on options	17,225.0	25,350	33,475.0
Cost of options (premium)	(6,012.5)	(9,100)	(13,162.5)
Net cost	(159,412.5)	(154,375)	(150,312.5)

The 95750 exercise price has the lowest net cost, with a worst case effective interest rate of **4.625%** $(150,312.5/6,500,000) \times 12/6 \times 100\%)$. This is better than the expected effective rate using futures to hedge.

However, the spot futures price at the time when the option would be exercised/sold is not certain.

If interest rates were to fall rather than increase the option could be allowed to lapse (or sold for time value if any) and advantage taken of the lower cash market borrowing rates.

(c) A payment of $4.3 million dollars is due in three months' time. The company therefore needs to buy dollars in exchange for sterling, in order to make the payment.

Hedging with a forward contract

A forward contract to buy $4.3 million could be arranged at a rate of 1.4632.

Tutorial note: If you are in doubt about which rate to use, the rate on the left or the rate on the right, remember that the bank will quote the rate that is more profitable for itself. Here, it will quote the rate that gives it more sterling for the dollars it sells, which means the rate of 1.4632 rather than the rate of 1.4735 will apply.

Sterling cost of buying $4.3 million with a forward contract =

$$\frac{\$4,300,000}{1.4632} = £2,938,764.$$

Hedging with currency options

As the option contracts are denominated in sterling, the company must purchase March put options (giving it the right to sell sterling in exchange for dollars). March contracts are used because they are the closest maturity date after the date of the transaction (1 March).

Any of three option exercise rates could be chosen for buying put options.

Number of contracts:

Exercise rate 1.45

$4,300,000/1.45 = £2,965,517/31,250 = 94.90 or 95 contracts (£2,968,750)

Exercise rate 1.46

$4,300,000/1.46 = £2,945,205/31,250 = 94.25 or 94 contracts (£2,937,500)

Exercise rate 1.47

$4,300,000/1.47 = £2,925,170/31,250 = 93.61 or 94 contracts (£2,937,500)

Option premiums

Exercise rate 1.45

1.56 cents × £2,968,750 = $46,312/1.4692 = £31,522

Exercise rate 1.46

1.99 cents × £2,937,500 = $58,456/1.4692 = £39,788

Exercise rate 1.47

2.51 cents × £2,937,500 = $73,731/1.4692 = £50,185

The option premium will be payable upfront, hence the sterling cost is estimated using the spot rate.

The effect of the hedge with options

The possible spot rates in three months' time for the purchase of dollars are:

(i) $1.4350/£1

(ii) $1.4780/£1.

If the spot rate is $1.4350

The options would be exercised at all three of the exercise prices.

Exercise rate	*1.45*	*1.46*	*1.47*
Number of option contracts purchased	95	94	94
Sterling value (£31,250 per contract)	£2,968,750	£2,937,500	£2,937,500
Dollars purchased at option rate	$4,304,687	$4,288,750	$4,318,125
Dollars required	$4,300,000	$4,300,000	$4,300,000
Surplus/(shortfall) in dollars	$4,307	$(11,250)	$18,125
Sell surplus or buy to make up shortfall:			
Spot rate	1.4386	1.4350	1.4386
Income/(cost)	£2,994	£(7,840)	£12,599

The surplus dollars will be sold at the spot rate in three months, or the shortfall in dollars will be purchased at the spot rate in three months, because it is not until then that the company knows whether or not the options will be exercised.

Total costs with options, in sterling, if the spot rate is $1.4350

Exercise rate	*1.45*	*1.46*	*1.47*
	£	£	£
Cost of exercising options and buying $	(2,968,750)	(2,937,500)	(2,937,500)
Income/(cost) of surplus/shortfall in $	2,994	(7,840)	12,599
Cost of option premiums	(31,522)	(39,788)	(50,185)
Total cost	(2,997,278)	(2,985,128)	(2,975,086)

All of these are much more expensive than hedging in the forward market.

If the spot rate is $1.4780

If the spot rate were $1.4780, none of the options would be exercised. The $4.3 million would be purchased at the spot rate, at a cost of:

$$\frac{\$4,300,000}{1.4780} = £2,909,337.$$

Total costs with options, in sterling, if the spot rate is $1.4780

Exercise rate	1.45	1.46	1.47
	£	£	£
Cost of buying $ at 1.4780	(2,909,337)	(2,909,337)	(2,909,337)
Cost of option premiums	(31,522)	(39,788)	(50,185)
Total cost	(2,940,859)	(2,949,125)	(2,959,522)

All of these are still worse than hedging with a forward contract. The spot price of the dollar in three months' time would need to weaken further for options to be the cheaper hedge.

(d) A straddle involves the simultaneous purchase of call and put options at the same exercise price. Straddles are undertaken if the buyer of the straddle believes that the currency prices are going to be volatile, but is not sure whether a currency is going to appreciate or depreciate.

As two options are purchased, two option premiums are payable. Here, the straddle would involve buying a call at $1.460 for 2.55 cents and buying a put at $1.460 for 1.99 cents. The total payable would therefore be (2.55 plus 1.99 =) 4.54 cents per pound.

A straddle would not be appropriate for Autocrat plc. As the company is trying to hedge against a future exposure in dollars, a one-way option to purchase dollars is all that is necessary to protect the exposure.

Straddles are suited to traders (speculators) who are trying to profit from volatile currency movements but do not have a future commitment in the currency. If the exchange rate rises above or falls below 1.460, one of the options will be exercised, but the other will be allowed to lapse. In this example the exchange rate would have to move out of the range $1.460 plus or minus 4.54 cents (i.e. below $1.4146 or above $1.5054), in order for the straddle to show a net profit.

Tutorial note: Since the spot exchange rate is quoted in dollars per £1, a fall in the rate below 1.460 means that the dollar is strengthening and sterling is weakening. The call options in the question are for buying sterling in exchange for dollars and put options give the right to sell sterling. A call option on sterling at 1.460 will be exercised) if sterling strengthens and the rate rises above 1.460. A put option will be exercised if sterling weakens and the rate falls below 1.460. To make a net profit, the profit on exercising an option needs to be at least the combined cost of the two options, which here is 4.54 cents/£1.

ACCA marking scheme		
		Marks
(a)	Futures	3
	Options	3
(b)	Futures:	
	Sell June futures	1
	Number of contracts	1
	Hedge, with outcome	3
	For full marks basis must be included	
	Opions:	
	Buy 26 June puts	1
	Premium costs	1

	Overall costs with options	3
	Conclusion	1
	Comment about interest rates falling	1
	For full marks all exercise prices should be considered	
(c)	Forward contract	1
	Buy March puts	1
	Correct number of contracts	1
	Option premiums	2
	Outcomes at 1.4350	2
	Outcomes at 1.4780	2
(d)	Understanding of straddle	2
	Value to Autocrat	1-2
	Situation when it would be profitable	2
Total		30

78 HYK COMMUNICATIONS PLC

(a) HYK can currently borrow at LIBOR + 0.75 or 7.25%.

Using a futures hedge the company will attempt to make a futures gain in order to offset a possible cash market loss if interest rates rise. As the primary concern is an interest rate rise, the company will **sell futures contracts**.

Cash market

Current cost of borrowing for four months is:

£18,000,000 × 7.25% × 4/12 = £435,000

If interest rates increase by 150 basis points, or 1.5%, the new cost of borrowing will be:

£18,000,000 × 8.75% × 4/12 = £525,000

This represents a cash market 'loss' of £90,000.

Futures market

Sell March futures contracts (as March is the nearest expiry after the borrowing commences).

In order to hedge a 4-month risk:

$$\frac{£18,000,000}{£500,000} \times \frac{4}{3} = 48 \text{ contracts are required}$$

Basis is the March futures price (%) less the current LIBOR rate. The current futures price is (100 − 93.10) = 6.90%. Basis = 6.90% − 6.5% = 0.40%.

At maturity of the futures contract at the end of March, the basis will be zero. Assuming basis risk falls at a constant rate, the expected basis risk when the loan is taken at the start of February will be 0.20% or 20 basis points. (The contract matures in four months time, and the loan is taken out in two months time, so basis will be 2/4 × 40 = 20).

Interest rates rise by 1.5%

The expected futures price in two months will be 93.1 − 1.50 + 0.20 = 91.80.

The futures position will be closed by buying 48 contracts at 91.80. The gain on closing out will be (93.10 − 91.80) = 1.30 or 130 points.

The total expected futures gain if the 48 contracts are closed out in 2 months time is:

48 × 130 × £12.50 per point = £78,000.

The overall cost of the loan is expected to be:

	£
Cost of borrowing at 8.75%	525,000
Gain on futures hedge	78,000
	447,000

£447,000 represents an effective interest rate on borrowing £18 million for four months of:

$$(£447,000/£18 \text{ million}) \times (12/4) \times 100\% = 7.45\%.$$

Interest rates fall by 0.5%

If interest rates fall by 50 basis points, the new cost of borrowing will be:

$$£18,000,000 \times 6.75\% \times 4/12 \quad £405,000.$$

This is a cash market 'gain' of £30,000 on the cost of borrowing at the current interest rate (which is £435,000, see above).

The same futures contract will have been used to hedge the risk, and the expected basis risk at the start of February will still be 0.20%.

The expected futures price in two months is therefore 93.1 + 0.50 + 0.20 = 93.80.

The futures position will be closed by buying 48 contracts at 93.80. The expected futures loss if the 48 contracts are closed out in 2 months time is (93.10 − 93.80) = 0.70 or 70 points. The total loss on the futures position will be:

$$48 \text{ contracts} \times 70 \times £12.50 = £42,000.$$

The overall cost of the loan is expected to be:

	£
Cost of borrowing at 6.75%	405,000
Loss on futures hedge	42,000
	447,000

This is the same as if interest rates went up by 1.5%, and represents an effective interest rate of 7.45% per annum.

No matter how interest rates move the futures hedge should keep the cost of borrowing below the desired 7.50% maximum.

(Note. In reality any futures gains or losses would occur on a daily basis, not at the end of the period, and basis risk may not fall at a constant rate.)

Options

March put options are required. (The company would want to exercise the right to sell futures contracts, so it should buy put options.) HYK will buy 48 put options on March futures.

The worst case scenario for HYK is if interest rates rise and the options have to be exercised.

Cash market

If interest rates increase by 150 basis points, or 1.5%, the new cost of borrowing will be £525,000 (calculation shown earlier).

Options market

Using the 93.00 exercise price

Buy 48 March put options contracts, at a cost of £18m × 0.20% p.a. × 4/12 = £12,000.

If interest rates increase by 1.5%, the options will be exercised and 48 futures contracts will be sold at the exercise price of 93.00. (Note: It might be possible to sell the options themselves at a better rate as they still have some time value.)

Expected profit = 93.00 – 91.80 (the expected futures price in two months) = 120 points per contract.

The total expected gain is 48 contracts × 120 × £12.50 = £72,000.

The overall cost of the loan is expected to be:

	£
Cost of borrowing at 8.75%	525,000
Cost of option premiums	12,000
Gain on options hedge	(72,000)
	465,000

This represents an effective interest rate on a four-month loan of £18 million of:

(£465,000/£18 million) × (12/4) × 100% = 7.75% p.a.

Using the 93.50 exercise price

Buy 48 March put options contracts, at a cost of £18m × 0.60% p.a. × 4/12 = £36,000.

The expected profit is 93.50 – 91.80 (the expected futures price in two months) = 170 points.

The expected total gain is 48 × 170 × £12.50 = £102,000.

The overall cost of the loan is expected to be:

	£
Cost of borrowing at 8.75%	525,000
Cost of option premiums	36,000
Gain on options hedge	(102,000)
	459,000

A net cost of £459,000 represents an effective interest rate on a four-month loan of £18 million of:

(£459,000/£18 million) × (12/4) × 100% = 7.65% p.a.

Using the 94.00 exercise price

Buy 48 March put options contracts, at a cost of £18m × 1.35% p.a. × 4/12 = £81,000.

The expected profit is 94.00 – 91.80 (the expected futures price in two months) = 220 points.

The expected gain is 48 × £12.50 × (94.00 – 91.80) × 100 = £132,000.

The overall cost of the loan is expected to be:

	£
Cost of borrowing at 8.75%	525,000
Cost of option premiums	81,000
Gain on options hedge	(132,000)
	474,000

A net cost of £474,000 represents an effective interest rate on a four-month loan of £18 million of:

(£474,000/£18 million) × (12/4) × 100% = 7.9% p.a..

If interest rates fall by 50 basis points, the new cost of borrowing will be:

£18m × 6.75% × 4/12 = £405,000.

The expected futures price will be 93.80 (see earlier).

The 93.00 and 93.50 options will not be exercised and the overall cost will be:

(1) *93.00 exercise price*: £405,000 + £12,000 = £417,000 or 6.95%

(2) *93.50 exercise price*: £405,000 + £36,000 = £441,000 or 7.35%

The *94.00 contract* will be exercised giving an expected profit of 94.00 – 93.80 (the expected futures price in two months) = 20 points.

The expected total gain is 48 × 20 × £12.50 = £12,000.

The overall cost of the loan is expected to be:

	£
Cost of borrowing at 6.75%	405,000
Cost of option premiums	81,000
Gain on options hedge	(12,000)
	474,000

A net cost of £474,000 represents an effective interest rate on a four-month loan of £18 million of 7.9% p.a.

Conclusion

If basis risk is expected to fall to 0.20, none of the option contracts has a maximum expected interest rate (including option premium) of 7.5%, although the 93.50 exercise price is close to it. If the finance director does not wish to pay more than 7.5%, hedging with futures should be selected.

An **option collar** might also be possible in this situation, if HYK is prepared to limit the benefit from any fall in interest rates.

(b) Market traded interest rate options have several advantages over OTC options:

(i) There is greater price transparency, with current prices on the market immediately available and widely disseminated, which facilitates the management of option positions.

(ii) Exchange traded options offer greater liquidity, with easy sale or purchase of options of a known standard quality.

(iii) There is a central marketplace, with quick access to large numbers of buyers and sellers.

(iv) Lower counterparty risk. Contracts are marked to market on a daily basis, and a central clearing house monitors the ability of all counterparties to meet their obligations.

(v) Better regulation. Most options exchanges are subject to stringent regulation by government authorities.

(vi) Market traded options are normally American style and may be exercised at any time. OTC options are often European style, and can only be exercised at their maturity date.

Advantages of OTC options include:

(i) OTC options offer a much larger choice of contract size, maturity, and type of interest option which allows the purchaser of the option to tailor the option much more specifically to individual needs.

      (ii)   Option sizes are typically much larger on the OTC market.

      (iii)   Options may be arranged for longer periods than is possible on traded options markets.

  (c)   Option prices are influenced by the following factors:

      (i)   The price of the underlying security, in this case a specific interest bearing instrument.

      (ii)   The exercise price of the option.

      (iii)   The time until expiry of the option.

      (iv)   The risk of the option, as normally measured by the historic volatility of a similar option.

      (v)   The level of interest rates within the economy.

      (iv)   Whether the option is European style or American style, the American style being more flexible and slightly more expensive.

Whether or not the option is expensive will depend upon whether it has been correctly priced, which will itself largely depend upon what assumptions have been made by the seller of the OTC option about the volatility of the option. OTC options are not very price transparent, but there is a competitive market in such options, and reputable banks and other sellers of options have little to gain in the long run by overpricing options. There is, however, evidence that some forms of options, e.g. underwriting fees on stock market issues, have been substantially more expensive than would be expected from option pricing models.

79   COLLAR HEDGE

  (a)   Interest rate caps and collars are available as over the counter (OTC) transactions with a bank, or may be devised using market-based interest rate options (options on interest rate futures). They may be used to hedge current or expected interest receipts or payments.

An **interest rate cap** is a series of call options on a notional amount of principal, exercisable at regular intervals over the term to expiry of the cap. The effect of a cap is to place an upper limit on the interest rate to be paid, and is therefore useful to a borrower of funds who will be paying interest at a future date. By purchasing a cap, a borrower will limit the net interest paid to the agreed cap strike price (less any premium paid for the cap). OTC caps are available for periods of up to ten years and can thus protect against long-term interest rate movements. As with all options, if interest rates were to move in a favourable direction, the buyer of the cap could let the option lapse and take advantage of the more favourable rates in the spot market.

The main disadvantage of options is the premium cost. An **interest rate collar** option reduces the premium cost by limiting the possible benefits of favourable interest rate movements. A collar involves the simultaneous purchase and sale of options, or in the case of OTC collars the equivalent to this. The premium paid for the purchase of one option would be partly or wholly offset by the premium received from the sale of another option. A borrower using an OTC collar would in effect buy a cap at one strike price, to secure a maximum interest cost, and sell a floor at a lower strike rate, which sets a minimum interest cost. The effective interest cost would be somewhere between the exercise price for the floor and the exercise price for the cap. The premium cost would be the cost of the cap less the selling price of the floor. A zero cost collar is a collar for which the cost of the cap is offset exactly by the sales value of the floor.

(b) For the company to earn interest of £6,750,000 it would need to earn an annualised interest rate, after premium costs of $\dfrac{£6,750,000}{£400,000,000} \times \dfrac{12}{5} = 4.05\%$.

The collar needs to produce a minimum of more than 4.05% including premium costs, allowing for the fact that the company can invest at 0.25% below LIBOR.

As Troder plc is investing, a lending collar will be required. To create a lending collar with options on interest rate futures, the company will simultaneously buy a floor and sell a cap. (*Tutorial note*: A borrower would buy a cap and sell a floor, but an investor should buy a floor and sell a cap.)

- *Buying a floor.* To buy a floor, the company should buy a call option on interest rate futures (giving it the right to buy futures). The call option will increase in value if interest rates fall. This will set the floor, or minimum interest rate.

- *Selling a cap.* The cap is created by selling put options. This sets the maximum interest. If interest rates rise, the market price of the option (and the underlying futures) will fall. The buyer will exercise the option (or the options position will be closed at a loss). As a result the company would forgo any higher interest rate than the put option exercise price.

- *Premium.* The overall cost of the collar will be the call option premium paid less the put option premium received.

In order to achieve a return of more than 4.05% (£6,750,000) a collar needs to be arranged with the call strike price higher than the put strike price (in order to set the maximum interest that can be received).

Alternatives are:

Call strike price	Put strike price	Minimum interest rate secured by call	Less call cost	Plus put receipt	Minimum LIBOR rate secured
95750	95500	4.25%	(0.165)%	0.170%	4.255%
95750	95250	4.25%	(0.165)%	0.085%	4.170%
95500	95250	4.50%	(0.280)%	0.085%	4.305%

Call strike price	Put strike price	Minimum LIBOR rate secured	Invest at LIBOR minus 0.25% Minimum net yield
95750	95500	4.255%	4.005%
95750	95250	4.170%	3.920%
95500	95250	4.305%	4.055%

Tutorial note:

The maximum net yield obtainable from the collar hedge is determined by the put option exercise price. It can be calculated as the minimum net yield, as shown in the table above, plus the difference between the put option interest rate and the call option interest rate.

Of the alternatives considered above, only the purchase of a call at 95500 and sale of a put at 95250 will result in a minimum return of £6,750,000. The actual minimum return (ignoring any possible remaining time value that might increase the return) is:

£400,000,000 × $^5/_{12}$ × 4.055% = £6,758,333.

However, there is a possibility that the net yield will be 0.25% higher (the difference between the call option and put option rates, in which case the return would be £400,000,000 × $^5/_{12}$ × 4.305% = £7,175,000.)

Examiner's note

If a collar is set with the same put and call price the return will be:

Strike price	Interest rate	Less call cost	Plus put receipt	Less 0.25%	Investment return
95250	4.75%	(0.445)%	0.085%	(0.250)%	4.140%
95500	4.50%	(0.280)%	0.170%	(0.250)%	4.140%
95750	4.25%	(0.165)%	0.305%	(0.250)%	4.140%

This would achieve the required 4.05%, but would not allow Troder to take advantage of any favourable movement in interest rates.

(ii) The maximum return would occur if market interest rates are at least 4.75% and the call option were allowed to lapse. The put option would be exercised by its buyer and the maximum overall return would be:

Call option strike price	Interest rate (call not exercised)	Less call cost	Plus put receipt	Less 0.25%	Investment return
95500	4.75%	(0.280)%	0.085%	(0.250)%	4.305%

This would yield:

$$£400,000,000 \times {}^5/_{12} \times 4.305\% = £7,175,000.$$

ACCA marking scheme		Marks
(a)	Advantages of caps	3
	Advantages of collars	3
(b)	Required interest yield	1
	Collar calculations	6
	Give credit for technique	
		7
(c)	Maximum yield if option is not exercised	2
Total		15

80 LEADING NEWSPAPERS

The term structure of interest rates is revealed by the redemption yield data. As the term to maturity increases, so does the redemption yield, indicating *an upward sloping yield curve*. There are several theories which might explain the shape of the yield curve.

(1) *The expectations theory* suggests that if the yield curve is upward sloping, this may reflect the expectation that inflation levels, and therefore interest rates, will increase in the future.

(2) *The liquidity preference theory* considers that even if there is no expectation of a change in inflation levels the yield curve will still be upward sloping. This is because investors have a natural preference for more liquid investments and, will need to be compensated if they are derived of their cash for a longer period. Hence the longer dated the stock, the higher the redemption yield, leading to an upward sloping yield curve.

(3) *The market segmentation theory* suggests that the shape of the yield curve is in part influenced by the size of activity of investors in various segments of the market. For example, pension funds would tend to invest in long-term maturities to match the long-term nature of their liabilities.

The supply and demand forces in various segments of the market in part influence the shape of the yield curve. If there is an increased supply in the long-term end of the market because the government needs to borrow more, this may cause the price to fall and the yield to rise and may result in an upward sloping yield curve.

(a)   As the financial manager does not expect interest rates to rise next year, rather than invest in the one-year bond with a yield of 8.43%, he could invest in the two-year maturity bond and sell it after one year.

The total expected return if the bond is sold at the end of the first year is:

$$\frac{1.0901^2}{1.0843} - 1 = 9.59\%$$

This is a substantially higher expected yield than the yield from investing in the one-year maturity bond. However, if interest rates increase during the year the return could be much lower.

Note: The redemption yield on the two year bond implies that the market expects interest rates to rise from their current level of 8.43% to 9.59%, as the capital plus interest received from an investment in a two-year bond should be the same as the capital plus interest received from investing in two consecutive one-year bonds.

$$1.0901^2 = 1.0843 \times 1.0959$$

81   FOLTER PLC

(a)   Folter can protect against possible falls in the share price either by buying put options or selling call options in Magterdoor's shares. Ideally a put option would be purchased at the money i.e. at the current market price of the shares. This opportunity is not available. If an in the money price of 550 pence is selected, the outcome with a market price at the end of October of 485 pence would be:

550 (exercise price) – 51 (option premium) = 499 pence × 2 million shares = £9.98m.

If the exercise price of 500 pence is used the outcome would be:

500 – 24.5 = 475.5 × 2m = £9.51m

If no hedge were undertaken the shares would be worth £9.70m.

The success of the hedge would depend upon the exercise price selected.

However, if the price at the end of October was not 485, but was in excess of the relevant exercise price of the option, then the option would be allowed to lapse.

(b)   The purpose of a delta neutral hedge is to set up a riskless portfolio. Any adverse movement in a share price would be offset by a similar favourable movement in the option price. A delta of 0.47 means that for every share held 1/0.47 call options would need to be sold to establish the delta neutral hedge.

$$\frac{2,000,000}{1,000 \times 0.47} = 4,255 \text{ call options would need to be sold}$$

Delta hedges are only valid for small movements in the share price. As the share price changes, so will the relevant delta, and the hedge would need to be frequently rebalanced in order to maintain the delta neutral position.

(c)   The intrinsic value of the January 550 call option is zero, as the exercise price exceeds the current market price. The option premium of 34 pence is the time value of the option. The time value depends upon the remaining time to the expiration of the option, the volatility of the option and the level of interest rates. As these variables increase, so will the time value of the option.

(d)   Apart from the obvious cost and risk associated with increasing the holding, an increase to six percent means that Folter would have to publicly declare its holding in Magterdoor, which might reveal that a take-over is being considered. Under the City Code on Take-overs and Mergers any holding over 3% must be disclosed to the target company.

The main advantage of increasing the percentage holding is that it makes achieving the ownership of more than 50% of the shares easier. It might be argued that if Folter has to reveal its holding to Magterdoor, a larger holding than 6% should be considered.

Tutorial note: While this is not a particularly difficult question it does require a broad understanding of the various issues associated with options.

ACCA marking scheme			
			Marks
(a)		Traded option hedge with comment on exercise price	4
(b)		Number and type of contracts	2–3
		Practical problems	1–2
			4
(c)		Reward understanding, especially intrinsic value and the causes of time value	4
(d)		Comments about the City Code implications	1–2
		Other comments	1–2
			3
	Total		15

82   INTEREST RATE HEDGES

Key answer tips

A technical but routine question on hedging interest rate risk. It is vital that all calculations are clearly explained and interpreted.

(a)   The company is worried about a fall in interest rates during the next five months. It will need a long futures hedge, with December futures purchased at 96.60. If interest rates fall the futures price will rise and the contracts may be closed out at a higher price to partially offset the cash market interest rate fall. For a risk of £7.1 million to protect a four month period the company will need to buy:

$$\frac{£7,100,000}{£500,000} \times \frac{4}{3} = 18.93, \text{ or 19 contracts, a slight over hedge.}$$

Basis is futures rate less spot rate, or 96.60 – 96.00 = 0.60% (The current LIBOR of 4% is equivalent to a futures price of 96.00).

The time to expiry of the December futures contract is seven months. Remaining time at the close out date (five months' time) is two months.

The expected basis for two months is $0.60\% \times \frac{2}{7} = 0.171\%$

The expected LIBOR lock-in rate is 96.60 – 0.171 = 96.429 or 3.571%

The company will invest in commercial paper at LIBOR + 0.60%. The overall expected lock-in rate is 4.171%.

(b)   The relevant FRA rate is 5 v 9. The company would sell the FRA to a bank to fix the interest rate at 3.45%. This is a lower rate than the expected futures LIBOR lock-in rate of 3.571%.

(c)   **Cash market**:

Expected receipts from the investment on 1 November: £7.1m x 4.1% x $\dfrac{4}{12}$ =

£97,033 (4.1% is LIBOR of 3.5% + 0.6%)

Futures market:

1 June: Buy 19 December contracts at 96.60

1 November: Sell 19 December contracts at 96.671 (spot of 96.50 plus expected remaining basis of 0.171).

Profit from futures is 7.1 basis points × £12.50 × 19 = £1,686

Overall receipts are £97,033 + £1,686 = £98,719

(N.B. $\dfrac{£98,719}{£7,100,000} \times \dfrac{12}{4}$ = 4.171%, the expected lock-in rate).

FRA:

The FRA fixed rate is 3.45%. Actual LIBOR is 3.5%. The company will therefore have to make a payment to the bank.

This will be: £7.1m $(3.50\% - 3.45\%) \times \dfrac{4}{12} \times \dfrac{1}{1 + (3.5\% \times 4/12)}$ or £1,169.65

This will be deducted from the actual receipts of £97,033 (estimated above) to give a net £95,863, a return of 4.05%. (N.B. this is the FRA rate of 3.45 plus the 0.6% over LIBOR from the commercial paper).

(d)   The futures market outcome might differ because:

(i)   The hedge is not exact. 19 contracts is a slight over hedge.

Basis risk might exist. The basis at the futures close out date might differ from the expected basis of 0.171.

Commercial paper interest rates might not move exactly with LIBOR rates.

(iv)   Any gains or losses on futures contracts would be taken/payable daily when the futures contracts are marked to market. The interest effect of such receipts or payments is ignored in the calculations.

(v)   The above analysis ignores transactions costs.

ACCA marking scheme			
			Marks
(a)		Hedge details	2
		Expected lock-in rate	2
			4
(b)		Higher income – with evidence	2
(c)		Cash market	1
		Futures market	3
		FRA	2
			6
(d)		1 mark for each good point Maximum	3
		Total	15

THE GLOBAL ECONOMIC ENVIRONMENT AND GLOBAL FINANCIAL MANAGEMENT

83   IMF

Key answer tips

The first part of the answer contains a clear and comprehensive explanation of the functions of the IMF – this attracts the majority of the marks so do not be vague here. The discussion following on the possible impact on multinationals also requires a clear understanding of how the IMF works.

The International Monetary Fund (IMF) was established at the Bretton Wood Conference of 1945. Its initial tasks were to promote world trade and to help support the fixed exchange rate system that existed at that time. Support was mainly in the form of temporary loans to member countries which experienced balance of payments difficulties. Such loans were financed by member countries' quota subscriptions. Although floating exchange rates and exchange rate agreements between blocs of countries have replaced the fixed exchange rate system, the IMF still provides loans to many of its members, particularly developing countries. Today loans are also granted to help countries repay large commercial debts that they have built up from the international banking system.

An important feature of most IMF loans is the conditions attached to the loans. Countries receiving IMF loans are required to take strong economic measures to try to improve or eliminate the economic problems that made the loans necessary, and to stimulate medium to long-term economic development. These conditions typically include currency devaluation, controls over inflation via the money supply, public expenditure cuts to reduce government budget deficits and local tax increases.

Loans of up to 25% of a member country's quotas are given without condition. A further 25% is available to countries that 'demonstrate reasonable efforts' to overcome balance of payments difficulties. Upper credit tranches of up to a further 75% of quota, normally in the form of standby facilities, are available subject to conditionality agreements. Most loans are for a period of up to five years.

The IMF also offers loans under the Compensatory Financing Facility to cover unforeseen problems such as crop failure, medium-term loans of up to ten years via the Extended Fund Facility in order to overcome severe structural balance of payments problems, and special supplementary borrowing facilities, often at concessionary rates of interest, to countries with severe problems.

The IMF has undoubtedly been successful in helping to reduce volatility in international exchange rates, and in facilitating world trade. This has beneficial effects on the trading activities of multinational companies. However, the strong influence of the IMF on the macro-economic policies of developing nations often leads to short term deflation and reductions in the size of markets for multinational companies' products. Conflicts may exist between multinationals, who wish to freely move capital internationally, and governments trying to control the money supply and inflation. Tax increases often accompany economic austerity measures, import tariff quotas may make operations more difficult and increases in interest rates raise the cost of finance. In the medium to long term it is hoped that the structural adjustments will stimulate economic growth and will increase the size of markets for multinational companies, but IMF economic conditions may cause significant short to medium term difficulties for subsidiaries of multinationals in the countries concerned.

84   CURRENT ACCOUNT DEFICIT

A large current account deficit means that the value of exports of goods, services, investment income and current transfers is much less than the value of imports of these items. If the government believes that the deficit is not a temporary phenomenon, which will be largely self-correcting, it may attempt to reduce the deficit by taking one or more of a selection of economic measures. However, a country with large foreign currency reserves may decide to finance the deficit by running down some of those reserves and may not take significant additional actions for some time.

Economic measures include:

1   Monetary policy. A government will often take deflationary measures to reduce the money supply. This may be through increases in interest rates, or attempting to reduce the money supply through actions such as credit restrictions, wage and/or price controls and reductions in government expenditure. Increased interest rates will tend to reduce local borrowing and demand for imports, and attract overseas funds into the country to take advantage of the higher interest rates (until interest rate and exchange rates are in equilibrium once more).

2   Fiscal policy. Governments often reduce consumer spending, including spending on imports, by increasing taxation.

3   Devaluation. If the country is part of a fixed exchange rate system the currency may be devalued in order to make imports more expensive and exports more competitive.

4   Exchange controls, tariffs, and quotas are all measures, which may be used to reduce imports, and to reduce a current account deficit. However, these may be contrary to World Trade Organisation (WTO) agreements.

5   Export stimulation through government subsidies, although these too are often restricted by the WTO.

6   Borrowing. The government may finance the deficit by borrowing from international commercial banks or international organisations such as the IMF. Such borrowing, however, may not tackle the underlying symptoms of the deficit.

The IMF may provide loans to help finance a balance of payments deficit. An important feature of most IMF loans is the conditions attached to the loans. Countries receiving IMF loans are required to take strong economic measures to try to improve or eliminate the economic problems that made the loans necessary, and to stimulate medium to long-term economic development. These conditions typically include currency devaluation, controls over inflation via the money supply, public expenditure cuts to reduce government budget deficits and local tax increases. Most loans are for a period of up to five years. The IMF also offers loans under the Extended Fund Facility in order to overcome severe structural balance of payments problems, and special supplementary borrowing facilities, often at concessionary rates of interest, to countries with severe problems.

The actions of the IMF help to reduce volatility in international exchange rates, and to facilitate world trade. This has beneficial effects on the trading activities of multinational companies. However, the strong influence of the IMF on the macroeconomic policies of developing nations often leads to short term deflation and to reductions in the size of markets for multinational companies' products. Conflicts may exist between multinationals, who wish to freely move capital internationally, and governments trying to control the money supply and inflation. Tax increases often accompany economic austerity measures, import tariff quotas may make operations more difficult and increases in interest rates raise the cost of finance. In the medium to long term the structural adjustments might stimulate economic growth and increase the size of markets for multinational companies, but IMF economic conditions may cause significant short to medium term difficulties for subsidiaries of multinationals in the countries concerned.

Most of the government policies discussed above tend to reduce domestic economic growth and increase unemployment, and are detrimental to a multinational company operating in the country concerned. For example, the impact of higher interest rates usually results in higher borrowing costs for a multinational company.

A possible beneficial effect is when the multinational exports a high proportion of its products, and the incremental demand stimulated by the devaluation/fall in value of the local currency results in an overall increase in the present value of cash flows to the multinational.

ACCA marking scheme	
	Marks
Measures to reduce the deficit: for very high marks most of the alternatives must be discussed	5
Role of the IMF. Impact of government actions and of the IMF on multinationals	10
Total	15

85 FOREIGN TRADE RISKS

The management of risk associated with foreign trade will depend upon the nature of the risk:

Commercial risk is risk that the client will not pay or will only pay after the due date. It may be managed by:

(i)   Credit screening prior to the contract being signed. This might include formal credit evaluation through a credit agency, use of information from trade associations, government databases (e.g. the DTI in the UK), bank references or trade references.

(ii)   The terms of sale. Some terms of sale involve much less risk than others. Most secure (but not common) is cash in advance. Others, in order of increasing risk include cash on delivery, documentary letters of credit, bills of exchange and open account.

(iii)   The method of payment. The quicker and more secure the method of payment, the lower the risk. Extremes range from secure electronic funds transfer to sending a cheque in the post.

(iv)   Insurance against non-payment or late payment. In many countries this is offered through government agencies. In the UK short-term insurance providers include NCM and Trade Indemnity.

Physical risk, the risk of damage or theft in transit is best managed through insurance cover.

Political risk is risk of non-payment or late payment as a result of the actions of a foreign government, e.g. through the introduction of exchange controls, tariffs or quotas. Political risk protection is often offered by the same insurers as commercial risk. Political risk might also be avoided by using different forms of international activity, e.g. tariffs and quotas might be avoided by direct investment in the country concerned, exchange controls might be avoided by engaging in countertrade rather than cash trade.

Cultural risk is risk associated with different cultures, ways of doing business, attitude to religion, colours, gender, food and drink etc. In order to reduce such risk thorough research of the local market, culture, and business practices should be undertaken prior to trading.

ACCA marking scheme	
	Marks
Identification of risks	2
Management of risks	8
For very high marks all of the main forms of risk must be discussed. The majority of marks should relate to the management of commercial and political risk.	
Total	10

86   POLITICAL RISK

(a)   The consultant's report should not be used as the only basis for the African investment decision, for the following reasons.

    (i)   The decision should be taken after evaluating the risk/return trade-off; financial factors (e.g. the expected NPV from the investments); strategic factors; and other issues including political risk. Political risk is only one part of the decision process (although in extremely risky countries it might be the most important one).

    (ii)   The scores for the three countries are, giving double weighting to economic growth and political stability:

Country 1	29
Country 2	24
Country 3	28

Just because previous clients have not invested in countries with scores of less than 30 does not mean that Beela should not. The previous countries may not have been comparable with these in Africa. This decision rule also ignores return. If return is expected to be very high, a relatively low score might be acceptable to Beela.

    (iii)   The factors considered by the consultant might not be the only relevant factors when assessing political risk. Others could include the extent of capital flight from the country, the legal infrastructure, availability of local finance and the existence of special taxes and regulations for multinational companies.

    (iv)   The weightings of the factors might not be relevant to Beela.

    (v)   Scores such as these only focus on the macro risk of the country. The micro risk, the risk for the actual company investing in a country, is the vital factor. This differs between companies and between industries. A relatively hi-tech electronics company might be less susceptible to political actions than, for example, companies in extractive industries where the diminishing bargain concept may apply.

    (vi)   There is no evidence of how the scores have been devised and how valid they are.

(b)   Prior to investing Beela might negotiate an agreement with the local government covering areas of possible contention such as dividend remittance, transfer pricing, taxation, the use of local labour and capital, and exchange controls. The problem with such negotiations is that governments might change, and a new government might not honour the agreement.

The logistics of the investment may also influence political risk:

    (i)   If a key element of the process is left outside the country it may not be viable for the government to take actions against a company as it could not produce a complete product. This particularly applies when intellectual property or know-how is kept back.

    (ii)   Financing locally might deter political action, as effectively the action will hurt the local providers of finance.

    (iii)   Local sourcing of components and raw materials might reduce risk.

    (iv)   It is sometimes argued that participating in joint ventures with a local partner reduces political risk, although evidence of this is not conclusive.

(v)   Control of patents and processes by the multinational might reduce risk, although patents are not recognised in all countries.

Governments or commercial agencies in multinationals' home countries often offer insurance against political risk.

ACCA marking scheme		
		Marks
(a)	Conclusion that the report should not be used	1
	1 – 2 marks for each relevant point. For 2 marks, look especially for financial/strategic factors, macro versus micro risk and mention of other possible relevant influences on political risk	7
(b)	1 mark for each good point. 2 if very well explained	7
Total		15

87   GLITOR PLC

Tutorial note: The question goes against standard practice in the foreign exchange markets for quoting exchange rates. In the foreign exchange markets, the 'base' currency is stated first and the 'variable' currency second. So the USD/EUR exchange rate is the number of euros for one US dollar. The question in fact means the opposite, so that the $/Euro rate is meant to be the number of dollars for one euro. Similarly, the £/Euro rate is the number of pounds sterling for one euro. The examiner's intention is perhaps obvious when you look at the Yen/$ rate, which is clearly the number of yen for one US dollar. Even so, the tendency for examination questions to go against market practice is confusing and difficult to understand.

Solution

Report

To: Managing director

From: Accountant

Date: xx/xx/xx

Subject: **Banks' forecasts of exchange rates.**

The three banks have produced widely differing forecasts, which even involve forecasts of exchange rates moving in opposite directions from the current spot rate.

The banks' forecasts are likely to differ for the following reasons:

(i)   Different models may be used by the banks to produce their forecasts. For example, models may be based on either technical analysis or fundamental analysis. Technical analysis involves the use of charts of past price movements to try to establish future trends. Fundamental analysis normally involves economic/econometric modelling based on past and current economic and financial information.

(ii)   Different assumptions about the economic and other variables that influence future exchange rates. For example, the banks could easily have different views on the future level of interest rates, inflation, economic growth, government spending, unemployment, taxation, balance of payments, international capital movements or other key economic indicators.

There is nothing unusual about banks producing different forecasts of exchange rates.

The financial information would suggest the following expected one-year spot exchange rates should be based on either Purchasing Power Parity or the International Fisher Effect.

	Purchasing Power Parity	*International Fisher Effect*
$/€	0.8800	0.8721
£/€	0.6140	0.6234
Yen/$	120.15	121.08
$/£	1.4339	1.3997

Even these traditional economic explanations of exchange rates give conflicting evidence, suggesting that the markets are in disequilibrium. For example, the inflation rate in the UK is lower than in the USA, suggesting that the £ will strengthen relative to the $. However, interest rates in the UK are higher than in the USA, suggesting that the £ will weaken relative to the $. The forecasts of the banks are significantly different from the above forecasts, suggesting that the banks have used other models to predict future exchange rates.

If foreign exchange markets are efficient, future foreign exchange rates will result from new relevant information reaching the market. At the present time this information is unknown. Who can forecast a natural disaster, such as a flood, drought, or earthquake, or even when a change in government will occur? Future economic information is also not known. When announced, economic information frequently differs from market expectations, and will result in changes in exchange rates.

The type of exchange rate system that exists will influence the ability to forecast future exchange rates. Freely-floating exchange rates are the most difficult to forecast as they directly respond to economic events and relevant new information. If governments intervene in the currency markets in a managed float, unless the intervention rules are known then accurate forecasts are impossible. Even if the rules are known the size of the currency markets make it difficult for governments to protect currency values against speculative attacks. At the other extreme fixed exchange rates, where one currency is pegged to another (often the US dollar) should, in theory, be easier to forecast. Unfortunately fixed exchange rates do not remain fixed forever; devaluation or revaluation is likely eventually, as inflation and interest rates between the two countries diverge. With fixed exchange rates the direction of a possible change in rates is quite easy to predict, but not the exact time a devaluation or revaluation would take place, or the magnitude of any change in values.

Accurate forecasts of future exchange rates are very difficult, if not impossible. Key economic variables, political developments etc. will provide information at the present time on the likely direction and magnitude of movement in exchange rates. However, events change quickly and current expectations may be reversed by unpredictable future events.

Workings

PPP theory

Predicted $/€ rate in one year = $0.8800 \times (1.03/1.03) = 0.8800$.

Predicted £/€ rate in one year = $0.6200 \times (1.02/1.03) = 0.6140$.

Predicted Yen/$ rate in one year = $125 \times (0.99/1.03) = 120.15$.

Predicted $/£ rate in one year = $1.42 \times (1.03/1.02) = 1.4339$.

(The currency with the lower inflation rate has a stronger value in the future.)

International Fisher Effect

Predicted $/€ rate in one year = $0.8800 \times (1.0325/1.0418) = 0.8721$.

Predicted £/€ rate in one year = $0.6200 \times (1.0475/1.0418) = 0.6234$.

Predicted Yen/$ rate in one year = $125 \times (1.0001/1.0325) = 121.08$.

Predicted $/£ rate in one year = $1.42 \times (1.0325/1.0475) = 1.3997$.

(The currency with the lower interest rate has a stronger value in the future.)

ACCA marking scheme	
	Marks
Explanation of why banks' forecasts differ	3-4
Relevant calculations and comment	4-5
Discussion of exchange rate forecasts. Look for market efficiency, different exchange rate systems etc	6-7
Total	15

88 DEBOIS SA

(a) The overall tax liability of Debois SA could, in theory, be reduced by minimising tax liability in Norway, a higher-taxed country.

The current position is:

		UK €000	Norway €000	Total €000
Sales		18,000	43,750	61,750
Expenses	(UK 80% of 1,800)	14,400	35,000	49,400
Profit before tax	(Norway 12,500 × €70)	3,600	8,750	12,350
Local corporate tax	(25% UK, 40% Norway)	900	3,500	4,400
Profit after corporate tax = dividend		2,700	5,250	7,950
Withholding tax	(0% UK, 8% Norway)	–	420	420
French taxation:				
Taxable profit		3,600	8,750	
Tax at French tax rate	(33.3%)	1,199	2,914	
Tax credit		900	2,914	
Tax paid in France		299	–	

Total tax paid	£000	£000
In Norway		
Corporate tax	3,500	
Withholding tax	420	
		3,920
In the UK		900
In France		299
Total		5,119

If the transfer price between the UK and German subsidiaries is increased by 20%:

		UK €000	Norway €000	Total €000
Sales	(18,000 × 1.20 in UK)	21,600	43,750	65,350
Expenses	(Norway: + 20% of 18,000)	14,400	38,600	53,000
Profit before tax		7,200	5,150	12,350
Local corporate tax	(25% UK, 40% Norway)	1,800	2,060	3,860
Profit after corporate tax = dividend		5,400	3,090	8,490
Withholding tax	(0% UK, 8% Norway)	-	247	247

French taxation:

Taxable profit		7,200	5,150
Tax at French tax rate	(33.3%)	2,398	1,715
Tax credit		1,800	1,715
Tax paid in France		598	–

Total tax paid	£000	£000
In Norway		
Corporate tax	2,060	
Withholding tax	247	
		2,307
In the UK		1,800
In France		598
Total		4,705

The total tax payable by Debois SA is reduced by €414,000.

(b)   Although taxation can theoretically be reduced in this way, most governments seek to prevent multinational companies from manipulating transfer prices to reduce taxation. Multinationals are often assessed for tax purposes on the arm's length price of the goods being sold rather than an artificial transfer price. Where no market based arm's length price exists there may still be some scope for tax reduction by manipulating transfer prices.

The impact of altering transfer prices on other aspects of a company's operations must also be considered, including:

(i)   The effect on motivation and the performance evaluation of managers in the foreign subsidiaries, especially if subsidiaries are regarded as profit centres.

(ii)   The international location of funds within the group will be altered by transfer pricing.

(iii)   The change in the reported profit of foreign subsidiaries could alter the credit rating and cost of finance of those subsidiaries in the foreign money and capital markets where they are located.

89   COUNTRIES

(a)   Country political risk scores are widely used as part of the international investment decision process. However, the table provided is only one possible political risk measure. It contains only a limited number of factors that might influence political risk, and does not include factors such as currency convertibility, social conditions, the legal and financial infrastructure, transfer pricing and taxation all of which may significantly affect risk. Using different factors might result in different country rankings. There is no information about how the weightings for the factors were decided. These weightings are likely to be to some extent subjective, and different weightings might lead to different country rankings.

Other techniques have been suggested to measure political risk such as 'grand tours', seeking the opinions of academics, journalists or diplomats who are experts on the countries, measures based upon socio-economic, social conflict, and governmental process characteristics, or the gap between aspirations and expectations in a country. Each of these techniques might assist in the risk measurement process, and add to the information provided by the country scores.

(b)   Political risk scores focus upon the macro environment of a country; they do not directly measure the potential political risk facing an individual industry or company.

This micro focus is important. Some industries are much more prone to political risk than others, for example, extractive industries and financial services. High technology industries which require highly skilled labour and heavy investment in R&D tend to be less at risk. A country may appear risky according to its score, but a company investing in certain industries in that country may face relatively little risk.

On the basis of the scores provided Forland looks to be easily the best investment, but it scores badly on economic performance, which might adversely affect the future potential of the subsidiary. Settia, for example, might have far better prospects.

More importantly, decisions about foreign direct investment should not be made with reference only to political risk. The expected cash flows from the investment are fundamental to the investment decision, as is the strategic fit of the potential investment with the company's existing and planned operations.

90   GROWTH OF MULTINATIONALS

Multinational companies are normally able to take more advantage of imperfections in product markets, factor markets or financial markets than companies that only operate in a domestic market. Taking advantage of market imperfections gives a competitive advantage and facilitates the organic growth of multinationals. By virtue of their size they are also well placed to grow through acquisition, often in the form of vertical or horizontal integration.

Many market imperfections result from government actions, for example through tariffs, quotas, exchange controls, and investment incentives. Multinationals often avoid government imposed barriers through foreign direct investment, and may take advantage of favourable tax and other incentives.

Multinationals may benefit from locating production in different countries in order to take full advantage of economies of scale and scope, low labour costs, and control of raw material supplies. Economies of scale and scope may be in production (operating at an optimum unit size, and specialising production in those countries where comparative advantages are greatest), purchasing (quantity discounts and use of market power), marketing (utilising an internationally known brand image, and an efficient international marketing structure), research and development (superior technology and/or differentiated products) or financing (access to international financial markets with the potential to raise finance at relatively low cost, and to earn higher yields on financial investments). Multinationals also often have the ability to reduce their global tax payments by locating activities in tax efficient countries, reducing taxable income or shifting tax liability from one country to another through devices such as transfer pricing, royalty fees and management fees, and eliminating or deferring taxation through the use of tax havens.

In many countries multinationals may be in an oligopolistic or even monopolistic situation, which may be exploited to generate abnormally good profitability and growth.

Internalisation of comparative advantages

Competitive advantage can be maintained by possession of unique information and skills which employees can use to create further advantage through research and development, marketing and other commercial skills. The multinational company is motivated to create an internal market for this information and to keep possession of their unique advantage specific to the firm.

Taking advantage of market imperfections is important, but a prerequisite for a successful multinational is high quality management, and the ability to survive against other multinationals in a competitive world.

91 TRANSFER PRICING STRATEGIES

Tutorial note: This question, set in the December 2002 examination, is very challenging for the number of marks available. Work through the solution carefully, to make sure that you understand the issued that are being examined.

(a) The objectives of transfer pricing include:

(i) The reduction of overall corporate income taxes, primarily by manipulating the transfer price to divert taxable income from high tax countries to low tax countries.

(ii) The minimisation of import duties. A low transfer price into a country with import duties will reduce the level of duty paid.

(iii) The avoidance of exchange controls or other restrictions such as dividend remittance restrictions. A low transfer price to the parent company might be attempted as an alternative to a dividend payment.

(iv) To improve the appearance of the financial performance of a subsidiary. If profits are increased through transfer pricing this might help satisfy any earnings criteria set by lenders to the subsidiary, or make the acquisition of a new loan easier.

(b) (i) **Transfer price at fixed plus variable cost:**

The fixed cost/unit in Umgaba is $1.8 million/400,000 units = $4.50.

Fixed plus variable cost = $4.50 + $16 = $20.50.

In the table below, the columns for Mazila and Bethuna show figures calculated on the assumption that all 400,000 units are assembled and sold in that particular country.

	Umgaba $000	Mazila $000	Bettuna $000
Sales ($20.50, $40, $37)	8,200	16,000	14,800
Variable costs	6,400	3,600	3,000
Fixed costs	1,800	700	900
Transfer price 'expense'	-	8,200	8,200
Import duty (10%)	-	820	-
	8,200	13,320	12,100
Taxable profit	0	2,680	2,700
Tax (25%, 32%)	0	(670)	(864)
Income after tax	0	2,010	1,836
Remitted to UK (60%)	0	1,206	1,102
Retained locally	0	804	734

Transfer price cost plus 30%

The transfer price from Umgaba is $20.50 plus 30% = $26.65/unit.

	Umgaba $000	Mazila $000	Bettuna $000
Sales ($26.65, $40, $37)	10,660	16,000	14,800
Variable cost	6,400	3,600	3,000
Fixed cost	1,800	700	900
Transfer price 'expense'	-	10,660	10,660
Import duty (10%)	-	1,066	-
	8,200	16,026	14,560

Taxable profit	2,460	(26)	240
Tax (40%, -, 32%)	(984)	0	(77)
Income after tax	1,476	(26)	163
For remittance (60%)	886	0	98
Withholding tax (15% in Umgaba)	(133)	0	-
Remitted	753	0	98
Retained profit	590	(26)	65

Summary of net position

	Retained (after local tax) $	Remitted (net) $	UK tax (see note) $	Overall position $
Fixed plus variable cost				
Umgaba plus Mazila				
Umgaba	0	0	-	0
Mazila	804,000	1,206,000	(134,000)	1,876,000
				1,876,000
Umgaba plus Bettuna				
Umgaba	0	0	-	0
Bettuna	734,000	1,102,000	-	1,836,000
				1,836,000
Cost plus 30%				
Umgaba plus Mazila				
Umgaba	590,000	753,000	-	1,343,000
Mazila	(26,000)	0	-	(26,000)
				1,317,200
Umgaba plus Bettuna				
Umgaba	590,000	753,000	-	1,343,000
Bettuna	65,000	98,000	-	163,000
				1,506,000

Note:

UK tax. As full credit is given by the UK tax authorities for tax paid overseas, UK tax liability will only exist for countries where the tax rate is lower than in the UK, in this case Mazila. For the fixed plus variable cost alternative, effectively tax at 5% of the taxable income (30% – 25%) will be payable in the UK. This amounts to 5% of $2,680,000 = $134,000.

This is the only situation where tax would be payable in the UK.

Conclusion

The maximum possible cash flow is from using the fixed plus variable cost transfer price, with assembly of the product in Mazila. This is $40,000 better than assembling in Bettuna (with the same transfer price).

The use of the fixed plus variable cost transfer price is more beneficial because no taxes are payable in the highest tax country, Umgaba.

(ii) The choice between Mazila and Bettuna is indicated in the answer to (i) above. However, it is useful to look at the total tax payable by the group in each case. Mazila has the lowest corporate tax rate, but also levies an import duty, meaning that the total tax paid if assembly takes place in Mazila is more than it would have been in Bettuna. (However, this is offset by the larger gross profit in Mazila, resulting from the higher sales price in that market.)

Tax paid in the four countries	Tax ($)			
	Umgaba	*Mazila*	*Bettuna*	*UK*
	$	$	$	$
Fixed plus variable cost				
Umgaba plus Mazila	0	1,285,000[1]	-	134,000
Umgaba plus Bettuna	0	-	864,000	0
Cost plus 30%				
Umgaba plus Mazila	1,117,000[2]	799,500[3]	-	0
Umgaba plus Bettuna	1,117,000		77,000	0

[1] After tax relief on the import duty. Total tax therefore (75% of 820,000) + 670,000 = $1,285,000.

[2] $984,000 plus withholding tax of $133,000 = $1,117,000.

[3] After tax relief on the import duty. Total tax therefore (75% of 1,066,000) + 0 = $799,500.

(c)   If the transfer price is at fixed plus variable cost, and assembly takes place in Mazila, the likely attitudes of the governments are:

Umgaba: The government of Umgaba would not receive any tax, and would probably try to ensure that any transfer price included an element of profit.

Mazila: Tax is maximised for Mazila, as well as jobs provided by the assembly. The government is likely to regard this favourably.

Bettuna: No tax is received or jobs created as assembly would take place in Mazila. Unless the government offers incentives to attract the assembly there is little it can do.

UK: This is the only situation in which the UK government would receive any tax on the income.

ACCA marking scheme		
		Marks
(a)	One mark for each relevant objective	4
(b)	Fixed plus variable cost data for each country	2-3
	Plus 30% data for each country	2-3
	Overall cash flows and conclusion about transfer price and assembly	2-3
(c)	Tax calculations and attitude of governments	
	Reward technique, especially with respect to taxation	3
Total		15

92   HGT

Key answer tips

What appears to be an amazingly complex question for 10 marks is nothing much more than a relevant cost exercise. That said, the numbers take time and it would be sensible, if short of time, to cover the discussion points with assumed numbers if necessary.

Under the current scheme:

		Glinland £000	Rytora £000
Sales	(150,000 units)	<u>1,575</u>	<u>4,500</u>
Variable costs		900	1,350
Costs from Glinland		-	1,575
Fixed costs		<u>140</u>	<u>166</u>
Profit before tax		535	1,409
Local corporate tax	(40% Glinland, 25% Rytora)	<u>214</u>	<u>352</u>
Profit after corporate tax		321	1,057
Withholding tax	(Glinland: 10% of 50% of 321)	16	-
Import tariff	(10% of 1,575)	-	157
Retained	(Glinland: 50% of 321)	161	-
Remitted	(Glinland: 321 – 161 – 16)	144	900
UK taxation:			
Taxable profit		<u>535</u>	<u>1,409</u>
Tax at UK tax rate	(30%)	160	423
Tax credit	(Rytors: limited to Rytora tax)	<u>160</u>	<u>352</u>
Tax paid in the UK		<u>0</u>	<u>71</u>

Total tax paid	£000	£000
In Glinland		
Corporate tax	214	
Withholding tax	<u>16</u>	
		230
In Rytora		
Corporate tax	352	
Import taxes	<u>157</u>	
		509
In the UK		<u>71</u>
Total		<u>810</u>

If goods are sold at cost by the Glinland subsidiary (i.e. at variable cost of 900 + fixed costs of 140 = 1,040):

		Glinland £000	Rytora £000
Sales		<u>1,040</u>	<u>4,500</u>
Variable costs		900	1,350
Costs from Glinland		-	1,040
Fixed costs		<u>140</u>	<u>166</u>
Profit before tax		0	1,944
Local corporate tax	(25% Rytora)	-	<u>486</u>
Profit after corporate tax		-	1,458

		Glinland	Rytora
Withholding tax		-	-
Import tariff	(10% of 1,040)	-	104
Retained		-	-
Remitted	(1,458 – 104)	-	1,354
UK taxation:			
Taxable profit		-	1,944
Tax at UK tax rate	(30%)	-	583
Tax credit	(limited to Rytora tax)	-	486
Tax paid in the UK		0	97

Total tax paid	£000	£000
In Glinland		0
In Rytora		
Corporate tax	486	
Import taxes	104	
		590
In the UK		97
Total		687

The proposed change would result in an overall saving of £123,000 per year.

The proposal might not be acceptable to:

(i) The tax authorities in Glinland, where £230,000 in taxation would be lost. The tax authorities might insist on an arms length price for transfers between Glinland and Rytora.

(ii) The subsidiary in Glinland, which would no longer make a profit, or have retentions available for future investment in Glinland. Depending upon how performance in Glinland was evaluated, this might adversely affect rewards and motivation in Glinland.

93   LDC DEBT

Key answer tips

Straightforward marks are available if you have covered this topic. Never be tempted to select questions like this if you are not sure of the subject. The examiner is skilled at detecting 'waffle' and you would be better off attempting a more 'demanding' question on a topic you have revised.

(a) The LDC debt problem has existed for at least 20 years, although the countries experiencing the most difficulties have varied. Measures to alleviate the debt problem focus upon both internal measures by the countries themselves, and external measures or support provided by the international community and/or international organisations such as the IMF and World Bank Internal and external measures are frequently interrelated; for example the IMF will often impose stringent economic conditions on countries to which it provides assistance.

Methods used to reduce the debt problem include:

(i) Debt rescheduling. This involves relaxing the conditions for repayment of the debt, typically by lengthening the period over which the debt is to be repaid in order to reduce the annual interest burden. Debt rescheduling is normally accompanied by externally imposed economic conditions such as tight monetary control, reduction in government deficits, and devaluation of the country's currency.

(ii)   Debt moratorium. This is the suspension for an agreed period of time of contractual debt service payments. The hope is that the country's economy will improve to allow the successful servicing of debt after the moratorium period.

(iii) Debt forgiveness. The outright cancelling of and writing off of debt by lenders such as major banks.

(iv)   Sale of debt on the secondary markets, at a discount to its face value. Such debt may be bought and redeemed by the government that issued it subject to sufficient foreign currency being available, or bought by a third party. In the latter case there might be a debt fur equity swap, whereby the debt is swapped for equity in local companies, allowing the debt to be extinguished. Other alternatives include debt for nature swaps where the country agrees to engage in environmental protection projects in exchange for debt forgiveness, or debt for education swaps where the government agrees to invest in significant education development programs.

(v)   The Baker Plan and the Brady Plan. The Baker Plan of 1985 focused on assistance by banks to the 15 most indebted countries. However, many banks were unwilling to extend further loans to highly indebted countries. The Brady Plan focused on countries engaging in significant economic reforms to alleviate underlying problems in exchange for debt forgiveness. Part of this debt forgiveness was funded from official sources such as the IMF, World Bank and individual governments.

(vi)   Encourage and aid high debt countries to invest in people and education, deregulate controls on market entry and prices, invest in infrastructure, reduce tariffs and other restrictions on trade. All of these measures are aimed at helping the country to enhance its development and growth, and to be in a position to more easily service its debt.

(b)   The LDC debt crisis has lead to a number of difficulties for multinational companies wishing to operate in high debt countries. Investment risks tend to be higher as such countries have lower international credit ratings. Political risks are often greater; as countries may experience more frequent changes in government or governments are forced to impose stringent monetary and fiscal controls. High debt countries often have relatively high rates of inflation and are prone to devaluation of their currency leading to higher costs and possible loss of export income for the multinational. Restrictions on the movement of funds are often imposed through exchange controls and dividend remittance restrictions.

However, there may also be benefits for multinationals as high debt countries will seek to attract multinationals and their capital, employment creation potential, technology and skills.

Very attractive incentives may be offered to multinationals including subsidies, tax concessions, and the ability to establish operations with little formality or 'red tape'.

94   GLOBAL DEBT PROBLEM

(a)   The 'global debt problem' has existed for some countries for nearly thirty years. It developed partly as a result of a massive increase in petrol and other commodity prices during the 1970s and 1980s. This together with widespread economic recession, reductions in the imports of many advanced countries from developing countries, and relatively high levels of international interest rates, meant that many countries were forced to borrow internationally in order to meet their import requirements of essential goods such as fuel and foodstuffs. Such countries often experienced large current account deficits, and could not get access to the necessary hard currency to pay for imports other than by borrowing. Many also suffered from capital flight, with funds leaving the country to find what was perceived to be a safer international home. Major international banks were very willing to lend to sovereign nations, as historically country default risk had been low. Arguably banks' risk assessment took too optimistic a view and vast amounts of sovereign loans were agreed, with countries such as Mexico and Brazil borrowing in excess of 100 billion dollars. Debt servicing payments in some countries exceeded 50% of total export earnings, and domestic savings were insufficient to provide the necessary funds to repay international debts. Continuing current account deficits made the situation even worse in many countries. Many countries had insufficient hard currency to meet the debt servicing conditions of their loans.

Financial contagion refers to the spread of economic and financial problems from one country to another. As barriers to trade, investment and capital flows are reduced or eliminated the resultant more 'global' economy is more susceptible to contagion. As can be seen from the problems of the Thai baht in 1997, the problems of even a relatively small economy can easily have severe economic impacts on neighbouring countries and even upon larger countries such as Brazil and Russia. Financial contagion potentially worsens the impact of the international debt problem. If financial problems in one country directly lead to similar problems in several others it accentuates the debt servicing difficulties.

(b)   Attempts to resolve the international debt problem have included:

   (i)   Lending additional funds to the countries, sometimes to meet current interest payments and prevent default. Most lending has been accompanied by suggested or imposed economic reforms to try and address the fundamental causes of the problem. Such reforms are often based upon stringent conditions set by the IMF.

   (ii)   Rescheduling the repayment of debt to extend the repayment period and reduce current cash outflows.

   (iii)   Writing off some or all of the debt. Where lenders are institutions such as international banks this naturally requires their agreement, and has substantial cost for them.

   (iv)   Sale of debt for less than face value.

   (v)   Swapping debt into some other form of commitment. This includes swaps from debt into the equity of local companies, or even promises to reduce pollution, provided enhanced education etc.

Financial problems are most often experienced in those countries that have fixed exchange rates and an overvalued currency; suffer from large short-term capital outflows; or have overheated parts of the economy (especially the property sector). Fixed exchange rate systems are also much more likely to be the subject of speculative attacks. Financial crises are also associated with weak economic fundamentals such as high unemployment, low growth in GDP, high short-term debt to currency reserves, balance of payments deficits and high real interest rates.

Governments might reduce the risk of financial problems and the potential associated contagion by altering the exchange rate system and trying to address these economic issues. For example, the government might adopt a floating rate regime (although this will impact upon other aspects of the economy), or possibly a currency board system. Governments should closely monitor important sectors of the economy to assess the risks within those sectors, and consider the use of taxation, monetary policy and/or exchange controls to prevent a crisis occurring.

ACCA marking scheme		
		Marks
(a)	Reasons for the global debt problem	4–5
	Financial contagion and its links to global debt	3
		———
		7
(b)	Attempts to resolve the debt problem	4–5
	How financial contagion might be limited	3–4
		———
		8
Total		15

95 EXCHANGE RATE SYSTEMS

Key answer tips

This question is standard bookwork. It is vital that you discuss the implications of each system to multinationals.

Managed floating exchange rate

A managed floating exchange rate will be mainly influenced by the market supply and demand for a currency, but is also subject to intervention by the relevant government. The government will buy or sell the currency in order to influence the exchange rate, often to keep it within a desired range against the dollar or other key currency. The government will not normally reveal how or when it will intervene in the foreign exchange market, and floating exchange rates such as this are difficult to forecast as they directly respond to economic events, relevant new information and to government intervention. This could lead to volatility in foreign exchange rates, which might be a deterrent to foreign trade.

In theory, managed exchange rates should gradually adjust to changing economic relationships between nations. For example, as a country moves into a balance of trade deficit, this would normally lead to a fall in the value of the country's currency, which in turn will make the country's exports more attractive, and will reduce the trade deficit. Floating exchange rates should prevent persistent deficits, and result in fewer large speculative international movements of funds. From a multinational company's perspective the difficulty in forecasting such rates makes accurate cash budgeting for international activities more onerous, increases currency risk, and in many cases makes some form of currency hedging essential.

Fixed exchange rate linked to a basket of currencies

An economy that fixes its exchange rate against the dollar or other major currency will inevitably be affected by the state of the economy and the policies of the country to which it has linked. For example, if inflation or the money supply increases in the USA, similar effects may be experienced in countries which have their currencies tied to the dollar.

An exchange rate linked to a basket of currencies is less susceptible to economic influences from a single country, although if the basket is weighted by international trade, a dominant trade partner might still have a major influence. In theory, fixed exchange rates offer greater stability, and future rates should be easier to forecast, which reduces risk and aids international pricing and cash budgeting. However, fixed exchange rates do not remain fixed forever; devaluation or revaluation may occur if inflation, interest rates and other economic variables diverge between the relevant countries. The direction of a possible change in rates is quite easy to predict, but not the exact timing of devaluation or revaluation, or the magnitude of any change in currency values. Fixed rates are also more susceptible to currency speculation.

Fixed exchange rates backed by a currency board system

This type of exchange rate regime shares many characteristics of other fixed exchange rate systems, but the currency board means that any domestic currency issues are backed by an equal amount of some 'hard' currency, such as the dollar. In theory the domestic currency could be converted at any time into the hard currency at a fixed exchange rate. This backing by a 'hard' currency is aimed at achieving greater economic stability, and less exchange rate volatility. A currency board system might result in a fall in the domestic money supply, high interest rates, and thus high 'local' financing costs for multinational companies. For some countries, such as Hong Kong, a currency board has proved successful. For others, such as Argentina, it has failed. A multinational company will normally experience lower inflation and more stable economic conditions when a currency board exists.

ACCA marking scheme		
		Marks
(a)	Managed floating exchange rate	5–6
(b)	Fixed exchange rate linked to a basket of currencies	5–6
(c)	Fixed exchange rate backed by a currency board system	4–5
	Maximum	15

96 BOSTER PLC

Key answer tips

Part (a) involves portfolio calculations and is straightforward as long as you treat "political" risk in the same way you would treat 'risk' normally.

Part (b) looks at how useful the results of part (a) are. You need to focus here on the extent to which the full political risk faced by the firm has been reflected in the calculations specified in the question.

Part (c) asks for other ways of measuring political risk and should be bookwork.

(a) Portfolio theory for a two asset portfolio may be used to estimate the risk and return combinations.

Portfolio return

Expected return Ammobia/Flassia (0.5) (21) + (0.5) (18) = 19.5%

Expected return Ammobia/Hracland (0.5) (21) + (0.5) (28) = 24.5%

Expected return Flassia/Hracland (0.5) (18) + (0.5) (28) = 23%

Portfolio risk:

As the investments are expected to be independent the final term of the two asset portfolio equation will be zero.

Ammobia/Flassia

$[(33)^2 (.5)^2 + (29)^2 (.5)2]^{/2}$ $\sigma_p = 21.96$

Ammobia/Hracland

$[(33)^2 (.5)^2 + (42)^2 (.5)2]^{1/2}$ $\sigma_p = 26.71$

Flassia/Hracland

$[(29)^2 (.5)^2 + (42)^2 (.5)2]^{1/2}$ $\sigma_p = 25.52$

The coefficient of variation shows the amount of risk per pound of expected return

Ammobia/Flassia

$$\frac{21.96}{19.50} = 1.13$$

Ammobia/Hracland

$$\frac{26.71}{24.50} = 1.09$$

Flassia/Hracland

$$\frac{25.52}{23.00} = 1.11$$

(b)   The Ammobia/Hracland combination has the lowest coefficient of variation, and hence the lower risk relative to expected return. However, there is little to choose between the alternatives.

This information is of relatively little use to Boster plc and may be criticised for a number of reasons:

(i)   The analysis only considers a sub-set of Boster's overseas investments. Portfolio theory should examine the risk/return relationships of all the company's investments.

(ii)   Historic evidence of political instability and other political risk factors does not necessarily mean these will be repeated in the future.

(iii)   The measures of political risk ignore many important variables such as economic growth, unemployment, GDP, legal and financial infrastructure, debt servicing capacity, capital flight, government type (democracy, autocracy etc.), and global risks such as terrorism and cyber attacks.

(iv)   The political risk variables attempt to measure risk at the macro level. The actual risk faced by a company at the micro level may be quite different, and depend upon the commercial sector in which the company operates.

(v)   Overseas investment decisions should not be made on the basis of political risk alone. This might be an important part of the decision process, but other issues such as financial and strategic implications must also be considered.

(c)   Political risk assessment is often two stage. First a macro analysis of the country's risks, then a micro analysis focusing upon the risks of the specific company, trying to identify where conflicts might occur between the company and host government.

Macro analysis will often involve the use of political risk measures, such as those produced by Euromoney, BERI (Business Environmental Risk Intelligence), and The Economist Intelligence Unit.

Micro analysis might involve:

(i)   Using the expertise of companies, journalists, diplomats and others who have first hand experience of the country.

(ii)   Undertaking detailed fact finding visits to the countries.

(iii)   Commissioning quantitative or qualitative consultancy reports on political risk specific to the company and its activities.

ACCA marking sheme			
			Marks
(a)	Return		1
	Risk		3
	Coefficient of variation		2
			—
			6
(b)	Look for critical analysis. 1–2 marks for each good point. Look especially for strategy and finance Maximum		5
(c)	Look for mix of micro and micro. Main focus should be on micro risk		4
			—
	Total		15

97 WORLD TRADE ORGANISATION

Key answer tips

A detailed question on protectionism and the role of the WTO, highlighting the need for students to learn the 'bookwork' aspects of the syllabus.

(a) Historically, the most important protectionist measures were tariffs, a levy or effectively a tax on imports, and quotas, which restricted either the volume or value of imports. In most recent years import barriers have tended to become more subtle, largely in response to the actions of GATT (General Agreement on Tariffs and Trade) and the WTO, which sought to promote free trade. Such barriers include explicit or 'hidden' subsidies favouring local companies, and regulations/red tape that made access to markets by importers difficult. These might include onerous environmental or health regulations, very lengthy bureaucratic process before permission to import is given, and very slow customs procedures which delay the entry of goods into a market. All of these measures are intended to deter overseas companies from exporting to the country.

(b) The World Trade Organisation (WTO) in 1995 succeeded GATT (General Agreement on Tariffs and Trade) as the major world forum for international negotiations and agreement in trade. It now encompasses almost 150 countries, which represent the vast majority of world trade. In contrast to GATT, which focused on the trade in goods, the WTO also covers trade in services including banks, insurance companies, telecommunications and hotels, intellectual property and agriculture.

The WTO's overriding objectives are to promote freer trade and thereby to help trade flow smoothly, and to reduce or eliminate protectionist barriers. It administers trade agreements, acts as a forum for negotiations and settles trade disputes. Its activities involve:

(i) Extending trade concessions equally to all members of the WTO.

(ii) Encouraging lower tariffs and fairer trade around the world, including anti-dumping measures and subsidies.

(iii) Introducing rules that make trade more predictable.

(iv) Stimulating competition through cutting subsidies.

(c) A developing country that had recently joined the WTO would be expected to gradually reduce any barriers to trade of its goods and services. However, because it is a developing country it would be permitted a much longer time to undertake such measures. The effect on multinational companies could vary. If the multinational currently takes advantage of protectionist barriers that exist in the country, such barriers would be gradually removed exposing the multinational to more competition. However, freer trade might facilitate the expansion of the multinational's exports into more markets and stimulate demand for its products. In either case the multinational company would normally have a considerable period of time in which to modify its operations in response to the reduction in barriers to trade.

ACCA marking scheme		
		Marks
(a)	Protectionist measures. Max 3 if only tariffs and quotas are discussed	5
(b)	Role of WTO and effect on protectionist measures	6
(c)	Effects on multinational. Look for reasoned discussion. Answers could vary	4
Total		15

Section 3

JUNE 2006 EXAM QUESTIONS

1   VADENER PLC

Vadener plc has instigated a review of the group's recent performance and potential future strategy. The Board of Directors has publicly stated that it is pleased with the group's performance and proposes to devote resources equally to its three operating divisions. Two of the divisions are in the UK, and focus on construction and leisure respectively, and one is in the USA and manufactures pharmaceuticals.

Recent summarised accounts for the group and data for the individual divisions are shown below:

Group data £ million

Profit and loss accounts:	2003	2004	2005
Turnover	1,210	1,410	1,490
Operating costs	800	870	930
Operating profit	410	540	560
Net interest	40	56	65
Profit before tax	370	484	495
Tax (30%)	111	145	149
Profit after tax	259	339	346
Equity dividends	146	170	185
Retained earnings	113	169	161

Balance sheets:			
Fixed assets:			
Tangible fixed assets	1,223	1,280	1,410
Intangible fixed assets	100	250	250
Current assets:			
Stock	340	410	490
Debtors	378	438	510
Cash	10	15	15
Total assets	2,051	2,393	2,675

Less current liabilities:

Creditors	302	401	430
Short term loans	135	170	201
Taxation	55	72	75
Dividends	73	85	93
	1,486	1,665	1,876

Financed by:

Long term liabilities	400	410	470
Shareholders' equity	1,086	1,255	1,406
	1,486	1,665	1,876

Note;

The 2005 amount for shareholders' equity includes a £10 million loss on translation from the US division due to the recent weakness of the $US.

Other group data at year end:	2003	2004	2005
Share price (pence)	1,220	1,417	1,542
Number of issued shares (million)	300	300	300
Equity beta			1.10

The company's share price has increased by an average of 12% per year over the last five years.

Other data at year end:	2003	2004	2005
FT 100 index	3,700	4,600	4,960
PE ratio of similar companies	15:1	14:1	15:1
Risk free rate (%)			5
Market return (%)			12

Divisional data 2005	Construction	Leisure	Pharmaceuticals
Turnover (£m)	480	560	450
Operating profit	160	220	180
Estimated after tax return (%)	13	16	14

Data for the sector:	Construction	Leisure	Pharmaceuticals
Average asset beta 2005	0.75	1.10	1.40

Required:

(a) Evaluate and comment on the performance of Vadener plc and each of its divisions. Highlight performance that appears favourable, and any areas of potential concern for the managers of Vadener. Comment upon the likely validity of the company's strategy to devote resources equally to the operating divisions.

All relevant calculations must be shown. Approximately 19 marks are available for calculations, and 9 for discussion **(28 marks)**

(b) Discuss what additional information would be useful in order to more accurately assess the performance of Vadener plc and its divisions. **(6 marks)**

(c) Discuss the possible implications for Vadener plc of the £10 million loss on translation, and recommend what action, if any, the company should take as a result of this loss. **(6 marks)**

(Total: 40 marks)

2   LAMMER PLC

£

(a)   Lammer plc is a UK based company that regularly trades with companies in the USA. Several large transactions are due in five months' time. These are shown below. The transactions are in '000' units of the currencies shown. *— do not spot in Smtws*

Assume that it is now 1 June and that futures and options contracts mature at the relevant month end. *— December*

Receipt   Payment

	Exports to:	Imports from:
Company 1	$490	£150
Company 2	–	$890
Company 3	£110	$750

Net %

Exchange rates: *$US/£*

Spot	1.9156 – 1.9210
3 months forward	1.9066 – 1.9120
1 year forward	1.8901 – 1.8945

Money market   Forward market

Annual interest rates available to Lammer plc

Deposit   Money Market

	Borrowing	Investing
Sterling up to 6 months	5.5%	4.2%
Dollar up to 6 months	4.0%	2.0%

CME $/£ Currency futures (£62,500)   *— Currency Hedge*

September 1.9045
December 1.8986

CME currency options prices, $/£ options £31,250 (cents per pound)   *— Option Hedge*

	CALLS		PUTS	
	Sept	**Dec**	**Sept**	**Dec**
1.8800	4.76	5.95	1.60	2.96
1.9000	3.53	4.70	2.36	4.34
1.9200	2.28	3.56	3.40	6.55

Required:

Prepare a report for the managers of Lammer plc on how the five-month currency risk should be hedged. Include in your report all relevant calculations relating to the alternative types of hedge.   **(20 marks)**

(15 marks are available for calculations and 5 marks for discussion)

(b)   In a typical financial year Lammer plc has net dollar imports of $4.2 million. This is expected to continue for five years.

The company's cost of capital is estimated to be 11% per year. Taxation may be ignored, and cash flows may be assumed to occur at the year end.

Required:

Assuming that there is no change in the physical volume or dollar price of imports, estimate the effect on the expected market value of Lammer plc if the market expects the dollar to strengthen by 3% per year against the pound.   **(5 marks)**

(c)   Briefly discuss how Lammer plc might manage the economic exposure of any foreign subsidiaries in the USA.   **(5 marks)**

(Total: 30 marks)

SECTION B – TWO QUESTIONS ONLY TO BE ATTEMPTED

3 EWADE PLC

Ewade plc has recently issued £100 million par value of £100 zero coupon convertible debentures 2013 at a price of £71.10 per debenture. The debentures are redeemable at their par value of £100.

Conversion may take place at any time after three years from the issue date. The conversion terms are 12 ordinary shares of Ewade for each debenture. The current redemption yield on Ewade's 8% coupon straight debt with seven years until maturity, and redeemable at the par value of £100, is 6%. The straight debt pays semi-annual interest.

Required:

(a)   Estimate the redemption yield on the zero coupon convertible debentures, and the difference between the market price of the seven year straight debt and the seven year zero coupon convertible debt. Explain the reasons for the different market prices and yields. **(6 marks)**

(b)   Assume that in three years' time the redemption yield of the zero coupon debt is 6% and the price of an ordinary share of Ewade is:

(i)   550 pence

(ii)   710 pence

Required:

For each share price, estimate the minimum price of the zero coupon convertible debentures.
(4 marks)

(c)   If Ewade held a portfolio including bonds with attached warrants and wished to protect the value of the warrants, explain how the knowledge of the delta value and theta value might assist in this. **(5 marks)**

(Total: 15 marks)

4 ARNBROOK PLC

Arnbrook plc is considering a £50 million three year interest rate swap. The company wishes to have use of floating rate funds, but because of its AA credit rating has a comparative advantage over lower rated companies when borrowing in the domestic fixed rate market. Arnbrook can borrow fixed rate at 6.25% or floating rate at LIBOR plus 0.75%.

LIBOR is currently 5.25%, but parliamentary elections are due in six months' time and future interest rates are uncertain. A swap could be arranged using a bank as an intermediary. The bank would offset the swap risk with a counterparty BBB rated company that could borrow fixed rate at 7.25% and floating rate at LIBOR plus 1.25%. The bank would charge a fee of £120,000 per year to each party in the swap. Arnbrook would require 60% of any arbitrage savings (before the payment of fees) from the swap because of its higher credit rating.

Any fees paid to the bank are tax allowable. The corporate tax rate is 30%.

Required:

(a)   Discuss the risks that Arnbrook and a participating bank might face when undertaking an interest rate swap. **(3 marks)**

(b)   Evaluate whether or not the proposed swap might be beneficial to all parties.

(6 marks)

(c)   If LIBOR was to increase immediately after the forthcoming election to 5.75% and then stay constant for the period of the swap, estimate the present value of the savings from the swap for Arnbrook plc. Interest payments are made semi-annually in arrears. Comment upon whether the swap would have been beneficial to Arnbrook plc.

The money market may be assumed to be an efficient market.   **(6 marks)**

(Total: 15 marks)

5   STAFER PLC

Stafer plc, a UK company, is proposing to invest in two overseas countries. The first country, Xendia, has introduced protectionist barriers and there are severe restrictions on the movements of funds between Xendia and other countries.

The government of Xendia wishes to encourage investment by Stafer plc and is prepared to relax these rules for the proposed investment.

The second investment will be in Germany, where there are no restrictions on the movement of foreign exchange or capital into or out of the country.

	UK	Germany	Xendia	World capital markets[1]
Risk free rate (%)	5	4	7	4.5
Market return (%)	11	9	14	10
Equity beta for the relevant industry	1.2	0.9	1.4	0.95
Long term borrowing rate (%)	7.5	6.5	10	7
Corporate tax rate (%)	30	28	35	29
Pre-tax cost of debt (%)	6.5	5.5	9.0	6.0

[1]World capital markets refers to markets where no significant barriers to the movement of foreign exchange or capital exist.

Stafer's capital structure if the two investments are undertaken is expected to be 50% equity, 50% debt by book values, and 65% equity, 35% debt by market values. The debt would be borrowed in the relevant local capital market.

Required:

(a)   Calculate and discuss what discount rates should be used in the evaluation of the investment opportunities in Xendia and Germany.   **(8 marks)**

(b)   Explain possible inaccuracies of the estimates in (a) above.   **(3 marks)**

(c)   Briefly discuss whether or not the overseas subsidiaries should use the same capital structure as the group as a whole.   **(4 marks)**

(Total: 15 marks)

6   SERVEALOT PLC

Servealot plc has issued the following statement as part of its annual report:

'This company aims at all times to serve its shareholders by paying a high level of dividends and adopting strategies that will increase the company's share price. Satisfying our shareholders will ensure our success. The company will reduce costs by manufacturing overseas wherever possible, and will attempt to minimise the company's global tax bill by using tax haven facilities.'

Required:

Discuss the validity and implications of each of the comments and strategies in the above statement.

(15 marks)

Section 4

ANSWERS TO JUNE 2006 EXAM QUESTIONS

SECTION A

1 VADENER PLC

Key answer tips

Requirement (a) is standard corporate appraisal. To achieve a good answer ensure that you discuss all ratios calculated and conclude by commenting on the firm's resource allocation plans.

Part (b) is easier if you think of issues as you approach part(a), rather than as a separate exercise.

In part (c) the key issue is that translation losses are unrealised unless the division or asset concerned is sold.

(a) Group performance may be analysed by using financial ratios, growth trends and comparative market data. Alternative definitions exist for some ratios, and other ratios are equally valid.

Operating and profitability ratios:

		2003	2004	2005
Return on capital:	$\dfrac{\text{EBIT}}{\text{M \& LT capital}}$	$\dfrac{410}{1,486} = 27.6\%$	$\dfrac{540}{1,665} = 32.4\%$	$\dfrac{560}{1,876} = 29.9\%$
Asset turnover:	$\dfrac{\text{Sales}}{\text{Capital employed}}$	$\dfrac{1,210}{1,486} = 0.81$	$\dfrac{1,410}{1,665} = 0.85$	$\dfrac{1,490}{1,876} = 0.79$
Profit margin:	$\dfrac{\text{EBIT}}{\text{Sales}}$	$\dfrac{410}{1,210} = 33.9\%$	$\dfrac{540}{1,410} = 38.3\%$	$\dfrac{560}{1,490} = 37.6\%$

Liquidity ratios:

		2003	2004	2005
Current ratio:	$\dfrac{\text{Current assets}}{\text{Current liabilities}}$	$\dfrac{728}{565} = 1.29$	$\dfrac{863}{728} = 1.19$	$\dfrac{1,015}{799} = 1.27$
Acid test:	$\dfrac{\text{Current assets - stock}}{\text{Current liabilities}}$	$\dfrac{388}{565} = 0.69$	$\dfrac{453}{728} = 0.62$	$\dfrac{525}{799} = 0.66$

Market ratios:

		2003	2004	2005
Dividend yield:	$\dfrac{\text{Dividend per share}}{\text{Market price}}$	$\dfrac{48.7}{1,220} = 4.0\%$	$\dfrac{56.7}{1,417} = 4.0\%$	$\dfrac{61.7}{1,542} = 4.0\%$
Ernings per share:	$\dfrac{\text{Earnings after tax}}{\text{Number of shares}}$	$\dfrac{259}{300} = 86.3$	$\dfrac{339}{300} = 113.0$	$\dfrac{346}{300} = 115.3$
PE ratio	$\dfrac{\text{Market price}}{\text{Earnings per share}}$	$\dfrac{1,220}{86.3} = 14.1$	$\dfrac{1,417}{113} = 12.5$	$\dfrac{1,542}{115.3} = 13.4$
Gearing:	$\dfrac{\text{Total borrowing}}{\text{Borrowing + equity}}$	$\dfrac{535}{1,621} = 33\%$	$\dfrac{580}{1,835} = 32\%$	$\dfrac{671}{2,077} = 32\%$

It is difficult to reach conclusions about the performance of Vadener without more comparative data from similar companies.

Return on capital at around 30% is dominated by the effect of high profit margins, but the split between divisions is not provided. Asset utilisation is well below 1, which implies relatively inefficient utilisation of assets. Vadener might investigate whether this could be improved.

Liquidity has improved during the last year, and although below some commonly used benchmarks might be satisfactory for the sectors that Vadener is involved with. However, some aspects of working capital require attention. Stock levels have increased from 28% of turnover in 2003 to 33% in 2005, and the collection period for debtors has similarly increased from 114 days to 125 days. Creditors have also increased more than proportionately to turnover. Vadener should take action to improve the efficiency of its working capital management.

In contrast operating costs have fallen over the three years from 66% to 62% of turnover, indicating greater efficiency. Gearing appears to be relatively low at around 32%, but comparative data is needed, and Interest cover is high at more than eight times in 2005.

Investors do not appear to be entirely satisfied with group performance. The FT market index has increased by 34% between 2003 and 2005, whereas Vadener's share price has only increased by 26%. With an equity beta of 1.1 Vadener's share price would be expected to increase by more than the market index. Vadener's PE ratios are also lower than those of similar companies, suggesting that investors do not value the company's future prospects as highly as those of its competitors.

The required return from Vadener's shares may be estimated using the capital asset pricing model (CAPM).

Required return = 5% + (12% – 5%) 1.1 = 12.7%

An approximation of the actual return from Vadener's shares is the 12% average annual increase in share price plus 4% annual dividend yield, or 16%. The total return is higher than expected for the systematic risk. Given this, Vadener should investigate the reasons why its share price has performed relatively poorly. One possibility is the company's dividend policy.

Dividends have consistently been more than 50% of available after tax earnings, which might not be popular with investors.

Divisional performance.

The information on the individual divisions is very sparse. All divisions are profitable, but the return from the pharmaceutical division is relatively low for its systematic risk.

Using CAPM to approximate required returns:

	Required return	Actual return
Construction	5% + (12% – 5%) 0.75 = 10.25%	13%
Leisure	5% + (12% – 5%) 1.1 = 12.7%	16%
Pharmaceuticals	5% + (12% – 5%) 1.40 = 14.8%[1]	14%

[1] It is assumed that the same market parameters are valid for the US based division.

The construction and leisure divisions appear to have greater than expected returns (a positive alpha) and the pharmaceutical division slightly less than expected for the risk of the division. The pharmaceutical division has recently suffered a translation loss due to the weakness of the US dollar, and the potential economic exposure from changes in the value of the dollar should be investigated.

From a financial perspective it would appear that the company should not devote equal resources to the divisions, and should focus its efforts on construction and leisure. However, the future prospects of the sectors are not known, nor the long term strategy of Vadener, which might be to expand international operations in the USA or elsewhere. The strategic use of resources should not be decided on the basis of the limited financial information that is available.

(b)   Other information that would be useful includes:

(i)   Cash flow forecasts for the group and the individual divisions.

(ii)   Full product and market information for each of the divisions.

(iii)   Details of recent investments in each of the divisions and the expected impact of such investment on future performance.

(iv)   Detailed historic performance data of the divisions over at least three years, and similar data for companies in the relevant sectors.

(v)   Competitors and potential growth rates in each of the sectors.

(vi)   The economic exposure of the US division

(vii)   The future strategic plans of Vadener. Are there any other proposed initiatives?

(viii)   How the company's equal resource strategy will be viewed by investors. The company has performed worse than the market in recent years despite having a higher beta than the market.

(c)   A translation loss of £10 million is not necessarily a problem for Vadener plc.

Translation exposure, sometimes known as accounting exposure, often does not reflect any real cash flow changes. It is changes in cash flow that, in an efficient market, will impact on the share price and value of a company. For example, a translation loss might in part reflect a lower home currency value of an overseas factory, but the factory will still be the same and will still be producing goods. It is the impact on the home currency cash flows from the continuing operations of the factory that will affect share price.

However, if the market is not efficient, investors might not understand that there are no real cash flow implications from the exposure, and might be worried about the effect of the translation loss on Vadener, and possibly sell their shares. If this is the case Vadener might consider internal hedges to reduce translation exposure. In most cases this would not be recommended, and companies must also be careful that hedges to manage translation exposure do not adversely affect the efficient operations of the business, or be contrary to hedges that are being undertaken to protect against other forms of currency exposure such as transaction exposure.

ACCA marking scheme		Marks
(a)	Criterion (a) for performance evaluation	1
	Group performance	
	Financial ratios	9
	For full marks a range of ratios over three years is required	
	Growth trends	3–4
	Required return/share performance	3
	Discussion and analysis of ratios and other data. Look for comments about favourable and problem areas	6–7
	Operating divisions:	
	Financial analysis	3
	Discussion including strategy	3–4
	Max	28

(b)	One mark for each valid point	Max	6
(c)	Discussion of implications Realistic recommendation of action		4 2
			6
		Total	40

2 LAMMER PLC

Key answer tips

In requirement (a) ensure you only hedge the **net** dollar exposure. Apart from the need to prorate some figures (forward rates and futures basis); the calculations for each hedging technique are fairly typical. Ensure you reach a conclusion.

In part (b) the relevant cash flow to discount is the difference between the forecast flow using a strengthening dollar and a forecast flow at spot

Part (c) is standard bookwork.

(a) Report on possible hedging strategies for the foreign exchange exposure in five months' time.

Only relevant net dollar exposures should be hedged. Net dollar imports in five months time are $1,150,000. This is the amount to be hedged. The transactions in sterling are not exposed and should not be hedged. The exposure may be hedged using the forward foreign exchange market, a money market hedge, currency futures hedge or currency options hedge. A combination of these hedges is also possible, or alternatively a partial hedge may be selected that protects only part of the exposure.

Forward market hedge:

No five month forward rate is given. The rate may be interpolated from the three month and one year rates for buying dollars.

The estimated five month forward rate is:

$$1.9066 \times \frac{7}{9} + 1.8901 \times \frac{2}{9} = 1.9029$$

Hedging with a forward contact will fix the £ payment at:

$$\frac{\$1,150,000}{1.9029} = £604,341$$

Money market hedge:

In order to protect against any future strengthening of the dollar, Lammer could borrow £ now and convert £ into dollars to ensure that the company is not exposed if there are changes in the $/£ exchange rate.

Borrow £595,373 at 5.5% per annum for five months, total cost £609,017

Convert into $ at the spot rate of $1.9156/£ to yield $1,140,496

Invest in the USA at 2.0% per annum to yield a total of $1,150,000 which will be used to make payment for the imports.

($1,140,496 × 1.008333 = $1,150,000)

A money market hedge is more expensive than the forward hedge.

Currency futures hedge:

The currency exposure is in five months' time. To protect against the risk of the dollar strengthening December futures should be sold.

The basis is $1.9156 - 1.8986 = 1.7$ cents. This relates to a futures contract maturing in seven months' time.

The expected basis in five months' time is $1.7 \times \dfrac{2}{7} \times 2 = 0.486$ cents

The expected lock-in futures rate may be estimated by:

$1.8986 + 0.00486 = 1.9035$

This is slightly more favourable than the forward market rate, but there are a number of possible disadvantages of using currency futures:

(i)   Basis risk might exist. The actual basis at the close out date in five months' time might be different from the expected basis of 0.486 cents.

(ii) Currency futures will involve either underhedging or overhedging as an exact number of contracts for the risk is not available.

$$\frac{\$1,150,000}{1.9035} = £604,150 \quad \frac{£604,150}{£62,500} = 9.67 \text{contracts}$$

(iii) Currency futures involve the upfront payment of a margin (security deposit). If daily losses are made on the futures contracts additional margin will need to be provided to keep the futures contracts open.

Currency options hedge:

As $ need to be purchased, Lammer will need to buy December put options on £.

Exercise price	$	£	No. of contracts
1.8800	1,150,000	611,702	19.57
1.9000	1,150,000	605,263	19.37
1.9200	1,150,000	598,958	19.17

It is assumed that Lammer will underhedge using 19 contracts and will purchase the remaining dollars in the forward market (in reality it would probably wait and use the spot market in five months' time). 19 contracts is £593,750.

Exercise price	$	Premium $	Premium £ at spot	Underhedge $
1.8800	1,116,250	17,575	9,175	33,750
1.9000	1,128,125	25,769	13,452	21,875
1.9200	1,140,000	38,891	20,302	10,000

Worst case outcomes if the options are exercised:

Exercise price	Basic cost (£)	Premium	Underhedged £ at forward	Total
1.8800	593,750	9,175	17,736	620,661
1.9000	593,750	13,452	11,496	618,698
1.9200	593,750	20,302	5,255	619,307

As is normal, the currency options worst case outcomes are much more expensive than alternative hedges. However, if the dollar weakens relative to the pound, option contracts allow the company to purchase the required dollars in five months' time in the spot market and let the options lapse (or alternatively sell the options to take advantage of any remaining time value). In this situation the dollar would have to weaken to about 1.98/£ before the currency options became more favourable than the forward contract or futures hedge. This is possible, but unlikely, especially as the forward market expects the dollar to strengthen rather than weaken.

Forward contracts or futures contracts appear to be the best form of hedge.

(b)   Estimated effect on value:

Exchange rate $/£	£ equivalent of $4.2m	£ difference to spot	DF (11%)	PV
Spot 1.9156	2,192,525			
1 year 1.8581	2,260,374	67,849	0.901	61,132
2 years 1.8024	2,330,226	137,701	0.812	111,813
3 years 1.7483	2,402,334	209,809	0.731	153,370
4 years 1.6959	2,476,561	284,036	0.659	187,180
5 years 1.6450	2,553,191	360,666	0.593	213,875
				727,370

The strengthening of the dollar is expected to reduce the present value of cash flows, and, if the market is efficient, the market value of Lammer, by £727,370.

(c)   Economic exposure relates to the change in the value of a company as a result of unexpected changes in exchange rates.

Unless there are known contractual future cash flows it is difficult to hedge economic exposure using options, swaps, or other financial hedges as the amount of the exposure is unknown.

Economic exposure is normally managed by internationally diversifying activities, and organising activities to allow flexibility to vary the location of production, the supply sources of raw materials and components, and international financing, in response to changes in exchange rates.

To some extent multinational companies may offset economic exposure by arranging natural hedges, for example by borrowing funds in the USA, and then servicing the interest payments and the repayment of principal on the borrowing with cash flows generated by subsidiaries in the USA.

Marketing strategies may also be used to offset the effects of economic exposure. For example if UK products were to become relatively expensive in the USA due to a fall in the value of the dollar, a UK company might adopt an intensive marketing campaign to create a better brand or quality image for its products.

ACCA marking scheme		*Marks*
(a)	Netting exposures	1
	Forward market:	
	Five month rate	2
	Correct hedge (for rate used)	1
	Money market hedge	4
	Futures hedge:	
	Basis	1
	Expected lock-in rate	3
	Other issues with futures	1–2

	Currency options:		
	December puts		1
	Options calculations		4–5
	Discussion of benefit of options if dollar weakens		2
	Conclusion		1
		Max	20
(b)	Present value estimates		4
	Conclusion		1
			5
(c)	Reward focus on diversification, production/marketing strategies, and natural hedges	Max	5
		Total	30

3 EWADE PLC

Key answer tips

In requirement (a) the yield on the convertibles is an IRR calculation. An alternative approach to calculating the MV of the straight debt would be to use a 6 monthly yield calculated by

1+ 6monthly yield = $(1.06)^{1/2}$ = 1.0296. However, 3% is close enough.

When explaining the differences in yields, ensure that you focus on risk.

In part (b) the share value is only relevant to the debenture price if investors **would** convert.

In part (c) only a basic explanation of delta and theta is required here.

(a) The redemption yield on the convertible zero coupon debt may be found by solving:

$$£71.10 = \frac{100}{(1+r)^7}, (1+r)^7 = 1.4065, r = \text{approximately } 5\%$$

The current annual yield on straight debt is 6%. This yield will comprise the present value of the semi-annual interest payments, and of any capital gain or loss on redemption in seven years' time. The market price may be found by solving:

$$\text{Market price} = \frac{4}{1.03} + \frac{4}{(1.03)^2} + \dots \frac{4}{(1.03)^{14}} + \frac{100}{(1.03)^{14}}$$

From PV and annuity tables:

	£
$4 \times 11.30 =$	45.20
$100 \times 0.661 =$	66.10
	111.30

The yield on a zero coupon bond and coupon bearing bond of the same maturity might differ slightly according to the preferences of investors for regular interest payments (coupon bearing), or a definite capital sum at the end of a period (zero coupon). Zero coupon bonds are not subject to reinvestment risk, but are subject to significant price risk if not held to maturity.

Because of the existence of the conversion option, the 5% redemption yield on the zero coupon bond is less than would be expected for a zero coupon bond without the conversion option. This lower yield affects the price of the bond. The main reasons for the £40.20 difference between the prices of the bonds are that the zero coupon is issued at a significant discount to the par value, and the coupon bearing bond has a coupon interest rate higher than the current redemption yield, meaning that its market price will be above the par value.

(b)   The minimum price of the zero coupon bond will be the greater of its value if converted immediately, and its value as a bond with fours years until maturity.

The value as a bond is: $\dfrac{100}{(1.06)^4} = £79.21$

If converted:

At a price of 550 pence, the value is 12×550 pence $= £66.00$

At a price of 710 pence, the value is 12×710 pence $= £85.20$

With a share price of 550 pence the value will be the bond value of £79.21

With a share price of 710 pence the value will be the value if converted of £85.20

(c)   A warrant is an option to purchase additional securities, at a specified price and time. If warrants are held as part of a portfolio, the delta and theta values are useful in developing hedging strategies.

The delta value shows the change in the price of the option (warrant) relative to the change in the price of the underlying share. It is possible to use the delta value to devise a delta neutral hedge which means that the total value of the options and underlying shares held is not expected to change as the price of the underlying share changes.

The theta value shows how the price of an option (warrant) changes over time.

$$\text{Theta} = \dfrac{\text{Change in option price}}{\text{Change in time}}$$

The nearer to the maturity date of the warrant, the lower will be the time value associated with the warrant.

ACCA marking scheme		Marks
(a)	Estimate of the redemption yield	2
	Market price of straight debt	2
	Reasons for different prices and yields	2–3
		Max 6
(b)	Minimum price of zero coupon:	
	At 550 pence, bond value with calculations	2
	at 710 pence, share value, with calculations	2
		4
(c)	Understanding of delta value	3
	Theta value	2
		5
	Total	15

4   ARNBROOK PLC

Key answer tips

Some students make the error in this question of constructing the swap in detail. This is not necessary to answer all requirements.

In part (a) ensure that you consider the bank's perspective as well as Arnbrook's. Similarly in part (b) ensure you consider all three parties.

In part (c) an alternative approach to calculating discount rates after 6 months is to incorporate both the 5.7% and 6.2% rates. For example, the discount rate for 2 years = $1/(1.057^{0.5} \times 1.062^{1.5})$

(a)   The risks faced by Arnbrook and the bank include:

(i)   Default risk by the counterparty to the swap. If the counterparty is a bank this risk will normally be very small. A bank would face larger counterparty default risk, especially from counterparties such as the BBB company with a relatively low credit rating.

(ii)   Market or position risk. This is the risk that market interest rate will change such that the company undertaking the swap would have been better off, with hindsight, if it had not undertaken the swap.

(iii)   Banks often undertake a 'warehousing' function in swap transactions. The size and/or maturity of the transactions desired by each counterparty to the bank often do not match. In such cases the bank faces gap or mismatch risk which it will normally hedge in the futures or other markets.

(b)

	Fixed rate	Floating rate
Arnbrook	6.25%	LIBOR + 0.75%
BBB company	7.25%	LIBOR + 1.25%
Difference	1.00%	0.50%

There is a potential 0.50% arbitrage saving from undertaking the swap.

On a £50 million swap this is £250,000 per year.

Arnbrook would require 60% of any saving, or £150,000 annually. The BBB company would receive £100,000 annually.

The bank would charge each party £120,000 per year. After tax this is a cost of £84,000 each. This would leave a net saving of £16,000 for the BBB rated counterparty company.

The swap is potentially beneficial to all parties, but the counterparty company might press for a larger saving than £16,000.

(c)   Arnbrook will pay floating rate interest as a result of the swap. If Arnbrook receives 60% of the arbitrage savings, it will save 0.5% (0.60) on its interest rates relative to borrowing directly in the floating rate market, and effectively pay LIBOR + 0.45%, or 5.70% at current interest rates. If LIBOR moves to 5.75% in six months' time, Arnbrook will then pay 6.20% floating rate interest for the remaining period of the swap.

Interest savings in each six month periods are £50 million × 0.30% × 0.5 = £75,000

If the money market is efficient, the relevant discount rate will be the prevailing interest rate paid by Arnbrook.

Period:	Savings £	Discount factor	Present value (£)
0–6 months	75,000	0.972 (5.7%)	72,900
6 months–1 year	75,000	0.942 (6.2%)	70,650
1 year–18 months	75,000	0.913 (6.2%)	68,475
18 months–2 years	75,000	0.887 (6.2%)	66,525
2 years–30 months	75,000	0.860 (6.2%)	64,500
30 months–3 years	75,000	0.835 (6.2%)	62,625
Total present values			405,675

The interest rate swap is estimated to produce interest rate savings with a present value of £405,675 relative to borrowing floating rate directly. The swap would be beneficial, and, with hindsight, would result in lower interest costs than would have been available by borrowing at 6.25% in the fixed rate market.

ACCA marking scheme			
			Marks
(a)	1 mark for each valid point	Max	3
(b)	Swap calculations, with arbitrage savings		5
	Discussion of how beneficial		1
			6
(c)	Calculations of the present value of savings		5
	Comment upon whether it would have been beneficial		1
			6
		Total	15

5   STAFER PLC

Key answer tips

This is a tricky question that requires some thought as the discount rate depends on the investment appraisal method used:

1. Each investment could be assessed by converting foreign cash flows into Sterling and using a UK based rate. This would be difficult in Xendia with restrictions on the movement of funds.

2. An APV approach would involve discounting cash flows using a cost of equity derived from ungeared (asset) betas to determine a base case NPV before including financing side-effects.

3. The simplest approach (used in the answer below) is to calculate a wacc for each country to apply to local cash flows.

With the segmented nature of Xendia it is reasonably obvious that Xendia data should be used. With Germany, the cost of capital should be lower as it is part of an integrated market. Companies whose shareholders are international investors would consider applying the international cost of capital to investment appraisal, rather than using domestic rates.

(a)   Xendia and Germany are examples of segmented and integrated markets respectively. Where a segmented market exists, the capital asset pricing model should focus upon local factors when assessing the required return from an investment. The relevant risk free rate and market return will be the local rates in Xendia, and the beta that best reflects the risk of the investment is, in theory, the Xendian beta for the sector.

Cost of equity in Xendia:

Ke = Rf + (Rm – Rf) beta = 7% + (14% – 7%) 1.4 = 16.8%

$$\text{WACC} = \text{ke} \ \frac{E}{E + D} + \text{kd} \ (1 - t) \ \frac{D}{E + D}$$

WACC in Xendia is estimated to be:

16.8% × 0.65 + 9%(1 – 0.35) × 0.35 = 12.96%

Cost of equity in Germany:

As there are no restrictions on the movement of capital or foreign exchange the German market may be regarded as part of an integrated 'world' market, and the relevant data when assessing the required return will be the world data.

Ke = Rf + (Rm – Rf) beta = 4.5% + (10% – 4.5%) 0.95 = 9.725%

WACC in Germany is estimated to be:

9.725% × 0.65 + 5.5% (1 – 0.28) × 0.35 = 7.7%

As debt is borrowed in Germany, the German cost of debt and corporate tax rate have been used, but it might be argued that the world rates are a valid alternative.

Adjusted present value is an alternative method that might be used to appraise overseas investments. This would require an estimate of the base case NPV for each project, using an estimate of the ungeared equity beta, and discounting any financing side effects by a discount rate that reflects the risk of each individual financing side effect.

(b) Possible errors include:

(i) The markets are unlikely to be either perfectly segmented or perfectly integrated. Most markets fall between these extremes. A margin of error will exist in these estimates.

(ii) The International capital asset pricing model assumes that investors are well diversified internationally. In reality many are not, and there is a tendency for investors to hold a higher than expected proportion of their assets in their own domestic capital market.

(iii) The betas provided are average equity betas for the relevant sector. Such betas will reflect the average gearing of the relevant sector. If the gearing of Stafer differs from the relevant average gearing, it is necessary to ungear the sector beta and then regear for Stafer's gearing in order to reflect the financial risk of Stafer.

(c) Stafer should use the capital structure that is best suited to the individual market, even if that means a very different capital structure from that used in the home country. For example, if subsidised loans are available in the overseas country it might be better to take full advantage of such loans and adopt a high level of gearing. Similarly if there are restrictions on dividend remittances but not on interest payments, high gearing might be appropriate. If necessary the parent company can provide a guarantee for interest payments where unusually high gearing levels exist in a foreign subsidiary. Gearing is likely to vary considerably between overseas subsidiaries. The crucial factor is that the overall group gearing remains at a level that is satisfactory to lenders and other investors.

<table>
<thead>
<tr><th colspan="3">ACCA marking scheme</th><th></th></tr>
</thead>
<tbody>
<tr><td></td><td></td><td></td><td>Marks</td></tr>
<tr><td>(a)</td><td>Discussion of principles relating to discount rates in segmented and integrated markets</td><td></td><td>3</td></tr>
<tr><td></td><td>WACC estimates</td><td></td><td>5</td></tr>
<tr><td></td><td></td><td></td><td>—
8</td></tr>
<tr><td>(b)</td><td>One mark for each valid point</td><td>Max</td><td>3</td></tr>
<tr><td>(c)</td><td>Reward sensible discussion that focusses on the best choice of capital structure for the individual circumstance/country</td><td></td><td>4</td></tr>
<tr><td></td><td></td><td>Total</td><td>—
15</td></tr>
</tbody>
</table>

6 SERVEALOT PLC

Key answer tips

This was a relatively straightforward question focussing on shareholder wealth. It is essential that your answer encompasses the views of other stakeholders and ethical considerations as well as the more obvious drivers of shareholder value.

There are several aspects of the statement that might not be valid.

'The company aims to serve its shareholders by paying a high level of dividends.'

Not all shareholders would favour a high level of dividends. Where dividends are taxed at a higher rate than capital gains there might be a preference for low or no dividends to be paid in which case the payment of high dividends might be unpopular with shareholders and have a detrimental effect on share price.

'Adopting strategies that will increase the company's share price'.

This is problematic for at least two reasons. Firstly, according to financial theory a company should attempt to maximise the returns (wealth) to shareholders. Increasing the share price is not the same as maximising the returns. Secondly, the objectives of most companies are much broader than a single objective of shareholder wealth maximisation. Companies have many stakeholders, including their customers, suppliers, employees, lenders of funds to the company, and normally the government and the local community. The objectives of companies will normally be influenced by such stakeholders. Additionally environmental issues and other aspects of corporate social responsibility are increasingly influencing the objectives and strategies of companies in many countries, and there are strong ethical grounds for companies to be sensitive to such issues.

'Satisfying our shareholders will ensure our success'.

As mentioned above there are many other stakeholders that the company might need to satisfy. Satisfying shareholders is not likely to ensure success as actions that satisfy shareholders might be at the expense of other stakeholders.

'The company will reduce costs by manufacturing overseas wherever possible'.

This strategy is contentious, as it normally means a loss of employment, wealth generation, and possibly taxation, in the home country. It is true that costs can often be reduced by manufacturing overseas, but there is an ethical question of how loyal a company should be to its local employees and the local community.

'Adopt a strategy of attempting to minimise the company's global tax bill through the judicious use of tax haven facilities'

As long as the tax reduction is by means of legal tax avoidance then this strategy should lead to an increase in cash flow and share price. Many governments try to restrict the use companies make of overseas tax havens but they are not illegal. Government restrictions mean that it will not always be possible for companies to make use of tax havens.

ACCA marking scheme	
	Marks
Discussion of dividends	3–4
Strategies to increase share price	4–5
Satisfying shareholders	2–3
Manufacturing overseas	3–4
Minimise tax bill by using tax havens	3–4
Total	15
Note: Reward broad discussion that includes governance and ethical considerations. Allow for overlap between sections	